THE COVERT SPHERE

THE COVERT SPHERE

Secrecy, Fiction, and the National Security State

TIMOTHY MELLEY

CORNELL UNIVERSITY PRESS
ITHACA AND LONDON

First published 2012 by Cornell University Press
First printing, Cornell Paperbacks, 2012
Printed in the United States of America

Library of Congress Cataloging-in-Publication Data

Melley, Timothy, 1963–
    The covert sphere : secrecy, fiction, and the national security state /
Timothy Melley.
        p. cm.
    Includes bibliographical references and index.
    ISBN 978-0-8014-5123-2 (cloth : alk. paper)
    ISBN 978-0-8014-7853-6 (pbk. : alk. paper)
  1. Spy stories, American—History and criticism.   2. American
fiction—20th century—History and criticism.   3. Espionage in
literature.   4. Terrorism in literature.   5. Secrecy in literature.
6. World politics in literature.   7. Literature and history—United
States.   8. National security—Social aspects—United States.
9. Popular culture—Political aspects—United States—History—
20th century. 10. Popular culture—Political aspects—United States—
History—21st century.   I. Title.
    PS374.S5M45   2013
    813′.087209—dc23   2012026271

Cloth printing   10 9 8 7 6 5 4 3 2 1
Paperback printing   10 9 8 7 6 5 4 3 2 1

CONTENTS

PREFACE

As I was finishing this book, I had the good fortune to receive a kind of unsolicited endorsement from the U.S. Department of State. On December 7, 2010, the U.S. Embassy in Kabul acknowledged that it was providing major funding for thirteen episodes of *Eagle Four*—a new Afghani television melodrama based loosely on the popular U.S. series *24*. According to National Public Radio, *Eagle Four* "tracks the fictional adventures of an elite police unit that chases terrorists, kidnappers and smugglers in the midst of a war zone." An embassy spokesperson refused to divulge the cost of the project but acknowledged its military purpose. *Eagle Four* is part of a strategy to transform Afghani suspicion of security forces into something like awed respect.[1] What does it mean when a wartime government chooses to spend valuable resources on a melodrama of covert operations? Among other things, it means that fiction has a powerful ability to shape the real world.

This book began as a public lecture on that proposition. I was speaking to a general audience, and my aim was to challenge the still widely held notion that studying literature and culture is a noble but fundamentally unserious pursuit, far removed from "real" political, diplomatic, and military conflicts. I could have used any number of historical examples, but because I was speaking at the height of public concern about the Bush administration's "Global War on Terror," I decided to focus on popular discourse about terrorism and U.S. antiterror policy. Several features of this discourse struck me as notable at the time. First, it was difficult to find historical, scholarly, and legal approaches to terrorism in the popular press. Several years into the War on Terror, many commentators still seemed genuinely perplexed about the nature, aims, and grievances of those who had recently attacked New York and Washington. Second, the most visible representations of the subject seemed to be films and television series, most of which were melodramatic thrillers. Third, and most striking of all, many commentators and important public figures had explicated or defended U.S. policy on the basis of these melodramas. While there is nothing unusual about the use of fiction in political debate, a number of things about this case seemed singular, and they all had to do with the role of covert action and state secrecy in the War on Terror. Why, I wondered, was there so little historical and political analysis of the state's new enemies? And why so little objection to a counterstrategy rooted in Cold War protocols, particularly given the widespread public sense that the post–Cold War era was a radical departure from the Cold War? Had the substantially covert nature of the U.S. response shaped the political and cultural dynamics of the moment?

The Covert Sphere pursues these questions through the cultural history of the Cold War and the War on Terror. My central claim is that the development of the National Security State, with its emphasis on secrecy and deception, helped transform the cultural status of fiction as it relates to discourses of "fact," such as journalism and history. As state secrecy shifted the conditions of public knowledge, certain forms of fiction became crucial in helping Americans imagine, or fantasize about, U.S. foreign policy. This transformation had a powerful role in fostering the forms of suspicion, skepticism, and uncertainty that would eventually find their fullest expression in postmodernism.

As I worked on this book, I incurred many debts. I would not have been able to complete it without generous grants from Miami University. Karen Schilling, dean of the College of Arts and Sciences, gave me a leave of absence just when I needed it, despite tough financial times. A number of people invited me to present parts of my argument as it developed. I am grateful to Andreas Killen and Stefan Andriopoulos for inviting me to speak at Columbia University, and to Andreas Huyssen for his generous response; to Eva Horne and Anson Rabinbach for bringing me to the University of Konstanz, Germany, for a superb conference on conspiracy theory and history; to Michael Prince for an invitation to address the Annual American and Canadian Studies Conference in Kristiansand, Norway; to Elisabeth Davies for the chance to speak at the Duke workshop on "Security, Suspicion, and Intelligence"; and to Molly Hite for an invitation to Cornell. The feedback I received on these occasions was invaluable. Though he may not remember it, Anson Rabinbach was the one who noticed my use of the phrase "covert sphere" and suggested I make more of it. Portions of this book have appeared elsewhere in slightly different form. Much of chapter 5 appeared as "Postmodern Amnesia," *Contemporary Literature* 44, no. 1 (2003): 106–31. Some of chapter 1 appeared in "Brainwashed! Conspiracy Theory and Ideology in the Cold War United States," *New German Critique* 35, no. 1, 103 (Spring 2008): 145–64. A different portion of the same chapter appeared as "Brain Warfare: The Covert Sphere, Terrorism, and the Legacy of Cold War," *Grey Room* 45 (2011): 18–39. Quotations from *The Public Burning* by Robert Coover, copyright 1976, 1977 by Robert Coover, have been reprinted by permission of Georges Borchardt, Inc.

My friends and colleagues have given me a lot of help and encouragement. I am deeply grateful to Mary Jean Corbett for her support, guidance, and careful reading over several years. Special thanks as well to Peggy Shaffer, Madelyn Detloff, Elisabeth Hodges, Jonathan Strauss, and Andrew Hebard, all of whom read portions of this book in draft and made excellent suggestions for improvement. At important moments along the way, Susan Morgan, Jim Creech, Erik Rose, Drew Cayton, Allan Winkler, Fran Dolan, Scott Shershow, Barry Chabot, and Jim Curell were invaluable interlocutors and advisers. I am grateful to my fellow members of the Miami University American Cultures Seminar and English Department for their feedback. At Cornell University Press, Peter J. Potter has been an incisive, critically engaged, and supportive editor from the start, and I was very lucky to have the help of Susan Specter, Susan Barnett, Dave Prout, and Marie Flaherty-Jones in getting this book to press. I am especially grateful to Brian McHale and an anonymous reader at the press for their thoughtful suggestions for improvement.

This book simply would not have been possible without the patience, wisdom, and love of my parents, Ellen and Dan Melley; my brother, Brian; my sister, Kathy; my son, Liam; and my wonderful partner, Katie Johnson, who is a devoted listener, an attentive reader, and a tireless source of encouragement. I am forever grateful.

THE COVERT SPHERE

INTRODUCTION

The Postmodern Public Sphere

Cold War Redux

On September 17, 2001—six days after terrorists slammed jetliners into the World Trade Center and Pentagon—President George W. Bush signed a Memorandum of Notifications authorizing the Central Intelligence Agency (CIA) to launch what the correspondent Jane Mayer called "the most aggressive, ambitious covert-action plan seen since the Cold War, maybe ever." The document, Mayer argued, was "nothing less than a global plan for a secret war, fought not by the military with its well-known legal codes of conduct and a publicly accountable chain of command, but instead in the dark by faceless and nameless CIA agents following commands unknown to the American public."[1] Calling for paramilitary squads with the authority to hunt and kill major terrorist suspects in eighty countries around the world, the memo also authorized the CIA to break and enter private property and to monitor financial transactions and communications worldwide, including within the United States. To guarantee

presidential deniability, the memo assigned blanket authority over assassination, kidnapping, and interrogation to the head of the CIA. Thus began
what Bush would later call his "invisible" war on terror.[2]

Yet how secret was this campaign? Only two years after Bush's decision,
the first of Mayer's riveting *New Yorker* articles began to reveal it to the
public. These stories testify to Mayer's journalistic grit, but they also illustrate the paradoxical openness of the covert state. Indeed, given the shock
with which many in the United States greeted the operational details of
Bush's plan, it seems important to note that in certain respects it had never
been secret. Less than a week after the attacks of 9/11, Vice President Dick
Cheney told a national television audience in his trademark deadpan that
"a lot of what needs to be done will have to be done quietly, without any
discussion,... in the shadows in the intelligence world."[3] Four days later,
President Bush confirmed this approach, promising a joint session of Congress that he would wage war not only through "dramatic" military strikes
but also through "covert operations secret even in success."[4] It was clear
from the beginning that the War on Terror would be conducted outside the
public sphere. In fact, Cheney's phrase "without any discussion" precisely
evoked, and swept aside, Jürgen Habermas's original definition of the public sphere as a forum for the rational, public discussion of state policy.[5]

The declaration of a War on Terror was thus marked by a paradoxical epistemology. It was to be a mighty struggle whose two shadowy
protagonists—"the global terror network" and the state's vast security
apparatus—would remain largely invisible to the democratic public on
whose behalf the war would be waged.[6] Yet the intention to work in secret was publicly announced. This oxymoronic strategy of *open secrecy*
provoked little public notice. Only several years later, when the press exposed the extraordinary rendition, detention, and torture of prisoners, did
a broad sector of the public express uneasiness about the arrangement.

How should we understand the odd conjunction of publicity and secrecy in this case? Why was there so little visible objection to an antiterror strategy that ceded public oversight of state activity? And why, when
the public glimpsed the state's clandestine operations, was it so shocked at
what it discovered?

The answers to these questions lie in the state and cultural institutions
of the Cold War. In tracing the dynamics of the War on Terror back to the
architecture of the Cold War, I do not intend to brush aside the way the

world has changed since the fall of the Berlin Wall. It has not escaped any-one's notice that the world is no longer bipolar or that conflicts increasingly involve the David-and-Goliath dynamic of "asymmetrical warfare," in which the putative enemies of state are often geographically mobile, non-state actors embedded in civilian populations. Domestic discourse about terrorism, moreover, has often taken as a starting point the fundamental importance of the Cold War's end. Nonetheless, the War on Terror has been articulated largely along Cold War lines: as a global ideological con-flict with embedded "hot" wars and religious dimensions. In both conflicts, a distant and mysterious enemy became the object of extraordinary pub-lic concern and the state responded to this enemy through an open-ended "peacetime" mobilization, extreme domestic hypervigilance, and a massive program of covert action.[7]

The institutional foundations of this approach were laid down in the Truman administration. In 1947, the National Security Act established the CIA and placed it under the guidance of a new National Security Coun-cil (NSC) within the executive branch. The NSC soon issued NSC-4A, among the first of many secret memorandums, directing the CIA to launch a program of "covert psychological operations" against the Soviet Union.[8] A year later, George Kennan—head of the State Department's Policy Planning Staff, former chargé d'affaires at the U.S. Embassy in Moscow, and arguably the chief architect of the Cold War—insisted that the United States embrace "covert political warfare" and "propaganda as a major weapon of policy."[9] Although Kennan claimed he was promoting "organized *public* support of resistance to tyranny in foreign countries," he secretly crafted NSC-10/2, which transformed the CIA from an intelligence-gathering agency to an operational outfit with a charter to engage in "pro-paganda, economic warfare; preventive direct action, including sabotage, anti-sabotage, demolition and evacuation measures; subversion against hostile states, including assistance to underground resistance movements, guerrillas and refugee liberation groups, and support of indigenous anti-Communist elements in threatened countries of the free world." More im-portant, NSC-10/2 specified that such actions must be carried out so that "if uncovered the U.S. Government can *plausibly disclaim any responsibility for them.*"[10] When President Truman signed this directive on June 18, 1948, he institutionalized not simply secret warfare but also public deception as a *fundamental* element of U.S. policy.[11]

Thus began a fundamental transformation of U.S. government. In the next three years, the CIA's covert operations section grew by 2,000 percent. By 1950, Paul Nitze, Kennan's successor as head of the Policy Planning Staff, was crafting NSC-68, the crucial policy paper that would cast the Cold War as a "total" struggle between "freedom" and "slavery." NSC-68 called for "a rapid and sustained buildup of the political, economic, and military strength of the free world, and ... an affirmative program intended to wrest the initiative from the Soviet Union." Crucially, as Gregory Mitrovich observes, Nitze understood this military buildup less as an offensive capacity than as "a shield behind which we must deploy all of our nonmilitary resources."[12] In other words, NSC-68's plan for a massive arms race enabled "containment" not only as a global military strategy but also as a means of "containing" the conflict to *covert* methods.

In so doing, NSC-68 ensured that what first seemed a minor exception to democratic oversight would eventually become a major basis for U.S. foreign policy. The scale of psychological operations in the early Cold War so overwhelmed the CIA that Truman was forced to create a Psychological Strategy Board packed with public relations and advertising executives. President Eisenhower enhanced these capacities dramatically. In 1953, his CIA director, Allen Dulles, publicly warned that psychological operations were not simply an "*indirect* weapon" but were in fact the Soviets' "*major* weapon in this period."[13] So dramatic was the growth of the clandestine state that by 1964 David Wise and Thomas Ross were criticizing what they called "the Invisible Government"—"a massive, hidden apparatus, secretly employing about 200,000 persons and spending several billion dollars a year," all "out of public view and quite apart from the traditional political process."[14] Only sixteen years after he had signed this system into existence, Harry Truman expressed second thoughts in the *Washington Post:* "For some time I have been disturbed by the way CIA has been diverted from its original assignment. It has become an operational and at times a policy-making arm of the Government."[15] While there was nothing new about espionage, the degree to which foreign policy matters were sequestered from the public sphere during the Cold War fundamentally—and perhaps permanently—transformed U.S. democracy.

Fifty years later, the United States has sixteen intelligence agencies employing untold civilian and military personnel at a public cost of $75 billion per year—a figure that, while only recently disclosed and almost certainly understated, is still more than any other nonmilitary discretionary budget item and more than the total spent on intelligence by all other world governments combined.[16] A total of forty-five U.S. agencies, 1,271 government organizations, and 1,391 private corporations now do intelligence and counterterrorism work. Over 850,000 U.S. citizens—one in every 181 U.S. workers—hold a "top secret" clearance. Since September 11, 2001, report Dana Priest and William M. Arkin, the U.S. government has created 263 new security bureaucracies.[17] Yet the proliferation of such agencies cannot be understood simply as a response to the events of 9/11. It is a structural legacy of Cold War counterespionage tactics, which require extraordinary compartmentalization of knowledge. Even in 1997, nearly a decade after the end of the Cold War, the Moynihan Commission on government secrecy lamented the fact that the United States was still keeping four hundred thousand new "top secrets" per year and sitting atop 1.5 billion pages of material classified twenty-five years earlier.[18]

In short, the covert sector has increasingly become a version of the state itself. It has its own bureaucracies (the intelligence services, shell companies), its own laws (NSC memorandums, secret authorization directives, covert rules of engagement), and its own territories (remote airstrips, Guantánamo Bay, rendition sites). It is the institutional sedimentation of what Giorgio Agamben calls "the state of exception"—the paradoxical suspension of democracy as a means of saving democracy.[19]

What are the political and cultural consequences of this transformation? The most important is the rise of what I call *the covert sphere*. The covert sphere is a cultural imaginary shaped by both institutional secrecy and public fascination with the secret work of the state. If, as Nancy Fraser puts it, the public sphere "designates a theatre...in which political participation is enacted through the medium of talk," then the covert sphere is a more specific theater for the deliberation of clandestine policy from the Cold War to the present.[20] The covert sphere is not a set of government agencies, nor is it what Michael Warner so usefully calls a "counterpublic."[21] It is an array of discursive forms and cultural institutions through which the public can "discuss" or, more exactly, fantasize the clandestine dimensions of the state. The covert sphere is an important locus of what Donald Pease calls "state fantasy." It is a cultural apparatus for resolving the internal contradictions of democracy in an age of heightened sovereignty.[22] Unlike the supposedly "rational-critical" public sphere, the covert sphere is dominated by narrative fictions, such as novels, films, television series, and electronic games, for fiction is one of the few discourses in which the secret work of the state may be disclosed to citizens. The projection of strategic "fictions," in fact, is a primary goal of clandestine agencies.

In my treatment of this concept, I frequently distinguish between state institutions—which constitute the *covert sector* of government—and the broader cultural arena of the *covert sphere*. Yet these two fields overlap and influence one another. Despite the significant barrier of state secrecy, information leaks constantly from the covert sector into the covert sphere, where it is reported journalistically and converted into fiction; meanwhile, the extraordinary compartmentalization of the covert sector—the fact that each operational secret is restricted to those very few who "need to know"—means that even covert agents are stuck mainly in the covert sphere. The covert sphere is thus much more than simply the cultural "reflection" of real covert actions or a collection of diversionary fantasies about secret government. It is an ideological arena with profound effects on democracy, citizenship, and state policy. While state secrecy makes such effects hard to trace, each chapter of this book contains examples of ways the cultural imaginary of the covert sphere has shaped U.S. foreign policy.

At first glance, the covert sphere may seem a relatively a minor lacuna in the public sphere, the "necessary" exception to public deliberation. But as Agamben and others have shown, "states of exception" and "emergency politics" are remarkably stable elements of modern democracy.[23] They prompt relatively little public critique—not because the state suppresses it, but because the covert sphere is an efficient ideological system. Through a combination of state secrecy and public representation, the covert sphere not only smooths over the central contradiction of the Cold War state— that Western democracy can preserve itself only through the suspension of democracy—but it turns this troubling proposition into a source of public reassurance and even pleasure.

In the pages that follow, I argue that this system has had major political and cultural consequences. It has inspired a large body of narrative and visual culture; generated cynicism about government; fostered skepticism about historical narrative; and contributed significantly to the rise of postmodernism. Before I turn to the details of these arguments, I want to be clear at the outset that I do not mean to draw too sharp a distinction between the covert and public spheres. My goal is neither to suggest a

means of "healing" the wounded public sphere—as if the revelation of secrets would suddenly restore "real" democracy (a notion proffered by covert-
sphere narratives like *Three Days of the Condor, Hopscotch, The Package,*
and *Green Zone*)—nor to depict the public sphere as a transparent, democratic ideal that has been sullied primarily by the rise of Cold War secrecy. Government has always had secret components, and as so many of
Habermas's interlocutors have shown, the democratic public sphere has
long seemed "secret" or off-limits to large segments of the public, particularly women, minorities, and the lower classes.[24] State secrets, moreover,
are not the only kinds of important social knowledge routinely excluded
from public discourse. In fact, so many historians have unearthed stories
lost to cultural memory in recent decades that it is now a cliché to subtitle
one's monograph "a secret history."[25]

In concentrating on the representation of covert state agencies, then, I
do not want to suggest that knowledge suppressed by the security state is
more important than other "repressed" social content. Yet the astonishing growth of clandestine institutions since World War II has produced a
qualitative change in the structure of public knowledge about U.S. foreign
affairs. The institutional infrastructure of the covert state—particularly its
commitments to "plausible deniability," hypercompartmentalization, psychological warfare, and covert action—is a significant barrier to certain
forms of public knowledge. As the ideal of *rational democracy* came into
increasing tension with what can be called *psychological operations,* the result was not simply a reduction of public knowledge but a transformation
of the discursive means through which the public "knows," or imagines,
the work of the state. As I will explain in detail later, this change provided
a heightened—though certainly not unique—stimulus for the production
of postmodernism.

We Now Know

In an era of covert action, citizens are offered a modified social contract
in which they are asked to trade democratic oversight for enhanced security. In so doing, they tacitly acknowledge that their elected leaders will deceive them about some actions taken on their behalf. The growth of this
arrangement since the Cold War has institutionalized certain forms of

deception and suspicion in U.S. political culture. "Major decisions involving peace and war," observed Wise and Ross almost fifty years ago, "are taking place out of public view. An informed citizen might come to suspect that the foreign policy of the United States often works publicly in one direction and secretly through the Invisible Government in just the opposite direction."[26] The declassification of NSC-4A and NSC-10/2, among other notable directives, confirmed this suspicion. Public deception was not an occasional political tactic (i.e., "all politicians lie") but a *structural requirement* of U.S. policy (what George Kennan called "the necessary lie").[27] Once a significant portion of government work becomes top secret and "plausibility of denial" becomes state policy, the belief that political power is wielded by powerful, invisible actors can hardly be called paranoid. The covert sector, in fact, has made a certain kind of paranoia a condition of good citizenship.[28]

It would be a mistake, however, to understand the covert sector as an invisible locus of power. For all its operational secrecy, covert government is *not* secret. In fact, it is the subject of constant speculation and representation. We know covert agencies exist; we speak of them endlessly; we know some things they have done, and we think we know many more. Their secrecy is like that of Victorian sexuality in Foucault's famous account: purportedly repressed but endlessly discussed. Is it any surprise that they, too, have come to seem "the explanation for everything"—"the omnipotent cause, the hidden meaning, the unremitting fear"?[29]

Covert government, then, is not so much a secret as what Michael Taussig calls a "public secret"—"that which is generally known, but cannot be articulated." Public secrets are "the basis of our social institutions," Taussig claims. They invite "active not-knowing" and require "knowing what *not* to know."[30] They are a paradoxical mix of awareness and disavowal that illuminates the sources of value and power in a society. Public secrecy is a regime of half-knowledge. It allows the public to know on the level of fantasy what it cannot know in an operational sense. This half-knowledge facilitates public acceptance of initiatives that seem "necessary" even though their specific details are not debated in the rational forms crucial to Habermas's description of the bourgeois public sphere.

But how does the public acquire even "half-knowledge" about state secrets? First, state secrets leak incessantly into the public sphere. They are disclosed not only by aggressive guardians of the public interest—journalists, historians, activists—but also by state and enemy agents for a wide variety of motives, including both public welfare and public deception.[31] Second, the covert state *intentionally* reveals some of its activities. It is a paradoxical monster whose need for massive public investment conflicts with its need for operational secrecy. Covert work cannot continue without public approval, but it also cannot be disclosed, and thus the covert state has an interest in generating a public that *thinks* it has a general knowledge of such work but *does not* and *cannot* know in detail. This is why military agencies routinely permit the use of their equipment in Hollywood films and why the CIA has a large public relations division. The history of the covert sector overflows with paradoxical cases in which state agencies shielded material already in the public domain or publicized material that other agencies aggressively guarded.[32] As I explain in chapter 2, for instance, the Rosenbergs were executed in 1953 for providing the USSR with "atomic secrets" that were nonetheless made public during their trial and immediately published around the world. Such anomalies are not simply relics of the Cold War. In May 2012, members of Congress were outraged to learn that the Pentagon and CIA had secretly given classified information to the Oscar-winning director Kathryn Bigelow and screenwriter Mark Boal for "Zero Dark Thirty," a thriller about the 2011 Navy Seal operation that killed Osama bin Laden. One of the most interesting features of the National Security State is the vexed relation of publicity and secrets.[33] As Trevor Paglen has shown, the entanglement of covert agencies with the public sphere (for instance, the CIA's use of civilian aircraft and publicly registered shell companies) permits new groups of "black watchers" to track certain forms of clandestine state activity.[34] The surprises of the covert sphere often lie less in the revelation of secrets than in the public's astonishment at "discovering" what is already public.

Third, and most important, the public "knows" about covert action through popular *fiction*. A key cultural consequence of covert warfare, in fact, is that fiction is one of the few permissible discourses through which writers can represent the secret work of the state, which the public must ultimately approve "sight unseen." Foreign and domestic intelligence is thus a major subject of popular culture, central to thousands of films, television serials, novels, comics, and electronic games.[35] These representations are artistically and politically diverse. Some are brilliant literary experiments or carefully researched historical novels on the political consequences of "the invisible government." Others are melodramas—spy thrillers, counterterrorism flicks, black ops and paramilitary fictions. The political and philosophical issues of covert government have also occasionally been displaced onto the landscapes of science fiction and the western, to a variety of political ends. Some covert-sphere representations function as virtual propaganda for the National Security State, while others satirize or soberly critique the "body of lies" that has led to intelligence failures, human rights violations, and the growth of sovereign state capacities in the democratic West. For a number of influential literary figures, the covert state has become a central object of reflection and, I will argue, a major stimulus of postmodern epistemological skepticism. These writers include Kathy Acker, Margaret Atwood, William S. Burroughs, Robert Coover, Don DeLillo, Philip K. Dick, Joan Didion, E. L. Doctorow, William Gibson, Graham Greene, Michael Herr, Denis Johnson, Tony Kushner, John Le Carré, Norman Mailer, Joseph McElroy, Tim O'Brien, Thomas Pynchon, Ishmael Reed, Robert Stone, Jess Walter, and John A. Williams.

The remarkable dominance of men as both creators and subjects of this corpus is a reflection partly of intelligence history and partly of the traditionally male genres that center on war and espionage. As I will explain in detail later, this body of work highlights a crisis of masculinity connected to the transformation of Cold War democracy. While the state increasingly shelters citizens from the dirty work of foreign policy, the fictions of the covert sphere compensate for this structural "feminization" with fantasies of masculinist bravado and heroic agency.

Unlike the "rational-critical" public sphere, then, the covert sphere is marked by a structural irrationality, for the democratic state prohibits citizens from engaging in public oversight of its covert activities. A primary consequence of this strange epistemology is that the covert sphere is shaped less by the dominant discourses of the public sphere—journalism, history, jurisprudence, and other approaches grounded in an ethical insistence on "truth as correspondence to fact"—than by fiction, which is not subject to the state's prohibitions.[36] To put it crudely, it is illegal to disclose state secrets but not illegal to write espionage fiction. The Valerie Plame Wilson affair offers a telling illustration of this institutional effect. In 2002, the Office of the Vice President misrepresented CIA analysis to the public, suggesting that Niger was shipping five hundred tons of yellow cake uranium to Iraq. President Bush reiterated this erroneous claim in his 2002

State of the Union address. The misrepresentation was possible partly because the CIA is prohibited from presenting its own analysis to the public. Only when the agency contracted with a civilian expert—Joseph Wilson, a former ambassador and the husband of the CIA officer Valerie Plame Wilson—did the door open to a public rebuttal in the form of Wilson's op-ed piece, "What I Didn't Find in Africa."[37] The subsequent public humiliation of Valerie Plame Wilson became the basis of her 2007 memoir, *Fair Game,* and the 2010 Doug Liman film of the same title. But even this memoir, though already the subject of massive newspaper coverage, was heavily edited by the CIA. Is it any surprise that Plame Wilson in 2011 signed a deal with Penguin to write a series of spy novels with a female protagonist? As she put it when announcing her decision to abandon the memoir genre for fiction, "I'm going for redaction-free.... I've had enough trouble."[38]

This is not to say that the discourses of "fact" have no place in the covert sphere. But in its precincts they are more likely to take on fictional qualities—a reliance on anonymous sources, speculation, invention, and confabulation. Daniel Ellsberg, who in 1971 leaked the top secret Pentagon Papers to the *New York Times,* describes how his top secret clearance made him "really look down on the *New York Times* readers." Once granted access to "whole libraries of hidden information," Ellsberg began to see the *New York Times* as "fantasies basically" and read it "just to see what the rubes and the yokels are thinking." From inside the secret archive of the security state, in other words, the most serious institutions of the public sphere seemed vehicles of fiction. And yet the inside knowledge afforded by a top secret clearance did not open a special pathway to Habermasian public reason. Over time, in fact, Ellsberg came to believe that his profound isolation from the public sphere had made him "something like a moron...incapable of learning from most people in the world, no matter how much experience they may have."[39]

Indeed, the deeper one digs in the clandestine archive, the more one doubts that public reason can be guaranteed by the institutions of the public sphere. One of the most important functions of the intelligence services is to manipulate public opinion through propaganda and disinformation, which is most effective when circulated by unwitting civilian journalists and presses. As I show in chapters 1–3, some journalistic representations of the covert state turn out to be in fact strategic *fictions* produced by state agencies for instrumental purposes. Such influences create confusion and, when discovered, foster public skepticism, distrust, and uncertainty—a sense that the business of covert warfare can never be publicly known. My argument, in short, is not that the covert sphere represses discourse while the public sphere circulates it. It is rather that institutional constraints on public knowledge shift discourse in the direction of fiction.[40]

Before I go further down this road, I want to address several conceptual matters related to my argument. First, I am aware that it is reductive to speak of the state as monolithic, when in fact it is a byzantine hodgepodge of bureaucracies and individuals with competing goals, interests, and beliefs. Second, it is an even grosser oversimplification to speak of "the public" and "public knowledge." To say that "the public knows" about certain matters of state certainly does not mean that *everyone* knows. The extraordinary diversity of knowledge among sectors of the public means that virtually anything known by one person or group is unknown by others. A traditional solution to this problem is to use the term "public" to refer to those citizens who pay close attention to public affairs—the intelligentsia outside of the state.[41] But this solution is doubly problematic. For one thing, the public is larger than the citizenry, for it includes noncitizens living within and without the nation's borders who have a major stake in national policy. And for another, the public is a conceptual apparition. "Publics," as Michael Warner points out, "do not exist apart from the discourse that addresses them."[42] It is important not only to heed this warning but to insist on Warner's association of publicness with discourse. The notion of "public knowledge" is best understood as shorthand for the social circulation of ideas—particularly for their visibility within mass media. This sense is already implicit in popular usage. To say that "the public knows" something usually implies that the idea has been widely mentioned in the mainstream press, whereas to say something is "secret" means it has fallen outside these circuits. As Noam Chomsky observes of Nixon's 1970 "secret bombing" of Cambodia, for example, "the bombing was 'secret' because the press refused to expose it."[43] Secrecy, in this instance, is not simply a matter of state repression but also of media circulation—though the two are clearly related. It is this sense of secrecy that explains the recent explosion of "secret histories."

My uses of "the state," "the public," and "public knowledge" thus constitute deliberate oversimplifications. The lines between "the state" and "the public," and between "classified information" and "public knowledge," are fluid and difficult to chart. Yet the concept of public knowledge is none-theless a useful way of recognizing that, within a regime of state secrecy, certain ideas are easier to come by than others. Some forms of knowledge receive wide public airing; others are carefully guarded or disavowed.

Chomsky's remark about Cambodia brings a third consideration for-ward: the line between the "overt" and the "covert" shifts in relation to both the scale and recency of events. Whereas small operations often remain se-cret, larger initiatives are more difficult to conceal, particularly over time. Secrecy, that is, has a temporal dimension. Hence, the distinguished con-servative historian John Lewis Gaddis called his 1998 reexamination of the Cold War *We Now Know,* a title that simultaneously articulates an original public unknowing and a subsequent process of disclosure by which state secrets eventually come to "public consciousness."[44]

I make these distinctions to address a question lingering over my argu-ment: To what extent is public knowledge of covert action controlled by state secrecy and to what extent is it governed by more ordinary ideologi-cal or discursive mechanisms? To put it another way, am I attempting to resuscitate the "repressive model" of power that Foucault associated with state sovereignty and replaced with a discursive model?[45] Not quite. My argument is not that power is *primarily* "repressive" but that state secrecy is a crucial part of a larger ideological system for managing the contradic-tions of U.S. empire. It makes a profound difference that the state con-ducts much of its foreign policy through covert institutions, particularly when people (here and abroad) *know* that the state is acting secretly, for they begin to suspect that all kinds of world events are being secretly or-chestrated by covert agencies. At the same time, much public unknowing seems less a matter of state secrecy per se than of garden-variety "histori-cal amnesia." It is no longer secret, for instance, that the CIA successfully overthrew the popularly elected governments of Iran in 1953 and Gua-temala in 1956. Yet most U.S. citizens seem no more aware of this his-tory than of other "national shames."[46] The effects of state secrecy are of course most powerful while covert actions are being taken, but even then the "public secret" of the covert state itself must be understood within an ideological and discursive framework. Only a hybrid approach, recogniz-ing the effects of state repression within a larger ideological system, can explain the vitality of American exceptionalism amid an extensive (and expensive) form of state sovereignty.

A good starting point for such an approach is Slavoj Žižek's brilliant reconceptualization of ideology as a matter of action rather than knowledge. For Žižek, the sign of an effective ideology is not "false consciousness" in the classic Marxian sense but rather the expression of belief through actions. Žižek's basic "formula" for ideological disavowal is "*I know very well...but just the same...*" Under the spell of this formula, we may "know very well" that something is wrong, but "just the same" we continue to act as if all is well.[47] Fantasy is the mechanism that smoothes the contradiction between knowledge and action. Within a powerful enough fantasy, simply knowing that something is wrong is not enough to change behavior. Indeed, the cynicism that was once the hallmark of enlightened ideology critique is for Žižek the very essence of contemporary ideology, for cynicism ("I know very well what is wrong, but there is nothing I can do") results in the same inaction as classical ideological delusion ("nothing *is* wrong, all *is* well").

In the covert sphere, however, the question of public knowledge is complicated by the tension between state secrecy and its popular representation. On the one hand, the public "knows very well" that the state has adopted methods at odds with its public commitment to democracy and human rights. The reason U.S. citizens did not protest domestic NSA "data mining" in 2005, notes a character in William Gibson's *Spook Country,* is that "they'd already been taking it for granted, since at least the 1960s, that the CIA was tapping everybody's phone. It was the stuff of bad episodic television. It was something little kids knew to be true."[48] On the other hand, the public does *not* know the details of most covert actions, particularly as they unfold. Knowing, for instance, that enemy combatants are being interrogated in military prisons is not the same as knowing *how* they are being interrogated or *why.* This gap explains the public shock when news outlets began to report the abuse and torture of enemy prisoners several years into President Bush's War on Terror. Yet it would be wrong to conclude that the public knew nothing of U.S. policy, for it had long enjoyed popular *fictions* (*The Siege, 24, Patriot Games, The Sum of All Fears, The Unit,* the *Bourne* trilogy, and many others) that depicted the grim horrors and miraculous efficacy of covert action, extraordinary rendition, and brutal interrogation (see chapter 6). These entertainments suggested the state's covert methods, but the knowledge came in the form of melodrama and narrative fantasy. In an era of covert action, such fantasies are crucial vehicles of public half-knowledge.

The epistemology of the covert sphere can thus be further specified in two modifications of Žižek's general formula, *I know very well...but just the same*. The first of these is *I can't know, and I don't want to know*. The second is *I believed I knew, but I am shocked to discover...!* The contradiction between these two positions reflects the gap between juridical-historical and "fictional" sources of knowledge about the covert sector. The first statement converts the state's prohibition on knowledge into a desire not to know. This stance represents an inversion of Althusser's classic example of ideological interpellation; instead of the subject answering when the state says, "Hey, you!" the subjects of the covert sphere close their eyes when the state says, "Don't look!" The state's position here is epitomized by Nathan R. Jessup, the haughty colonel (played by Jack Nicholson) in *A Few Good Men:* "You want the truth? You can't *handle* the truth!"[49] This is the original "don't ask, don't tell" policy of the Cold War state. It captures not only the state's prohibition of public knowledge but also the public's desire to disavow its knowledge of undemocratic state means. It transforms cynicism (I *know* but cannot act) into mystified submission (I *cannot* and *should not* know).

But this formula alone cannot explain the powerful expressions of shock when the undemocratic activities of the covert state are revealed in

Figure 1. In *A Few Good Men*, Colonel Nathan R. Jessup (Jack Nicholson) articulates the security state's contemptuous dismissal of public half-knowledge: "You can't *handle* the truth! . . . You have the luxury of not knowing what I know! . . . My existence, while grotesque and incomprehensible to you, saves lives!"

the nonfiction press. Here we must turn to the second statement, which suggests that, despite prohibitions on "real" knowing, *some* channels of knowledge remain open between the public and the covert state. This knowledge, however, comes substantially through fiction, which the public can dismiss as an amalgam of possibility, fantasy, and dramatic hyperbole. As Žižek observed only days after September 11, 2001, the events of 9/11 came as "a shock" even though they had been uncannily anticipated for years in films depicting the violent destruction of iconic U.S. institutions. Popular film displayed an awareness that the world was poised to strike the United States, and yet this awareness was disavowed as *mere fiction.*[50] As Michael Taussig notes, when public secrets concern state institutions, "only the movies tell it like it is.... But that's fiction."[51] The phrase "but that's fiction" is a familiar dismissal—a reminder that fiction is what the philosopher John Searle (following J. L. Austin) famously called "nonserious" discourse.[52] But it is precisely fiction's status as nonserious that has made it the privileged discourse of the covert sphere. Unlike the "serious" discourses of the rational-critical public sphere, fiction can reveal the public secrets of the covert state without appearing to reveal any "real" secrets, for its knowledge is invented, not found.

One way to recognize the power of these epistemological conditions is to observe that they affect not only the public but also the agents of the state. While Habermas draws a sharp distinction between the public sphere and the state proper, the institutions of the National Security State erode this distinction, trapping citizens and state officials alike in a condition of unknowing. In fact, ranking administrators, including the president of the United States, sometimes do not know the operational details of important intelligence initiatives. As the CIA officer Joseph B. Smith puts it in *Portrait of a Cold Warrior,* "One of the ironies of the Bay of Pigs, CIA's greatest fiasco, was that so few of the Agency's professional staff knew anything about the preparation and launching of the operation while almost every Cuban exile in Miami knew practically everything."[53] The unknowing of covert agents is the basis of Harry Mathews's arch memoir, *My Life in CIA,* which describes how Mathews, tired of being a suspected CIA agent, decides to embrace the role, setting up a phony travel business and poking around in matters of Soviet geography. He is soon treated as a serious spy by many intelligence agents.[54] How could they know otherwise?

Such oddities are the result of two institutional hallmarks of the security state: "plausible deniability" and the compartmentalization of knowledge, which is a bulwark against counterespionage. These structures have profound effects not only on public knowledge but also on the knowledge of state officials and agents. Consider, for example, President Dwight Eisenhower's speech to the American Society of Newspaper Editors on April 16, 1953, "The Chance for Peace," which took the recent death of Joseph Stalin as an opportunity to argue against a massive arms race with the USSR. Standing at the symbolic center of the U.S. public sphere, the president reaffirmed every nation's "inalienable...right to form a government and an economic system of its own choosing," and he declared that "any nation's attempt to dictate to other nations their form of government is indefensible." Yet on March 18, 1953, one month prior to this speech and two weeks after Stalin's death, the Director of Central Intelligence (DCI) Allen Dulles had committed $1 million to the CIA's Tehran Station for the overthrow of the Iranian prime minister Mohammad Mossadeq. At an earlier meeting of the NSC, on March 4, 1953, Eisenhower had rejected the idea of overthrowing Mossadeq and suggested giving him a loan instead. Nonetheless, CIA planners, working with the British Secret Intelligence Service (SIS), scripted an elaborate simulated coup d'état: a "terrorist gang" (in the words of the in-house CIA historian Donald Wilber) would pose as Communists and attack religious leaders; a $150,000 psychological warfare campaign would use paid Iranian "actors" to protest against Mossadeq's policies; and a band of mercenaries would then seize government and media sites, deposing Mossadeq. Once the plan had been approved by the British prime minister, Winston Churchill, Eisenhower approved it on July 11, 1953. Five weeks later, the phony revolution installed Shah Mohammad Reza Pahlavi in Mossadeq's place, where he would remain for the next twenty-five years.[55] Although Eisenhower eventually "knew very well" about this plot, his knowledge of its details was at best fragmentary, managed by the epistemology of NSC-10/2 and the compartmentalization of the CIA. As Eisenhower watched Operation Ajax unfold from Washington, it had the quality of *fiction* for him. In his 1963 memoir he remarks that the "reports from observers on the spot in Teheran during the critical days sounded more like a dime novel than historical fact."[56] While this comment mocks the imaginative excesses of CIA reports, it correctly discerns the surprising link between covert action and fiction, which I take up in detail later.

An even more instructive example can be drawn from President John F. Kennedy's remarks to a Seattle audience on November 16, 1961: "We cannot, as a free nation, compete with our adversaries in tactics of terror, assassination, false promises, counterfeit mobs, and crises. We cannot, under the scrutiny of a free press and public, tell different stories to different audiences, foreign, domestic, friendly, and hostile."[57] On the day before this speech, William Harvey, the CIA's point man on Cuba, and Richard Bissell, the CIA deputy director of operations, met to plan the assassination of Fidel Castro through a new version of operation ZR/RIFLE, which had earlier been used in an unsuccessful attempt on the life of the Congolese prime minister, Patrice Lumumba. Harvey had already found Mafia hit men for the mission. Two weeks prior to Kennedy's speech, the president's aide, Richard Goodwin, had urged a covert program against Cuba, and two weeks after the speech, Kennedy himself directed his cabinet to "use our available assets . . . to help Cuba overthrow its Communist regime." Yet when the president and the attorney general, Robert Kennedy, learned the specific details of this and other anti-Castro operations, they expressed surprise and anger to the president's staff. Like the public, in other words, the Kennedys "knew very well but were shocked to discover . . ."[58]

"Deniability," then, is not simply a structure for insulating the nation-state from culpability in embarrassing strategic actions. It is also an institutionally supported form of official disavowal, a general way of managing knowledge. It shields not only the public *but also administration officials* from the disturbing details of U.S. covert action. Deniability is the hinge between the institutional and cultural features of the covert sphere. It allows the public and its representatives to "disappear" the contradiction between principles and actions, permitting the rhetoric of democracy to flourish amid the use of undemocratic tactics.

I am not suggesting, of course, that state officials know as little as John Q. Public—only that they too face, and invite, restrictions on their knowledge. There is no "deeper level" or ultimate "inside position" from which *all* the secret work of the covert state is visible. Like the public, state agents are caught up in the cultural imaginary of the covert sphere. It is no accident that Kennedy, a notorious devotee of Ian Fleming's fiction, kept searching for "our James Bond" (see chapter 3), or that Ronald Reagan articulated his foreign policy through the terminology of *Star Wars,* or that Bill Clinton and Antonin Scalia, among others, have defended U.S.

antiterror policy on the basis of examples from the FOX terror melodrama *24* (see chapter 6).[59] When popular fiction becomes a vehicle through which the state's own agents imagine their work, then representations stand in a puzzling relation to the real and the work of national security begins to take on a postmodern quality—an effect to which I will return later in this introduction.

Public Secrets

Six blocks from the White House stands a major institution of the covert sphere. The building that once housed the Washington chapter of the American Communist Party is now the International Spy Museum. A reminder of the once-powerful antagonisms tolerated within democracy, in other words, has been converted into a monument to the secret methods by which the Cold War security state eliminated those antagonisms.

Founded in 2002 by the former NSA employee and media magnate Milton Maltz, the Spy Museum is one of DC's most popular tourist sites with seven hundred thousand visitors a year (by comparison, visits to the White House surged in 2009 to 614,000).[60] "People like to learn secrets," says the Spy Museum's director, Peter Earnest, a decorated thirty-six-year veteran and former public relations officer of the CIA.[61] The museum trades aggressively on this desire and, in the process, struggles to understand whether its mission is the promulgation of facts or fictions. On the one hand, the museum purports to reveal the secrets of the intelligence business. It displays six hundred artifacts—mainly high-tech gadgets— and claims to relate the history of spying "from the Bible to Bond." Its board of directors, moreover, is packed with accomplished former intelligence officials such as William Webster (former head of both the Federal Bureau of Investigation [FBI] and the CIA); R. James Woolsey (former FBI director); and Maj. Gen. Oleg Kalugin (former KGB chief of foreign counterintelligence), among others.[62]

On the other hand, the museum is fun. Its deepest commitment is to the celebration of the individual espionage agent as depicted in popular fiction. Visitors are invited to take on a "cover identity" and attend "spy school." During their tour, they learn basic elements of spycraft (dead drops, lock picking, etc.). For an extra fee, visitors can indulge in the "great game" of espionage, entering a high-tech "themed environment" where they must "locate a missing nuclear device on the verge of being sold to a rogue nation." And for $10,000, four visitors can enjoy a weekend of such simulations while also hobnobbing over cocktails and meals with the "extraordinary spymasters [on] the museum's board of directors."[63] There is nothing here about the political or human costs of covert action—no exhibit on the CIA's adventures in Guatemala or Iran, no Bay of Pigs, Cambodia, or Laos, no paramilitary operations in Latin America. The ISM is a fast-paced, multimedia advertisement for the intelligence services. Visitors are invited to awe-filled contemplation of the state's most vital work in a setting that markets this work as a series of thrilling but dismissible fantasies. Could there be a better illustration of the logic of the covert sphere?

This is not a rhetorical question—for only seven miles away by jetpack sits the even more paradoxical CIA Museum. Locked in the secure perimeter of the agency's Langley, Virginia, campus, this oxymoronic museum of secrets proudly commemorates selected efforts of men and women sworn never to disclose their work to the public. The CIA Museum is the secret doppelgänger of the wildly popular International Spy Museum, for while it is "the preeminent national archive" of intelligence history, it is also *closed*

Figure 2. The International Spy Museum invites visitors, especially children, to "come to an actual covert ops playground" where they can engage in espionage fantasy.

to the public. Created in 1972 at the suggestion of the CIA director William Colby, it was part of the CIA's public relations effort amid the embarrassing revelations and investigations of the Vietnam era (an effort that was, interestingly enough, a major duty of Peter Earnest, the current curator of the International Spy Museum).[64] According to promotional documents, the self-defeating mission of the CIA Museum requires it, on the one hand, to "promote a wider understanding of the craft of intelligence and its role in the American experience," and on the other, to "remind CIA officers of their history." While the former task requires public outreach to make a case for public funding, the latter requires shuttering the museum, for anything detailed enough to inspire agency insiders is classified. A 2008 *Voice of America News* report on the museum's new Afghanistan gallery (clearly a CIA public relations piece) claimed to reveal some items in the gallery "for the first time." But it also digitally obscured the faces of officers (and a dog) depicted in the exhibit.[65] Unlike the artifacts in the International Spy Museum, in other words, the contents of the CIA Museum are so "real" that they cannot become fully public.[66]

The CIA Museum is thus the quintessential emblem of the covert sphere—haunted through-and-through by the state's competing needs for publicity and secrecy. It is thus doubly revealing to examine the three dozen or so "declassified" artifacts that the museum makes available for public viewing on its website. What are these public secrets? They include a predictable array of gizmos almost worthy of Q., the techno-wizard of James Bond fame: an enigma machine, a microdot camera, a robotic fish, and a "dragonfly insecthopter." The capacities of the agency's current enemy, meanwhile, are depicted by this bizarre trio: an Al Qaeda training manual, a gas mask, and a hunk of lapis lazuli said to illustrate the financial strength of the Taliban. The rest of the online artifacts are so absurdly quotidian (Allan Dulles's ID card! Ike's groundbreaking trowel!) that they seem mainly to illustrate the impossibility of finding publishable secrets.[67]

There is one telling object in the collection, however: the "SPY-Fi Archives," a collection of images and objects from popular spy films and television programs. This collection emphasizes melodrama and lighthearted fare—the James Bond films, *The Man from U.N.C.L.E., Get Smart, Mission Impossible, The Avengers, Wild Wild West, Our Man Flint, The Silencers,* even the Austin Powers films. Notably, the museum does not represent

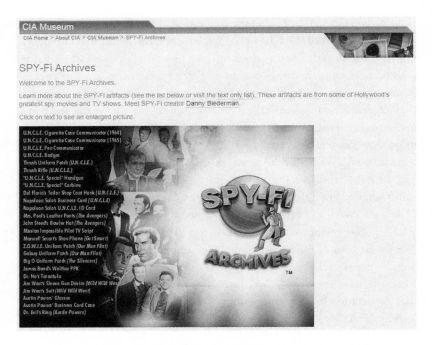

Figure 3. Museum of secrets. Alongside gadgets like those used in spy thrillers, the online CIA Museum proudly displays the "SPY-Fi Archives," suggesting that the agency's representation in popular fiction is crucial to its mission.

such narratives as a trivializing *misrepresentation* of the agency's gritty and difficult real work. On the contrary, like the International Spy Museum, it pays *homage* to these entertainments.

What, then, is the "secret" revealed in both the CIA and Spy Museums? The secret is that there is no secret—or, to be more exact, that the most important secrets are public secrets. Like Poe's "Purloined Letter," the covert state is hidden right out in the open, made endlessly public in the popular fictions of the covert sphere—melodramas of Cold War espionage, counterterrorism, Western technological superiority, and individual masculinist bravado. Why is this fiction the central content of both the nation's popular spy museum and its "premiere intelligence archive"? The intelligence officials who curate these institutions clearly recognize the crucial role of fiction in the work of the state. Fiction "reveals" covert action in a form dismissible as fantasy, melodrama, mere entertainment. It satisfies the public desire to know the work of the state while also pretending not to know what the state does in the public's name.

Mere Entertainment

I have stressed the enhanced role of fiction in the covert sphere, but I want to be clear that the covert sphere is the sum of public discourse about secret government. In addition to popular and "literary" fiction, this discourse includes histories, documentaries, journalism, professional intelligence and diplomatic writings, unclassified or declassified government documents, conspiracy theories, blog posts, WikiLeaks, water-cooler conversations, and the book you are reading right now.[68] This body of discourse is politically and aesthetically diverse. While much of it provides political support to the National Security State, it also includes many incisive critiques. Although popular films, spy novels, television shows, comic books, and electronic games have a large role in shaping public attitudes, I spend many of the pages that follow on writing by Coover, DeLillo, Doctorow, Didion, and others whose historical fictions of Cold War secrecy are as illuminating as anything on the subject.

Despite the remarkable scope and variety of covert-sphere narrative, it has several defining general features. First, it is overwhelmingly white and male, both in terms of authorship and content. Its principal popular genres—the spy thriller, the western, the detective and combat narratives—were the crucible of Cold War hypermasculinity, part of what Ellen Tyler May and Alan Nadel have both described as a domestic "containment culture" that mirrored the logic of U.S. foreign policy in a gendered form of domestic hypervigilance.[69] As Michael Davidson and Robert Corber have so compellingly shown, an entire poetics of masculinity and homophobia developed in response to the apparent dangers of enemy "penetration," "thought-control," and subversion. While rugged male agency became articulated as a defense against creeping socialism, metaphorically "leaky" forms of identity came under strict scrutiny: mothers were chastised for mollycoddling their sons; women experienced extraordinary feminizing pressures; gay and effeminate men were viewed as insufficiently tough to prevent the spread of socialism, liberalism, and even cooperation.[70]

This spectacular intensification of traditional gender concepts has too often been viewed as a "mere" cultural effect of "real" political conflict. But as Amy Kaplan notes, the already-gendered relation of the (masculine) geopolitical to the (feminine) cultural sphere is what produces the erroneous assumption that real geopolitical conflict is always the cause, and not the effect, of "mere" domestic culture.[71] It is important to heed this warning. A number of important studies have shown that U.S. policy was directly affected by a culture of masculinity among the architects of the Cold War.[72] The CIA in particular was a clandestine form of what Michael Davidson calls the "boy gang"—one of the many 1950s-era insular cohorts of elite, artistically inclined men.[73] The representations of covert action concentrate on this priesthood through traditionally male genres and the familiar rhetoric of a carefully bounded body that does not leak its secrets into the public.

More surprising, perhaps, is what this hypermasculine imaginary suggests about the transformation of the Cold War public sphere. As the Cold War covert sector became the arena in which foreign policy was made, U.S. citizens were shuttled into a more passive civic role. By offering security in exchange for submission to the inscrutable will of a state protector, this new social compact placed the public in an increasingly feminized relation to a paternalistic state. This is a significant shift, for the public has historically been associated with masculinity. As Habermas's critics have often pointed out, the eighteenth-century public sphere is a flawed ideal because its institutions were dominated by men of privilege. Through at least the nineteenth century, a cult of domesticity construed the public sphere as male space and the domestic sphere as a zone of female influence outside the rough-and-tumble world of political conflict and policymaking.[74] As the Cold War state concealed important political knowledge, however, the public increasingly took a position "out of the know" and reliant on the clandestine agents of the state to act in its best political interests. In other words, the public sphere was tacitly reconceived along the lines of the feminized domestic sphere. This transformation might have provoked more notice had it not been accompanied by the rise of a new cultural imaginary for the contemplation of clandestine policy. This imaginary, the covert sphere, offered an anxious *recognition* of, and imaginary *compensation* for, the feminization of the public sphere. The anxiety came in the nightmarish form of brainwashed assassins, pliant citizens, and a security state run amok; the compensation was a steady diet of masculinist fantasy—heroic violence, individual agency, and rogue bravado.

The compensatory fantasies of the covert sphere are among its most powerful cultural effects, and an entire cultural machinery is now in place to cultivate such fantasies. An astonishing array of toys—including cameras, listening devices, and robotic vehicles—encourage Western children, especially boys, to view covert action as a fact of life and a privileged form of subjectivity. Youth fiction not only makes "spycraft" a popular fantasy but it normalizes the idea of foreign policy as a set of exceptions to democracy. At seven years old my son selected for a school assignment the novel *NERDS: National Espionage, Rescue, and Defense Society.* This tale of a kid spy agency that is secret even to the president of the United States begins with a portrait of "the United States' most valuable spy," Alexander Brand: "He had saved the world on more than a dozen occasions. He had stopped three invasions of the United States by foreign powers. He had helped depose six dictators and four corrupt presidents.... Plus, he looked awesome in a tuxedo."[75] Here, the celebration of covert action and plausible deniability is decidedly "nonserious," allowing readers (and their parents) to laugh off the implications of a world where U.S. agents routinely manipulate foreign governments. Within the fantasy of secret agency, as every child knows, the secret agent *always* has the power and moral rectitude to compensate for the abrogation of democracy.

For the past several decades, video gaming has offered an even richer field for compensatory fantasy. In hundreds of complex simulations, these interfaces invite users to imagine that they are hardened special operations forces engaged in dangerous foreign missions. With several billions of dollars in sales and approaching one billion user hours, the Activision *Call of Duty* series is, according to Activision CEO Bobby Kotick, "likely to be one of the most viewed of all entertainment experiences in modern history."[76] Such entertainments not only market a fantasy of hypermasculine combat on the frontiers of empire but also critique the public sphere as a domestic fantasy. A trailer for *Call of Duty: Black Ops* informs the viewer, over a montage of air strikes, detonations, and small-arms fire, "A lie is a lie. Just because they write it down and call it history doesn't make it the truth. We live in a world where seeing isn't believing, where only a few know what really happened. We live in a world where everything we know is wrong." While making an argument about the public's utter deception, the trailer invites us to pierce the deceptive veil of the domestic sphere and enter "the real world" of hypermasculine racialized combat, political power, and secret knowledge. Another trailer explicitly connects this fantasy to state sovereignty and the state of exception: "You will move without boundaries," intones the grave, bass voiceover. "You will act above the law. You will use every means necessary to stop the wars that are hidden from the world. And if you succeed, you will do so without recognition because *you... do not... exist.*"[77] Activision knows that most of its players are the antithesis of the hardened male action hero, hence a major advertising campaign for the games—"There's a soldier in all of us"—shows civilian men, women, and children on the simulated battlefield, awkwardly but enthusiastically engaged in mortal combat. This advertisement concisely registers the gender dynamic of the covert sphere, which invites feminized civilians to project themselves into the hypermasculine bodies of professional warriors. The result is not merely a fantasy of masculine agency but also a *fantasy of citizenship* in which the middle-class descendants of "the greatest generation," safe on their living room sofas, imagine risking their lives on behalf of a grateful nation.

Such fantasies facilitate what Susan Jeffords calls "the remasculinization of America"—in which hair-raising combat fictions resuscitate a wounded national masculinity—and also the social transformation that

Figure 4. In this trailer for *Call of Duty: Modern Warfare* 3 a hardened special-ops veteran (Sam Worthington, right) schools a comically inept "nOOb" (Jonah Hill, left), who is a stand-in for the sheltered Western consumer. The trailer, like the game, allows consumers to fantasize real citizenship through the simulation of heroic male action.

Ann Douglas calls the "feminization of American culture."[78] These two social changes are in fact part of the same general transformation in which an increasingly passive citizenry is recompensed by the fantasies of the covert sphere. This is why it seemed so natural to President George W. Bush to suggest that the public respond to the events of 9/11 by visiting Disney World and *going shopping*.[79] The work of the post–Cold-War public is to keep the home well stocked, recall an upbeat version of U.S. history, and not worry its pretty little head about the grim and secret work of the state.

A second defining feature of covert-sphere narrative is its organization around two rival anxieties: on the one hand, a serious external threat to the nation; on the other, the threat of the U.S. security state itself. In both cases, the primary object of interest—the external enemy or the vast security apparatus itself—tends to be seen as a source of irrationality, mystery, or supernatural agency. Narratives dominated by a concern with external enemies tend to enact the racialized logic Michael Rogin calls "demonology"—the tradition of shoring up U.S. identity through a paranoid scapegoating of Native Americans, immigrants, Communists, and now jihadists. This dynamic is especially notable in narratives of Third World combat, where demonology not only provides a source of national identity and purpose but also registers the unknowability of covert warfare. In the massive body of work on the U.S. war in Vietnam, Southeast Asia is routinely rendered as radically other, a site of surreal horror where the enemy is invisible and the mission vague (see chapter 3). In such cases, the distant frontiers of U.S. empire become a screen for the racialized projection of Cold War epistemological uncertainty.

A similar quality marks narratives of the security state itself, which is usually depicted as a vast, mysterious, and astonishingly powerful apparatus. It is striking how many popular representations of this system depict its negative consequences for U.S. citizens: its potential for technological catastrophe (from *Fail-Safe* [1964] and *Dr. Strangelove* [1964] through *Eagle Eye* [2008] and *Echelon Conspiracy* [2009]); its labyrinth of cynical, pointless, and ultimately fatal spy games (from *The Spy Who Came in from the Cold* [1963] through *Syriana* [2005] and *The Good Shepherd* [2006]); its violent disregard for human rights (from *Three Days of the Condor* [1975] through *Rendition* [2007] and *Body of Lies* [2008]); or its wholesale undoing of democracy (*Seven Days in May* [1964], *Executive Action* [1973], *The Conversation* [1974], *The Parallax View* [1975], *Hangmen* [1987], *The Package* [1989],

The Siege [1998], *Enemy of the State* [1998], and many others). Despite their profound anxiety about the National Security State, these critiques are hardly rooted in solidarity with those historically affected by U.S. intervention. They are, on the contrary, concerned that the security state might be a danger to U.S. citizens. Indeed, as I explain in chapter 6, one of the distinctive features of covert-sphere melodrama is that its hero usually takes the place of the state's enemies, doing battle with the U.S. security apparatus in an effort to save the world. Like demonological fantasies, these narratives are narcissistic expressions of American exceptionalism shaped by the epistemology of the covert sphere. When the state engages covertly with a distant and inscrutable enemy, both the state's enemies *and* its own methods become a source of mystery, fascination, speculation, and anxious projection. This structure fosters public ignorance about U.S. policy and supports the disavowal of U.S. empire.[80] This is one reason why there are such striking differences between U.S. and postcolonial narratives of U.S. foreign engagement.[81]

Third, the discourse of the covert sphere is marked by a general sense of epistemological uncertainty, a feeling that Cold War secrecy has made it difficult to know what is true or to narrate events as history. As Tobin Siebers writes in his compelling study of Cold War literary criticism, the Cold War ushered in a generalized state of "distrust, suspicion, paranoia, and skepticism": "It is a state that requires skepticism, and this skepticism in turn preserves the state. This is the cold war effect." As a result of these general conditions, Siebers suggests, Cold War literary study began to describe textual "tactics, strategies, and maneuvers" and made a "virtue of cold war paranoia" by cultivating theoretical suspicion.[82] Similar forms of skepticism are the hallmark of writing by Pynchon, Heller, Didion, DeLillo, Mailer, Atwood, Coover, Acker, Burroughs, and other important postmodern literary figures. Conspiracy films such as *The Conversation, The Parallax View,* and *Syriana* convey a haunting sense that no amount of exposure can reveal the state's terrifying security capabilities. More conventional espionage plots tend to end with a fantasy of public revelation, when their protagonists deliver evidence to the press or testify to Congress (notable cases include *Three Days of the Condor, Hopscotch* [1980], *The Package, Enemy of the State,* and *Green Zone* [2010]). But even these "heroic public sphere" narratives lavish considerable attention on the difficulty of discovering what is real and true. Their protagonists uncover the nature of the covert state only through exceptional courage and heroism. As Sergeant Johnny Gallagher puts it in the covert-ops thriller *The Package,* "Who the hell knows what's real?"[83]

It is significant that such expressions of skepticism haunt not *only* postmodern historiographic metafiction—where confusion about reality is an aesthetic strategy—but also more conventional forms like *The Package.* What does it mean that Sergeant Gallagher's question could serve as a crude précis of Baudrillard's "Precession of Simulacra"? It suggests a connection between the representation of state secrecy and postmodernism, for the conditions of public knowledge under a regime of state secrecy generate forms of suspicion and unknowing uncannily similar to those typically associated with postmodern representation.

I will turn to this matter momentarily. Before I do, however, I need to complicate my account of covert-sphere fiction by pointing to the epistemological effect of a very different, and more literal, sort of state fiction. The construction of *strategic fictions* is a crucial element of intelligence work. A "cold" war, after all, is fought substantially through elaborate simulations and invented plots—propaganda, psychological operations, and public deception. It is hence no accident that the early CIA was packed with literature students and writers. When the CIA decided it "wanted a terror campaign" against the left-wing Árbenz regime in Guatemala, as the operative E. Howard Hunt put it, the agency hired the professional actor David Atlee Phillips to broadcast fabricated news stories over Voice of Liberation Radio. These stories were the stuff of pulp fiction: they falsely reported that Árbenz was meeting with visiting Soviet officials, that Árbenz would soon confine all sixteen-year-olds to concentration camps for "reeducation," and so on. The CIA supplemented such operations by planting phony caches of Soviet arms in the country (Operation WASHTUB), and it later concocted the even more cynical Operation PBHISTORY, which planted fabricated "historical proof" of Soviet influence in Guatemala.[84]

As many novelists have noted, such operations require the mind of a novelist; they often require the fabrication of imaginary characters and false documents so rich in detail that unknowing investigators will be able to "reconstruct" an entirely fictional event and believe it really happened (see chapter 3). The Cold War archive overflows with such plots. It resembles the private papers of a postmodern fabulist whose unpublished sketches are regularly unearthed by persistent biographers. To take merely one example, after scrapping a proposal to blow John Glenn's February 20, 1962, space flight out of the sky and blame the disaster on "electronic interference on the part of the Cubans," the Joint Chiefs of Staff formally recommended to President Kennedy, on March 13, 1962, a campaign of fabricated domestic terrorist attacks called "Operation Northwoods." The goal of this false flag operation was to simulate "a Communist Cuban terror campaign in Miami" in order to provide grounds for the invasion of Cuba. According to JCS documents, covert U.S. operatives would "make it appear that Communist Cuban MiGs have destroyed a USAF aircraft over international waters in an unprovoked attack"; detonate "plastic bombs in carefully chosen spots" in the United States; and "[shoot] down a chartered civil airliner en route from the United States to Jamaica, Guatemala, Panama, or Venezuela." Still smarting from the 1961 debacle of the CIA's simulated "Cuban uprising" at the Bay of Pigs, Kennedy rejected the proposal.[85]

If the Cold War state was in part a fiction-making machine designed to sway enemies and citizens alike, it was also a "literary agent" and "arts patron." During the 1950s and '60s, the CIA was almost certainly the largest sponsor of serious art and literature in the Western hemisphere. As Frances Stonor Saunders has shown, "the CIA was in effect acting as America's Ministry of Culture" through a series of front organizations, most notably the Congress for Cultural Freedom.[86] Over seventeen years, the CIA spent tens of millions of dollars funding an astonishing array of journals, exhibits, societies and other creative and critical works that projected what it viewed as a strategically favorable view of Western liberal capitalism. By 1977, the agency had underwritten the publication of over one thousand books, including many modernist classics, new antisocialist fiction, and works by current and former agency employees such as John Hunt, Peter Matthiessen, James Michener, Howard Hunt, and William F. Buckley Jr. As the chief of the CIA's covert action staff explained, books were "the most important weapon of strategic (long-range) propaganda." Hence the CIA developed a way not only to "get books published for operational reasons, regardless of commercial viability" but also to "[stimulate] the writing of politically significant books by unknown foreign authors—either by directly subsidizing the author, if covert contact is feasible, or indirectly through literary agents or publishers."[87]

In short, the work of the Cold War state was quite frequently literary and cultural work. And while this work often involved the promotion of modernism (the CIA air-dropped Eliot's *Four Quartets* behind the Iron Curtain, for instance), its public effect was oddly similar to that of post-modernism.[88] Its operational goal, after all, was often to blur the authentic and the fabricated, reality and representation—precisely the sort of onto-logical confabulation that has come to define postmodernism. This is certainly not to say that the state's work was "postmodern"—only to note that the Cold War state made a considerable investment in transforming the conditions of public knowledge at home and abroad. It seems more than a coincidence that this subject would become the dominant concern of post-modern expression—a subject I now address in detail.

Strategic Irrationalism

In Habermas's classic account, the bourgeois public sphere emerged specif-ically as a check on state secrecy: "against the reliance of princely author-ity on secrets of state," Habermas explains, a new public "articulated the concept of and demand for general and abstract laws and...came to as-sert itself (i.e., public opinion) as the only legitimate source of this law."[89] This change in the public's conception of itself was famously fostered not only by liberal capitalism but also by new social organs—literary societ-ies, salons, coffeehouses, libraries, concert halls, theaters, and museums. By allowing debate on matters of social importance, such institutions cre-ated the conditions in which the public could conceive of itself as a source of power opposed to "the secret chanceries of the prince."[90] The primary social consequence of such interactions was what Habermas calls public "reason": "The bourgeois public sphere may be conceived above all as the sphere of private people come together as a public...against the public au-thorities themselves, to engage them in a debate over the general rules gov-erning relations in the basically privatized but publicly relevant sphere of commodity exchange and social labor. The medium of this political con-frontation was peculiar and without historical precedent: people's public use of their reason."[91] In this context, "reason" is the result not simply of a particular intellectual procedure but of a general social condition in which information is both "accessible to the public" and publicly discussed.

Obviously, then, the growth of Cold War state secrecy threatens "rea-son" and poses a serious problem of legitimation for Western democracy.

But Habermas is only marginally concerned with state secrecy. His primary concern is the rise of pathological forms of *publicity*—particularly strategic mass communications. These new institutions, Habermas argues, have undermined reason and led to the "refeudalization" of society. "In the measure that it is shaped by public relations, the public sphere of civil society again takes on feudal features"—particularly in the personal "aura" and "prestige" of celebrities.[92] This argument—that mass culture has swung the rational Enlightenment back toward the irrationality of the premodern or feudal—is a version of what Horkheimer and Adorno called "the dialectic of Enlightenment." Interestingly, while Habermas focuses primarily on new forms of publicity, he repeatedly notes that these forms have the same effect as an increase of secrecy. "At one time," he observes, "publicity had to be gained in opposition to the secret politics of the monarchs.... Today, on the contrary, publicity is achieved with the help of the secret politics of interest groups.... The very phrase 'publicity work' betrays that a public sphere...has to be 'made,' it is not 'there' anymore." Indeed, Habermas notes, quoting M. L. Goldschmidt, the problem of the postwar public sphere stems from two, opposite, "disturbing tendencies...: first a tendency toward *too much publicity* with a consequent disregard of the individual's right of privacy; and second, a tendency toward too little publicity, with a consequent *increase of secrecy* in areas hitherto considered public."[93]

These two changes—a new regime of publicity and a rise in secrecy—are not as separate as Habermas makes them seem. One of the decisive cultural shifts of the twentieth century was the bureaucratization of strategic communications by *both* the market and the state. In the middle of the century, the dissemination of mass messages became increasingly institutionalized and compartmentalized not only in private institutions designed to stimulate consumption (public relations, marketing, advertising) but also in a culturally and psychologically oriented National Security State devoted to strategic deception, propaganda, and psychological operations. While the private sector undoubtedly had a larger overall effect, it is important to note that the Cold War state employed the same methods as private public-relations firms and indeed the *same personnel*. To build his massive new U.S. psychological warfare program, for instance, President Dwight Eisenhower hired the most celebrated public-relations experts of Madison Avenue. His most important psychological warfare adviser, for example ("America's single most influential cold warrior," according to

Saunders), did most of his work for the U.S. government while simultaneously overseeing the publication of *Time* and *Fortune* magazines as a vice president at Time-Life (see chapter 2).[94] "Intelligence," remarks one of William Gibson's spies, "is advertising turned inside out."[95]

Such relations between the covert and private sectors point to the far more important way in which the U.S. National Security Council committed itself to worldwide control of public messages. The CIA became a massive sponsor of Western art and writing; it employed untold numbers of journalists, editors, novelists, and public-relations officers for the production of both domestic and foreign copy; and it spawned an elaborate apparatus of "white," "gray," and "black" propaganda agencies—including the United States Information Agency, the United States Information Service, Voice of America, and Radio Liberty—that worked tirelessly with the CIA to weave strategic messages into the fabric of public communications around the globe.[96] As Kenneth Osgood compellingly shows, these efforts were colossal and decisive. It would thus be a profound misconception to see the transformation of the postwar public sphere as a process separate from the rise of the National Security State.

One of the major consequences of these institutional shifts is a widespread suspicion of mass-mediated messages and a concomitant uncertainty about what is real and true. While there is nothing new about advertising or political deception, the *institutionalization* of corporate and state models of psychological influence requires a major shift in the public conception of messages and their relation to reality. The Cold War public sphere was awash in messages ghostwritten by functionaries with little personal investment in the content of those messages and minimal reason to guarantee their truth. The state had in fact *openly* embraced a paradoxical policy of public deception in the purported defense of openness and democracy. When messages propagated by both the market and one's own government are widely known to be instrumental in nature and widely suspected to be manipulative or misleading, then a strange condition arises in which the savvy citizen regards all statements as potentially fictional—or potentially true—and cynicism flourishes.[97] In the midst of a conflict with the potential to end life on earth, is it any surprise that postwar discourse soon began to express the difficulty of knowing what was real and true?

With this question, we arrive at the intersection where democracy's ongoing crisis of legitimation meets the *other* major crisis of legitimation of the twentieth century—the problem of legitimating modern knowledge that is the basis of Lyotard's *Postmodern Condition*.[98] For Lyotard, the postmodern condition is rooted in a crisis of modern knowledge. The most important sign of this crisis is that rational science, the dominant model of modern knowledge, realizes it cannot legitimate itself without recourse to the traditional *narrative* knowledge that it displaced and devalued as "primitive." The result is a crisis of legitimation marked by a resurgence of traditional, narrative knowledge—or what Habermas would call "feudal" forms.[99]

These twin crises of legitimation suggest a powerful connection between postmodernism and state secrecy. If the problem facing Western rationality is that scientific knowledge cannot make known that it is the true knowledge without resorting to narrative knowledge, then the problem facing the state is that the purported survival of democracy rests on the suspension or erosion of democratic procedure. When the democratic public cannot know the methods by which the state guarantees its right to be a public, public "reason" itself is jeopardized and the state becomes increasingly irrational. In both cases, a fundamental irrationality or "feudal" quality haunts the emblems of modern rationality.

But can the Cold War really be understood through the model of "refeudalization" and the suppression of public "reason"? In fact, that is precisely how the chief architect of the Cold War conceived it. In a 1947 speech to the National War College, George Kennan advanced the concept of the "necessary lie" as a major plank of U.S. foreign policy. The Communists, Kennan argued, had established a "strong position in Europe...through unabashed and skillful use of lies. *They have fought us with unreality, with irrationalism.* Can we combat this unreality successfully with *rationalism*, with truth, with honest well-meant economic assistance?"[100] The implicit answer was no. Lies called for counterlies. Unreality would be fought not with reality and truth but with more unreality. In a specific opposition of rationalism to irrationalism, Kennan evoked the ideal of the public sphere and then drove another nail into its coffin. If the watchwords of the Enlightenment public sphere were rationality and publicity, then the watchwords of the Cold War covert sphere would be irrationalism, secrecy, uncertainty, and suspicion.

This "irrationalism" is widely visible in the culture of political suspicion and conspiracy theory, where large swaths of the public feel that one story is as good as another, that important historical information is hidden, that powerful but invisible agents are the motive forces of history. If such suspicions are, at one level, attempts to restore public reason through the unearthing of secrets, they seem, at another level, signs of profound "irrationality," because they are rarely grounded in the procedures of modern historiography.[101] Meanwhile, the "secret chanceries of the prince" acquire feudal qualities in the public imagination. Secrecy, noted the Senate Foreign Relations Committee chairman J. William Fulbright in 1971, "has become a god in this country."[102] In a stunning rebirth of the "Elizabethan world picture," the early modern place of God has been assumed by the CIA, which is now seen not only as a symbol of public unknowing and state sovereignty but as a sort of magical being with extraordinary powers of surveillance, knowledge, and control.[103] For the former CIA analyst Victor Marchetti and the journalist John D. Marks the CIA is "a powerful and dangerous secret cult" whose "holy men are...a secret fraternity of the American political aristocracy."[104] For the characters of Don De-Lillo, it is "America's myth," a "theology of secrets."[105] In short, the covert state has become a primary force in the postmodern "reenchantment of the world."[106]

Could the growth of the National Security State really be the crucible of postmodernism? Chronologically, the answer is yes. Postmodernism arose as the Cold War consensus of the 1950s disintegrated amid social upheaval and protest in the 1960s.[107] Many of its early practitioners—Joseph Heller, Thomas Pynchon, Kurt Vonnegut, Philip K. Dick, Ishmael Reed, and Vladimir Nabokov—wrote explicitly about Cold War themes in texts that emphasize epistemological or ontological confusion. A number of excellent studies, moreover, suggest compelling connections between postmodernism and the institutions of the Cold War. As Andreas Huyssen notes, postmodernism has a "specifically American character" rooted in a rejection of the modernist canon that became "domesticated in the 1950s" and "turned into a propaganda weapon in the cultural-political arsenal of Cold War anticommunism."[108] Alan Nadel persuasively connects early postmodernism to the "epistemological nightmare" created by Cold War containment and more explicitly to the institutional duplicity revealed in incidents like the U.S. failure at the Bay of Pigs.[109] Jean Baudrillard's account of postmodern simulation relies heavily on Cold War examples, especially the essential strategy of nuclear deterrence, which stakes the fate of the earth on the inability to distinguish between real threats and pretended ones.[110] As Ann Douglas puts it in a landmark essay, "The extreme skepticism about the possibility of disinterested knowledge and language that postmodernism sponsors...makes the most sense when taken as a straightforward description of the extremes of official dishonesty characteristic of the cold war era."[111]

Still, it would be a mistake to trace the advent of postmodernism simply to the Cold War or the National Security State. After all, a great deal of postmodern art and literature has little to do with the Cold War. The representations of the covert sphere, moreover, are not *primarily* postmodern; if anything they tend toward realism or romantic melodrama.

My claim, then, is not that postmodernism is a simple product of the Cold War, but rather that national security institutions were among several crucial factors—including the postwar triumph of new mass media, strategic communications, and multinational capitalism—that altered the conditions of public knowledge in postwar Western societies, generating a pervasive skepticism about the public's ability to know what is real and true. A good deal of U.S. postmodernism expresses this epistemological skepticism.

This claim is not an attempt to dismiss other influences. Over the past several decades critics have explained postmodernism as both a set of discursive shifts and a material transformation of the social and economic order. In doing so, they have used dramatically different artifacts and even media as examples, and they have disagreed over many important issues: whether postmodernism is problematic or salutary; whether it is a decisive response to modernism or merely the "leading edge" of a longer reaction against modernity; whether it has particular aesthetic features and political implications; whether it has gone through different phases; whether it has ended; and whether it exists or ever existed.[112]

My goal is neither to settle these disputes nor to offer a new general theory of postmodernism. Hence I want to concentrate on what seems largely settled about postmodernism. Its central quality is skepticism about how to know and represent the world, particularly as history. Postmodernism emphasizes the constructed nature of narratives, philosophical and social structures, and even persons. It reflects the institutions of mass culture, and it thematizes the artifice of nearly everything, especially nature (or "nature") itself. Its distinctive effect on readers and observers is disorientation or confusion about the nature of the real. For Brian McHale, the hallmark of postmodern fiction is the simultaneous presence of competing ontologies, a plurality of worlds that makes it difficult to know which "reality" is the *real* reality.[113] In a very different account, Fredric Jameson also sees postmodernism as a "new and historically original dilemma...that involves our insertion as individual subjects into a multidimensional set of radically discontinuous realities."[114] Jameson illustrates the "depthlessness" and ahistoricity generated by this dilemma through the "disturbing sense of unreality" experienced by a schizophrenic who feels suddenly "apart from the rest of the world."[115] Linda Hutcheon emphasizes similar effects in postmodern historiographic metafiction, which is torn between a desire to depict real events and an "intensively self-reflexive" sense that reality cannot be transparently represented.[116]

What material social conditions might have produced such aesthetic features? The answer depends in part on whether one emphasizes postmodernism as a fundamental crisis of modernity or a specifically postwar phenomenon. Although my argument concerns the postwar era, I believe postmodernism is at bottom an expression of skepticism about the project of modernity, particularly its commitments to scientific rationality, individualism, and universalism. Postmodernism intensifies a critique mounted earlier by romanticism and modernism. While it is often evinced by ontological questions, as Brian McHale argues, these questions stem from a crisis of knowledge. As McHale notes, "Intractable epistemological uncertainty becomes at a certain point ontological plurality: push epistemological questions far enough and they 'tip over' into ontological questions."[117]

If postmodernism registers an epistemological crisis within modernity, it nonetheless has specific roots in postwar society. What material conditions inspired a pervasive cultural impulse to question foundations, expose the constructedness of discourse, and emphasize the difficulty of knowing what is real? A number of brilliant studies have compellingly linked postmodernism to the emergence of new technologies of information, mass culture, global capitalism, post-Fordist production, time-space compression, monetary inflation, and the collapse of the modern utopian state. Before adding to this list, I want to observe the degree to which these powerful accounts are concerned with not only material conditions but also conditions of knowledge. One of the powerful features of Fredric Jameson's account of postmodernism's roots in late capitalism, for example, is his challenge to midcentury descriptions of "postindustrial" or "consumer" society. The notion that advanced economies had fundamentally changed, Jameson shows, was an illusion created by the large-scale movement of labor to developing countries. What had been transformed, in other words, was not the basic nature of capitalism but rather the geography of class division. Yet, *from a U.S. perspective,* this new geography appeared to transform the nature of the economy because it had changed the conditions of knowledge in advanced Western societies, where consumers were increasingly unaware of how their products were made. This new level of mystification is crucially linked to Western postmodernism, which Jameson describes as a difficulty "mapping" the new global reality. In this sense, postmodernism reflects the epistemological conditions created by late capitalism from a perspective *inside* an advanced "postindustrial" Western economy.

This is an exceptionally powerful approach, particularly if we turn our attention to the way state institutions reshaped the conditions of knowledge in the United States. The emergence of a Cold War security state is in some ways inseparable from the growth of global capitalism, not only because U.S. "national interests" so often included the protection of colonialist business ventures, but also because of the way in which *both* the state and the corporate realm began to articulate their missions to the public.

Perhaps this is why the specter of the covert state haunts Jameson's resolutely economic account of postmodernism. Consider, for example, Jameson's oft-cited description of the Westin Bonaventure Hotel, an emblem of postmodern Los Angeles architecture. Inside the "reflective glass skin" of the building, designed by John C. Portman, Jameson feels a "bewildering immersion" like "the suppression of depth [in] postmodern paint or literature."[118] Significantly, what this "bewilderment" and "milling confusion" brings to mind for Jameson is Michael Herr's dizzying account of the Vietnam War, *Dispatches,* which Jameson calls the hotel's "analogue in . . . postmodern warfare." The pairing is not coincidental, for Jameson returns to it at the very end of *Postmodernism,* again comparing the experience of "wandering through a postmodern hotel" to "undergoing the multiple shocks and bombardments of the Vietnam War as Michael Herr conveys it to us." Jameson's point is that the "postmodern hyperspace" of the hotel makes it difficult "to map [one's] position in a mappable external world."[119]

If geographical confusion is the essential effect of postmodernism, then it is particularly important that Jameson should simultaneously evoke both a temple of capitalist leisure *and* a hot zone of the U.S. Cold War. While each artifact—the Bonaventure, *Dispatches*—is a discrete example of postmodernism, his pairing of them is among the most significant features of his entire account, for it exemplifies his claim that postmodernism "involves our insertion as individual subjects into a multidimensional set of radically discontinuous realities."[120] What could be more "radically discontinuous" than a paradise of U.S. civilian consumerism on the one hand, and the grim horrors of a Cold War "conflict" on the other? The Vietnam War seemed incomprehensible not only to U.S. civilians but also to participants and witnesses like Herr, who portrays it as a surreal nightmare, an otherworldly violation of the U.S. sense of "reality" (see chapter 3). And yet the logic of the Cold War insisted on the theoretical connection between such disparate realities. The Vietnam War was the semi-public extrusion of an initially subterranean state effort that purported to defend capitalism and that, by extension, protected its celebrated temples like the Bonaventure Hotel. The war takes place to protect the hotel, and the hotel is part of a glittering veneer that shields U.S. citizens from the grim global reality that underpins their consumerist paradise. The disorientation Jameson finds in each artifact is in part a reflection of their incomprehensible codependence. In short, the central effect of the postmodern—a difficulty mapping incompatible ontologies—was a basic condition for trying to understand the Cold War from a U.S. perspective. Cold War consciousness involved a quintessential sense that Western economic reality itself was underpinned by another terrible but vague reality—the distant and often secret business of cold warfare. A growing awareness of and discomfort with these two fundamentally incompatible "worlds" is one way to mark the emergence of postmodernism.

It is also, finally, a way to describe the primary experience of the Cold War by its practitioners. The Cold War not only divided the world into two "incompatible" worlds, but also divided the public sphere into overt and covert components. For those who traversed these worlds, the experience was often uncannily similar to the ontological befuddlement that literary critics have tied to postmodernism. The legendary CIA counterintelligence giant James Jesus Angleton, for example, described Cold War espionage as a "wilderness of mirrors" in which it was virtually impossible to separate the reality from fabrication, history from fiction. In his 1965 novel, *The Looking Glass War,* the former intelligence operative and premier spy novelist John Le Carré famously associated this same problem with the surrealism of *Alice in Wonderland*.[121] The notion that intelligence work puts one "through the looking glass"—into a zone of radical uncertainty—has since become a commonplace in the history and fiction of espionage. Robert Littell's historical novel, *The Company* (2002)—which draws heavily on David Martin's excellent biography of Angleton and William Harvey (the CIA mastermind behind the Berlin Tunnel)—makes the looking glass of espionage its central figure. When Littell's major Soviet contact turns out to go by the name "Dodgson," Angleton notes that Dodgson, "curiously, happened to have been the real name of Lewis Carroll, the author of *Alice in Wonderland*. It makes you wonder if the KGB...isn't, like Dodgson, creating worlds within worlds within worlds for us to get lost in."[122] At this moment, Littell has not only fictionalized a real spymaster reading an opposing spy's allusion to surreal fiction, but he has repurposed the metaphors of Le Carré, Angleton, and Don DeLillo, whose CIA novel *Libra* makes "a world inside the world" its primary metaphor for plotting in both the authorial and conspiratorial senses. A "world inside the world" is also the basic form of ontological plurality that Brian McHale calls the essence of postmodern fiction.[123] Littell's novel, however, is not postmodern. It is realist, spy-genre fiction. And yet it has a certain "postmodern" quality that comes less from literary allusion than from the supposed experience of espionage as a practice. The point here is not that the clandestine world is "postmodern" but that it produces the sort of extreme epistemological uncertainty that postmodernism would later convert into an aesthetic.

Representations of the Covert State

In this book I trace these dynamics through the cultural history of the Cold War and the War on Terror. My methodological assumption is that it is possible to say interesting and useful things only when looking in detail at particular historical cases and texts. While the book moves chronologically from the early Cold War through Vietnam to the present, it is not a comprehensive history of national security in this era. It is a set of case studies designed to explore the cultural, political, and philosophical consequences of a substantially covert foreign policy.

In chapter 1, "Brainwashed!" I argue that the strange and fascinating history of brainwashing opens a window onto the covert sphere. Brainwashing has long been seen as a product of the Korean War, when purportedly brainwashed U.S. POWs confessed to war crimes. The idea has had an astonishing cultural afterlife in hundreds of medical and psychiatric studies, popular books and articles, novels, films, and popular theories about public events (such as the Patty Hearst affair, the Jonestown suicides, "cult" movements, and acts of terrorism). Yet brainwashing was actually a CIA propaganda fiction. It was also the subject of a clandestine research program on "brain warfare" that predated the Korean War and eventually led to a military program that simulates capture for at-risk U.S. troops. I track these two histories toward the unfortunate moment when the Bush administration converted this training simulation into an *actual* method of interrogating detainees in the War on Terror. At every turn in this story, the epistemology of the covert sphere fomented an astonishing conflation of reality and fantasy—the secret funding of "journalism," clinical studies based on dystopian fiction, the supposed implantation of a fictive worldview, and the conversion of a Cold War–era simulation into a real program of "enhanced interrogation."

In the second chapter, "Spectacles of Secrecy," I return to the domestic scene to examine how the state gains public support for covert institutions. The spy trials of the 1950s were instrumental in fulfilling this social function. But because these trials publicly revealed clandestine activity, they were haunted by a fictional quality. The Rosenberg trial, for example, relied on simulated evidence and staged testimony. This quality helps explain the trial's privileged place in postmodern historiographic fiction (where it is the basis of major works by E. L. Doctorow, Robert Coover, and Tony Kushner). After an opening discussion of these issues, I turn to Coover's brilliant satire of the Rosenberg case, *The Public Burning*. Among the most important examples of postmodern U.S. fiction, this novel repeatedly associates its own narrative experimentation with the confusion of the Rosenberg trial and the ideological system that supports the National Security State. In so doing, it illustrates a common paradox of much Cold War avant-garde writing: because writers cannot know state secrets, they must limit themselves to representing (and perhaps imitating) the radical unknowing produced by the security state.

In chapter 3, "False Documents," I address the fiction-making capacity of covert institutions and link this capacity to the postmodern revaluation of fiction. In influential essays, E. L. Doctorow, Don DeLillo, and Tim O'Brien have all contended that fiction can be "truer" than history and journalism—and they specifically relate this claim to the problem of deception in Cold War government. Major novels of espionage (such as Norman Mailer's *Harlot's Ghost* and Don DeLillo's *Libra*) repeatedly stress the parallels between fiction writing and spycraft. The Cold War CIA relied implicitly on such parallels when it shifted emphasis from intelligence gathering to covert operations, which are often strategic fictions that place the state into a new and disdainful relation to the public sphere. This shift is a major subject of Denis Johnson's novel of psychological operations, *Tree of Smoke* (2007). Johnson's novel, I argue, depicts the atmosphere of public and military confusion during Vietnam in order to comment on the Bush administration's War on Terror. In so doing, Johnson reveals how the entire Western canon of Vietnam literature (Greene, Burdick and Lederer, Herr, Kubrick, Coppola, Stone, and others) develops from public incomprehension rooted in the war's secret origins.

In chapter 4, "The Work of Art in the Age of Plausible Deniability," I locate the roots of postmodern historiographic skepticism in representations of a dysfunctional public sphere. Beginning with Charles Baxter's claim that Cold War duplicity has produced widespread "narrative dysfunction" in U.S. culture, I trace links between state secrecy and historiographic uncertainty through Mailer (*Armies of the Night*) and Atwood (*The Handmaid's Tale*). Many postmodern novels develop intentionally incomplete or "dysfunctional" narratives to critique the conditions of knowledge in a regime of state secrecy. My central examples come from the novels of Joan Didion, which allegorize the Cold War public sphere through a female protagonist who is romantically involved with both a public servant and a secret agent. By emphasizing the difficulty of producing a clear explanation of events, Didion's elliptical style brilliantly diagnoses the exclusion of the Cold War public from the male realm of state policymaking. In a brief coda, I take up John Barth's "Lost in the Funhouse" to suggest that even metafiction not primarily about state secrecy is nonetheless entangled with the problems of public knowledge in the covert sphere.

In chapter 5, "Postmodern Amnesia," I begin by asking why so many stories of covert action are also about amnesia. I suggest two answers. First, amnesia is a popular way of exploring the historical implications of postmodern theory. Second, the amnesic assassin, from *The Manchurian*

Candidate to the Bourne trilogy, is a figure for public half-knowledge of U.S. foreign policy. The connection between postmodernism and covert action in such narratives is not incidental. Approaches to postmodernism have repeatedly addressed both the problem of cultural memory and the dialectic of spectacle and secrecy at the heart of the covert sphere. To explore these relations further, I turn to Tim O'Brien's unsettling novel of the My Lai massacre, *In the Lake of the Woods*. Through a story of profound individual and national amnesia, O'Brien attempts to conceptualize the effects of covert state action on U.S. cultural memory. His novel and its source materials suggest that public amnesia about U.S. foreign policy must be remedied by a combination of narrative "trickery" and a postmodern emphasis on the difficulty of knowing. This contradiction, I argue, is a symptom of covert-sphere postmodernism, which encourages the writer to critique the epistemological conditions of the Cold War by reproducing them in fictional form.

In the final chapter, "The Geopolitical Melodrama," I return to the opening pages of the book by inquiring how the covert sphere influenced U.S. reactions to the attacks of September 11, 2001. If the covert sphere is indeed the primary way in which the public conceptualizes covert activity, then its effect on the War on Terror should be evident. By examining dozens of remarkably similar films and television series, I argue that these melodramas explain much of the early U.S. response to 9/11. Although there have been notable changes in such narratives since 2001, the continuities between the two periods are striking and instructive. The ideological function of the geopolitical melodrama, I argue, is to defend the operation of a Cold War security state in a post–Cold War climate. I support this position by demonstrating that numerous political pundits and national leaders publicly explained U.S. strategy after 2001 through reference to such popular melodramas of terrorism.

1

BRAINWASHED!

The Faisalabad Candidate

On October 2, 2005, three months after the coordinated bombing of the London transportation system and three days before the U.S. Senate overwhelmingly approved John McCain's Detainee Treatment Act, the British home secretary, Charles Clarke, attempted to explain terrorism by invoking a specter of the Cold War. Islamic terrorists, Clarke argued, should not be seen in the "'classic' mould of revolutionaries fighting for a political cause." Rather, they are like educated youths "brainwashed" into joining cults. Perhaps, Clarke added, "anti-brainwashing techniques" could be used to "deprogramme" terrorists—converting them back to productive citizens essentially by running brainwashing protocols in reverse.[1]

If this "Manchurian candidate" theory of terror illustrates the tenacity of Cold War concepts in contemporary responses to terrorism, it also hints at the odd persistence of brainwashing in the world of the covert state. What Clarke probably did not know is that the CIA had been test-ing this very idea—with far less therapeutic aims—in its interrogation of "high value" terrorism suspects. The agency began with Abu Zubay-dah, the man it erroneously believed to be Al Qaeda's head of logistics. Shot and captured in Faisalabad, Pakistan, on March 28, 2002, Zubay-dah was flown around the world continuously for three days by differ-ent aircrews so that almost no one in U.S. intelligence would know his whereabouts. (This counterespionage tactic itself illustrates the strange anachronism of so much of the U.S. War on Terror. On the one hand, Al Qaeda hardly has the technological capability to track CIA rendition flights; on the other hand, Zubaydah's eventual destination—a secret Thai prison—would be published only a few years later in one of Jane Mayer's invaluable *New Yorker* articles on President Bush's program of "enhanced interrogation.")[2]

In Thailand, Zubaydah was first interrogated by Ali Soufan and Steve Gaudin, FBI agents with extensive experience in Islamic terror. A surpris-ingly voluble Zubaydah disclaimed membership in Al Qaeda but divulged information implicating Khalid Sheikh Mohammed in the 9/11 attacks and leading to the arrest of José Padilla for planning a radiological attack in the United States. Days later, however, the investigation took a turn for the worse when the Bush administration handed it to a special CIA unit. Heading the CIA team was a former military psychologist, James Mitch-ell, who immediately got Pavlovian on Zubaydah, demanding that he be treated "like a dog in a cage."[3] Mitchell meant this literally. Zubaydah was stripped naked and placed inside what he came to call his "tiny coffin." Deeply disturbed, the FBI agents protested, and the FBI director, Robert Mueller, soon barred bureau personnel from participating in what he saw as an illegal and counterproductive interrogation. Meanwhile, an increasingly uncooperative Zubaydah was shuttled from coffin to frigid cell, deprived of sleep for up to ninety-six hours straight, placed in agonizing "stress posi-tions," blasted with loud music, and eventually waterboarded eighty-three times, as often as three times a day. Weeks of this "*Clockwork Orange* kind of approach," as one CIA officer called it, produced exactly the response Mitchell and his staff had hoped for. Zubaydah confessed to membership in Al Qaeda and to a horrifying array of terror plots—including plans to blow up "American banks, supermarkets, malls, the Statue of Liberty, the Golden Gate Bridge, the Brooklyn Bridge, and nuclear power plants." On investigation, however, all of these confessions proved fictitious. Zubaydah, it turned out, was not even a member of Al Qaeda.[4]

Why, then, had the most critical early investigation of the War on Terror been placed in Mitchell's hands? Mitchell had no knowledge of Islam or the Middle East, no counterterrorism experience, and no Arabic language skills. He had never conducted an interrogation. In fact, he had never *witnessed* a real interrogation. His particular skill lay in the *simulation* of torture. Before contracting privately with the CIA, Mitchell was a military psychologist involved in the Survival, Evasion, Resistance, Escape (SERE) program. Never intended for use on foreign detainees, SERE was developed at the end of the Korean War to protect U.S. troops from enemy "brainwashing." The theory was that a program of simulated capture and coercive interrogation could inoculate U.S. troops against Communist mind control in the event of their real capture.[5] In its interrogation of Abu Zubaydah, then, the CIA had essentially subjected him to its own notion of midcentury Chinese "brainwashing."

But how could *brainwashing* have come to be the model on which the United States built a crucial part of its twenty-first-century antiterror program? And how, for that matter, could commentators and politicians like Clarke have come to see brainwashing as both a cause of terrorism and a potential solution to it? Brainwashing would seem at most a strange footnote in the history of the Cold War—a marginal anxiety at the lunatic fringe of the Korean War era.

Yet brainwashing turns out to be among *the* quintessential fantasies of the postwar period. The subject of scores of novels and films, congressional hearings, and government research projects, brainwashing has for sixty years been a persistent vehicle through which citizens and government officials have imagined global ideological conflict. Insofar as "cold" warfare implies a conflict of ideas and persuasion fought not on the battlefield but through propaganda, psychological warfare, and other ideological weapons, brainwashing is the essence of cold warfare. It is no accident that U.S. military leaders explicitly embraced the notion as both a metaphor for psychological warfare and a literal weapon in the U.S. arsenal. In popular discourse, the notion of brainwashing provoked crucial questions about the nature of U.S. democracy in the age of the National Security State. Was the postwar public sphere a "marketplace of ideas" or a field in which new social institutions—including covert government agencies—controlled human thought and action?

Brainwashing became a meaningful cultural fantasy because it adjudicated such questions through the thematics of secret agency and ideological conversion at the heart of cold warfare. In the following pages, I suggest that its cultural history powerfully illustrates the role of fiction in the covert sphere. Brainwashing was widely understood to produce a bizarre amalgam of reality and fiction. It thus conjured up perhaps the first full-blown postmodern subject, a person utterly constructed and controlled from without. This nightmare of masculinity undone was among the first major ways in which the Cold War public came to conceive its own relation to the Cold War. It was also a major influence on U.S. security policy, whose architects (like the public) turn out to be trapped in the epistemology of the covert sphere. Because the history of brainwashing divides along the fault line between the covert and public spheres, I must offer two different renditions of its history, beginning first with the popular, or public, version—which, of course, is not the whole story.

Brain Warfare

Brainwashing has always been associated with the Korean War, even though fears of a more vague form of Communist "thought control" became a U.S. obsession as early as the Eastern bloc show trials of the late 1940s. As Stephen Whitfield notes, the United States Chamber of Commerce so worried about "thought-control" that its Committee on Socialism and Communism "proposed in 1946 and 1948 to remove liberals, socialists, and Communists from opinion-forming agencies," including libraries, schools, newspapers, and "the entertainment industries."[6] Among the most memorable moments of Ellen Schrecker's outstanding history of McCarthyism is her anecdote about Judge Harold Medina, who presided in the 1949 case that effectively outlawed the Communist Party as a criminal conspiracy to overthrow the government (*Dennis v. U.S.*). At a dinner party one evening, Schrecker reports, Medina explained "that whenever he looked at the spectators during the trial, he consciously forced himself to keep his eyes moving so that he wouldn't let himself be placed in a trance by the hypnotists that the party might have placed in the courtroom."[7] Clearly, fears of mind control were in the air long before the outbreak of war in Korea.

But the more specific concept of brainwashing was first popularized by the journalist Edward Hunter three months after the start of the Korean War. In September 1950, the *Miami News* published Hunter's article "'Brain-Washing' Tactics Force Chinese into Ranks of Communist Party." Hunter would go on to publish two books on the subject: *Brain-Washing in Red China: The Calculated Destruction of Men's Minds* (1951) and *Brainwashing: The Story of Men Who Defied It* (1956).[8] Hunter initially conceived of brainwashing to explain the mass "reeducation" of civilians in Maoist China. Largely on the basis of interviews with Chi Sze-chen, a recent graduate of North China People's Revolutionary University, Hunter claimed to unearth a complex system of ideological indoctrination. The system was notable not so much for its scathing anti-American ethos as for its coercive methodology, which combined mind-numbing repetition with rewards and punishments in order to force a wholesale shift in worldview. This approach, Hunter explained, was "psychological warfare on a scale incalculably more immense than any militarist of the past has ever envisaged." Still, at this early juncture in its history, brainwashing had not yet come to seem the nightmare of total mental control into which it would soon be transformed. It was rather a mix of familiar techniques for coercion on the one hand and pedagogy on the other—a tool "for political indoctrination" in which the "medium for this learning is propaganda, and propaganda is applied to everyone.... Even the word [learning], used this way, is a propaganda term."[9] If this system was innovative, it was so only because of its scale and the ruthlessness of its proponents, who aimed to install a new worldview in an entire population.

The transformation of brainwashing from a system of coercive interrogation and propaganda to a supposed program for human enslavement reflects the cultural demands placed on the idea by the Korean War. In 1952, a group of U.S. Air Force pilots—most famously, Colonel Frank Schwable—confessed to dropping anthrax, typhus, cholera, and plague on North Korea. Thirty-five other captured pilots substantiated these confessions in great detail. By 1953, to the embarrassment of many in the United States, almost 5,000 of 7,200 U.S. POWs had signed confessions or petitions calling for an end to the war. Evidence emerged that U.S. troops engaged in criminal behavior detrimental to their compatriots. While most veterans recanted their confessions on repatriation, some did not. Most disturbing of all, twenty-one POWs refused repatriation entirely—actions a disgusted Eisenhower attributed to a U.S. "propaganda disadvantage" with the East. "A basic truth," noted Eisenhower, is that "the minds of all men are susceptible to outside influences." In keeping with this theory, Eisenhower dramatically enhanced U.S. military capacities in once-scorned avenues such as public relations, propaganda, and psychological warfare. The United States, he told a San Francisco crowd in October 1952, was locked in a "struggle for men's minds," and what was needed was a "psychological effort put forth on a national scale."[10]

But most of this campaign would not be conducted in front of the nation. Eisenhower asked specifically for "subversion and propaganda weapons" with "no govt [sic] connection."[11] Ike's theory of "outside influence" could not be a plank of his *public* policy. The notion that individuals were the products of social influence flew in the face of Cold War domestic ideology, which saw American individualism as a bulwark against Communist conformity. An *open* campaign of influence, moreover, would discredit the ideology of American exceptionalism. The resulting division between public and covert policy is among the reasons Americans came to see brainwashing less as a tool in a propaganda war than as a deadly threat to the rugged individualism that would win the Cold War. This view was held not only by the public but also by military and intelligence officials, who took seriously the idea that Communist states had developed a terrifying form of mind control. In 1953, for instance, the CIA Psychological Strategy Board recommended that U.S. politicians be monitored for "signs of a changed personality" so that they could be quarantined and tested for Soviet drugging.[12] After the British launched their version of SERE training, the United States soon followed suit.

Yet the end of the Korean War did not calm the brainwashing scare. Five years after Hunter's initial article, in fact, the notion had grown into something far more bizarre and terrifying than it originally seemed. In Hunter's 1956 volume—this one published not by Vanguard but by the large New York house of Farrar, Straus, and Cudahy—brainwashing had become the stuff of science fiction, "some form of mass hypnosis" capable of fostering "unthinking discipline and robotlike enslavement." A mysterious mix of oriental mystery and Soviet rationality, the technique now seemed "like witchcraft, with its incantations, trances, poisons, and potions, with a strange flair of science about it all, like a devil dancer in a tuxedo carrying his magic brew in a test tube."[13] The "flair of science" in this increasingly occult practice came from the Russian behavioral psychologist Ivan Pavlov, whose discoveries had supposedly made it possible to supplant an individual's consciousness with fabricated beliefs, memories, and even traits. "Conditioned reflexes," Hunter explained, "could conceivably be produced to make [a man] react like [a] dog that rolled over at its trainer's signal.... The Kremlin could use words as signals—any words would do—*imperialism, learning, running dog of the imperialists, people, friend of the people, big brother,* without any relationship to their actual meaning. The Kremlin's plan was to make these reflexes instinctive, like the reactions of…animals," until subjects were "no longer capable of using free will." According to this account, brainwashing could "change a mind radically so that its owner becomes a living puppet—a human robot—without the atrocity being visible from the outside. The aim is to create a mechanism in flesh and blood, with new beliefs and new thought processes inserted into a captive body. What that amounts to is the search for a slave race that, unlike the slaves of olden times, can be trusted never to revolt, always amenable to orders, like an insect to its instincts."[14] If U.S. POWs proved weak, it was because they had been subjected to a mind-control weapon of extraordinary power.

Such notions proved hugely attractive to conservative anti-Communists, who came to see brainwashing as both a cause of communism's perplexing appeal in the Far East and a potential threat at home. Hunter's sense that "brainwashing would inevitably cause a national neurosis" in any country "afflicted" with it echoed the claim of national psychopathology in George Kennan's 1946 "Long Telegram"—arguably the most important document of the Cold War—which painted Soviet leadership as "neurotic," "insecure," "fanatical," and "impervious to the logic of reason."[15] The discovery of a vast brainwashing program in China seemed further proof that more subtle forms of influence were already at work on the unwitting U.S. masses. Cold warriors like the FBI director, J. Edgar Hoover, railed against the Communist "thought-control machine" that allowed Communists "to wield influence entirely out of proportion to their actual number" and "control, in various degrees, the thinking of many Americans."[16]

Had the notion of brainwashing simply been confined to right-wing arguments of this sort, it might have had a trajectory much like McCarthyism—increasingly marginalized by the mid-1950s as a symbol of anti-Communist hyperbole. But that is not what happened. Although

Hunter had essentially modernized the ideas of demonic possession, mesmerism, and hypnosis in an orientalist fiction, his concept gained broader traction for several reasons. First, as I will explain in more detail later, the notion of brainwashing sketched the vague outlines of a new Cold War world whose clandestine agents and exotic powers could never be fully known by the public. Second, the notion of an easily influenced subject echoed scholarly and popular accounts of waning individualism and masculinity, such as David Riesman's *Lonely Crowd* (1950), William Whyte's *Organization Man* (1956), and Vance Packard's *Hidden Persuaders* (1958).[17] If people were becoming "other-directed," as Riesman argued, then no more histrionic example could be found than the brainwashed. It is notable how many early commentaries on the Korean War brainwashing scandal saw it as evidence of a national crisis of masculinity. Initial Defense Department reports claimed that insufficiently tough U.S. POWs offered less resistance to their captors than the forces of all other nations and all previous U.S. POWs.[18] As Edward Hunter warned a Senate subcommittee in March of 1959, "A man who has been deprived of convictions and standards...will accept a quack faith.... That is how we in America are falling into a trap, and the way in which we softened up our boys for brainwashing before they went to Korea or were captured by the Communists."[19]

Third, and most important, influential scholars and writers lent credibility to the concept of brainwashing. Their testimony is particularly notable for the way it reveals the epistemology of the covert sphere. Chief among these were two prominent psychologists, William Sargant and Joost Meerloo. Meerloo, a former chief psychiatrist for the Dutch military and a faculty member of the Columbia medical school, became an expert defense witness in the highly publicized trial of Colonel Frank Schwable. By signing a detailed statement accusing the United States of using biological weapons in the war, Schwable had made himself perhaps the most notorious POW in U.S. history. Meerloo offered a vigorous defense of Schwable and thereby became instrumental in framing POW confessions within the discourse of brainwashing. Meerloo's 1956 book, *Rape of the Mind,* popularized his earlier work on the totalitarian practice he called "menticide" or "psychic homicide."[20] *Rape of the Mind* depicts this nightmare of beset manhood with an odd mixture of clinical dispassion and anxious speculation. On the one hand, Meerloo offers a sensible explanation of Pavlovian conditioning—which he sees as no cause for alarm, because it "occurs everywhere people are together in common interaction"; on the other hand, he offers anxious warnings about the power of totalitarian states to "make conditioned zombies out of people" (52–53). The goal of this conditioning, for Meerloo, is to enforce ideological conformity but it also destroyed its victim's ability to know the world. "The panic of the 'brainwashee,'" he explains, "is the total confusion he suffers about all concepts" (29). And because a victim's testimony could later be "used for propaganda," brainwashing could ultimately cause "great confusion...in the mind of every observer, friend or foe. In the end no one knows how to distinguish truth from falsehood" (28).

Brainwashing, in other words, was both the sign and the engine of an epistemological crisis. It unsettled a stable sense of reality and legitimated a generalized paranoia in which not even sworn testimony could be trusted. Thus, as I will explain later in detail, brainwashing ushered in a kind of experience that would become a goal of some postmodern fiction: the deliberate conflation of fact and fiction, reality and fantasy. As Robert Lifton notes, westerners subjected to Chinese "thought reform" often suffered an "inability to distinguish the real from the unreal." As one of Lifton's subjects explained, after brainwashing, "I was mixed up between real and imaginary things and persons. I was no longer able to distinguish what was real and what was imaginary....I had the notion that many things were imaginary, but I was not sure. I could not say, 'This is real,' or 'This is not real.'"[21]

Despite its initial focus on the coercion of individuals, *Rape of the Mind* ends up devoting considerable energy to "techniques of mass submission." Meerloo saw such techniques, which included new mass cultural forms of "simple advertising and propaganda," creeping into Western society, and he feared they would pave the way to a socialist political transformation. These techniques, he wrote, "exist all around us, both on a political and a nonpolitical level and they become as dangerous to the free way of life as are the aggressive totalitarian governments themselves" (*RM* 93, 95). "In our epoch of too many noises and many frustrations," he went on, "many 'free' minds have given up the struggle for decency and individuality. They surrender to the *Zeitgeist,* often without being aware of it. Public opinion molds our critical thoughts every day. Unknowingly, we may become opinionated robots" (99). Until the melodramatic final phrase, what Meerloo describes here seems to be nothing more sinister than socialization. He freely admits that even the strong-minded—himself included—are subject to social influences. And yet, because he struggles to separate such ordinary forms of social influence from "brainwashing," he regularly expresses a sense of panic about external influences. He understands the formation of cultural differences, for example, through the concepts of "mental contagion" and "mass delusion." "The fakir lying on his bed of nails," he notes by way of example, might seem "eminently sane" among his own people but "deluded...if he exhibited his devotion on Fifth Avenue" (202).

Meerloo here goes beyond the reasonable view that sanity is culturally determined to the more anxious proposition that culture is a set of delusions fostered by something akin to brainwashing. For Meerloo, such delusions are not confined to totalitarian nations; every nation has forces capable of converting its average citizen into "Robot Man," a subject who "no longer feels himself an *I,* an ego, a person" and has "no personality of his own...no morality, no capacity to think clearly and honestly" (*RM* 117, 202). Meerloo sounds in such moments as if his clinical observations were made during a screening of *Invasion of the Body Snatchers,* the 1956 thriller about zombie conformism.[22] "Our present-day civilization is full of mass delusions, prejudices, and collective errors," Meerloo writes, and "there actually exists such a thing as mass brainwashing" (105). This argument couches a potentially useful insight about the ubiquity of ideological conditioning in profoundly anxious terms. Meerloo is not unaware of his own hysteria. "All this may sound extreme," he notes, yet "any influence which tends to rob man of his free mind can reduce him to robotism" (217).

Of course, this *is* an extreme proposition, for it sweeps aside the notion of the public sphere as a marketplace of ideas for a view in which public debate hides a nearly magical means of manipulating human thought and behavior. Meerloo's all-or-nothing thinking—the view that *any* influence can lead to *total* control—is a symptom of his commitment to the cultural fantasy that individuals are *wholly* responsible for their own beliefs and actions. Only in the context of this belief can any external influence be construed as invasive and dangerous. The apparent emergence of brainwashing thus makes possible a conception of social or ideological influence while also providing the basis for an energetic defense of individual autonomy against such influence.[23] This conception in turn relies on a vision of the public sphere haunted by the covert. Meerloo's encounter with wartime incarceration has destroyed his faith in what Habermas calls the "rational-critical" public sphere. Public reason is incessantly undermined by subtle forms of influence, manipulation, and even delusion.

Meerloo's basic claims about Communist brainwashing were swiftly reinforced by William Sargant, an Oxford-educated psychiatrist with significant experience treating World War II veterans for battle stress. Sargant's 1957 *Battle for the Mind* would be in its fourth printing by 1959. Like Meerloo, Sargant found Pavlov persuasive and understood brainwashing as a plausible and terrifying operation. And like Meerloo, he found much more ordinary forms of mental conditioning at work all around him. But unlike Meerloo, he tended to locate such conditioning in the activities of religious leaders and clinicians such as himself. "Politicians, priests and psychiatrists often face the same problem," he notes, "how to find the most rapid and permanent means of changing a man's beliefs."[24] This insight would later become a source of the countercultural critique of psychiatry as a repressive, normalizing practice. It would also permit Sargant to construct a genealogy of mind control, which he saw as the basis for religious conversion. Charismatic religious figures like John Wesley and Jonathan Edwards, Sargant believed, had used physical privation and ritual to create highly suggestible subjects—precisely the technique perfected in Communist brainwashing. Sargant, again like Meerloo, emphasized the public sphere's irrational underbelly, and he hinted at the eventual cultural trajectory of brainwashing—which would live on primarily as an explanation of religious conversion in so-called cults, especially the Unification Church of Reverend Sun Myung Moon and certain sects of radical Islam.

Two notable features thus characterize the early scholarly discourse on brainwashing. First, brainwashing quickly emerged as a model of *both* secret warfare *and* a more ordinary sort of social or ideological conditioning. This duality reflects the nature of the Cold War security state and the emerging covert sphere. The growing division between public and clandestine warfare made it difficult to know the nature of the battle. Was cold war a matter of covert action or mass mediated influence? The public fascination with brainwashing derived in part from this conundrum.

Second, the scholarly discourse on brainwashing regularly cited, and at times even resembled, *fiction*. Sargant, for example, based most of his analysis not on clinical cases but on distant historical summaries and contemporary literature—particularly the dystopian *fiction* of Aldous Huxley, Arthur Koestler, and George Orwell, which, Sargant believed, accurately reflected reports filtering from the East. This assumption is a crucial epistemological effect of the covert sphere. The structural barriers to knowing the enemies of state made a small number of representations extremely influential. Among these were official documents like Kennan's "Long Telegram" and fictions about Stalinist social engineering (Koestler and Orwell particularly).[25] The extraordinary role of such fictions in the covert sphere helps explain why serious, *clinical* writing came to rely so heavily on dystopian *fiction* for illustration and support. Meerloo's *Rape of the Mind* not only cites the same novels as Sargant but at times reads like a dystopian novel. Noting that "leading authors, among them H.G. Wells, Huxley, and Orwell, grow more and more concerned about the ghastly future of the robotized man," Meerloo concocts his own speculative narrative, "Totalitaria and Its Dictatorship," a detailed portrait of coming conformity and repression (*RM* 117).

Decoupled from communism and endorsed by experts like Meerloo and Sargant, brainwashing eventually became a powerful and long-lived cultural fantasy. By 1960, brainwashing had been the subject of over two hundred articles in popular U.S. magazines, including *Time* and *Life*.[26] Thereafter it entered an astonishing array of fiction, from popular films to literary works by Thomas Pynchon, Don DeLillo, Sylvia Plath, Kurt Vonnegut, Philip K. Dick, Ken Kesey, William Burroughs, Allan Ginsberg, Kathy Acker, Ralph Ellison, E. L. Doctorow, and Ishmael Reed.[27] Many of these narratives converted brainwashing from a conservative hysteria about foreign enemies to a liberal attack on corporate power, political conformity, and social conditioning. The problem with mainstream Americans, Norman Mailer railed in *The Armies of the Night* (1968), was that "the authority had operated on their brain with commercials, and washed their brain with packaged education, packaged politics." Here the idea of brainwashing has become shorthand for a general sort of ideological conditioning. "Anyone who has passed through the educational system of America is in unconscious degree somewhere near half a patriot," Mailer explained. "The brain is washed deep, there are reflexes: white shirts, Star Spangled Banner, saluting the flag."[28]

Ironically, just as celebrated fiction began to associate brainwashing with terrifying depictions of electroshock therapy and invasive psychiatry, the American Psychiatric Association gave the concept its ultimate stamp of approval by including it in the 1980 *Diagnostic and Statistical Manual of*

Mental Disorders (DSM), under the heading "dissociative disorders," a definition often cited in lawsuits aimed at religious "cults."[29] But the concept never left the domain of the covert sphere. At the end of the Cold War, cult specialists such as Margaret Singer and Steve Hassan assimilated the theory to the emerging threat of post–Cold War terrorism, where it is a surprisingly persistent topic. "Studies of charismatic religious cults" like the Unification Church, writes the Yale psychiatrist (and CIA consultant) Jerrold Post in an important anthology on terrorism, "contribute usefully to our understanding of the dynamics of the terrorist group."[30] For Steve Hassan, "terrorist cults" operate primarily through "mind-control techniques [such as] hypnosis, sleep deprivation,…and the programming of phobias into the minds of members."[31] Such views have informed many representations of terrorism (see chapter 5). Perhaps the most important postwar U.S. novel of terrorism, Don DeLillo's *Mao II* (1991) explicitly juxtaposes the story of a brainwashed Moonie with the lone agency of both the terrorist and the novelist. In 2011, the Showtime series *Homeland* brought the discourse on brainwashing full circle by reprising *The Manchurian Candidate* as a tale of Islamic terrorism in which a U.S. POW is converted to Islam, returned to the United States as a military hero, and secretly tasked with the assassination of the vice-president.[32]

Like their Cold War predecessors, many expert explanations of terrorism are marked by a striking reliance on fiction. In his account of "Terrorist Psycho-Logic," for instance, Post rests his argument about terrorist motives on a purely invented scenario, which begins "Consider a youth…"[33] Similarly, the Oxford psychologist Kathleen Taylor, who is the author of a book on brainwashing, used a fictional brainwashing scenario to explain the 2005 London Tube bombings. In a *Guardian* article published only a week after Secretary Clarke offered his own brainwashing hypothesis, Taylor described how an imaginary charismatic leader, whom she calls "Mr. X." (interestingly, the very name under which George Kennan republished his "Long Telegram" in *Foreign Affairs*), could have used psychological techniques to "transplant" a set of new ideas into the "brain" of a young man named Adam. As in Meerloo's dystopia, Taylor's "Brainwashed Adam is no longer able to think" clearly enough "to reject [Mr. X's] twisted terrorist logic."[34]

What does it mean when expert commentary from academics at the world's best universities relies heavily on invention, hypothetical scenarios, and dystopian fantasies? It means that we are in the covert sphere, where the enemies of state are hard to study and "proof" tends to come in the form of fiction. Should we be surprised that public officials like Secretary Clarke explain terrorism as the result of brainwashing?

Little Shop of Horrors

Far from being a marginal subject, then, brainwashing has been a remarkably vital and tenacious concept since the Cold War. But the brief history I have just related is not the whole story. Brainwashing, it turns out, was also the subject of considerable U.S. state activity, and the story that emerges from the annals of covert government differs substantially from the public history I have just sketched.

First, as is increasingly well-known, Edward Hunter was not simply a journalist. He was a CIA propaganda specialist, a former member of the Office of Strategic Services (OSS), and eventually the editor of the psychological-operations journal *Tactics*.[35] Thus the concept of brainwashing was from the beginning a creation of the CIA, which invented and disseminated the idea as part of a propaganda campaign to fuel public anxiety about Communist methods.

Second, as one arm of the CIA worked to foment public alarm about Communist brainwashing, another arm worked secretly to develop a *real* mind-control weapon of its own. The most important study of this effort is still John Marks's *Search for the "Manchurian Candidate"* (1979), a gripping account of the costs of state secrecy in the early Cold War. As Marks shows, the CIA "started preliminary work on drugs and hypnosis shortly after the Agency's creation in 1947." These efforts intensified after the 1949 trial of the Hungarian cardinal József Mindszenty, whose trancelike confession to highly improbable crimes against the Communist government appeared to have been forced by some mysterious process of mind control. Not long after the Mindszenty trial, the CIA director Rosco Hillenkoetter directed unvouchered funds to project BLUEBIRD, a mind-control initiative later renamed ARTICHOKE. These "black psychiatry" projects explored whether drugs or hypnosis could, in the words of project documents, "[control] an individual to the point where he will do our bidding against his will and even against such fundamental laws of nature as self-preservation."[36] BLUEBIRD documents ordered CIA officers to investigate, on "resident [redacted] aliens,... special or unorthodox methods, such as brain damage, sensory stimulation, hypnosis, so-called 'black psychiatry,' Pavlovian conditioning, 'Brain-washing' or any other methods having pertinence for such procedures as interrogation, subversion, or seduction."[37]

The plot gets thicker, however, for the U.S. attempt to develop and test an operational mind-control weapon preceded even the publication of Hunter's "groundbreaking" article on the subject. In July 1950, three CIA employees traveled to Tokyo to study whether various drugs could enhance "intensive polygraph" testing or be used to induce amnesia in human subjects. Three months later, CIA officers returned to Japan to conduct "advanced" mind-control tests on what appears to have been a group of twenty-five North Korean prisoners of war. These tests took place only four months after the start of the Korean War, a month after the publication of Hunter's brainwashing story, and a full two years *before* the 1952 panic about purported Chinese brainwashing of U.S. POWs. In other words, it may be that the *CIA,* and not the Chinese, launched brain warfare in the Far East. In a near-perfect example of Cold War "demonology"—Michael Rogin's term for the simultaneous demonization and imitation of a dreaded enemy—the CIA attempted to beat Chinese brainwashers to the punch, experimenting on North Korean POWs for what agency documents call "defensive purposes."[38]

The CIA's race to develop this mind-control weapon was, in fact, fueled by its own propaganda campaign about the terrifying use of enemy brainwashing techniques. By 1953, CIA officials were so worried about a "mind-control gap" with the Soviets and Chinese that the CIA director Allen Dulles made a rare public speech on the subject.[39] In it, he attributed Eastern bloc consolidation to the molding of a "parrotlike" population conditioned to "repeat thoughts which have been implanted in their minds by suggestion from outside." "We in the West," Dulles added, "are somewhat handicapped" in understanding "brain warfare" because "there are few survivors and we have no human guinea pigs, ourselves, on which to try these extraordinary techniques."[40] But guinea pigs were soon found when Dulles issued two secret directives. First, he commissioned the Cornell neurologists Harold Wolff and Lawrence Hinkle to study Communist techniques for a secret CIA report. Second, he directed secret funds toward the now infamous MK-ULTRA project, which studied the effects of sensory deprivation, hypnotism, drugs, and electroshock on unwitting prisoners, Soviet defectors, resident aliens, recovering drug addicts, hired prostitutes, and even fellow CIA operatives.[41] Eventually these experiments mushroomed into what the historian of torture Alfred McCoy calls "a veritable Manhattan Project of the mind," a scandalous program of behavioral research that cost a billion dollars a year.[42] So powerful was the appeal of acquiring a mind-control weapon that MK-ULTRA would continue to be funded long after the agency's own investigators, Hinkle and Wolff, concluded that brainwashing relied on "physiological deprivation" and thus had to be distinguished from "thought-control or mass indoctrination." Hinkle and Wolff also found that "neither the Chinese nor the Russians made appreciable use of drugs or hypnosis, and…certainly did not possess the brainwashing equivalent of the atomic bomb (as many feared)."[43]

By the early 1960s, these assessments of brainwashing were independently confirmed by three civilian researchers—Albert Biderman, Edgar Schein, and Robert Jay Lifton—each of whom conducted extensive interviews with former POWs and showed that, contrary to previous allegations, so-called brainwashing neither placed prisoners in a permanently altered state of consciousness nor resulted in the creation of a permanent "new self." It was, in fact, not the result of a radically new technology or method—just a brutal regimen of age-old interrogation tactics. Prisoners were subjected to lengthy periods of isolation and extreme physical deprivation, during which they were endlessly forced to revise a personal confession that would eventually be adequate to terminate the interrogation.[44] Moreover, because thought reform combined *"external force of coercion"* with *"inner enthusiasm through evangelistic exhortation,"* as Lifton put it, the human response to the experience was surprisingly diverse: "Some people considered it a relentless means of undermining the human personality; others saw it as a profoundly 'moral'—even religious—attempt to instill new ethics into the Chinese people. Both of these views were partly correct, and yet each, insofar as it ignored the other, was greatly misleading.…In all of this it is most important to realize that *what we see as a set of coercive maneuvers, the Chinese Communists view as a morally uplifting, harmonizing, and scientifically therapeutic experience.*"[45] Equally impressive to Lifton was the varied U.S. response, which ranged from terror and outrage to profound soul-searching about the ways in which Western society—from its early modern witch trials to McCarthyism to its methods of education more generally—had engaged in the equivalent of Chinese thought reform. Little did U.S. citizens know that their government was exploring similar questions in a much less self-effacing manner.

The fascinating and horrifying tale of the CIA's search for a mind-control weapon is usually narrated as a story of colossal failure because the CIA never found a truth serum or a mechanism for reliable human control. But this impression is an artifact of the CIA's own propaganda wing. That is, MK-ULTRA seemed a failure only because it did not produce the kind of magical and total mental control described by the propagandist Edward Hunter and his alarmist cohort. But Hunter's vision of total control was from the beginning a fiction designed to stir public fear.

When judged against less sensational standards, MK-ULTRA, for all its grotesque excesses and empty results, *did* succeed in two ways. First, it revealed the mystery of Communist brainwashing—which is that there never was any mystery. Brainwashing relies on torture. Second, and more important, MK-ULTRA led to a U.S. model of brainwashing that, like its Communist counterpart, is also essentially a form of torture. The U.S. model, now euphemized as "enhanced interrogation," was consolidated in the CIA's compact 1963 *KUBARK Counterintelligence Interrogation Manual*. ("KUBARK" is the CIA's cryptonym for CIA itself). "There is nothing mysterious about interrogation," the *KUBARK* manual explains, borrowing the language of Hinkle and Wolff.[46] Effective interrogation, the manual explains, simply requires "regression of the [subject's] personality." And "psychological research" shows that the best way to regress a human being is through extreme sensory deprivation, self-inflicted pain, and "a confusion technique designed not only to obliterate the familiar but to replace it with the weird" until this interrogation becomes "mentally intolerable."[47] This method became the basis for the U.S. military's SERE program of simulated interrogation.

To state the implications of this brief history another way, the only reason Abu Zubaydah confessed to being a member of Al Qaeda and to plotting the destruction of U.S. monuments is that he had been "brainwashed." If this claim seems melodramatic, it seems that way only because the CIA's propaganda wing succeeded so spectacularly in popularizing the notion of a magically effective brainwashing process. One of the most important aspects of the CIA's bipolar brainwashing effort—part propaganda, part "black psychiatry"—was the power of its propaganda fictions over its *own operations personnel.* Allen Dulles's public anxiety about "brain warfare" was, in other words, partly the fruit of the CIA's own propaganda campaign. But how could Edward Hunter and company have "implanted" a fear of brainwashing in the minds of CIA insiders like Dulles? The answer lies in the hypercompartmentalization of the CIA, which makes many intelligence actions operationally secret for virtually everyone, including agency executives and political leaders. While agents have a much greater inside knowledge of certain matters, there is no special inside position from which the *entire* covert machinery of the state is visible.[48]

Let me then recap the history of brainwashing in a way that emphasizes my point: brainwashing began as an orientalist propaganda fiction created by the CIA to mobilize domestic support for a massive military buildup. This fiction proved so effective that elements of U.S. intelligence believed it and began a furious search for a *real* mind-control weapon. While the search did not produce a miraculous form of total mind control, it did produce a method of coercive interrogation and a program of *simulated* brainwashing designed as a prophylactic against enemy mistreatment. Fifty years later, this simulation became the *real* basis for interrogating detainees in the War on Terror. In this way, the demonology of the Cold War took a surreal and bodily turn, as the institutions of the United States first imagined, then simulated, then projected onto a new enemy their worst fears of Cold War communism.[49]

How do we explain the dizzying relation here between fiction, simulation, and torture? Why does the covert story of brainwashing sound like the plot of a postmodern novel? The answer is that elements of the National Security State were themselves committed to the production of strategic fictions, simulations, and deceptions—psychological operations whose strategic goals were sometimes to produce confusion about what was real and true. The crucial policy document NSC-68, for example, advocated a domestic campaign to strengthen U.S. "moral fiber." Even before this campaign was approved, the State Department developed plans for what Assistant Secretary of State Edward Barrett called a domestic "psychological 'scare campaign.'"[50] Whether or not Hunter's September 1950 and 1951 writings on brainwashing were explicitly part of this initiative, they must be understood as part of the U.S. government's general embrace of what Allen Dulles called "brain warfare." In a climate where some obscure compartments of the state are frightening citizens and others are dabbling in mind control, the ideal of the bourgeois public sphere seems the stuff of distant fantasy.

Softening Up Our Boys

The constraints on knowledge in the Cold War, I have been suggesting, undermined the ideal of a public sphere in which individuals are the masters of their ideas and desires. This concern engendered a crisis of masculinity that found one of its purest forms in the discourse on brainwashing. No text demonstrates this effect better than John Frankenheimer's *Manchurian Candidate,* which is among the most enduring films of the late twentieth century. Based on the 1959 Richard Condon novel of the same name, *The Manchurian Candidate* depicts a Sino-Soviet conspiracy to co-opt the presidency of the United States through the use of brainwashed Korean War veterans.[51] A captured patrol of U.S. troops is airlifted to Manchuria, where they are conditioned by psychologists from the Soviet Pavlov Institute. Sergeant Raymond Shaw, the stepson of a U.S. senator, is programmed as an unwitting assassin who can be mobilized to kill by viewing the queen of diamonds in a deck of playing cards. The other POWs, meanwhile, are conditioned to tell a fabricated story about how Shaw's heroism saved the patrol—which earns Shaw the Congressional Medal of Honor and puts him above suspicion.

The signature scene of Frankenheimer's film reveals the supposed effect of brainwashing. A sensational rotating shot depicts a recurrent nightmare suffered by some members of the patrol, including the protagonist, Major Ben Marco. The camera pans across Marco's men, who sit lazily listening to what appears to be a lecture on hydrangeas at a New Jersey garden club. As the camera makes a second sweep of the room, however, the garden club is revealed to be a stark and imposing lecture hall full of Communist leaders who are impatiently awaiting a demonstration of brainwashing. The jovially sinister Chinese doctor leading the demonstration informs his comrades that the Americans have been brainwashed to believe they are at a garden club lecture. He then commands Raymond Shaw to kill two of his comrades, which Shaw does without hesitation or interference from his compatriots.

Frankenheimer's rotating shot is a stunning emblem of the Cold War covert sphere. It extends to their limit assumptions about brainwashing's power over the agency of individuals. Not only are the men completely controlled by external suggestion, but their consciousness and perception are replaced by an allegory of reality itself. This fictional consciousness converts men into women and a site of Cold War intrigue into a commonplace domestic scene. Frankenheimer's rotating shot asks viewers to overlay these two radically distinct worlds—one the inmost chamber of the Communist covert sector, the other a humdrum slice of bourgeois America. As subjects unwittingly trapped within the former reality, but convinced they inhabit the latter, the brainwashed soldiers allegorize the feminized Cold War public. They believe themselves safe amid the trappings of bourgeois domesticity, completely unaware of Cold War dangers that literally surround and manipulate them. They are cold warriors who have forgotten that they are cold warriors—which is another way of saying that they are typical Americans as seen from the perspective of the Cold War state. If this scene depicts the essence of brainwashing, then brainwashing is the essence of cold war— an international contest of ideology that plays out *undetected* at home.

This is partly why Condon and Frankenheimer locate a dire foreign threat within the guise of female domesticity. The choice of a women's club as the central delusion of the brainwashed is not incidental, for it seems to confirm J. Edgar Hoover's assertion that many "attractive," "smartly-dressed," apparently patriotic U.S. women were actually Communist agents.[52] Indeed, it turns out that Raymond Shaw's Communist handler is none other than his own *mother,* who is also the wife of McCarthyite Senator Johnny Iselin. Mrs. Iselin is the film's *real* queen of diamonds—the red ice queen—and she has been quite effective at controlling Raymond long before any of his Pavlovian conditioning. Raymond, moreover, is not the only one she manipulates. She also seduces and berates the clownish Senator Iselin into carrying out her every wish. After shepherding this incompetent Communist hunter into position as a vice-presidential nominee, she activates Raymond's mechanism and directs him to kill off both Senator Iselin's chief rival and the presidential nominee so that Johnny Iselin will rise as a puppet president under her control.

For all its concern about a Communist conspiracy to seize control of the U.S. political system, in other words, *The Manchurian Candidate* is equally worried about the influence women—especially mothers—exert over men

Figure 5. In John Frankenheimer's *Manchurian Candidate* (1962) brainwashed men experience a delusion of feminine domesticity (top) that masks the brutal reality of international cold warfare (bottom).

in the U.S. domestic scene. In fact, the film is deeply conflicted in its stance on communism. On the one hand, it takes seriously the worst fears of anti-Communists like McCarthy and Hoover, who claimed that a Communist "Trojan horse" strategy had placed "concealed members in sensitive positions in government."[53] On the other hand, the film is a scathing satire of U.S. anti-communism. It depicts anti-Communists as witting and unwitting Communist agents. It savages Senator McCarthy through the fictional figure of Senator Johnny Iselin, a drunken blowhard who cannot remember, from one moment to the next, the number of Defense Department officials he has accused of being Communists. (His exasperated wife finally allows him to settle on "exactly 57 card-carrying Communists" because he is fond of Heinz 57 ketchup.)

What does it mean that this film weds a fear of secret, foreign influence to a fear of ordinary, "domestic" influence ("domestic" in both senses of the word)? The conflation of the domestic and the foreign suggests that this war is fought invisibly at all times. To put the same thing another way, matters of seemingly ordinary social influence are crucial to winning a cold war, for a "cold" war is a war won by influencing the majority of a population (convincing it, for instance, that socialism might not be so bad or that socialism is evil). As many excellent studies have shown, the U.S. Cold War was significantly waged among the U.S. population as a war of ideas and social norms, particularly gender and sexual norms.[54] Like many postwar narratives, *The Manchurian Candidate* is notable for the way it employs a model of malevolent, external control to raise questions about much more ordinary and pervasive forms of social influence. To the extent that the film *is* about communism, it is about the ways in which both Communist and anti-Communist propaganda might undermine male autonomy—and it suggests that responsibility for such hostile takeovers is the fault of both insufficiently masculine men and inappropriately masculine women. Mrs. Iselin is the epitome of the domineering mother excoriated in Phillip Wylie's popular "momism" theory—the notion that overbearing and over-protective mothers emasculated their sons and thereby the nation.[55] It is no accident that Mrs. Iselin eventually reveals that she is not working for the Communists so much as for her own aggrandizement.

The film's two other assertive blondes—uncannily named Rosie and Josie—have inexplicable power over their male love interests, Marco and Shaw, respectively. When Rosie meets Marco on a train, Frankenheimer evokes the earlier brainwashing scenes. Rosie aggressively questions Marco, who seems both half asleep and profoundly disturbed just as he does in the glare of the Communist amphitheater. He sweats profusely, mumbles, and averts his gaze from Rosie's intense stare. After lighting Marco's cigarette, Rosie hypnotically repeats her address and asks, "Can you remember that?" "Yes," mumbles Marco, staring glassy-eyed into the distance. In case we have missed the point, Rosie then gives her phone number and again asks, "Can you remember that?" Marco again mumbles, "Yes." Rosie's suggestions work almost magically. When Marco is arrested in New York he inexplicably calls Rosie, whom he has met only once and who not only rushes to bail him out but explains that she has just broken up with her fiancé. As they drive away, Marco again hypnotically recalls her apartment number, "3B," to which she replies, "Very good." It's not very long before Marco has proposed to her, suggesting they start a family.

Frankenheimer develops similar associations between hypnotic suggestion and female sexuality in Josie Jordan, who in all apparent innocence arrives at Mrs. Iselin's costume party dressed as none other than the queen of diamonds, a costume she claims she bought whimsically from a store window. On first glance, this astonishing coincidence—the daughter of the Democratic senator Jordan dressed in the very symbol that activates the unwitting Communist assassin—would seem to make Josie part of the conspiracy. But this turns out not to be the case. Her costume is purely coincidental, a feminine whim that trumps Mrs. Iselin's deck of playing cards and inspires the repressed Raymond to elope immediately with Josie. Josie has inexplicable influence over Marco, too. When Marco tracks the newlyweds down, Josie easily persuades him to let her and Raymond take a honeymoon—even though Marco knows Raymond has been programmed as a high-level political assassin.

What are we to make of these puzzlingly suggestive scenes? The film associates all three of its major female characters with Communist brainwashing and creates a foreboding sense that all three are potential agents engaged in a mysterious form of human control. Their three male counterparts, moreover, are exceptionally compliant and suggestible. Ultimately, the uncanny sense of control attributed to both Rosie and Josie does not indicate their participation in Mrs. Iselin's plot—but the strange associations with foreign espionage are hard to shake. All the women in this film carry a residue of the clandestine—and the implication of this residue is

Figure 6. *The Manchurian Candidate* insistently depicts female aggression as
a threat lurking in the U.S. domestic sphere.

that "ordinary" American life conceals the extraordinary, covert activities
of cold war. The public sphere increasingly seems a deceptive screen covering mysterious forms of powerful influence.

Hypnotic suggestion, moreover, ultimately seems an ordinary feature of
social relations between men and women. Like Meerloo, in other words,
Frankenheimer suggests that Pavlovian brainwashing is not needed for
the most dangerous forms of influence. Mrs. Iselin easily controls the senator by ordinary suggestion and has long controlled Raymond in the same
way. What makes both men susceptible to conditioning is their insufficient
masculinity and the power of a pathologically aggressive mother. "My
whole life," Mrs. Iselin explains to Raymond before kissing him deeply and
erotically, "is dedicated to helping you and Johnny—my two boys, my two
little boys." This horrifying tendency, the film suggests, is the reason both
Raymond *and* Johnny become unwitting Communist agents: both are classic mama's boys, insufficiently sexually and emotionally autonomous, and
insufficiently bonded to other men. It is only a matter of completing the
psychic equation that Mrs. Iselin is herself a Communist.

This plot structure illuminates the masculinist logic of the covert sphere, which draws rigid lines between the male realm of state secrets and the female civilian world. *The Manchurian Candidate* exceeds even film noir in fantasizing a nightmarish reversal of these distinctions, a world in which men are sheep and aggressive women manage the Machiavellian domain of Cold War politics. The film's profound anxiety about gender norms is inseparable from its fear that Communist "thought control" is somehow like the ordinary forms of influence that exist in a "free society." The film conflates a fear that Communists are brainwashing young Americans with a more quotidian, but equally ludicrous, worry that U.S. society has allowed women, especially mothers, too much influence over men. In so doing, *The Manchurian Candidate* expresses something quite similar to Meerloo's anxiety about social conditioning. The epistemology of the covert sphere requires us to contemplate the secret activities of the Cold War through fictions, and hence to risk not knowing them at all. The latter possibility is suggested by the film's brilliant rotating shot: the naïveté of the brainwashed POWs is a result of clandestine enemy activity. But if we understand the POWs as figures for the U.S. public, then the naïveté must be attributed to *U.S.* state secrecy. In its fear of a frighteningly passive and pliant public, in other words, *The Manchurian Candidate* recognizes that the Cold War state demanded just such a public. It is this half-knowledge that illuminates the film's profound anxiety about feminization. The Cold War state placed U.S. citizens in a posture akin to that of women within the ideology of the nineteenth-century domestic sphere—a position of unknowing, "safe" from the rough-and-tumble realm of "real" political struggle, and highly reliant on men for both protection and information (which was, of course, provided on a "need to know" basis). In *The Manchurian Candidate,* the twin threats of female aggression and public feminization are the imaginary fruit of the Cold War's revised social compact.

Renditions

This brief history of brainwashing discourse suggests several important conclusions about Cold War U.S. culture. First, the notion of brainwashing was instrumental in shaping the cultural imaginary of the covert sphere.

The fundamental contradiction in U.S. foreign policy—the open secret that U.S. policy relied on undemocratic, secret means—contributed significantly to suspicion of government and fueled the representation of brainwashing as a practice of the U.S. security state. It is no accident that the story of brainwashing consists of both a public ("unclassified") story and a "secret history" of CIA experiments and Communist methods. Beneath the fantastical popular fictions of brainwashing schemes, there were real covert actions—both Eastern and Western. But many of these plots were themselves fictions and simulations. This is one meaning of the Colonel Schwable case. Chinese brainwashing was simultaneously all of the following: a real Chinese program of "thought reform"; a covert *U.S.* propaganda program designed to heighten public support for cold warfare; and a covert *Chinese* propaganda program designed to weaken U.S. interests through the publication of disinformation (the Chinese, for instance, successfully created the impression that the United States had used biological weapons in Korea). Despite the dizzying array of plots and counterplots, however, it is also clear that little coordination existed between different actors, and thus the phenomenon of brainwashing cannot be explained as the result of some single, overarching plot. Indeed, it seems relatively clear that the CIA's left hand was frequently doing things without the knowledge of its right hand, never mind its head.

Second, brainwashing became a popular notion because it provided a way of thinking about ideology and social influence. As *The Manchurian Candidate* illustrates, brainwashing specifically articulated how the framework of Cold War secrecy intersected with norms of gender and sexuality. Allen Ginsberg, for instance, associated mass culture's "identity brainwash" with both individual repression and the prosecution of the Cold War.[56] William S. Burroughs—who, like Ginsberg, underwent psychiatric treatment for homosexuality—drew even stronger connections between domestic social influence and clandestine military programs: "The technocratic control apparatus of the United States," he calmly declared, "has at its fingertips new techniques—brainwashing, psychotropic drugs, lobotomy and other more subtle forms of psychosurgery... which if fully exploited could make Orwell's *1984* seem like a benevolent utopia."[57] Sylvia Plath's Esther Greenwood associates femininity and motherhood with "being brainwashed" like "a slave in a totalitarian state"—a fate she tellingly connects to the execution of Ethel Rosenberg. Plath's contemporary,

Betty Friedan, not only associated brainwashing with the construction of Cold War femininity but explicitly understood femininity on the model of the U.S. Korean War POW, whom she called an "apathetic dependent, infantile, purposeless being,... the new American man ... strangely reminiscent of the familiar 'feminine' personality."[58]

What all these examples recognize is that "brain warfare" was simultaneously a quotidian fact of life in mass society *and* a primary form of the clandestine combat in which the nation was currently involved. It is noteworthy how regularly discussions of brainwashing, even in its most lurid orientalist constructions, provoked reflection on far more prosaic forms of ideological conditioning present in U.S. society. Even Hunter himself, as he developed the concept in 1951, immediately connected it to Western technological advances. "In effect," he writes, "our entire field of modern communications media, from public-opinion surveys to aptitude testing," has taught us not only "some of the theoretical processes that go on in a man's head but also how to direct his thoughts." These techniques, he adds, are "used by individuals..., by small firms and big corporations, and by political parties and governments."[59] Such ruminations on the relation between Communist brainwashing and the subtle effects of ordinary Western social institutions occupy a substantial portion of more thoughtful accounts of the subject. As Lifton notes, encounters with the concept of brainwashing routinely produce "tortured ... self-examination which leads professional people to ask whether they in their own activities might not be guilty of 'brainwashing': educators about their teaching, psychiatrists about their training and their psychotherapy, theologians about their own reform methods."[60]

In this way, brainwashing made culturally intelligible an enduring problem of U.S. political culture—on the one hand, a need to understand and explain social influence, and on the other hand, a rigid intolerance of the sociological and Marxist perspectives that could provide the theoretical basis for such an understanding. If brainwashing is ultimately a crude theory of ideology, it is also the brainchild of thinkers profoundly hostile to Marxist ideology critique—not only to Marxist economic assumptions but also to its emphasis on structural, rather than individual, causality. For U.S. cold warriors like Hunter, the tenets of liberal individualism— the view that persons are autonomous, rational agents wholly responsible for their own actions—were not only good philosophy but a crucial bulwark against totalitarianism. And yet it was precisely such thinkers who so floridly imagined the nightmare antithesis of the liberal self: the brainwashed subject. If individuals were truly capable of succumbing to wholesale external control, then liberal individualism was fatally flawed. Brainwashing theory seems to acknowledge this terrifying possibility while simultaneously providing a defense of individualism and a rationale for resisting the horror of external control. Crucially, the theory of brainwashing studiously avoids structuralism; it preserves the intentionality at the heart of individualism by understanding social control as the work of an exceptionally powerful, willful, rational, and malevolent human agent—the brainwasher. It was within this contradiction that a lurid idea like brainwashing could prove so compelling, for it permitted a crude form of sociological thinking that was still compatible with individualism. The idea of a malevolent and intentional program of mental conditioning permitted the fantasy that social conditioning could be explained without compromising the idea that, somewhere, a rational, motivated agent controlled the process.

Third, the discourse on brainwashing—at both its most serious and its most ludicrous—staged a debate between two competing psychological models at precisely the moment when critical fissures in the dominant U.S. model had opened. As Joost Meerloo put it in 1956:

> Western psychology...takes a much less mechanical view of man than do the Soviet Pavlovians. It is apparent to us that their simple explanation of training ignores and rejects the concept of purposeful adaptation and the question of the goals to which this training is directed.... The idea of Western democratic psychology is to train men into independence and maturity by enlisting their conscious aid, awareness, and volition in the learning process. The idea of the totalitarian psychology, on the other hand, is to tame men, to make them willing tools in the hands of their leaders. (*Rape of the Mind,* 51–52)

This is one way of understanding the central place of *The Manchurian Candidate* in the fiction of mind control. Raymond Shaw's Pavlovian conditioning in China is ultimately brought into the service of the very figure also responsible for most of his "Freudian training": his own domineering mother. When, at the conclusion of the narrative, Shaw's mother directs him to assassinate the Republican presidential nominee, Shaw breaks his

Pavlovian conditioning and instead shoots his mother and stepfather. The ultimate battle in the film, then, is not between Shaw and his mother, or even between capitalism and communism, but between a Freudian account of behavior and a Pavlovian one. In this narrative, the repressed returns. Not even the specialists at the Pavlov Institute can trump the Freudian family romance as a determinant of behavior.

The discursive rivalry between Freudianism and Pavlovianism was a model of the Cold War itself. It rearticulated long-standing aspects of individualism in a psychological framework.[61] Within the United States, individual autonomy was viewed as a key safeguard of capitalist democracy and liberty against the slavish conformity of socialism. Soviet behaviorism reinforced this cultural fantasy in the strongest of terms by seeming to explain how Communists had come to accept their own "enslavement." As Meerloo wrote in a 1954 article in the *American Journal of Psychiatry,* "It is accepted by Soviet theorists that just as animals can be trained and conditioned, so can man. The totalitarian wants to train and indoctrinate his fellow men in order to form a new society of conditioned human insects among whom every pattern of behavior is prefabricated."[62] Yet such statements also posed a serious problem for dominant U.S. thinking about subjectivity—particularly when they were offered in the context of Colonel Schwable's reduction to just such an "insect" in the face of Chinese brainwashing. If U.S. citizens were defined by their extraordinary autonomy, then how could they be brainwashed into Communist dupes? Obviously, they were not as autonomous as they wished to be. For Meerloo and Sargant, both of whom happily accepted Pavlov's account of behavioral influences, this fact in itself was not troubling. Indeed, one of the paradoxes of the brainwashing story is that the intellectual figures sounding the alarm—Meerloo and Sargant—were the ones criticized for defending Russian behavioralism to the U.S. public. Their influence reflected the contradiction between the assumptions of liberal individualism and the horrifying "discovery" that behaviorism provided a compelling account of human action—a contradiction, that is, between the assumption that persons *ought to be* rational, autonomous actors who determine their own fate and the fact that people are substantially constructed and controlled from without.

Finally, and most important, the centrality of fiction in the discourse on brainwashing reflects the problem of knowledge within the institutions of the Cold War and the War on Terror. In both conflicts, a distant and inscrutable enemy became the subject of extraordinary public concern, and the state responded through a massive program of covert action. The result, in both cases, was a political theater with a certain "postmodern" quality—a confusion of what is real and what is merely strategic fiction. In making this claim, I do not mean to suggest that brainwashing is a "postmodern" phenomenon or that brainwashing narratives have postmodern aesthetic features. My argument, rather, is that the Cold War security state transformed the conditions of social knowledge in a way that would later become a topic of central interest in postmodern narrative—in texts invested in demonstrating their own artifice and raising doubts about the nature of the real, the authentic, and the natural.

The notion of brainwashing literalizes the problem of knowledge under such a regime. Consider the way the brainwashed were thought to suffer the ontological uncertainty that would later typify postmodernism. In *Rape of the Mind,* for instance, Meerloo claims that "the panic of the 'brainwashee'...is the total confusion he suffers about all concepts"—a confusion that can be transmitted to other members of society until "no one knows how to distinguish truth from falsehood." Charles Mayo, of Mayo Clinic fame, testified to the United Nations in 1953 that new forms of torture could make a man the "seemingly willing accomplice to the complete disintegration of his integrity and the production of an elaborate fiction."[63] Edward Hunter told a Senate subcommittee in 1956 that brainwashing puts "a man's mind into a fog so that he will mistake what is true for what is untrue, what is right for what is wrong."[64] Testifying to Congress again in 1958, Hunter warned that brainwashing produced just the sort of moral relativism that would later come to be popularly identified with postmodernism.

> I see, primarily, as part of this softening up process in America, the liquidation of our attitudes on what we used to recognize as right and wrong, what we used to accept as absolute moral standards. We now confuse moral standards with the sophistication of dialectical materialism, with a Communist crackpot theology which teaches that everything changes, and that what is right or wrong, good or bad, changes as well. So nothing they say is really good or bad. There is no such thing as truth or a lie; and any belief we actually held was simply your being unsophisticated. They don't say this in so many words, except to those who are already indoctrinated in communism.[65]

This early testimony on brainwashing eerily anticipates the later critique of so-called postmodern relativism. Not only does Hunter's attack describe the hallmark epistemological skepticism of postmodern narrative but his description of the brainwashed subject is an anticipatory caricature of the postmodern subject—bereft of agency and other individuating qualities, socially constructed through and through.

The point of such comparisons is not to associate postmodernism with brainwashing per se but to find some of postmodernism's roots in the institutions of the Cold War. The conflicting demands of the Cold War state fueled an astonishing conflation of reality and fantasy in nearly every aspect of the brainwashing story—the secret funding of strategic "journalism," scientific analysis of dystopian fiction, the purported implantation of a fictional consciousness in hapless victims. Even if we return, finally, to the grim legacy of brainwashing—the business of psychologically "enhanced" interrogation, or torture—we remain in what Alfred McCoy calls "a kind of total *theatre,* a constructed unreality of lies and inversion": "To make their artifice of false charges, fabricated news, and mock executions convincing, interrogators often become inspired thespians. The torture chamber itself thus has the theatricality of a set with special lighting, sound effects, props, and backdrop, all designed with a perverse stagecraft to evoke an aura of fear."[66] The central principle of the *KUBARK* manual is to create radical ontological uncertainty in the subject by advancing and slowing clocks, preventing knowledge of day and night, feeding the prisoner at bizarre intervals, drugging and moving the prisoner during sleep, inquiring why he tried to hang himself (when he did not), and so on.[67] Successful psychologically oriented interrogation, in other words, produces the hallmark effect of postmodern metafiction—the complete upending of a stable sense of reality. When Hinkle and Wolff noted in 1956 that this form of interrogation swiftly produces a "loss of objectivity," they may as well have been describing the intellectual goals of postmodernism, which is rooted in a critique of objectivity and Enlightenment modernity.[68]

It may seem callous to trace the philosophical or aesthetic implications of a real form of bodily violence. "Enhanced interrogation" can lead to disabling trauma or psychosis. According to his lawyer, Abu Zubaydah has suffered hundreds of seizures and seems to have permanent physical and psychological disability.[69] Yet enhanced interrogation is itself the institutional legacy of "cold" warfare rooted in strategic fiction, simulation, and psychological influence. Ironically, by developing its model of enhanced interrogation in response to a fantasy about Communist brainwashing, the U.S. intelligence community forgot that this form of interrogation was never an effective way to produce *truth;* it was, on the contrary, an extraordinary machine for the production of *fictions.* The monstrous plots to which Zubaydah confessed were every bit as fictitious as the biological weapons Schwable and company admitted dropping on Korea. But we should not conclude therefore that brainwashing is completely ineffective; in fact it proved a highly effective propaganda weapon for the Chinese. And the *theory* of brainwashing was an equally effective domestic propaganda weapon for the United States.

Such fictions return us, finally, to the most important site of fiction in the story of brainwashing: the cell of the detainee. Among the remarkable features of the Abu Zubaydah story is how shocked FBI personnel were at CIA interrogation methods, which have been codified since 1963. At first glance, the bureau's horror seems to reflect an epistemological barrier between the public and covert agencies of government (the FBI and the CIA). Yet this reaction is so similar to the public response to the Abu Ghraib scandal and the CIA's use of torture that it suggests shock is itself an ideological effect of the covert sphere. The fictions of the covert sphere simultaneously make visible the secret work of the state and consign this work to the realm of fantasy. They confer a half-knowledge that makes government secrecy tolerable because it offers the public the opportunity to proclaim its official ignorance—and then to be shocked when the details of secret programs leak, via nonfiction discourse, into the "sheltered" public sphere.

This dynamic explains a final cultural function of brainwashing narratives. The fantasy of an esoteric and magical technique—a painless conversion effected through hypnosis or drugs—is much easier to stomach than an open defense of torture. Brainwashing suggests that the dirty details are best forgotten, seen as something forced on an innocent like Raymond Shaw, not adopted by a democratic state as a weapon of war. By understanding cold warfare through fiction, the U.S. public can disavow its own democracy's heart of darkness.

2

Spectacles of Secrecy

Trial by Simulation

Why has the Rosenberg affair been so important to postmodern U.S. historical fiction? While American slavery is the dominant subject of the genre, few events have drawn so much high-powered attention as the 1953 execution of Julius and Ethel Rosenberg for conspiracy to commit espionage. The subject of three of the most important literary achievements of the past fifty years—E. L. Doctorow's *Book of Daniel* (1971), Robert Coover's *Public Burning* (1977), and Tony Kushner's *Angels in America* (1991–92)—the Rosenberg affair has been rivaled in its fictionalization by only a few other postwar events: the assassination of John F. Kennedy, the Vietnam War, and the attacks of September 11, 2001.[1] One obvious reason for the attention to the Rosenberg case is its status as the "trial of the century" and a cause célèbre of the postwar Left. Even after the declassification of the National Security Administration's VENONA decrypts, which revealed that Julius Rosenberg was an active Soviet agent, there is still widespread agreement that the executions were a profound miscarriage of justice, a political spectacle rooted in hysteria, and a powerful register of the political energies of the Cold War.[2]

But there are two other reasons why the Rosenberg affair has been compelling to writers: first, like the Kennedy assassination, Vietnam, and 9/11, the Rosenberg case was a political spectacle of the covert sphere—a public drama of "atomic secrets," subversive citizens, and U.S. counterintelligence. Second, its development as both a juridical proceeding and a media spectacle had a postmodern quality in its own right. For Alice Jardine, in fact, "the Rosenberg Event is ... perhaps *the* initiatory postmodern event of the American fifties."[3] This second feature of the case is related to the first. Like other postwar historical events of interest to writers, the Rosenberg case had a "postmodern" quality because it erupted at the murky nexus of public culture and state secrecy. It was from the outset a drama of secrets. As the FBI chief J. Edgar Hoover declared after the stunning 1950 arrest of Harry Gold—the "atom spy courier" who would lead the FBI to David Greenglass and then to Greenglass's brother-in-law, Julius Rosenberg—"I doubt whether it will ever be possible to disclose publicly all of the factors involved" in the case.[4] This was itself an extraordinary understatement, for Hoover kept such "factors" secret even from President Eisenhower and the members of his cabinet. Hence, on the morning of the executions, when Attorney General Herb Brownell found himself reassuring Eisenhower that the government possessed evidence "[not] usable in court," Brownell did so not because he had actually *seen* the evidence but because Hoover had reassured him, via top secret memo, that the FBI had "information substantiating the Rosenberg's involvement in espionage" from "a confidential source of unimpeachable reliability whose identity cannot be revealed under any circumstances."[5]

But while the Rosenberg case purported to punish the theft of the nation's deepest secret, it was also a public spectacle. And like the other "atom spy trials" of the early 1950s, the thing it most spectacularized, paradoxically, was state secrecy itself. The dramatic revelation of a shadow world of covert agents and nuclear secrets made tangible the need for a vast apparatus of covert countermeasures. The state's need for secrecy thus competed with its need for publicity. These competing demands defined the Cold War atom spy trials, producing a political theater fraught with contradictions about the work of the state, the nature of evidence, and the blurry line between the public and covert spheres. In 1950, for instance, Abraham Brothman and Miriam Moskowitz were convicted of giving the Soviets plans for a synthetic rubber plant in 1941–42 even though their defense showed that Brothman had earlier published several articles on precisely the same "secret" rubber-making process. Even the defense missed the larger point, though, for as historians Walter and Miriam Schneir archly observe, in 1942 the U.S. government was providing the USSR with lend-lease shipments that included not only the blueprints and operating manuals for synthetic rubber factories but also *the very factories themselves*.[6] The covert activity for which Brothman and Moskowitz went to prison, in other words, was the transmission of already public information, which was simultaneously being transferred to the Soviet Union by its wartime ally, the U.S. government.

Brothman's prosecutors overcame this embarrassing fact by producing a spectacular witness—Harry Gold, a self-professed "courier" for Soviet agents, including Klaus Fuchs. Gold's astonishing testimony possessed a surreal and self-negating quality. In a bizarre but riveting appearance, he repudiated his earlier sworn testimony in support of Brothman and divulged his own lifelong habit of confabulation, melodramatic fantasy, and pathological deception. In the rational public sphere, such revelations of perjury and pathological lying might have sunk the prosecution's case. But the Brothman trial was a drama of the covert sphere, and in that strange space Gold's fantastic tale was sufficient to send Brothman and Moskowitz away. In the covert sphere, this case suggests, jurisprudence is transformed by the epistemology of state secrecy, which supplants traditional evidentiary procedures with the procedures of narrative *fiction*.

Similar peculiarities also governed the much grander spectacle of the Rosenberg trial. As in the brainwashing scare, the inquiry pointed to apparent gender traitors—the supposedly heartless, unmotherly, and selfish Ethel Rosenberg and a trio of mousy, unathletic men led by a paragon of Cold War "momism," Harry Gold.[7] Here, again, the prosecution built its case on Gold, who, amazingly, was never cross-examined by the defense. This omission is widely viewed as a sign of lawyerly incompetence, yet it must also be understood within the bizarre epistemology of the atom spy trials. In a proceeding where *nothing* could be substantiated by reference to physical evidence, every word out of Gold's mouth carried enormous power. "By an ironic quirk of Gold's testimony," the *New York Times* reported, "the cut-out portion of a Jello box became the first tangible bit of evidence to connect the Rosenbergs, the Greenglasses, Gold and Yakovlev."[8] But in fact, the Jell-O box introduced in court was not the one that purportedly identified David Greenglass to courier Harry Gold in Albuquerque. It was a *replica* purchased by prosecutors. Indeed, *all* the major physical evidence in the case consisted of replicas, not originals: the torn sheet of onion-skin paper that similarly identified Yakovlev to Gold; the comically crude "explosive lens mold" sketches by which David Greenglass purportedly transferred to his handler "the secret of the atom bomb"; the "Russian" console table that was in fact purchased by FBI agents at Macy's (and hence lacked the alleged secret compartment).[9]

This panoply of *simulations* defined the trial's contradictory drama of publicity and secrecy. In a bizarre but telling moment, prosecutor Roy Cohn presented the court with a replica of Greenglass's "cross-section sketch of the atom bomb." Instantly, defense attorney Emanuel Bloch leaped up and demanded that Judge Irving Kaufman "impound this exhibit so that it remains secret." Surprised, Judge Kaufman instantly sealed the courtroom, expelling spectators and the press. Like an actor reminded of forgotten lines, the chief prosecutor, Irving Saypol, chimed in, declaring Greenglass's drawing a matter "of such gravity that the Atomic Energy Commission held hearings...on the subject." Saypol must have felt chastened, for his entire case rested on the claim that this drawing contained "*the secret of the atomic bomb*"—and yet his junior colleague had just revealed this secret to the world press in open court. Everyone in the court knew that this claim was hyperbole, for only moments after this little melodrama of "top secrets," Judge Kaufman invited reporters back into court and urged them merely to use "good taste" in handling the stage props before them. Within a week, newspapers and magazines had published Greenglass's crude diagrams around the world. As *Scientific American* commented, the drawings were "not much of a secret" after all, because they conveyed only the widely known principle of implosion and lacked any "quantitative data" that would have conveyed how to implement this principle.[10]

What was most important about the "atom spy" trials, then, was not their secret *content*, but their purported revelation of the covert sector itself. They offered the public a window onto the shadow world of spies and government agents operating beneath the rational public sphere. In order to do so, however, the trials supplemented traditional juridical procedures

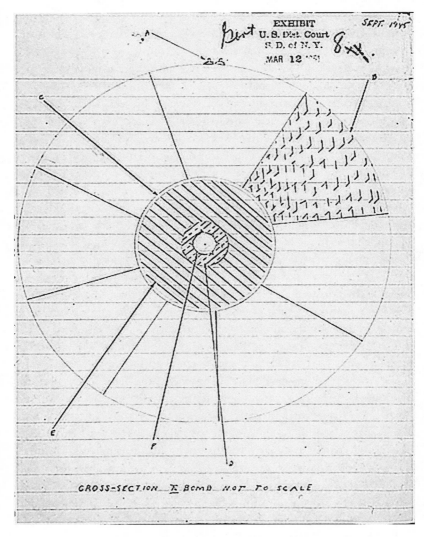

Figure 7. David Greenglass drew this replica cross-section of an A-bomb at the request of prosecutors, who then presented it during the Rosenberg trial as part of the "secret of the atom bomb."

with the procedures of narrative fiction, which requires far less rigorous correspondences between discourse and events. The result was a form of political theater marked by the major quality of postmodernism—a confusion of the real with its representations. It is in this sense that Jardine says the affair seems "to radiate simulationist postmodernism."[11]

What is the relation between secrecy, spectacle, and postmodernism? In his brilliant account of "covert spectacle" during the Reagan-Bush era, Michael Rogin offers a counterintuitive answer. For Rogin, political spectacle does not distract attention from the state's dirty secrets. It *reveals* them in an "easily forgettable series of surface entertainments—movies, television series, political shows." And such revelations lead not to democratic debate or public outrage but rather to something like "infantile amnesia"—an ahistorical numbness to certain facts of U.S. empire "that, if consciously sustained in memory over time, would have to be called into question." Paradoxically, the incessant *visibility* of the state's covert dimension "normalizes to invisibility" the undemocratic and often brutal work of the U.S. security state.[12]

This explanation upends the popular notion of state secrecy. The state's secrets, Rogin claims, are hidden in the open, like Poe's purloined letter, and what keeps them hidden is collective "amnesia." By amnesia, Rogin does not mean the total inability to recall mental content to consciousness. He means, rather, something like disavowal and the *conflation* of fact and fiction. "Covert spectacles," he explains, break down the distinction between politics and theater, causing citizens to confuse political events with fictional representations. Why, Rogin asks, "should the mass audience be able to tell the difference between TV series and movies and the political spectacles that also appear on the screen, so long as the reality principle never reaches, directly and forcefully, into their lives (as it did, for example, in the 1930s depression or the 1960s draft)?" Political amnesia, then, is a form of "motivated forgetting"—the ability "both to have [an] experience and not to retain it in memory."[13]

What makes this formulation so useful in understanding the Rosenberg case is its vision of "postmodern" theatricality as a core element of the National Security State. "The Cold War," Rogin notes, "was fought mainly with symbols and surrogates." U.S. foreign policy was simultaneously covert and spectacular, "conducted by theatrical events—Grenada invasion, Libyan bombing, Persian Gulf flagging, Honduran 'show of force'—staged for public consumption."[14] A similar sense of spectacle informs Jean Baudrillard's argument that Cold War deterrence is a primary example of postmodern simulation. While Rogin's focus is the Reagan-Bush era—during which a former actor and a former spymaster were themselves emblems of a strategy rooted in spectacle and secrecy—the same dynamic operated domestically during the early 1950s. The state's investment in strategic spectacle is a de facto endorsement of the power of representations to shape the world—a bedrock assumption of postmodernism.

The development of postmodernism must therefore be understood partly within this historical context, particularly when postmodern narrative addressed the Cold War as a subject. In explaining the genesis of *The Public Burning,* Robert Coover notes that the Rosenberg affair struck him as "the event that most dramatically encapsulated the Cold War madness. We were caught up in something that resembled myth more than reality."[15] This observation clearly locates the "postmodern" blurring of reality and myth in the hysteria of the event itself. Before I take up Coover's novel in more detail, I want to stress that this "postmodern" quality in the Rosenberg affair is not merely an artifact of its subsequent fictionalizations but an integral part of its original nonfictional representation, particularly as depicted in its most influential early history, Walter and Miriam Schneir's 1965 *Invitation to an Inquest.* The classic left-wing account of the affair, *Invitation to an Inquest* argues that the Rosenberg prosecution was an exercise in political theatrics and fictionality that resulted in a mockery of justice and perhaps even a deliberate scapegoating of innocents. The Schneirs advance several major claims: first, the difficulty of making an atomic weapon lay not in "atomic secrets" but in the immense industrial problem of safely isolating fissile material; second, 1950s media accounts of an "atomic spy ring" were fictions fueled by political hysteria; third, the supposed "atomic secrets" divulged by Greenglass were worthless versions of widely known scientific principles; and, finally, Harry Gold, the FBI's primary source in the atom spy cases, was an emotionally unstable fantasist and pathological liar.

In many ways Gold is the star of *Invitation to an Inquest.* His tendencies toward amnesia, confabulation, and revision in the state's favor echo similar tendencies in the Cold War public and media. When Gold was arrested three days after the FBI interrogated Klaus Fuchs in London, for instance, U.S. newspapers reported that that Fuchs had identified his courier as a "short, stocky, soft-spoken fellow with Slavic features, an oval face and a penchant for pin-striped suits"—a near-perfect description of Gold's picture as it appeared alongside these articles. A year later, however, J. Edgar Hoover revealed that Fuchs had actually described his courier as a tall, middle-aged, broadly built man—the virtual opposite of Gold. How, then, did the press almost uniformly report that Fuchs had described Gold as short and stocky? As the Schneirs observe, early press reports were based either "on FBI leaks or the *imaginative efforts* of reporters." In either case, they were fictions. *Invitation to an Inquest* details scores of such transformations of the record, and in doing so it powerfully suggests that the popular press influenced the atomic spy cases by abandoning evidentiary journalism for speculation and invention.[16]

Yet "we now know" that Julius Rosenberg was indeed a spy. As *Invitation to an Inquest* was moving toward reissue in 1983, it came under increasingly effective attack by the rival duo of Ronald Radosh and Joyce Milton, whose 1983 history, *The Rosenberg File,* relied more heavily on intelligence sources and declassified documents to argue that while the Rosenbergs were poorly served by the justice system, Julius Rosenberg was in fact a Soviet agent. In 1997, Radosh and Milton released a new edition of *The Rosenberg File* with powerful evidence from the declassified VENONA cables. These decrypted Soviet communiqués refer to a spy with the codename "Liberal," who was almost certainly Julius Rosenberg. Former KGB officers have since stepped forward to confirm that Rosenberg was a Soviet agent.[17]

My goal here is not to adjudicate between these two accounts but rather to suggest that their disagreement is symptomatic of the dialectic of spectacle and secrecy that defines the covert sphere. While the Schneirs worked largely from *public* information, Radosh and Milton eventually rested their case on formerly *classified* documents oozing from state archives. Radosh and Milton argue that the Schneirs pay insufficient attention to this material. But it was only after the Cold War, when state secrets began to trickle into the public sphere, that traditional historical evidence could confirm Julius Rosenberg's espionage. Writing within the constraints of the 1965 covert sphere, the Schneirs did not have access to the evidence eventually used by Radosh and Milton. If Radosh and Milton ultimately proved correct about Julius Rosenberg's identity as a spy, the Schneirs nonetheless diagnosed the symptoms of a public sphere whose legal and journalistic narratives of state secrecy are riddled with contradictions, inaccuracies, and a strange conflation of fact and fiction.

In the pages that follow, I trace these qualities through Robert Coover's treatment of the Rosenberg affair in *The Public Burning*. Coover's novel brilliantly critiques the state's "spectacle of secrecy" through a revolutionary postmodernism that stresses the fictional quality of the Rosenberg affair. By explicitly connecting the novel's literary form to Cold War institutions, Coover powerfully illustrates my claim that postmodern narrative is both a reflection of, and a response to, Cold War epistemology. As I flesh out this case, I take up the novel's various attempts to make visible the ideological work of the covert sphere—the state's reliance on popular entertainments, the influence of popular fiction and theater on national security actions, and the role of mass media in the creation of Cold War policy. While Coover indicts a wide variety of institutions, it is ultimately the figure of the *spy* and fabulator extraordinaire, Harry Gold, who embodies the central problem of the Cold War covert sphere and, remarkably, becomes a major inspiration for Coover's brand of postmodernism.

Political Theater

No novel in recent memory has insisted on the spectacular nature of political power more than *The Public Burning*. Written in the decade preceding Watergate and eventually published in 1977, Coover's novel recasts the Rosenberg executions as a carnivalesque historical pageant in Times Square. The novel is structured as a drama in four acts, each separated by an "intermezzo," a dramatic dialogue constructed of language mined from historical documents, including the letters of Julius and Ethel Rosenberg and the speeches of Dwight Eisenhower. The bulk of the novel consists of two alternating narratives. One is the first-person account of a bumbling and naive vice president Richard Nixon as he reviews the Rosenberg case with the hope of extracting confessions that will halt the executions and thereby alter the course of history. What Nixon uncovers, however, is the utter theatricality of the government's case—its sources in popular fiction and its reliance on political spectacle. The other major strand of the novel is an irreverent allegory of the Cold War as a melodrama of U.S. and Communist superheroes. In this narrative strand, a brash Uncle Sam, beset by the evil Phantom of Sino-Soviet communism, creates a grotesque spectacle of the Rosenberg executions in the hope "that a fierce public exorcism right now might flush the Phantom from his underground cells" and "give Uncle Sam something to swing at besides a lot of remote gooks."[18] Freely intermingling historical persons with allegorical figures—Betty Crocker, *Time* magazine ("the National Poet Laureate"), and the *New York Times* ("the Spirit of History")—this narrative presents a surreal, yet meticulously detailed, history of the Cold War through the masculinist rhetoric of comic books, sports commentary, and Christian fundamentalism. In alternating chapters, Coover uses these two narratives to shuttle the reader from Nixon's tortured reexamination of the case to a panoramic view of world events in 1953.

The novel thus literalizes the terms of Rogin's analysis. It depicts a culture of spectacle and secrecy that has utterly blurred the real and the theatrical, the geopolitical and the domestic. Moreover, it repeatedly links Cold War spectacle to problems of cultural memory. The more Nixon sees the Rosenberg affair as political theater, the more he questions his own memories; eventually he begins to experience "memories" of events he has never witnessed. If his story depicts individual amnesia and confabulation, the Uncle Sam narrative locates these problems at the national level, revealing an elaborate cultural machinery for maintaining American exceptionalism. Indeed, Coover wrote *The Public Burning* as a corrective to collective historical amnesia. Sensing that "we'd all repressed...a watershed moment in American history," he remarks, "it occurred to me...to restage it—with added attractions—right there in Times Square, where we could all have another look at it."[19] Together, then, the novel's twin narratives describe two sides of an ideological system that functions through political spectacle. While the Uncle Sam narrative illustrates the national construction of cultural memory through cultural institutions, the Nixon story illustrates the effect of these institutions on an individual mind.

Crucially, however, Coover's dual narratives are also organized around the division between the public and the covert, between the public burning of the Rosenbergs and the vice president's review of internal government documents. It is this relation between public and state, spectacle and secret, that gives purpose to Coover's account of the Rosenberg affair. The novel's absurd blend of fantasy and historical fact is not an exercise in postmodern "play" but a serious attempt to reveal the reliance of the Cold War security state on fiction-making operations. Like Rogin, Coover sees the state as a cultural producer in cahoots with the culture industry, and he understands domestic political spectacle as the vehicle by which much of the nation's "secret" work has its real effects. This vision of the Cold War state informs his particularly aggressive form of postmodernism—which, in turn, reflects the epistemological conditions in early Cold War culture. When the *real* work of the state consists substantially of theatrics, then fiction becomes a source of history and the Cold War becomes largely a domestic drama. By tracing the dizzying relation between fact and fantasy, public culture and covert manipulation, *The Public Burning* illustrates how the covert sphere shaped both Cold War ideology and postmodernism.[20]

The central innovation of *The Public Burning* is its rendering of the Rosenberg executions as a grotesque spectacle set in Times Square. Coover situates the executions in a three-day morality play, sacrificial rite, and festival of nostalgia called "The Sam Slick Show." This colossal spectacle— itself a "postmodern" blend of history and myth—entwines the political and theatrical, the juridical and fictional. Significantly, it is controlled not by the state but by an "Entertainment Committee" consisting of culture-industry figures like Cecil B. De Mille (chair), Betty Crocker, Conrad Hilton, Sam Goldwyn, Walt Disney, Ed Sullivan, and others. This group moves the entire cast of the Rosenberg trial—"the Judge and jury, prosecution team and witnesses, including Ethel Rosenberg's kid brother David Greenglass" (*Public Burning,* 6)—onto a Times Square stage. The resulting public spectacle not only simulates some real features of the trial but also incorporates popular fictions, including plays in which the real Richard Nixon and Ethel Rosenberg once starred. For example, the central stage includes replicas of both the Death House at Sing Sing prison and "the Warden's Office in *The Valiant,* a one-act melodrama by Holworthy Hall (*pseud.*) and Robert Middlemass about a condemned man wrongly accused, produced in the early thirties by the Clark House Players on the Lower East Side and featuring the starry-eyed sixteen-year-old Ethel Greenglass" (4).

The point of such historical-fictional connections, which Coover painstakingly locates in the historical record, is that *fiction* permeates political spectacle. It is not simply that a real case became "a courtroom drama," but that the case was scripted in advance and from the beginning conflated the theatrical with the real. Hence, when Sing Sing's Warden Denno complains in the novel that the artificial death house in Times Square may not function adequately, Cecil B. De Mille tells him not to worry. "See, life and the real stuff of life aren't always the same thing, Warden.... So sometimes, to get your story across you gotta...zap it up with a bit of spectacle" (281). It was, of course, the real death house at Sing Sing that malfunctioned, requiring three massive jolts to kill a badly burned Ethel Rosenberg. Coover's De Mille conveys the public's lack of interest in such matters. In his view, the opposite of life is not artifice but "the real stuff of life"— a form of spectacle that is nonetheless "real." This formulation recasts illusion as "real stuff," coding performance not as fakery but as hyperreality in Baudrillard's sense of the term.[21] This view concisely captures the strategy of the Eisenhower administration, whose theatrical brinkmanship— a public show to force Ethel to testify against her husband—ended up killing her.

In "The Sam Slick Show" Coover converts the execution into a self-congratulatory history of the United States, from the colonial era to the Cold War, told through games, skits, pageantry, and other entertainments. Everything in Coover's Times Square becomes repurposed for the promotion of American exceptionalism. Billboard and theater marquees are "consecrated to the display of homespun American wisdom" (5). Sideshows portray the United States as a "New Jerusalem," divinely ordained to extend *"Dominion over the Whole World"* (9). The performances include torch songs, choruses, literary readings, sporting events, marching bands, reenactments of the American Revolution and the Civil War, revivalist sermons decrying the Communist infestation of "guvvamint, schools, and churches...fanatically inspired by Satan" (417), a Fred Astaire and Ginger Rogers dance interpretation of Julius and Ethel's prison letters, sketch comedy routines of the Rosenbergs' domestic life, a public spanking of Supreme Court Justice William O. Douglas (for temporarily staying the execution), and a historical parade of famous Americans and American types: "Pilgrims, Pirates, Planters and Pioneers...Johnny Rebs and Damyankees,...Millionaires, Whalers, Cowboys and Indians and the U.S. Cavalry, Carpetbaggers and Ku Klux Klansmen,...Suffragettes, Rough Riders, Motorists, Movie Stars and Moonshiners," and so on (424). In short, Coover sets the executions in the equivalent of a historical theme park—"the American Showcase, Playland U.S.A., the Electrical Street of Dreams" (167).

This grotesque version of Disneyland develops a critique first made in E. L. Doctorow's *Book of Daniel*. In that novel, the narrator's quest to understand his parents' executions ends in Disneyland, which he describes as "totalitarian in nature."[22] It is no accident that both Doctorow and Coover trace a line from the drama of state secrets to the great American emblem of postmodern spectacle, for as Rogin suggests, the point of covert spectacle is to convert state violence into "a series of superficial entertainments." Coover stresses this function by repeatedly associating the spectacle of Disneyland with the nation's symbol of secrecy, J. Edgar Hoover. The career of "America's Top Cop," points out Coover's narrator, is "contemporaneous with that of Mickey Mouse" (15). Moreover, Walt Disney is the "genius behind the sideshows and vendors' gimmicks" of the Sam Slick Show, the narrator suggests, because he learned "from the great granddaddy of them all, J. Edgar Hoover of the FBI" (281).

Hoover was indeed a master of public relations, willing to make his case not only in anti-Communist tracts like *Masters of Deceit* but also though serial *fictions* like *I Was a Communist for the FBI*.[23] Coover mocks Hoover's showmanship in a sideshow exhibit of "Disney's giant Whale," which has become a detention center for "zanies, sick drunks, and pick-pockets" (469); there, as Richard Nixon ends his quest to understand the Rosenberg case, he discovers that his grandmother Milhous, who has been grilling him, is really Hoover in disguise. "*Goddamn you, Edgar!*" he shouts. "*It's been you all along!*" (529). Here, literally in the underbelly of Disney's whale, Nixon recognizes that his antagonist has not been the Soviet Phantom but the U.S. security state. State surveillance, moreover, is indistinguishable from Disneyesque spectacle. For Coover, the *real* work of the state is conducted in the covert sphere, which transforms the Cold War into a contest of representations fought on domestic turf.

Recovered (National) Memory

Coover develops this argument further through his treatment of Nixon. By the time of the novel's publication in 1977, ex-President Nixon was the U.S. poster boy for covert operations, but Coover paints a portrait of the younger vice president as an idealist whose penchant for deception ("Every student breaks into the Dean's Office to steal exams or find out results, most common prank in the world" [51]) is part of an obsession with acting and political theater. "My secret dreams," Coover's Nixon confesses of his youth, involved "being a playwright and actor" (138). The vice president understands acting as far more than a pastime. Identity itself, he believes, is a business of "having to adopt one role or another" (104). "You're not born with 'character,'" he argues; "you create this as you go along, and acting parts in plays helps you recognize some of the alternative options—most people don't realize this, and that's why they end up with such shabby characters" (295). This theatrical model of identity suggests Nixon's careful self-making through willful deception, but it also belies a deeper anxiety about theatricality itself, a fear that there is nothing deeper than acting. Nixon learns to cry, for instance, by acting in a college play (361). When giving himself to Jesus at a revival, he says, "I didn't really quite believe in what I was doing. It was like being in a play" (525). Eventually, he suffers profound doubts about his identity; by the time he is vice president, he admits, "Richard Nixon was already, even in my own mind, something other than myself" (367).

This concept of identity as performance underpins Nixon's understanding of the Rosenberg affair. Nixon sees his role in the case largely through his earlier roles in the plays *Bird-in-Hand, The Night of January 16th,* and *Tavern* (*Public Burning,* 362). The more he probes the case, the more it seems a piece of political theater in which *everyone* is acting out familiar fictional scripts. Attorney General Saypol's closing argument comes partly from Ayn Rand's *Night of January 16th.* At Sing Sing prison, Warden Denno notes that the Rosenbergs act "like they're on stage or something" (408). Julius looks "costumed," and Ethel's stylized approach to the prison building is like "seeing someone come out from behind the ... wings" (408). Recalling Eisenhower's youthful role as a buffoon in *Merchant of Venice,* Nixon asks himself, "What *about* all these plays? ... It was as though we'd all been given parts to play decades ago and were still acting them out on ever-widening stages" (361).

There are at least two ways to answer Nixon's question. The first would see acting as fakery or intentional political manipulation. This is the position taken by Uncle Sam when Nixon confronts him with the lack of hard evidence in the Rosenberg case: "Hell, *all* courtroom testimony about the past is ipso facto and teetotaciously a baldface lie. ... Like history itself—all more or less bunk, as Henry Ford liked to say, as saintly and wise a pup as this nation's seen since the Gold Rush—the fatal slantindicular futility of Fact! Appearances, my boy, appearances! Practical politics consists in ignorin' facts! *Opinion* ultimately governs the world!" (86).[24] This view of politics as cynical deception is the one suggested by the popular image of "tricky Dick Nixon," the emblem of government secrecy and deception.

But this view conflicts with a second model in which "performance" is not simply misrepresentation but rather an unavoidable social act conditioned by preexisting social scripts. This second view is akin to Judith Butler's conception of performative identity.[25] "Not only," observes Nixon, "was everybody in this case from the Judge on down—indeed, just about everyone in the nation, in and out of government, myself included—behaving like actors caught up in a play, but we all seemed moreover to be *aware* of just what we were doing and at the same time of our inability, committed as we were to some higher purpose, some larger script as it were, to do otherwise" (*Public Burning,* 117). Here, Nixon seems to be channeling not only Butler but also Žižek's view that ideology relies more on action than belief—that ideology functions when subjects *know* they are "only acting" or pretending to believe.[26] In this view, acting is not quite fakery but rather a general condition of sociality. This postmodern view recurs in Nixon's worries about the sources of his own identity, and it is a recurring theme in Coover's other writing. In his most anthologized story, "The Babysitter," for instance, human action is so heavily scripted by popular culture that it is virtually impossible to separate reality from fantasy.[27] Ubiquitous social scripting, in other words, unsettles what Baudrillard calls "the reality principle"—the ability to distinguish reality from mere representation—replacing it with a regime of simulation. Within such a regime it is no longer possible to make clear distinctions between reality and "fakery," or "mere" acting, since everyone is *always* performing.

Nixon struggles with this question throughout the novel, trying to retain the intentionalism of the first explanation against the postmodern sense that human identity and action are perpetually shaped by cultural narrative. As Nixon becomes increasingly aware that an ideological system may be controlling everyone's thinking and behavior, he finds himself in a full-blown crisis of historical agency. If the Rosenberg case is in fact a drama, then who has scripted it? And for what purpose? Initially, Nixon fantasizes that he himself is "a principal actor—if not...*the* principal actor" in the Rosenberg drama, perhaps even the "author of the trial itself...not of the words so much...but rather of the *style* of the performances, as though I had through my own public appearances created the audience expectation, set the standards, keyed the rhetoric" (120). But his study of the case prompts him to worry that perhaps spy courier Harry Gold—who suddenly "remembered" his meetings with Greenglass after weeks of FBI interrogation—is "the real playwright" (126). Nixon tries to reassure himself that "Uncle Sam [is] the maker and shaper of world history" (212), but eventually he rejects the very idea of a scripter itself and decides that he himself must "step in and change the script!" (363):

> And then I'd realized what it was that had been bothering me: that sense that everything happening was somehow inevitable, as though it had all been scripted out in advance. But bullshit! There were no scripts, no necessary patterns, no final scenes, there was just *action,* and then *more action!* Maybe in Russia History had a plot because one was being laid on, but not here—*that was what freedom was all about!*... This, then, was my crisis: to accept what I already knew. That there was no author, no director, and the audience had no memories—they got reinvented every day! I'd thought: perhaps there is not even a War between the Sons of Light and the Sons of Darkness! Perhaps we are all pretending! (362–63)

Here, Nixon recognizes that his vision of social scripting is a form of Marxist ideology critique. In a moment of nationalist fervor, he therefore dismisses the idea of ideology altogether and adopts a posture of heroic individual agency. Ironically, however, this new stance is itself the core of U.S. Cold War ideology, which celebrated individualism as a bulwark against Communist collectivism. Coover makes this point not long afterward, when Nixon asks, "Was my breaking out [of the script] a part of the script, too? Oh shit!" (367). Through such turns, the novel reinforces the postmodern view of political performance as a product of cultural narrative.

But there is another important feature of Nixon's great revelation. It connects social scripting to cultural memory. One of the notable oddities of the passage I just cited is Nixon's view that to say there is "no script" and "no author" also entails that the public has "no memories." By this logic, the script for a public spectacle is a form of cultural memory and thus a potential source of "cultural amnesia." Here, then, we return to the terms of Rogin's essay and indeed to the larger corpus of postmodern historiographic fiction, which has as a central trope the notion that ideological structures determine cultural memory. The closer Nixon moves to a vision of the Cold War as spectacle, the more he is haunted by the forms of amnesia and confabulation Rogin describes. After the execution, he remarks, "Time marches on. Shakespeare said that in some play, I believe. Some tomorrow would inevitably become today and we could start forgetting, that was the main thing" (524). Nixon not only forgets that Macbeth's famous speech is a eulogy ("She should have died hereafter," *Macbeth* 5.5.16–27), but he also converts its existential vision of life as theater into a plea for *amnesia*.

But forgetting is only one of Nixon's memory problems. The other is what the protagonist of Toni Morrison's *Beloved* calls "rememory"—the capacity to "remember" experiences from a collective past that one did not personally experience. As he pores over the Rosenberg case files, Nixon explains, "I seemed to remember things that had never happened to me, places I'd never been, friends and relatives I'd never met who spoke a language I didn't know" (144). Eventually, images of a youthful Ethel Rosenberg begin to enter his mind. Recognizing that the scenes are of an urban immigrant ghetto, Nixon asks, "Where did I get these memories? Me a farmboy, born in Yorba Linda, California" (145). Nixon here is not simply imagining Ethel's past; he is *remembering* it—or rather "remembering" it, since these are not individual but cultural memories from the repressed history of the U.S. working class.

The more Nixon deviates from the official governmental script for the executions, the more he is beset by these visions of Ethel's background. Soon he has begun to reimagine whole segments of her past—and to insert himself into them. He imagines protecting her from the water cannons at a 1931 strike and then making love to her. Like every intimate part of Nixon's self, these impressions are fabrications that conflate U.S. history and popular culture. In Nixon's memory, Ethel looks like the comic book character Ella Cinders, and later like Claudette Colbert (432, 433). Nixon's own words within these fantasies seem uncannily "familiar" to him, like "lines from some soap opera," or perhaps from *Aeneas and Dido* or even "some Horatio Alger novel probably" (434). Fueled increasingly by the content of the plays in which both Nixon and Ethel have acted, these fantasies eventually drive Nixon to visit Ethel in Sing Sing, in a vain attempt to talk a confession out of her. There, as he forces a kiss on a writhing Ethel, Nixon has a historical epiphany:

> I closed my eyes: my mind seemed to expand, it was as though her hand were kneading it, stretching it.... Oh what a mind! I hardly recognized it! It was full of hidden memories, astonishing thoughts, I'd never seen it like this before, a vast moving darkness and brilliant flickering pictures, new and

strange, called forth by the charged explorations of our mouths and hands. Some were frightening: girls knocked down by fire hoses, men gassed in trenches and run down by police on galloping horses, villagers buried in bomb-rubble, lives blighted by disease and poverty, children monstrously deformed by radiation or eaten up by vermin....I grasped Ethel's bottom and saw the face of a child. He seemed to live in a great city. I couldn't tell if he was black or white, Mexican, Italian, or Polish, but it didn't matter. I shared his dreams: he was a poet, a scientist, a great teacher, a proud crafts-man. He was America itself, everything we've ever hoped to be, everything we've dared to dream to be. But he awoke—we both awoke—to the night-mare of poverty, neglect, and despair. He failed in school. He ended up on welfare. He was drafted and died in Korea. I saw all this as my tongue roamed behind Ethel's incisors....I felt I'd reached some new plateau of awareness, of consciousness.... The real Ethel Greenglass, childlike, and ex-quisitely lovely—like Audrey Hepburn, I thought, whom I'd just seen on the cover of some magazine, though Ethel's bottom was softer—had come to the surface and absorbed all other emanations...and it was I who had called her out....I thought: *I am making history this evening, not for myself alone, but for all the ages!* (438–39)

Here, in a text dominated by the representation of spectacle, is the sort of postmodern confabulation that usually arises in fictions of historical trauma. Nixon's grotesque sexual fantasy stimulates his "rememory" of the U.S. underclass and becomes Coover's vehicle for the recovery of an "invisible" or "secret" history beneath the popular narrative of American exceptionalism, democracy, and opportunity. When Nixon punctures this ideological shell, the repressed content of U.S. history flows into his con-sciousness. This material—the history of people like the Rosenbergs—is the real state secret guarded by the Cold War ideological machine.

As I suggest more fully in chapter 5, this psychodynamic model of col-lective memory associates canonical history with national consciousness and countermemory with collective unconsciousness, repression, or amnesia. It is no accident that Nixon's strongest desire after the Rosenberg executions is to "start forgetting" (524). Like political spectacle, amnesia is a way of con-ceptualizing the ideological control of national consciousness. Both sets of tropes, however, rely on a postmodern vision of blurred ontological bound-aries and performative identity. In other words, Coover has made the Rosen-berg case a primary vehicle for articulating his own postmodern aesthetic.

The State's Two Faces

I have been suggesting that Coover understands cultural memory as an effect of political spectacle. What the public "remembers" and "forgets" is shaped in an ideological theater that blurs nationalist myth, popular fiction, and historical fact. Of course, publics do not really remember and forget. Conceiving of them that way requires a commonplace allegory, which Coover realizes in the figure of Uncle Sam. If Nixon is the individual who best represents the intersection between Cold War nation and Cold War state, then Uncle Sam is a collective, mythic figure for the same division. Uncle Sam's two-facedness reflects the nation's public celebration of democracy and the state's secret penchant for imperial power and undemocratic methods.

Coover's Uncle Sam is thus both a pastiche of famous presidential images and an arrogant, fast-talking hell-raiser who speaks in the vernacular of the early American frontier. He is "Sam Slick the Yankee Peddler," a colonizer whose parochial American chauvinism still has broad public appeal. "I can ride on a flash of lightnin'," Uncle Sam brags, "catch a thunderbolt in my fist, swaller niggers whole, raw or cooked,... and out-inscrutabullize the heathen Chinese—so whar's that Johnny Bull to stomp his hoof or quiver his hindquarters at *my* Proklymation? Whoo-*oop!*" (7). In this mode, Uncle Sam is a rambunctious optimist, a militant advocate of free-market capitalism, a vocal Christian, a misogynist, a racist, and ultimately a rapist. The other face of Uncle Sam, however, is more dignified: "A commanding figure, Uncle Sam; crowds have gathered in the Square to ogle him, root for him, worship him even, discovering in their Superhero all that's best in themselves.... One is reminded of Tom Jefferson...or perhaps of Handsome Frank Pierce...Old Hickory galloping up on Horseshoe Bend, T.R. throwing steers in the Badlands, Abe Lincoln splitting rails, or...George Washington crossing the Delaware"(171). The gap between these two aspects of Uncle Sam reflects division between the public and covert elements of the state.

Uncle Sam also represents both the demos and the president, the nation and the state. When Attorney General Herbert Brownell complains that "Uncle Sam's breathing hot down my neck," for example, it is not clear whether his chief concern is President Eisenhower or public opinion (69). Nixon spends a good deal of his time using "incarnation theory" to puzzle over the mysterious relation between the public, the president, and Uncle

Sam. In the manner of the Christian Trinity, Uncle Sam is simultaneously the spirit of the Cold War United States, incarnate in Dwight Eisenhower, his "new real-time disguise" (230), and a freestanding agent who presides over the Cold War, meets with Nixon, and sees all ("I was suddenly afraid Uncle Sam might be watching somewhere," Nixon admits [140]). "Whenever Uncle Sam shazammed himself back into the General," Nixon notes, "there was always a certain broadening of the nose, softening of the mouth, hair falling out" (260), indications that the president possessed by Uncle Sam is not quite himself. "The important thing," Nixon notes, "is that there be room for the Incarnation to take place.... Maybe Uncle Sam needed vacuity for an easy passage" (230–31). As Uncle Sam explains to Nixon, *"A nation, like a person, has got somethin' deeper, somethin' more permanent and pestifferous, somethin' larger than the scum of its parts, and what this nation's got is ME!"* (496). While Uncle Sam is thus represented by both the president and the populace, he is essentially a set of popular images and narratives of national identity—a version of the "script" that Nixon sees behind the Rosenberg case.

Coover models this ideology partly on an earlier allegory. "Sam Slick" was originally the creation of Thomas Chandler Haliburton, a conservative Nova Scotian judge whose *Sam Slick, the Clockmaker* series (1836–40) mocked the former colonies through the figure of a crude but wily traveling salesman.[28] It is significant that Coover characterizes Cold War ideology by borrowing from a conservative critic of early American democracy, for while Haliburton's politics are diametrically opposed to Coover's, both writers satirize U.S. populism, painting savage portraits of a nation ruined by a fickle and easily influenced demos. In Coover's version, the populace is ruled by nationalist narrative, and thus Uncle Sam's speech is often composed of famous statements by former U.S. leaders. For instance, his rousing call to arms at the outset of the Korean War is a patchwork of statements made by Patrick Henry, Ben Franklin, John Quincy Adams, David G. Farragut, William Howard Taft (satirizing the Progressivism of Theodore Roosevelt), John Adams, John L. O'Sullivan, Abraham Lincoln, George Washington, and John Dickinson:[29]

> Our brethren are already in the field, why stand we here idle? Time is money! No pent-up Utica contracts our powers, but the whole boundless continent is ours, it's as much a law of nature as that the Mississippi should

flow to the sea or that trade follers the flag! *Fear* is the fundament of most guvvamints, so let's get the boot in, boys, and listen to 'em scream, let us anny-mate and encourage each other—*whoo-PEE!*—and show the whole world that a Freeman, contendin' for Liberty on his own ground, can out-run, out-holler, out-finagle, and out-lick any yaller, brown, red, black, or white thing in the shape of human that's ever set his onfortunate kickers on Yankee soil! It is our manifest dust-in-yer-eye to overspread the continent allotted by Providence for the free development of our yearly multiplyin' millions, so damn the torpedoes and full steam ahead, fellow ripstavers, we cannot escape history! Boliterate 'em we must, for our cause it is just what the doctor ordered. (*Public Burning*, 8)

This speech fuses righteous militancy—the signature cries of the American Revolution (Henry, Washington, Dickinson) and the Civil War (Lincoln, Farragut)—with the rhetoric of U.S. empire and manifest destiny (Adams, Quincy Adams, Sullivan, and Taft). It converts conventional historical "facts" into a satiric précis of American exceptionalism as presented in a high-school history text.

It is this celebratory view of U.S. history that Richard Nixon increasingly comes to doubt as he digs into the Rosenberg case. Eventually, his view of the United States as a beacon of democracy and justice shatters as his scrutiny exposes the disturbing underpinnings of U.S. empire. *"You're no better than the Phantom,"* screams the horrified vice president as Uncle Sam electrocutes the Rosenbergs. "All they wanted was what you promised them, the Bill of Rights, the Declaration.... You're not the same as when I was a boy!" (531). It is no accident that Nixon associates his naive conception of the United States with boyhood. The "only version of the past that most citizens will ever know," remarks the Cold War historian Stephen Whitfield, "is what they picked up in the textbooks of their childhood."[30] In the history textbooks of the 1950s, argues Frances Fitzgerald in *America Revised,* "America was perfect: the greatest nation in the world and the embodiment of democracy, freedom, and technological progress. For [the histories of the fifties], the country never changed in any important way: its values and its political institutions remained constant from the time of the American Revolution.... There was no point in comparing these visions with reality, since they were the public truth,... the permanent expression of mass culture in America."[31] Coover holds this "public truth" up against a much uglier "reality." "You gotta love me like I really am," Uncle Sam tells Nixon, "Sam Slick the Yankee Peddler, gun-totin' hustler and tooth-'n'-claw tamer of the heathen wilderness, lusty and in everthing a screamin' meddler, novus ball-bustin' ordo seclorum, that's me, boy" (531–32).

This exchange comes at the climax of the novel, just as its twin narratives collide in Times Square. At this moment, Nixon realizes his lifelong dream to become an "incarnation" of Uncle Sam. But to Nixon's horror the incarnation occurs when he is sodomized by Uncle Sam (who snorts, "Drap your drawers and bend over, boy—you been ee-LECK-ted!" [530]). The climax of the novel links Nixon's rape to the traumatic replacement of his childhood fantasies of American exceptionalism with the terrible knowledge of U.S. power. "It ain't easy holdin' a community together," explains Uncle Sam, "and a lotta people gotta get killt tryin' to pretend it is, that's how the game is played" (531). Here, Nixon's entry into a fuller knowledge of the state's violent methods comes in the form of a feminizing trauma. "I felt like a woman," he complains as Uncle Sam rapes him (533). Nixon's passage through the veil of Cold War ideology requires a painful recognition of his feminization and naïveté as a mere citizen.

Through this traumatic sexual violation, *The Public Burning* connects spectacle as amnesia to secrecy as trauma. Coover's two-faced Uncle Sam simultaneously represents the popular history of the United States and its traumatic "secret history," the latter of which is kept from public consciousness by the former. The particular "public truth" that is shattered in Nixon's rape is a theocratic American exceptionalism that has converted the founding values of the republic into their very opposites and facilitated a stunning disavowal of undemocratic policy. Coover repeatedly shows how Cold War statecraft violates the principles of the republic's founding documents. "The Sam Slick Show," for instance, includes a reenactment of the American Revolution in which Minutemen and Green Mountain Boys square off against not only Redcoats but Winston Churchill (who looks "for all the world like John Bull himself" [423]). Like others, this scene relies on a postmodern blending of past events with the Cold War present. Churchill has just come onstage to deliver a speech stitched together from his 1946 "Iron Curtain" speech and his 1940 "Battle of Britain" ("Upon this battle depends the survival of Christian Civilization"). When the colonial troops then recite the portion of the Declaration of Independence that calls on citizens of a repressive regime "to abolish it, *and to institute new Government!*" Churchill roars, "What? What?" (422). Coover here smashes the liberatory rhetoric of the Revolution against repressive Cold War politics. In the skit, Churchill represents both Georgian Britain and Cold War conservatism. His denunciation of the Declaration's revolutionary zeal mocks the hypocrisy of Cold War conservatism. It was, after all, Ho Chi Minh who began his 1945 "Declaration of Independence of the Democratic Republic of Vietnam" by citing the opening of the American Declaration. As Coover reminds us repeatedly, moreover, it was Julius Rosenberg who had "the yellowed newspaper copy of the Declaration of Independence...taped up on his cell wall"—"just one more sign of his alienation," notes Coover's Nixon, for "the Declaration was never part of the mainstream" (*Public Burning,* 183). As Uncle Sam puts it, wedding the Declaration with the gospel of the free market, "We hold these truths to be self-evident: that God helps them what helps themselves" (7).

Ultimately, Coover depicts the Cold War state as a theocracy of the market, utterly devoid of its founding values. In the novel's first intermezzo, Coover borrows Eisenhower's proclamation that "we are Christian nations, deeply conscious that...our civilization and our form of government is deeply imbedded in a religious faith. Indeed, [our founders] felt that unless we recognized that relationship between our form of government and religious faith, *that form of government made no sense!*"(*Public Burning,* 150–51). Coover's satiric allegory literalizes this perversion of the nation's founding vision by casting the American story in the terms of the Old Testament. Uncle Sam is a version of Yahweh. The constitution is written on "stone tablets...that George Washington brought down off Bunkum Hill" (423). Supreme Court justices are guardians "of sacred laws and interpreter[s] of the Covenant" (65). Uncle Sam appears to Nixon at "Burning Tree" Golf Club to talk about "statecraft and incarnation theory, rules for the Community of God, the meaning of the sacred in modern society and the source of the Phantom's magical strength, the uses of rhetoric and ritual, and the hierology of free enterprise" (83). Within this religious framework, the Rosenberg executions are not simply state punishments but ritual murders, "a consecration...of the moral and social order of the Western World, the precedint on which the future is to be carn-structed to ensure peace in our time!" (91). In stressing the irrational bases of the executions, Coover concretizes the terms of Jean-Paul Sartre's widely publicized view that "by killing the Rosenbergs you have quite simply tried to halt the progress of science by human sacrifice. Magic, witch hunts, auto-da-fés, sacrifices...you are afraid of the shadow of your own bomb."[32] Or as Arthur Miller put it, "The execution of the Rosenbergs seems...a bleeding sacrifice on the altar of cold war politics."[33] What seems to have unraveled in the Rosenberg executions, in other words, is the rationality of the public sphere. The "dialectic of Enlightenment" has transformed the modern, rational justice system into a surreal carnival of nationalist mythos and religious irrationality.

Fakery in Allegiance to the Truth

Coover's postmodernism is specifically designed to mock this undoing of Habermasian public reason. With its surreal blend of historical precision and radical ontological dislocation, Coover's aesthetic parodies the irrationality of the Cold War covert sphere. Ironically, Coover's postmodernism critiques problems themselves associated with postmodernism—a confusion of the real and fictional, the hindrance of critical reason, and the conflation of distinct "realities" or ontological zones. This irony is what Linda Hutcheon means when she speaks of postmodernism's "complicitous critique."[34] Fredric Jameson notes a similar contradiction in E. L. Doctorow, who critiques postmodern ahistoricism in a (postmodern) form that is "itself the mark and symptom of his dilemma."[35] I point to this paradox not to dismiss Coover's approach. On the contrary, Coover's method permits a powerful critique of the conditions of knowledge in Cold War society. To make this case, I want to engage another aspect of the novel's dialectic of spectacle and secrecy, moving from its handling of the public press to its account of the covert agent, Harry Gold—who turns out to be a fiction writer of sorts and perhaps the ultimate scripter of the entire Rosenberg drama.

A strong public press is the chief requirement of a functional public sphere. In Coover's novel, however, the press is a site of irrationality and distortion. Drawing heavily from the scathing criticism of *Invitation to an Inquest,* Coover suggests that the major U.S. print organs—*Time* magazine and the *New York Times*—fomented hysteria, fictionalized certain "factual" reports, and ultimately helped hang the Rosenbergs. Coover's critique of the *New York Times,* the novel's "Spirit of History," anticipates Fredric Jameson's sense that postmodernism disables critical historiography. The newspaper's "mosaic" of hard news, entertainment, mundane

announcements, glamour, advertisements, sports, cooking, and so on results in "sequences but no causes, contiguities but no connections" (190).
"As in dreams," the narrator explains, "there is an impressive amount of
condensation on the one hand, elaboration on the other. Logical relationships are repressed, but reappear through displacement" (190). In using
Freud's primary mechanisms of dreamwork—condensation and displacement—Coover portrays the newspaper not as an objective record but a
site of national fantasy, a surreal mingling of the real and the fabulous.
While Coover's vision is a satiric exaggeration, it nonetheless bears considerable resemblance to Hayden White's account of the "analogy between
psychotherapy and historiography." Writing a history, White argues, is
like conducting psychoanalysis. "The therapist's problem . . . is not to hold
up before the patient the 'real facts' of the matter, the 'truth' as against the
'fantasy' that obsesses him" but rather "to get the patient to 'reemplot' his
whole life history in such a way as to change the *meaning* of those events for
him." In a similar way, White suggests, historians "seek to refamiliarize us
with events which have been forgotten through either accident, neglect, or
repression. Moreover, the greatest historians have always dealt with those
events in the histories of their cultures which are 'traumatic' in nature and
the meaning of which is either problematical or overdetermined in the
significance that they still have for current life."[36] Refamiliarization is not
a matter of unearthing some previously buried truth but rather of "reem-
plotting" history, situating historical content within a meaningful narrative structure and thus making a "literary artifact" of it.

In this influential rethinking of history, White articulates Coover's im-
petus for writing *The Public Burning:* "We'd all repressed it." Even more
important, White suggests that historiography is therapeutic in nature,
helping the social body work through traumatic events. In so doing, of
course, the historian risks compounding the problem that brought the
patient to therapy in the first place—"overemplott[ing] events, [charging]
them with a meaning so intense that . . . they continue to shape both his perceptions and his responses to the world long after they should have become
'past history.'"[37] But Coover's critique of the *Times* as Spirit of History is
precisely its *lack* of emplotment, its ahistoricism in Jameson's sense. The
paper's "mosaic" of elements can overwhelm readers, who "panic and race
recklessly through the [paper] as though lost in a circus or a ceremonial
abattoir" (*Public Burning,* 196). The problem for Coover is not that the

Spirit of History has overemplotted events that do not "speak for themselves" but that it has generated new forms of irrationality, disavowal, and mystification. For the public, he notes, the newspaper becomes more substantial than the world it represents: "The demand made by these tablets on the faithful is quite literally monumental, and they often experience the illusion suffered by mystics throughout the ages: the Spirit, annunciating reality, displaces it, and the tangible world dissolves even as it is being proclaimed" (193–94). Readers "press themselves against the Father's Day advertisements and crisis tabulations, fail to notice the people leaping out of buildings, girls being raped on subway platforms...[and] cannot see the crowds gathering outside the Supreme Court building" (194). In other words, the juxtaposition of ontologically incompatible materials lays the ground for what Rogin calls "spectacle as amnesia." As Don DeLillo notes, explaining the genesis of *Underworld* from a pair of incongruous *New York Times* headlines ("Giants Capture Pennant," "Soviets Explode Atomic Bomb"), "The newspaper with its crowded pages and unfolding global reach permits us to be ruthless in our forgetting."[38]

In short, Coover critiques the irrationality generated by the press's mixing of ontologically disparate narratives and images. Yet this very quality—the confusion of distinct realms—is the hallmark of his own aesthetic and arguably of postmodern narrative writ large.[39] Consider, for instance, the following description of the Rosenberg trial from the opening of *The Public Burning:*

> The bailiff pounds his knuckled fist on the door three times and calls out: *"Everybody please rise!"* There's a scraping of chairs, a scuffling of feet, the Strategic Air Command is put on alert, the Communist program for world domination is released by the House Un-American Activities Committee. A *New York Times* headline announces: DANGER OF ATOM BOMB ATTACK IS GREATEST IN PERIOD UP TO THIS FALL! The Judge enters—a ripple of surprise: Uncle Sam has chosen for his Easter Trial little Irving Kaufman, the Boy Judge, a stubby Park Avenue Jew and Tammany Hall Democrat...Julius and Ethel glance at each other, GIs lose another hill in Korea, and East Berlin policemen fire openly on U.S. Army sightseeing buses. The Russians are said to be massing troops on the Manchurian border. "God bless the United States of America!" cries the clerk. "Nobody will have to run if H-bombs start detonating. A big black cloud full of radioactive particles will get you even if...you happen to be browsing around the bottom of an abandoned

lead mine!"... The Judge climbs up into the big leather chair and sits down. Schoolchildren scramble under their desks in an atom bomb drill, and an entire Yank company is bogged down in a Korean rice paddy. (22–23)[40]

This exposition has precisely the dreamlike quality Coover associates with the *New York Times*. In fact, this passage was constructed partly from actual newspaper items.[41] But unlike the earlier examples focused on the *New York Times,* this passage is not a critique of the newspaper as an ideological screen. It is instead an *imitation* of the newspaper mosaic to illustrate the link between domestic spectacle, foreign conflict, and Cold War panic. Coover's interlacing of different ontological realms is a powerful way of insisting that the trial is inseparable from hysteria about foreign attack. Ironically, the aesthetic innovation that makes this argument possible— ontological mixing—is the very quality that makes Coover nervous about the *New York Times.* Coover's postmodernism, that is, simulates the problematic knowledge structures of the Cold War covert sphere.

My point, however, is not that Coover has reinforced the very logic he wishes to critique. On the contrary, his brilliant critique of Cold War hysteria reflects back the epistemological constraints of the covert sphere, in which state secrecy impedes the public's attempts to disentangle fact from fiction. If, as I suggested at the beginning of this chapter, there is a sort of "postmodern" quality to the Cold War security state, then Coover's work rearticulates this quality in order to expose and critique it. His most explicit treatment of this problem comes in a chapter on the 1953 three-dimensional film *House of Wax,* by André de Toth. Here, Coover makes 3-D technology a figure for *both* the irreconcilable ideologies of the Cold War and his own postmodern juxtaposition of irreconcilable realms. As the film lets out, a man leaves the theater unaware that he has forgotten to remove his 3-D glasses. Profoundly disoriented by the "two separate and unassimilable pictures" (284) he now sees, "he no longer trusts what his eyes tell him" (286). "Through one eye he learns that President Eisenhower has encouraged the reading of Marx and Stalin...and through the other reads about a plot to liquidate Senator McCarthy" (285). A moment later—as his right eye sees a sign urging "SAVE THE ROSENBERGS!" and his left sees "BOMB CHINA NOW!" and "ETHEL ROSENBERG BEWITCHED MY BABY!"—he decides "he is perhaps the only sane man left" (287). This final notion is crucial, for if sanity comes from the simultaneous perception of incompatible worldviews, then it can be attained only by a postmodern method. Postmodernism is thus the aesthetic that unveils the true nature of social reality in the Cold War United States. It does so by reproducing the "insane" or irrational epistemology of the 1950s public sphere in order to offer a "sane" position from which this irrationality can be critiqued.

This way of thinking informs Coover's treatment of *Time* magazine, which was the midcentury creation of Henry Luce and is the "Poet Laureate" in Coover's national allegory. As the novel opens, "*Time*'s Mother Luce" (presumed spinner of national fairy tales) "has been urging her son [*Time*] to push the idea of living with perpetual war as part of the American Way of Life" (21).[42] Coover's critique of *Time* rests partly on the real Henry Luce's commitment to "fakery in allegiance to the truth." Luce's chief desire as he unveiled *Life* magazine in 1936 was to convert image into narrative—to take "the cream of the world's pictures" and "edit [them] into a coherent story,...an effective mosaic."[43] On the one hand, this ambition addresses the very problem Coover attributes to newspapers like the *New York Times:* "Raw data is paralyzing, a nightmare, there's too much of it and man's mind is quickly engulfed by it" (320). On the other hand, Luce's goal seems to be a version of Cecil B. De Mille's illusionism. (His confidential prospectus for *Time* claimed it would be "the biggest picture show on earth.")[44] In *The Public Burning,* Coover emphasizes this aspect of Luce's program:

> It is not enough to present facts.... Poetry is the art of subordinating facts to the imagination, of giving them shape and visibility, keeping them *personal.* It is, as Mother Luce has said, "fakery in allegiance to the truth," a kind of interpretative reenactment of the overabundant flow of events, "an effective mosaic" assembled from "the fragmentary documents" of life.... Some would say that such deep personal involvement, such metaphoric compressions and reliance on inner vision and imaginary "sources," must make objectivity impossible, and *Time* would agree with them, but he would find simply illiterate anyone who concluded from this that he was not serving Truth. More: he would argue that objectivity is an impossible illusion, a "fantastic claim"..., and as an ideal perhaps even immoral, that *only* through the frankly biased and distorting lens of art is any real grasp of the facts—not to mention Ultimate Truth—even remotely possible. (320)

Coover's quotations of Luce here are all accurate, but Coover has drawn out their implications so that his Mother Luce seems to be a postmodernist *avant la lettre.*[45] In his suggestions that objectivity is "impossible" and that invention is essential for truth telling, Mother Luce sounds as though he had just invented the "new journalism," which Tom Wolfe described in 1973 as the use of narrative fiction techniques in fact-based journalism. "The most general feature of the New Journalism," notes Michael Wood in an early review of Wolfe's anthology, "is its insistence on the resemblances between fact and fiction—that fiction is the only shape we can give to facts, that all shapes are fictions."[46] This is similar to Hayden White's view that historical narrative is inevitably structured like fiction—arguably the primary insight of postmodern historiographic fiction—and to Tim O'Brien's defense of artistic invention in historical narrative. In a "true war story," writes O'Brien, "absolute occurrence is irrelevant. A thing may happen and be a total lie; another thing may not happen and be truer than the truth."[47] O'Brien's point is that fiction is sometimes more "truthful" than straight reporting because invention allows a writer to better evoke in the reader certain qualities of the original experience (see chapter 3).

Not only does Mother Luce's slogan reflect influential descriptions of postmodernism, but it seems to describe Coover's own novelistic method. After all, *The Public Burning* is wildly inventive in its effort to reveal the truth of the Rosenberg case. Yet Coover's novel also ruthlessly mocks invention as the source of injustice in the Rosenberg case. Mother Luce's mention of "imaginary 'sources,'" for instance, is clearly an indictment of TIME's role in the spy trials of the 1950s—a charge central to the Schneirs' history. In short, "fakery in allegiance to the truth" is both a strength of postmodern narrative *and* a serious challenge to the rationality of the public sphere.

But there is still more to say on this subject, for "fakery in allegiance to the truth" could very well be the motto of the CIA's psychological warfare unit. Eisenhower himself publicly promoted "psychological warfare" as a way not simply to tell the truth but to *"get the world,* by peaceful means, *to believe* the truth."[48] How did Ike implement this strategy? He hired Henry Luce's most important lieutenant—C. D. Jackson—to run his Psy-Ops program. According to the historian Frances Stonor Saunders, Jackson was "one of the most influential covert strategists in America" and "America's single most influential cold warrior."[49] After getting his start in advertising for *Time-Life* in 1931, Jackson became a leading psychological-warfare planner for Eisenhower during World War II. In the postwar period he returned to *Time-Life,* climbing the ladder to vice president while simultaneously becoming a major player in the new CIA. In 1953 Eisenhower appointed him special adviser to the president for psychological warfare—a sort of propaganda minister with broad powers. Jackson swiftly reorganized U.S. covert-warfare capabilities, beginning with a Psychological Strategy Board "blueprint" called PSB D-33/2. Although PSB D-33/2 is still classified, a leaked PSB memorandum reveals that it called for the use of "non-rational social theories" for the "doctrinal production" of "American objectives" in "all fields of human thought...from anthropology and artistic creations to sociology and scientific methodology."[50] The result was a monumental program of covert patronage designed to reshape all of Western art and thought, a program that would convert the CIA into one of the largest cultural influences in the West.

In associating this "machinery" with the "non-rational," PSB D-33/2 explicitly understood psychological operations as an inversion or perversion of the ideals of the *rational* public sphere. Yet its author, C. D. Jackson, sat at the controls of a major organ of the public sphere. After only a year in the White House, Jackson returned to *Time-Life* in 1954, where as one of the corporation's most important executives, he oversaw the publication of *Life* and *Fortune.* "Jackson's senior position in Luce's media empire," notes Kenneth Osgood, allowed Eisenhower to "count on *Time-Life* publications to sell his cold war policies to the American public and to the wider readership abroad."[51] "Enjoying unrivalled access to the secret machinations of the PSB," writes Saunders, "Jackson became the most sought-after figure in that tight circle of power which came to be known as 'the invisible government.'"[52]

To put it more bluntly, the most powerful architect of early CIA psychological operations also ran the *Time-Life* media empire. Could there be a better illustration of how the covert sector deforms the public sphere?

We thus arrive at the conundrum underlying both the representation of the covert sphere and the rise of postmodernism. "Fakery in allegiance to truth" is a strength of postmodern narrative *and* a serious challenge to the rationality of the public sphere. The strange combination of state secrecy and political spectacle produces epistemological barriers to knowing the work of the state. Historians and journalists cannot explore certain matters of state in the way they might approach other historical matters. The novelist, however, is not bound by an ethic of strict correspondence between narrative and "facts" or "primary sources." Although *The Public Burning* is meticulously researched and remarkably precise in its citation of primary material—despite its absurdist elements—Coover does not ground his critique in positivist historiography. His claims rest on a dizzying ability to connect apparently disparate events and discourses—an ability offered to his readers via a postmodern aesthetics. In other chapters I will show how other postmodern fiction redeploys the public unknowing within the security state as a form of radical political critique that cannot be rooted in exposure, documentation, or confidence. In the covert sphere, fiction writers and spies have a certain advantage over journalists and diplomats—for the logic of fiction ("fakery in allegiance to the truth") is also the logic of the covert state.

The Fabulist Spy

Luce's slogan points finally to the figure of the covert sphere par excellence— not Julius Rosenberg, but Harry Gold, the fabulist spy who was arguably the "author" of the Rosenberg drama. That, at least, is the position of the Schneirs, who place Gold's astonishing capacity for inventive storytelling at the center of the Rosenberg case. At his own sentencing, Gold admitted giving many "fictitious names" and fabricated reports to his Russian handlers. He would eventually reveal, under oath, that he had invented an imaginary wife, mother-in-law, and children and had managed to spin these inventions into an elaborate fantasy that deceived all his closest contacts "for a period of sixteen years." In 1956, in what the Associated Press called "fiction-rivaling" testimony, Gold told a rapt congressional committee that his "most valuable" theft was of an aerial photography process that Eastman Kodak later confirmed was widely available "in public literature or in published patent form."[53]

Gold's story-telling flair and remarkable capacity for invention made him a useful state witness and an attractive subject for Coover, whose fiction relentlessly explores the moral and aesthetic dimensions of fiction making itself. Borrowing heavily from *Invitation to an Inquest, The Public Burning* stresses that Gold was "used to living in make-believe worlds" and "at home within the artifice of a courtroom trial" (124). As Coover's Nixon notes, Gold "was an incorrigible fantasist, who in the course of his operations had invented a wife, twin children, and even a fictitious list of 'contacts' which he gave the Russians, sharing intimate moments from this fantasy life with friends and associates, acting it out for the world in all its bizarre details, while in fact living at home all the time with his mother" (124). Gold here seems the very antithesis of James Bond—a mama's boy so far from the rough-and-tumble world of supervillains and femmes fatales that he compensated by inventing an entire cosmology of imaginary beings. This quality is part of what compels Coover to see Gold as less a spy than a novelist. Gold's defense lawyer, muses Nixon, "told me he sometimes wondered if Gold was even a spy, maybe he was making the whole thing up," because even though Gold did have documents to support his contentions, he kept them "down in his basement, even the stuff he was supposed to have given the Russians, boxes of it, *like the raw materials of some novel*" (124, emphasis added).

Indeed, the real Harry Gold fantasized mightily about his own place in history. In the seventy-five-page autobiography he composed for his lawyers, he reported spending "a great deal of time in the very enjoyable pastime of imagining Harry Gold...always in a stern and self-sacrificing role."[54] Gold here sounds like a cross between Lee Harvey Oswald, who labored over his "Historic Diary," and Coover's Nixon, who incessantly fantasizes about his role in history. Gold is essentially another of the pathetic narcissistic male fantasists who populate so much of Coover's fiction.

But Gold's case is particularly noteworthy for another reason. In his autobiography, Gold explains that as a young man he amused himself by inventing "simulated games of football, baseball and boxing...with a single deck of Casino cards. In baseball, for example, I used a league of eight teams...which played a full schedule of games throughout the entire season, not forgetting double-headers on the weekends; the teams each had pitching staffs with imaginary hurlers, whose records and mound characteristics I carefully noted."[55] This is an astonishing revelation—itself just a footnote in the Schneirs' history—because the creation of a baseball "league of eight teams" is *also* the subject of Coover's 1968 novel, *The Universal Baseball Association, Inc., J. Henry Waugh, Prop.* The protagonist of that novel, moreover, is a dead ringer for Gold—a Walter Mitty–like figure who not only plays out full seasons of fantasy baseball at his kitchen table, using dice and statistical charts to determine the result of every pitch thrown, but invents "imaginary hurlers, whose records and mound characteristics" he catalogs in an increasingly elaborate history, until eventually he plunges into his fictional world entirely.[56]

It was thus the spy Harry Gold—and not Robert Coover—who conceived of the baseball game at the heart of Coover's second novel. The novel is among the finest examples of 1960s postmodernist metafiction. Like *The Public Burning* and much of Coover's other work, it is an allegory of creation. "J. H. Waugh"—a homonym for "Yahweh"—is a writer-creator who breaks the rules of his own creation, killing one of his best players (whose initials are J. C.) to redeem his game from meaninglessness. By casting God as a bumbling fantasist who seizes the power to rescript events in his world, *The Universal Baseball Association* takes up precisely the question of historical agency that Nixon addresses in *The Public Burning*. The novel's postmodernism is designed to explore this question by shifting us from Waugh's world to the world of his imaginary baseball players until it is difficult to keep the two realms separate. From the perspective of the players, the creator-author's "public burning" of his favorite pitcher (Jock Casey) cannot be historically verified, and hence public memory of the death takes on the character of religious ritual. As the players see it, the story of J. C.'s sacrifice is "nothing more than another of the ancient myths of the sun.... History: in the end, you can never prove a thing."[57]

Such claims are the stock-in-trade of postmodern metafiction. But if we understand Henry Waugh's character to be based partly on Harry Gold, then there would seem to be a spy in the house of Coover's postmodernism. Why is this important? Because it suggests that Coover recognized, long before the publication of *The Public Burning*, the fictional quality of the National Security State. Like the Schneirs, Coover understands Gold's fabulous imagination as the source of much of the "evidence" against the Rosenbergs. In *The Public Burning*, as Nixon reflects on Gold's "weird baseball games," he suspects that Gold's spy contacts are actually the imaginary characters in his fantasy baseball league. "It's a wonder one of his ace pitchers didn't turn up in the trial testimony" (124–26), he notes, unknowingly describing an almost daily occurrence in the life of Henry Waugh. This possibility—that a key witness might project his imaginary world into the most serious of state proceedings—requires more than the florid imagination of a Harry Gold; it also requires a legal arena in which only fantastic stories can supply the secret material hidden from a traditional jurisprudence.

The most important thing about Harry Gold, then, is his power to reveal the dynamics of the covert sphere. Although his capacity for invention, confabulation, and deception was a matter of public record, his capacity to spin fictions trumped these problems. In a regime of state secrecy, fakery in allegiance to the truth is king, and fiction writers of all sorts shape the cultural memory of the nation. On his arrest, Coover's narrator reports, "Harry Gold had forgotten about" the Greenglass connection, "but with the FBI's help he [began] to remember" (19). In a passage largely lifted from the Schneirs, Coover's Nixon later notes that, initially, Gold made no mention of secret signals with Greenglass—"in fact, no mention of Greenglass or A-bomb sketches either—all this had come later after Gold had had several helpful sessions with the FBI. But even after Gold had begun to 'remember' Greenglass, there had *still* been no Jell-O box and no Julius, just 'something on the order of Bob sent me or Benny sent me or John sent me or something like that'" (125).[58] In such moments, Gold's "forgetting" and "remembering" become the basis of a national spectacle that Coover, like Rogin, sees as a source of cultural amnesia.

This dynamic points, finally, to the basic strategic error of the Schneirs. In trying to discredit Gold, they presumed a rational public sphere in which the reality principle obtained. But the Rosenberg trial unfolded in the covert sphere, and in this strange space Gold's capacity for fabulation did not discredit him as either a spy or a witness. On the contrary, it suited him perfectly for both tasks, for narrative fiction makes claims on the basis of rich, convincing detail rather than correspondence to fact. In the end, the government needed only to assert the Rosenbergs' guilt and present a range of simulated, confabulated, and fictionalized evidence. The phantom public sphere did the rest.

3

FALSE DOCUMENTS

True Lies

In a 2006 panel discussion of the Rosenberg affair, E. L. Doctorow defended the inventions of historical novelists this way: "Our justification and our salvation is that people know we're liars.... The kind of genre-blurring done by the President of the United States is quite different. He is a storyteller, a fabulist, and presents as truth and fact stuff that is totally fictive."[1] This is a curious way to defend fiction, for it not only embraces "lying" as a moral act, but it explicitly relates the fabulation of the artist to the deceptions of the state. Both statecraft and fiction—particularly Doctorow's brand of inventive historical fiction—require the willful distortion of historical facts for strategic reasons.

This unexpected homology between the writer and the state is central to a surprising number of late twentieth-century U.S. narratives. Many influential writers explicitly theorize their own fiction in relation to state secrecy or draw comparisons between intelligence work and writing—especially writing that blurs the boundaries between history and fiction, reality and illusion or simulation. These connections suggest that the National Security State has powerfully influenced postwar U.S. fiction and postmodernism in particular. In this chapter I trace these influences through the writing of Doctorow, Tim O'Brien, Norman Mailer, and Don DeLillo. I then turn to Denis Johnson's 2007 novel, *Tree of Smoke,* which renarrates the cultural history of the Vietnam War as a tale of covert psychological operations. Like other important U.S. narratives of the war in Southeast Asia, this one swirls into surreality and epistemological confusion as it depicts a nation at war with itself. But it specifically associates these familiar aspects of postmodern representation with the business of Cold War intelligence—and it does so, I argue, to critique the George W. Bush administration's manipulation of intelligence before its 2003 invasion of Iraq. The novel thus lends support to several arguments of this book: first, that the security protocols of the Cold War state continue to shape U.S. policy and its cultural representations; second, that these representations associate secrecy and power with masculinity; and third, that the epistemological conditions generated by espionage and covert action provide a crucial, and mostly overlooked, basis for postmodern narrative.

How is the epistemology of state secrecy related to fiction writing? Doctorow provides another clue in his formal defense of historical fiction, the 1977 essay "False Documents."[2] In this essay, as in his 2006 public comments, Doctorow asserts that novelists are "born liars" in "a world made for liars," and he defends literature as a sort of deception that is "more valid, more real, more truthful than the 'true' documents of the politicians or the journalists or the psychologists" (164). For Doctorow, the novelist is a fabricator of "false documents," Kenneth Rexroth's term for the "lies" by which novelists claim the "additional authority" of historical documents. But what elevates the lies of the novelist above the lies of the state is their openness. As Doctorow puts it, "people know" that novelists invent details because "ours is the only profession forced to admit that it lies" (164). The open falsehoods of the fiction writer are thus a corrective to the deceptions of the state; the novel's lies are "true lies."

But Doctorow is perhaps too hasty to reintroduce the distance his own comparison has just eliminated between the writer and the state, for if people know fiction writers "lie," they *also* know their leaders lie. Once state policy relies on clandestine warfare and "plausible deniability," leaders *must* dissemble about foreign policy. The public, in turn, must entertain government statements with something like "the suspension of disbelief"—a simultaneous knowing and not knowing that is both the hallmark effect of ideology and the form of attention sought by fiction makers since time immemorial.

Doctorow's analogy between the state and the writer may thus be closer than he cares to admit. "False documents" are not just the work of writers; they are also a vital product of covert government, which regularly seeks to influence world events through deception, misdirection, and simulation. If the novelist is in the business of creating morally defensible fictions—"true lies"—then so too is the spy.

True Lies, it is worth recalling, is the title of James Cameron's 1994 Hollywood melodrama about a CIA operative, Harry Tasker, who must deceive his family in order to protect the nation. Like most such melodramas, *True Lies* makes the family an allegory of the nation, and it insists that the protection of the public (women and children in this allegory) requires the falsification of history by the (male) agents of the covert sector. While the politics of Cameron's film and Doctorow's fiction are quite different, both insist that blurring fact and fiction serves the greater good.[3]

So does Tim O'Brien, who has repeatedly defended his own trick of revealing that apparently autobiographical stories are in fact inventions containing a higher "truth." "I want you to know," he tells the reader of his celebrated collection of Vietnam stories, *The Things They Carried* (1990), "why story-truth is truer sometimes than happening-truth."[4] Fiction is truer than fact both because "it's difficult to separate what happened from what seemed to happen" (78) and because the "happening-truth" of war sometimes seems too absurd to believe. Above all, however, fiction more accurately simulates lived experience than does reportorial discourse. Good fiction, O'Brien argues, can "make things present" (204). Its ability to evoke lived experience is often impeded by a strict correspondence to events. Hence, telling a "true war story" may involve "making up a few things to get at the real truth." Indeed, it may be necessary to invent "every goddamned detail" (91).

Yet this tolerance of "lies" in the service of truth is not the whole story, for O'Brien does not quite dismiss the requirement that a story correspond to real events:

You'd feel cheated if it never happened. Without the grounding reality, it's just a trite bit of puffery, pure Hollywood, untrue in the way all such stories are untrue. Yet even if it did happen—and maybe it did, anything's possible—even then you know it can't be true, because a true war story does not depend upon that kind of truth. Absolute occurrence is irrelevant. A thing may happen and be a total lie; another thing may not happen and be truer than the truth. (*Things They Carried,* 89)

On the one hand, invention is "cheating"; on the other, it is the only way to guarantee the power of "story-truth," which "is truer sometimes than happening-truth" (203). It is not that truth-as-correspondence is unimportant, but rather that it is both unattainable and less important than the experience of "reliving" the original event through its fictionalization.

The blurring of "fact" and "fiction" is of course the central aesthetic strategy of postmodern historiographic fiction. It is thus doubly interesting that O'Brien and Doctorow should explicitly defend postmodern aesthetics in a critique of the National Security State. Doctorow mounts this defense by deconstructing the opposition between fact and fiction, beginning with the distinction between them. Whereas factual statements make "reference to the verifiable world," fictional statements describe a "private or ideal world that cannot be easily corroborated or verified" ("False Documents," 152). Although the discourses of fact have become the basis of modernity, of "scientific method and empiricism," Doctorow argues, the fictional statement (that is, "a sentence composed as a lie") has "some additional usefulness... that a sentence composed with the most strict reverence for fact does not" (152). Both fact and fiction, then, have distinct forms of power. By revealing "what we threaten to become," fiction contains "*the power of freedom.*" The discourses of fact, by contrast, carry "*the power of the regime*" (153, emphases in original). By "*the regime,*" Doctorow means "the modern consensus of sensibility that could be called *realism*"—not nineteenth-century literary realism but what Habermas calls "the project of Enlightenment" and its legacy of "empirical thinking and precise calculations... standards of measure, market studies, contracts, tests, polls," all of which constitute the dominant intellectual paradigm of modern Western societies ("False Documents," 152–53).[5]

There are two things to note about Doctorow's thinking here. First, through his unlikely phrase "*the regime,*" Doctorow associates realism and modernity with the ruling order and with the *state* in particular. Moreover, virtually every example of factual discourse in his essay—from its apparently random citation of a news story about military base closures to its invocation of the Rosenberg trial—concerns the institutions of the Cold War. Second, Doctorow sets the realism of the regime against a set of representational values that have since been associated with postmodernism. In other words, Doctorow understands "postmodern" aesthetics as a response both to modern epistemology and to the activities of the security state. In this regard, it is striking how precisely Doctorow's argument anticipates the central claims of Jean-François Lyotard's *Postmodern Condition* (1979), which associates postmodernism with a crisis in the dominant modern paradigm of scientific knowledge. The crisis stems from the recognition that science, the dominant form of modern knowledge, itself relies on the more traditional form of "narrative knowledge" in a postwar society dominated by scientific knowledge.[6] Like Lyotard, Doctorow describes narrative as the privileged form of traditional, premodern knowledge. For the ancients, Doctorow writes, narrative operated as both "metaphor and operative science" ("False Documents," 153); "the act of telling a story was in itself a presumption of truth" (154). Unlike the modern concept of "truth"—the verifiable correspondence of statements to what "really happened"—the ancient sense of "truth" was wisdom or good counsel. "If the story was good, the counsel was valuable and therefore the story was true" (154). For Doctorow, this value continues to inhere in narrative fiction despite its deliberate "mixing-up of the historical and the aesthetic, the real and the possibly real" (157). "Alone among the arts," Doctorow declares, "literature confuses fact and fiction. In the Bible the natural and the supernatural flow into each other, man and God go hand in hand. Even so, there are visible to our own time volcanoes that are *pillars of fire by night and pillars of cloud by day*" (154, emphasis added). The half-mythic status of this very "pillar" or "tree of smoke," as I will explain later, is the basis of Johnson's account of psychological operations.

The sort of fiction that most aggressively confuses "fact and fiction," "the real and the possibly real" is of course postmodernism—which is also Doctorow's sort of fiction.[7] It is thus no surprise that Doctorow's defense of literature against the modern "regime of facts" eventually becomes a précis of the philosophical underpinnings of postmodern historiography. Doctorow marshals an array of distinguished thinkers who have commented on the instability of facts: Nietzsche ("there are no facts in themselves"), Carl Becker ("the facts of history do not exist for any historian until he creates them"), and Roland Barthes ("historical discourse is essentially a product of ideology, or rather of imagination") ("False Documents," 160–61). If facts exist only within narrative, moreover, then they have a literary quality. "Facts," declares Doctorow, "are the images of history, just as images are the facts of fiction" (161). History and fiction, in other words, are much more alike than the realists would have us believe: "History is a kind of fiction in which we live and hope to survive, and fiction is a kind of speculative history, perhaps a superhistory" (162).

In all of these assertions, Doctorow sounds remarkably like Hayden White, who began to make more complicated versions of this argument in the mid-1970s. Insofar as history is "an image of some reality," White argues, "history is no less a form of fiction than the novel is a form of historical representation."[8] And because there is a "literary or fictive element in every historical account," as White claims elsewhere, "narrative is not simply a recording of 'what happened.'"[9] This is precisely Doctorow's point. In "False Documents," Doctorow eventually abandons his initial distinction between fact and fiction for "the proposition that there is no fiction or nonfiction as we commonly understand the distinction: there is only narrative" (163). By calling for a literary practice that resists the epistemology of science (and its humanistic cousin, realism), Doctorow anticipates the discourse of postmodern historiographic fiction.

But here it is crucial to recall that Doctorow's essay is not simply a defense of postmodern fiction. It is also a response to the Cold War state, and as it proceeds it increasingly positions the writer as an *enemy* of the state. "The novelist's opportunity to do his work today," writes Doctorow, "is increased by the power of the regime to which he finds himself in opposition" (164). In the United States, Doctorow explains, this power lies in the regime's ideology of facts. In many countries, the state views imaginary discourse as a threat and imprisons writers. But Western nations dismiss the idea that "literature is politics" (158). The control of writers here does not have to be violent; it operates on the assumption that aesthetics is a limited arena where we may be shocked or threatened, but only in "fun." "The novelist need not be taken seriously" in the United States, Doctorow writes, "because his work ... is not part of the relevant business of the nation (159). Thus, the "regime" that marginalizes the writer is not the state per se; it is rather the ideology of modern rationality with its aesthetic and philosophical adjuncts, realism and empiricism. The ideology of factual discourse accomplishes what other states ("Burma or Iran or Chile or Indonesia or the Soviet Union" [158]) must do by brute force; it does so merely through the widespread assumption that fiction is a "nonserious" form of discourse, as John Searle famously put it.[10] The work of the fiction writer is associated with the feminized public sphere, which, unlike the inside realm of real state policy, is widely seen as irrelevant to the serious "business of the nation" (159).

With this observation, Doctorow illuminates a central paradox of the covert sphere. Because the Cold War state prevents citizens from knowing much of its foreign policy, fiction is one of the only sanctioned ways in which citizens can "know" the covert activities of state. But by insisting that fiction is "nonserious" and "irrelevant," *the regime* consigns such "knowing" to the realm of fantasy and "mere entertainment." This is a superb ideological arrangement. Under it, the fiction writer is both the arbiter of truth about the covert sphere *and* a marginal figure whose "mixing of the historic and the aesthetic, the real and the possibly real" can be ignored. The knowledge offered by fiction is at once a major form of knowledge and yet not "real" knowledge.

Enemies of the State

Harry Hubbard, the protagonist of Norman Mailer's mammoth novel, *Harlot's Ghost* (1991), is a career CIA agent. He is also a prolific author of both narrative and analytic prose:

> Under one ghost's name or another, I was helping on a few pro-CIA spy novels...as well as overseeing one or two scholarly works, not to mention dashing off an occasional magazine piece on the new invidiousness of the old Commie threat. Will it help to explain that under various names I dealt with commercial publishers as agent, author, freelance editor, and even had my pseudonym on several books I did not write so much as midwife for others? Of course I did a few jobs as full ghost myself. If a prominent evangelist took a trip to Eastern Europe or Moscow, intermediaries called on me afterward to boil the sap of his taped meanderings into homiletic American for the patriotic subscribers of *Reader's Digest*.[11]

Part of the joke here is that "ghost-writing" is the only permissible writing for spooks. But like his peers, Mailer also suggests the special link between writing and intelligence work. Propaganda, it turns out, is not Hubbard's primary authorial endeavor. For many years, as part of his official duties, he has labored unsuccessfully to complete "a monumental work on the KGB whose in-progress title is *The Imagination of the State*" (30). At the same time, he has *secretly* written two memoirs of his life in the CIA, the publication of which would violate his CIA oath. One, "the Alpha manuscript," is a two-thousand-page account of Hubbard's CIA career from 1955–65; the other is the much shorter "Omega manuscript," which covers several years prior to 1983, when Hubbard's wife abandons him. *Harlot's Ghost* consists almost entirely of these two memoirs, which are presented in reverse order and framed by a brief narrative in which Hubbard reads the two texts during a final journey to Moscow. Both manuscripts are substantially about Hubbard's CIA boss, Hugh Montague ("Harlot"), and Montague's wife, Kittredge. Hubbard and Kittredge Montague carry on an extensive correspondence before having an affair in the early 1970s and eventually getting married.[12]

Hubbard is pitied by his colleagues, who correctly suspect that his masterwork, *The Imagination of the State,* will never materialize. But if Hubbard never brings his narrative to print, Mailer does the work for him. *Harlot's Ghost* is the real "Imagination of the State"—although the state in question is not the USSR but the United States and the "imagination" in question is that of the CIA not the KGB.[13] In the novel's afterword, Mailer admits as much, explicitly hoping that "the reader's imagination is rewarded with a large and detailed mural of a social organism [the CIA] moving through some real historical events" (1173). If Henry Hubbard is a figure for the author intent on representing this vast organism, then Mailer is a stand-in for the covert agent, the diviner and keeper of state secrets.

There has long been a strong connection between writing and spying.[14] Many well-known U.S. authors—Peter Matthiessen, Charles McCarry, James Michener, Howard Hunt, and William F. Buckley Jr., to take a few examples—wrote while working for the CIA. Many spies have gone on to be novelists. The list includes not only Ian Fleming, Graham Greene, and John Le Carré, but popular authors like Stella Rimington, the former director-general of MI-5 (and purported inspiration for Judi Dench's portrayal of "M" in recent Bond films).[15] The CIA aggressively recruited the students of influential literary scholars, like Norman Holmes Pearson at Yale, and poets, like John Crowe Ransom at Kenyon College. Peter Matthiessen founded *The Paris Review* while in the employ of the CIA.[16]

The towering figure of U.S. Cold War counterintelligence—James Jesus Angleton—was a Yale English major who cofounded *Furioso,* a major literary journal that published e. e. cummings, Ezra Pound, Archibald MacLeish, William Carlos Williams, and Wallace Stevens, among others. Angleton was "the very image of the poet-spy," writes Frances Stonor Saunders. He was so interested in literature that his OSS colleagues derisively called him "the Poet." In addition to running CIA counterintelligence for twenty years, he also single-handedly ran an ultrasecret group of journalist-operatives—a project that itself makes clear the vital connection between intelligence and writing.[17]

Trading on such connections, Mailer stresses the literary nature of intelligence work. Not only is Hubbard a prolific author with the sensibilities of a poet, but he and Hugh Montague persistently relate their work to classic literature. They compare intelligence plots to "Macbeth or Lear" (*Harlot's Ghost,* 28) and develop a cipher system based on T. S. Eliot's "The Waste Land" (which, not coincidentally, was one of roughly a thousand works the CIA translated and distributed abroad for strategic purposes).

The notions that the secret agent is a novelist and the novelist is a secret agent are fantasies rooted in the logic of the covert sphere, where the strictures of state secrecy often seem to make imagination more valuable than experience in the representation of the covert state. Hence, Mailer asserts his authority to represent the world's largest covert organization with astonishing confidence. Although *Harlot's Ghost* offers only "a fictional CIA" whose "only real existence is in my mind," Mailer states, "I would point out that the same is true for men and women who have spent forty years working within the Agency. They have only their part of the CIA to know, even as each of us has our own America, and no two Americas will prove identical. If I have an argument to make, then, on grounds of verisimilitude, I will claim that my imaginative CIA is as real or more real than nearly all of the lived-in ones" (1171). Here, Mailer first implies that the institutional structure of the CIA—its extraordinary compartmentalization—makes it unknowable to even its own agents. He then asserts—on the basis of reading hundreds of books and using "the part of my mind that has lived in the CIA for forty years" (1169)—his own power to imagine the agency more fully that its own employees. "How," people ask him, "do you understand enough to write about *them?*" (1169). "I did not have to be in the organization . . . to understand the tone of its inner workings," he argues, just as a "Russian Jew of the early nineteenth century...would not have had to be on intimate terms with a priest to feel that his comprehension of Russian Orthodoxy was possessed of some accuracy" (1170). This is an interesting assertion, not only because Mailer is a Jew writing about a blue-blood Christian CIA veteran, but also because it suggests the agency is a kind of religion or national unconscious—a site of *irrationality* unknowable through the organs of the public sphere.

This sense of the CIA as a vast social organism is an increasingly obvious element of U.S. culture. Popular narrative frequently represents the CIA as a quasi-divine being with extraordinary powers of surveillance. No one has captured this sense better than Don DeLillo, whose characters consistently view the agency as vast, omnipresent, and supernatural. The wife of a CIA officer in *Libra* calls it "the best organized church in the Christian world, a mission to collect and store everything that everyone has ever said and then reduce it to a microdot and call it God." Her husband seeks "the sheltering nave of the Agency" and believes its central work is to "resolve a nation's obsessions,...to remove the psychic threat."[18] James Axton of DeLillo's *The Names* calls the CIA "America's myth" and thinks of it as a "public dream," a national unconscious.[19] The CIA is so central to DeLillo's vision of the United States that it haunts even his satire of academia, *White Noise,* whose protagonist, Jack Gladney, keeps "stumbling into the company of lives in intelligence"; one of his ex-wives "reviewed fiction for the CIA, mainly long serious novels with coded structures," and another "came from a distinguished old family that had a long tradition of spying and counter-spying and...was now married to a high-level jungle operative."[20] The CIA has cultivated its own secular mythology in which it is a vast organism unknowable through the protocols of the rational public sphere. In this sense it is a locus of what Joseph Tabbi calls the "postmodern sublime."[21]

Confronted with this institutional dreamwork, Mailer casts himself in the role of the prophet Daniel; like the protagonist of Doctorow's *Book of Daniel,* he interprets the "dreams" of the Cold War sovereign. The hubris of this self-appointed role is fueled by the epistemology of the Cold War security state, where fiction trumps history. As Mailer puts it, novelists "create superior histories out of an enhancement of the real, the unverified, and the wholly fictional." Thus, Mailer asserts, "the imaginary world of *Harlot's Ghost* will bear more relation to the reality of these historical events than the spectrum of facts and often calculated misinformation that still surrounds them" (*Harlot's Ghost,* 1173). By this account, intelligence work and fiction writing are versions of the same thing: if the intelligence agent is a writer, then the writer is an agent.

This proposition is the often-overlooked conceit at the center of De-Lillo's *Libra,* which traces the assassination of John F. Kennedy to something like the writing of a novel.[22] In *Libra,* the plot against the president begins in the suburban study of a disgruntled CIA officer, Win Everett. Furious at the president's refusal to provide air support during the Bay of Pigs invasion, Everett concocts a fictional assassination made to look like "a Cuban response to repeated efforts of U.S. intelligence to murder Castro" (*Libra,* 139). In doing so, Everett takes a clearly literary approach, beginning with the construction of an imaginary assassin: "He would put someone together, build an identity, a skein of persuasion and habit, ever so subtle. He wanted a man with believable quirks. He would create a shadowed room, the gunman's room, which investigators would eventually find, exposing each fact to relentless scrutiny, following each friend, relative, casual acquaintance into his own roomful of shadows" (78). Everett sees people as "characters in plots" and believes that his creation will be read by forensic experts in the manner of a literary text. Like a novelist, he knows his work rests on the invention of rich, convincing details. He forges a top secret CIA memo on "the assassination of foreign leaders from a philosophical point of view"; he creates a trail of fake notes that will lead investigators to both "ordinary stops (florist, supermarket) as well as the home of an exiled leader in Miami"; and he plants a tiny news item in a Cuban exile magazine ("The story was fabricated but the plan itself was real, involving the assassination of Fidel Castro and his brother Raúl") to be "discovered" later among the supposed assassin's workaday possessions (138). The list goes on: "An address book with ambiguous leads. Photographs expertly altered (or crudely altered). Letters, travel documents, counterfeit signatures, a history of false names. He envisioned teams of linguists, photo analysts, fingerprint experts, handwriting experts, experts in hair and fibers, smudges and blurs" (78). Intelligence work here involves primarily the creation of *false documents,* to use Doctorow's term. It is essentially the work of the novelist.

By this account, fiction is not merely the imaginary representation of real events. It is a power within the real, a methodology for political transformation that is part and parcel of the "real" work of the covert agent. This proposition—which, in a more general form, is a central tenet of postmodern theory—tends to generate a serious historiographical problem, for if events are scripted in secret then how do we compose a history? This is precisely the question that stymies Nixon in *The Public Burning* when he begins to see history as scripted. *Libra* presses the question much further, persistently asking whether Lee Oswald is the author of his own actions or a "cardboard cutout" for the script Win Everett writes in his basement study.[23] The matter is complicated by the proliferation of authorship in the novel. Not only is everyone in *Libra* "a spook or dupe or asset, a double, courier, cutout or defector," as one CIA officer observes, but nearly everyone turns out to be an *author* as well (57). Lee Oswald is writing his historic diary and composing himself as a subject of history. Nicholas Branch, the CIA's internal historian, struggles to compose a reasonable narrative of the case. Like Mailer's Harry Hubbard, Branch is a figure for the historical novelist who wishes to reconcile the slew of historical material (some of it potentially false) with the demands of narrative and plot. Interestingly, while the fictional *historians,* Branch and Hubbard, are utterly blocked, their *fiction-writing* counterparts—DeLillo, Mailer, and Hubbard (as memoirist rather than KGB historian)—are anything *but* blocked. DeLillo's pairing of the intelligence agent and the author is the source of his relentless focus on "plots" and plotting. The basic concern running through all of DeLillo's middle-era fiction is the double-edged nature of plot as both a fictional form and a secret scheme. Plots, reflects Everett, "carry their own logic. There is a tendency of plots to move toward death. He believed that the idea of death is woven into the nature of every plot. A narrative plot no less than a conspiracy of armed men. The tighter the plot of a story, the more likely it will come to death. A plot in fiction, he believed, is the way we localize the force of the death outside the book, play it off, contain it" (221). Everett's comment here is a brilliant précis of *White Noise,* which meditates on the ways in which human beings manage the existential fear of death. Even the hapless Jack Gladney cannot escape the deathward movement of plot. When he decides to kill his wife's ex-lover, asserting that "to plot is to die," his colleague Murray Siskind corrects him, saying, "To plot is to live...to seek shape and control."[24] It is an act that demonstrates one's agency in the face of an overwhelming technological modernity or a vast "social organism" such as the CIA.

The anxiety about human agency points to the crisis of masculinity provoked by the covert sphere. As the historian Nicholas Branch finally realizes, the Kennedy assassination is ultimately the story of "men in small rooms," men struggling to find a space safe from social pressure where they can secretly shape history—something Branch is struggling to do in his own top secret study (*Libra,* 181). DeLillo repeatedly emphasizes this fantasy of the hermetic as a site of male agency and a defense against one's vulnerability in the public sphere. His Oswald, for instance, searches obsessively for a "world inside the world" (13, 47, 153, 277) where he can have "a say over men and events" through both violence and authorship (163). This is what "the melodrama of beset manhood" looks like in the imaginary of the covert sphere.[25] When history seems to be written by secret agents, recovering a sense of masculine agency is a matter of worming one's way into the esoteric precincts of the covert sector—whether as an agent or a writer.

Perhaps this is why DeLillo's fiction so often positions both writer and agent as rogue figures, enemies of state. *Mao II,* for instance, counterposes Bill Gray, a reclusive author in the mold of Pynchon or Salinger, to Abu Rashid, a charismatic Lebanese terrorist leader. DeLillo stresses the inverse fortunes of these two figures. "There's a curious knot that binds novelists and terrorists," explains Bill Gray. "Years ago I used to think it was possible for a novelist to alter the inner life of the culture. Now bomb-makers and gunmen have taken that territory."[26] By this account, both the novelist and the terrorist work in "opposition...to the power of the regime," to use Doctorow's terms ("False Documents," 64). But despite their similar work, Bill Gray sees them "playing a zero-sum game": "What terrorists gain, novelists lose" (*Mao II,* 157). The power of the novelist, Gray believes, has been sapped by the circulation of images and "the news, which provides an unremitting mood of catastrophe" (72). *Mao II* is thus about "the death of the author" as a meaningful enemy of state: Bill Gray literally dies on his journey to become a hostage for the terrorist group. By the end of the novel, the photographer Brita Nilsson has stopped photographing novelists and begun photographing terrorists, confirming the idea that terror has indeed replaced fiction as a primary shaper of mass consciousness. Kathleen Fitzpatrick convincingly argues that this arrangement is an expression of anxiety about the "obsolescence" of the writer in a technologically advanced society.[27] The idea of the novelist as intelligence agent or enemy of the state would thus seem a fantasy to compensate for the fear that writers no longer seem to possess what Doctorow calls the "power to do harm" ("False Documents," 158).

Here, then, is the argument offered by a number of brilliant contemporary novelists: the power of fiction lies in its ability to convey forms of truth beyond those contained in traditional history. This power derives in part from a type of falsification. "True"—that is, factually accurate—narratives are "dulled by the obligation to be factual," as Doctorow puts it ("False Documents," 159). Moreover, the realist view that events can be represented transparently is flawed. While an initial separation between fact and fiction seems possible and even desirable, it is in fact impossible. There is only narrative.

But this claim is haunted by two contradictions. First, the embrace of "true lies" is itself qualified by an underlying realism—an ethical commitment to alter factual detail in order to capture some essential truth of the original event. Second, and more important, the Cold War "regime" has also taken the position that the efficacy of communications is "dulled by the obligation to be factual." The state's agents create public illusions for what they also deem just reasons. The imaginative liberty that makes fiction a powerful discourse is also the source of the state's utilitarian investment in "necessary" deception.

Thus a postmodernism that rejects truth-as-correspondence in an attack on the state looks strangely similar to the state's attack on its putative enemies. In each case, the lies of a false regime must be fought with "true lies." This tactic may seem depressingly similar to the stance of the Cold War state (which claimed to embrace the "dirty" tactics of its enemy out of necessity). Yet it is not necessarily a capitulation to state values or claims. In fact, by tapping the source of the covert state's power, the writer can illuminate and critique the conditions of knowledge created by "the regime."

Psy Ops

One of the deep ironies of CIA history is that just when the Office of Strategic Services was reborn as *Central* Intelligence, it split in two. The CIA was created on July 26, 1947, by the National Security Act. Its mission as the nation's first peacetime intelligence agency was to coordinate military and diplomatic intelligence. But George Kennan, then director of the State Department's Policy Planning Staff, wanted the agency to have an operational capacity as well. On December 19, 1947, Kennan pushed Truman's National Security Council to approve memorandum NSC-4, whose secret appendix (NSC-4A) directed the CIA to conduct "covert psychological activities" to undermine communism around the world. Six months later, the NSC approved Kennan's more specific NSC-10/2, which directed the CIA to undertake propaganda, economic warfare, sabotage, demolition, subversion, and assistance to guerrilla groups so long as "the U.S. government can plausibly disclaim any responsibility" for such actions. The bureaucratic fruit of this memo was the creation of the Office of Policy Coordination (OPC), a deceptively boring-sounding bureaucracy that was in fact a "dirty tricks" department within Kennan's Policy Planning Staff.[28] Placed under the control of Frank Wisner, an investment lawyer and former military intelligence officer, OPC grew from just over three hundred workers in 1949 to almost six thousand in 1953. "I never had any thought," Harry Truman confessed a decade later, "when I set up the CIA that it would be injected into peacetime cloak and dagger operations."[29] But in 1978, according to the former CIA director William Colby, psychological and covert operations were consuming 40–50 percent of CIA resources.[30]

To put it crudely, then, the infant CIA developed a sort of split personality—one that symbolized the crisis of legitimation that secret government posed for democracy. The CIA's intelligence-gathering function is designed to unearth the truth about the world for U.S. leaders. It is a sort of global detective agency that gathers both secrets and publicly available information about other states. The operations function of the CIA, by contrast, conducts paramilitary actions, and it produces strategic fictions, deceptions, and propaganda for a range of purposes, including the deliberate creation of uncertainty about what is real and true.[31] If the work of intelligence gathering is to make the world transparent to U.S. leaders, the work of operations is often to make it opaque to outsiders. To put it another way, intelligence gathering implies a realist epistemology, operations suggests a postmodern one.

These are oversimplifications, but they suggest a relationship between the birth of the security state and the challenge to modern knowledge that Lyotard calls "the postmodern condition." In a quite literal way, the National Security State institutionalized a critique of modern *rational* knowing—which is epitomized by intelligence gathering—by engaging in what George Kennan called "irrationalism," "unreality," and "the necessary lie."[32] Indeed, the state's embrace of covert operations uncannily embodied the terms of Lyotard's *Postmodern Condition,* in which the modern paradigm of knowledge, science, gives way to the traditional forms of narrative. Within the rhetoric of the public sphere, this transformation produced a contest between *rational democracy* and *psychological operations.*[33]

In order to get a better sense of these relations, I turn now to Denis Johnson's 2007 novel, *Tree of Smoke,* which rewrites the Vietnam War as a story of psychological operations in order to critique the Bush War on Terror.[34] *Tree of Smoke* focuses on Skip Sands, an idealistic young CIA agent recruited by his uncle for a series of fruitless psychological operations in Southeast Asia. Beginning with the assassination of John F. Kennedy and moving through the 1968 Tet offensive to the evacuation of Saigon in 1975, the novel also relays the stories of two servicemen (James and Bill Houston), a Canadian missionary (Kathy Jones), a trio of Vietnamese men working with U.S. intelligence (Trung Than, Nguyen Hao, Nguyen Minh), and an assortment of spies, assassins, and special operations forces. Chief among these is Skip Sands' uncle, Colonel Francis Xavier Sands, the CIA liaison to the Psychological Operations Group in Vietnam. The Colonel, as he is known, is a legend in the U.S. intelligence community—a former Flying Tiger who escaped from a Japanese POW camp in Burma and went on to counterinsurgency warfare in Laos, Malay, and Vietnam. By the time we meet him, the Colonel is by turns a drunken blowhard and the philosopher king of U.S. military intelligence. He has used his charisma to acquire his own base of operations and platoon of marines for "Project Labyrinth," an attempt to map North Vietnamese tunnels in order to turn them "into a zone of psychological mental torture" (*Tree of Smoke,* 189). He has also raised the ire of his CIA supervisors by drafting a scholarly article on the contamination of intelligence by political influence. As the agency tries to rein him in, he recruits Skip for a series of fruitless tasks: the cataloging of his extensive intelligence files; the mistaken assassination of a pathetic and harmless Catholic priest named Carignan; and eventually his masterpiece—"Tree of Smoke." "Tree of Smoke" is an unauthorized psychological operation that would place a double agent, Trung Than, back in the hands of his North Vietnamese handlers with false information that a renegade U.S. commander plans to detonate a nuclear weapon in Haiphong Harbor.

"Wouldn't that mess with Ho's thinking just a little?" asks the Colonel. "If he thought a few lunatic bastards had decided to finish this thing without asking permission?" (255).

This rogue plot stems from the Colonel's lack of confidence in U.S. intelligence, which he articulates in a half-finished article on "cross-contamination" of "the two functions of the clandestine services—intelligence and analysis" (250). Theoretically, the Colonel argues, intelligence is gathered and moves up the chain of command. In practice, however, several kinds of problems mar this process: first, "the intelligence function [is] polluted by the analysis function"; second, "data from human sources, notoriously undependable, becomes the support for doubtful interpretations of documentary sources, and these interpretations come to be seen as shedding light, in turn, on data from human sources"; and most important, intelligence is corrupted when agents on the ground anticipate "the needs of command" and shape their reports to aid their superiors (251).[35] This final problem, "command influence," threatens to convert the search for truth into a form of political cover for leadership. To solve this problem, the article suggests, "a length of the communications chain must be insulated against the pressures from above and below" (253). But command would never permit such insulation, so it "must instead come as a result of the initiative of this Agency or members of it" (253). In other words, the solution lies in rogue operations. The Colonel's "Tree of Smoke" is just such a plan. He scrawls in the margins of his manuscript:

> Tree of Smoke—(pillar of smoke, pillar of fire) the "guiding light" of a sincere goal for the function of intelligence—restoring intelligence-gathering as the main function of intelligence operations, rather than to provide rationalizations for policy. Because if we don't, the next step is for career-minded power-mad cynical jaded bureaucrats to use intelligence to influence policy. The final step is to create fictions and serve them to our policy-makers in order to control the direction of government. ALSO—"Tree of Smoke"—note similarity to *mushroom cloud*. HAH! (254)

The Colonel's fear, in short, is that the CIA has ceased reporting inconvenient truths and has instead become a purveyor of "fictions."

This argument echoes critiques of Vietnam War–era intelligence gathering like William Lederer's 1961 *Nation of Sheep,* which described the result of U.S. intelligence capabilities as "government by misinformation."[36]

Johnson is clearly familiar with Lederer, the former navy captain whose novel *The Ugly American* (coauthored in 1958 with Eugene Burdick) is frequently on the mind of Skip Sands.[37] But ultimately the Colonel's article seems to be less about Vietnam than it is about the post-9/11 era in which it was written. The central critique of George W. Bush's justification for the 2003 Iraq War, after all, is that policymakers pressured the intelligence services to serve up fictions justifying the invasion of Iraq. According to the secret "Downing Street memo" prepared for the British prime minister Tony Blair on July 23, 2002, "Bush wanted to remove Saddam, through military action, justified by the conjunction of terrorism and WMD. But the intelligence and facts were being fixed around the policy."[38] The "power-mad cynical jaded bureaucrats" fixing policy in this case, as Colonel Sands might call them, included not only senior analysts but also the director of Central Intelligence, George Tenet. As Seymour Hersh reported in October 2003:

> In the view of many CIA analysts and operatives, the director was too eager to endear himself to the Administration hawks and improve his standing with the President and the Vice-President. Senior CIA analysts dealing with Iraq were constantly being urged by the Vice-President's office to provide worst-case assessments on Iraqi weapons issues. "They got pounded on, day after day," one senior Bush Administration official told me, and received no consistent backup from Tenet and his senior staff. "Pretty soon you say 'Fuck it.'" And they began to provide the intelligence that was wanted.[39]

At the heart of Johnson's 2007 novel, then, lies the Bush War on Terror and its strategic conversion of U.S. intelligence into propaganda fictions. The Tree of Smoke ("note similarity to *mushroom cloud*") dreamed up by Johnson's Colonel Sands was more famously dreamed up by Bush's national security adviser, Condoleezza Rice, who warned the nation on September 8, 2002, that Saddam Hussein was "actively pursuing a nuclear weapon" and added "we don't want the smoking gun to be a mushroom cloud."[40]

Crucial to Johnson's vision of intelligence is his description of it as a form of fiction. For Johnson, the historical shift that made intelligence work into something like novel writing was the shift from real, overt war to covert, or "cold," war. During World War II, the Colonel argues, the Office of Strategic Services (OSS) "remained almost untouched by policy, because policy is the game of peace, whereas the OSS served a command structure pursuing the objectives of war" (*Tree of Smoke,* 252). During the Cold War, by contrast, "the United States...does not enjoy the clarity of warlike goals. Ours is, in effect, a pawn's game played out with the not-quite-expressed priority that the back ranks, the powerful pieces, the world powers, should never be brought into play" (253). In other words, because intelligence work is no longer driven by a uniform, *public* objective, intelligence is increasingly subject to political pressure and more prone to consist of strategic fictions.

But the matter is a bit more complicated than the Colonel suggests, for the production of strategic fictions is the basic function of psychological operations—the Colonel's forte—and hence the colonel's solution to the problem he describes is simply to produce *more* strategic fictions (e.g., "Tree of Smoke"). Ironically, it is the Colonel's assistant and eventual nemesis, Rick Voss, who notes that the Colonel's critique is at odds with his own mission. While editing the Colonel's manuscript, Voss adds the following note: "One might hypothesize a step beyond the final one. Consider the possibility that a coterie or insulated group might elect to create fictions independent of the leadership's intuition of its own needs. And might serve these fictions to the enemy in order to influence choices" (289–90). This "final step" is exactly the one the Colonel eventually takes in "Operation Tree of Smoke"—a rogue psy op that, if successful, would be among the grandest fictions of the Cold War by making a tactical nuclear weapon operational without requiring its actual detonation. Of course, this very strategy lay at the heart of the Cold War, whose nuclear weapons were always already operational without their detonation. It is this fact that makes deterrence the ultimate symbol of postmodern simulation for Jean Baudrillard.[41]

There is thus a conflict between what can be called the *realist* desire to make intelligence reflect the world and something like the *postmodern* desire to question the supposed boundary between fiction and reality. This conflict is reflected in the very structure of the CIA, which is divided into a Directorate of Intelligence, charged with understanding the world, and a Directorate of Operations, charged with secretly changing it.[42] During the early years of the Cold War, CIA operations grew exponentially, launching many risky and often unsuccessful schemes.[43] As H. Bradford Westerfield notes, the CIA emerged "from the boom of the first cold war decade not central with regard to intelligence collection, not very central with regard to intelligence analysis...but truly central with regard to covert action (secret propaganda and political intrigue) and paramilitary operations."[44] This shift toward covert operations, I am suggesting, could not be accompanied without a corresponding crisis in intelligence, which is the central concern of the Colonel's essay in *Tree of Smoke*. On the one hand, the Colonel wants intelligence gathering to espouse the ethos of nineteenth-century realism or modern journalism. "I'm in intelligence," he tells Skip. "I'm after the truth" (*Tree of Smoke*, 57). On the other hand, the Colonel is also in Psychological Operations, which falsifies and simulates in order to instill anxiety and uncertainty in the enemy. Psy Ops, says Sergeant Storms, the Colonel's most trusted assistant, is "almost like yogic or spiritual work.... We're on the cutting edge of reality itself. Right where it turns into a dream" (255). If intelligence collection is the analogue of empiricism or realism, then covert operations, and Psy Ops in particular, abandon faithful representation for something akin to the postmodernist's deliberate conflation of reality, simulation, and myth.

The problem articulated by Colonel Sands thus reflects the postmodern crisis of knowledge that Lyotard attributes to a shift in the status of modern (scientific) and ancient (narrative) modes of knowledge. In the post–World War II era, Lyotard argues, narrative ("the quintessential form of customary knowledge" [*Postmodern Condition*, 19]) enjoys a resurgence, while rational science, still the dominant modern epistemology, undergoes a "crisis of legitimation." Scientific knowledge has become the dominant modern way of knowing in part by establishing rules of legitimacy that dismiss narrative knowledge: "The scientist questions the validity of narrative statements and concludes that they are never subject to argumentation or proof. He classifies them as savage, primitive...fables, myths, legends, fit only for women and children" (27). This assumption, Lyotard notes, underlies "the entire history of cultural imperialism from the dawn of Western civilization" (27). In this throwaway comment, Lyotard presciently aligns postmodernism with an emerging postcolonial critique of Western imperialism. He also identifies the patronizing masculinism implicit in the dismissal of "nonserious" discourse, a dismissal at the heart of what I am calling the feminization of the public sphere.

The problem facing modern Western rationality is that "scientific knowledge cannot know and make known that it is the true knowledge without resorting to the other, narrative, kind of knowledge, which from its point of view is no knowledge at all" (*Postmodern Condition,* 29). Modernity brushes off narrative knowledge, only to discover its own grounding in narratives about the liberation of the proletariat, the creation of wealth, the triumph of the human spirit, the creation of a just society, "better living through chemistry," and so on. The postmodern, then, is not only an "incredulity toward metanarratives" (xxiv), as Lyotard claims in his opening statement. It is, as Fredric Jameson notes, the paradoxical combination of a "revival of an essentially narrative view of 'truth'" *and* "a more global or totalizing 'crisis' in the narrative function."[45] The status of narrative is elevated in postmodernity, despite disappointment about its inability to legitimate itself through the "serious" procedures of rational science.

I dwell on this argument because Johnson depicts intelligence as haunted by the very conflict Lyotard finds between rational science and narrative. Colonel Sand's major critic at the CIA, Terry Crodelle, attacks his theory of "cross contamination" by suggesting that the Colonel conduct a scientific study of intelligence modeled on nineteenth-century epidemiology. "Let him propose a random-assignment study using two systems" like the "old proposals for the cause of polio" (418). The Colonel, however, is committed to a narrative approach. He is a devotee (and in some ways a version) of the legendary cold warrior Edward Lansdale, who became famous for his ethnographic approach to intelligence. For Lansdale, the key to intelligence was knowing "the people themselves...their songs, their stories, their legends" (49)—precisely the arena in which the United States so dramatically failed according to prominent critiques from *The Ugly American* to Frances Fitzgerald's magnificent 1972 history, *Fire in the Lake.* For the Colonel, "war is ninety percent myth," and thus the enemy must be "engaged at the level of myth" (54). Hence the Colonel assigns Skip and three other translators to extract an encyclopedia of mythological references from over seven hundred volumes of Vietnamese literature. His "Project Labyrinth" attempts to exploit native mythology to deter the North Vietnamese from using their own tunnels. And his grand plot— which he calls "embarrassingly poetic" (193)—comes from Old Testament references to God as a "pillar," "column," or "palm tree" of smoke.[46]

For all his insistence on the rational purification of intelligence, in other words, the Colonel sees his work as primarily humanistic or *literary* in character. Of course, so did the Cold War CIA, which spent massive sums sponsoring Western art and literature.[47] It is no accident that Skip's first

CIA assignment is as a literary critic who gets "a monthly stipend from the World Lit Foundation, a CIA front" (48). Early in the novel, he frets about being a mere librarian, and while he leaps at the opportunity to "create the fiction" of Tree of Smoke (342), he winds up doing little besides reading literature and cataloging the Colonel's nineteen thousand index cards. Even somewhere inside the Colonel, Skip later observes, "was this librarian" (491). Both men, that is, hover between the roles of author and archivist, novelist and historian. "The novelist," writes Doctorow, "deals with his isolation by splitting himself in two, creator and documentarian, teller and listener" ("False Documents," 157). In *Libra,* this division is represented by Win Everett, the CIA agent-author, and Nicholas Branch, the CIA historian crippled by the contradictory archive that threatens to entomb him.

This division of purpose within the intelligence agency is further symbolized in *Tree of Smoke* by the figure of the double agent. Because the Colonel's plot requires a double agent, Johnson's characters frequently discuss a real 1962 article for the CIA's secret journal, *Studies in Intelligence,* in which John Dimmer explains that "the double agent is, in effect, a condoned channel of communication with the enemy."[48] Johnson also stresses, through a pervasive theme of betrayal, that Trung should not be seen as the only double agent in this novel. The missionary Kathy Jones observes that "everyone's under cover" (87). As Sergeant Storms puts it, "In the shit-bucket of South Vietnam, every living thing is double" (478). Skip asks Trung, "What's it like to carry two souls in one body? It's the truth, isn't it. It's who we really are" (397). This sense of duplicity is related to a persistent conflation of the real and the fictional, overt and covert. Skip goes to Vietnam to be "shoved into the forge, an emphatically new order—so to speak a 'different administration'—where theories burned to cinders, where questions of morality became matters of fact" (196–97). But he later realizes that his craving for the real cannot be satisfied in the hallucinatory milieu of Vietnam. "He had come to war to see abstractions become realities. Instead he's seen the reverse. Everything was abstract now" (357).

The same conflation of reality and fiction haunts nearly everyone in *Tree of Smoke.* James Houston sees Vietnam as his "movie" (523). Another member of his platoon gets elements of battle "mixed up with the movies" (283). The novel's spies unwittingly adopt elements of Ian Fleming melodramatic spy novels. The Colonel smokes Bond's brand of cigarettes; they use the phrase "Eyes Only," which Voss points out is "not a legal classification" but "out of James Bond" (304); and Skip even momentarily thinks, "I am James Bond" (364). Is it any surprise to learn that President John F. Kennedy was a serious fan of James Bond novels or that he called Edward Lansdale, when naming him head of Cuba policy, "our answer to James Bond"?[49] And if the fictional seems to inform the real practice of spycraft, the reverse also seems true. As Skip tries to understand the violence of the era, the assassinations at home and the slaughter in Vietnam, "he devoured *Time* and *Newsweek* and found it all written down there, yet these events seemed improbable, *fictitious*" (329, emphasis added).

The epistemology of the covert sphere, in other words, disables the discourses of rationality and privileges "savage, primitive...fables, myths, legends, fit only for women and children" (Lyotard, *Postmodern Condition,* 27), which are a way of understanding not only the "mind" of the enemy but also the basic product of the Psychological Operations division. For the Colonel, Vietnamese mythology is not "primitive" or incorrect; it is simply the narrative form of knowledge through which war is waged. "The land is their myth," says the Colonel. "We penetrate their land, we penetrate their national soul. This is real infiltration. It may be tunnels, but it's in the realm of Psy Ops most definitely" (194). This view so conflates the real and the mythic, the physical and the psychological, that as Skip overhears it, he cannot tell whether to take it seriously. The same difficulty of knowing what is real eventually comes to shape nearly everything that happens in *Tree of Smoke*. Even the Colonel's reported death can never be fully accepted by his men because his deception operation creates conditions that prevent its rational confirmation. There are conflicting reports of his disappearance, burial, and possible resurrection. Storms believes the Colonel may have faked his own death so that he could be "captured and tortured" into "confessing" the same phony nuclear plot conveyed by the double agent, Trung, in Operation Tree of Smoke. When Storms tracks down one purported grave of the Colonel, he asks his guide, Anders Pitchfork, "What happened to him?"

> "Are you after the legend, or the fact?"
> "I'm after the truth, man."
> "I'd venture the truth is in the legend."
> "What about the facts, then?"
> "Unavailable. Obscured in legend." (587)

The very methodology of covert operations has turned the Colonel into a myth. "He'd written himself large-scale," realizes Skip, "chased his own myth down a maze of tunnels and into the fairyland of children's stories and up a tree of smoke" (451). Elsewhere, Skip muses:

> Uncle F.X, pillar of fire, tree of smoke, wanted to raise a great tree in his own image, a mushroom cloud—if not a real one over the rubble of Hanoi, then its dreaded possibility in the mind of Uncle Ho, the Enemy King. And who could say the delirious old warrior didn't grapple after actual truths? Intelligence, data, analysis be damned: to hell with reason, categories, synthesis, common sense. All was ideology and imagery and conjuring.... Fireworks, all of it, not just the stuff of history, but the stuff of reality itself, the thoughts of God. (345)

In the surreal world of Psy Ops, "actual truths" lie more in legend and "conjuring" than in data or analysis.

The Epistemology of Vietnam

Eventually this vision of covert warfare as a step beyond reason informs Johnson's entire portrait of Vietnam as a place that seems wholly other to its U.S. invaders. "It's not a different place," says the Colonel. "It's a different world under a different God" (188). There is a wonderland quality to Johnson's Vietnam. It is "Disneyland on acid," says the hipster Sergeant Storm, whose tour of duty turns into a bizarre spiritual odyssey (472). The novel's central vehicle for this portrait is the Colonel's oft-expressed understanding of Vietnam through a passage from First Corinthians:

> St. Paul says there is one God, he confirms that, but he says "There is one God, and many administrations." I understand that to mean you can wander out of one universe and into another just by pointing your feet and forward march. I mean you can come to a land where the fate of human beings is completely different from what you understood it to be.... So what's the point? The point is Vietnam. The point is Vietnam. The point is Vietnam. (63)[50]

Crucially, this remark links the radical otherness of Vietnam to the compartmentalization of government. The Colonel notes that he came upon the idea when traveling through a section of Alaska so "God-forsaken" that it suggested "the administration of an alien God" (63). Yet as Skip later notes, Paul's comment appeals to the "government man" in the Colonel, because it suggests "a cosmological bureaucracy" (110).

Lest we miss the connection between cultural difference and government compartmentalization, Johnson later has Kathy Jones mention the Colonel's beloved passage in a letter to Skip: "'And there are differences of administrations but the same Lord. And there are diversities of operations, but it is the same God which worketh in all.' That must appeal to a G-man like you!" (153). The appeal of the passage, Kathy correctly notes, is its emphasis not only on compartmentalization but also on "operations," both of which are essential to the work of the CIA. The CIA, moreover, conducts both the work of *the* administration and the work of other, smaller administrations, like the Colonel's rogue Psy Ops division. Kathy goes on, however, to make the Colonel's point about the Western experience of Vietnam. "If you want to believe that different angelic departments sort of run different parts of the show down here on earth, I don't blame you. Just going from the Manila airport to Tan Son Nhut airport in Saigon I'd be almost ready to call it diversities of deities, diverse universes, all on the same planet" (154). For North Americans, Vietnam feels like a place operating on a different set of natural laws.

What are we to make of this interesting constellation of ideas? It simultaneously reflects the apparent ontological otherness of Vietnam *and* the division of the state into separate "operations" with diverse goals and methods. But there is a third factor. It also reflects the discourse on postmodernism. Whether there is a single totalizing order ("one God") or multiple realities ("diverse universes") is among the central questions of postmodernism. In Brian McHale's influential account, modernism exploded into postmodernism when it ceased to depict radically different perspectives on a single reality and suggested something like the proliferation of distinct realities. In postmodern narrative, that is, "you can wander out of one universe and into another." The Colonel's approach may insist that ultimately there's a single order, but as Kathy Jones notes, Vietnam seems so utterly *other* that the question of one god or "diversities of deities" is essentially moot. Johnson's novel repeatedly depicts both Vietnam and covert government in language uncannily similar to McHale's descriptions of postmodern fiction as the elaboration of heterotopias, "worlds in collision," or ontologically incompatible "zones."[51]

The "hall of mirrors" created by Operation Tree of Smoke is thus something like an offshore version of John Barth's metafictional "funhouse," where the line between discourse and reality is insistently breached.[52] Covert warfare produces the same kinds of ontological disorientation described in Berger and Luckmann's famous account of social construction: "I am conscious of the world consisting of multiple realities. As I move from one reality to another, I experience the transition as a kind of shock."[53] Sergeant Storms tells a puzzled Trung, Vietnam is "a region that's completely basically dislocated from natural laws. That is, all the *laws* do apply *inside* Vietnam. But from the rest of planet Earth, those laws don't apply *to* Vietnam" (*Tree of Smoke*, 478). Despite Storms's hipsterish incoherence, his rant is not a bad description of postmodern fiction, in which discrete "worlds" seem to operate via different sets of "natural laws." Indeed, Storms's comment recalls Foucault's very definition of heterotopias as "the linking of things that are inappropriate" and "disturbing, probably because they secretly undermine language, because they make it impossible to name this *and* that, because they destroy the 'syntax' which causes words and things to… 'hold together.'"[54] As Storms says to Trung, "We are not getting through to each other.… I don't have the names for the entities in your language" (478).

What is the meaning of this similarity between foreign policy and the postmodern? First, it suggests that postmodern aesthetics derive partly from the covert projects of the Cold War—both its foreign adventures and its transformation of the state into public and secret compartments, with a high epistemological barrier between the two. Second, postmodernism renders the Third World, from a Western perspective, an incomprehensible parallel universe. One could say that the U.S. perspective on Vietnam literalizes the mythological. The colonial imagination—which perceives the Third World as a zone of superstition and myth—projects a demonological and racialized anxiety about unknowing onto the distant sites of Cold War battle.

Hence, while the Colonel wants to use mythology to make the tunnels frightening for the North Vietnamese, precisely the reverse happens. As James Houston is lowered face first into a tunnel, he thinks: "There were stories that the tunnels went for miles. There were monsters down there, blind reptiles and insects that had never seen the light, there were hospitals and brothels, and horrible things, piles of the offal from VC atrocities, dead babies, assassinated priests" (*Tree of Smoke*, 259). The U.S. marines project onto the tunnels a haunting otherness. They have a wonderland quality, as if they are wormholes to another world.

These effects are partly the result of an epistemology in which cold war seems distant and unknowable. For Johnson's American characters, the incomprehensibility of Vietnam makes it seem a place outside laws and reason altogether. The postmodern sense of different "realities" thus becomes a vehicle for managing racial and cultural difference. It permits Americans to recast Vietnam as a literal "state of exception," a place outside the law, a zone of supernatural horror in which every form of normality has been upended. "Ninety-nine percent of the shit that goes through my head on a daily basis is against the law," says one marine. "But not here. Here the shit in my head *is* the law and nothing *but* the law" (*Tree of Smoke,* 326). U.S. troops feel that Vietnam is "dislocated from natural laws" (478), because *they themselves* have transformed it into a site of extralegal sovereignty. *Tree of Smoke* is thus filled with American sociopaths who cannot understand or explain their world. One of the Colonel's tunnel patrollers cuts the eyeballs out of a prisoner and turns them around so the man can see his own evisceration. A similar group of Long Range Patrollers rapes a girl, and then James Houston "interrogates" her crazily at knifepoint, saying, "You're my mother, but who the fuck is my father?" (517). Back in the United States, other characters swirl into terror and insanity. This is the portrait of a nation that has lost its way.

It is also a remarkably familiar portrait—and this is perhaps the most interesting thing of all. Johnson's novel connects Cold War institutions not only to postmodernism but to an entire tradition of Vietnam narratives. Skip is aware that he's a version of Graham Greene's "Quiet American" (Alden Pyle) and Burdick and Lederer's "Ugly American" (Homer Atkins), but *Tree of Smoke*'s unacknowledged sources include Francis Ford Coppola's *Apocalypse Now,* Stanley Kubrick's *Full Metal Jacket,* Oliver Stone's *Platoon,* and the writings of Michael Herr and Tim O'Brien.

Herr, who did some screenwriting on both *Apocalypse Now* and *Full Metal Jacket,* is at the center of this group. His 1977 nonfiction book *Dispatches* first depicted the atmosphere of hallucinatory horror and insanity that is now a staple in the major fictions of Vietnam. For Herr, "Vietnam was a dark room full of deadly objects." Its Highlands "are spooky, unbearably spooky, spooky beyond belief.... The puritan belief that Satan dwelt in Nature could have been born here.... It is ghost-story country."[55] Herr beautifully illustrates Michael Rogin's argument that American "demonology" has its roots in the paranoid Puritan response to indigenous

Americans.[56] Like Johnson, Herr expresses a Puritan sense of alienation from the environment itself. "Forget the Cong," Herr writes, "the *trees* would kill you, the elephant grass grew up homicidal, the ground you were walking over possessed malignant intelligence" (*Dispatches,* 64).

This vision of a haunted jungle hiding invisible enemies would become a dominant feature of U.S. narratives of the Vietnam War. "The countryside itself seemed spooky," writes Tim O'Brien. "The land was haunted. We were fighting forces that did not obey the laws of twentieth-century science.... It was ghost country, and Charlie Cong was the main ghost.... He could blend with the land, changing form, becoming trees and grass. He could levitate. He could fly."[57] In the Western imagination, Vietnam becomes a Rorschach test onto which its would-be conquerors project their terror. By using the land to symbolize a mostly hidden human enemy and emphasizing the experience of desperate and confused Americans, these representations ultimately suggest a United States "at war with itself."

Tree of Smoke derives substantially from this way of thinking. Like *Apocalypse Now, Full Metal Jacket,* and *Platoon,* all of which relate the murder of one American by another, Johnson's novel is ultimately about conflicts *internal* to the U.S. security state.[58] The plot pits Skip and the Colonel against other elements of the CIA. The Colonel's protégé, Minh, eventually decides "the idea that they fought on anyone's side was foolish" (*Tree of Smoke,* 438). When Skip's CIA bosses threaten to polygraph him, they reassure him "we are not the enemy," but Skip replies, "'Enemy' is no longer a term I'd use in any case. Ever" (490). Similar confusion haunts the enlisted men. For one hardened veteran, when you "go up against Mr. Charlie...you swap yourselves," and the force attacking you "ain't him. It's you" (348). In the largest subplot of the novel, James Houston attacks a platoon of Green Berets who earlier killed one of his compatriots on a mission that "made no sense" (513). Houston's attack echoes Trung's earlier throwing of a grenade at his old friend Hao, who later in turn betrays Trung. At a deep level the novel is about various forms of betrayal. Father Carignan meditates on his status as a traitor; the Colonel accuses Skip of betraying him, saying, "You have no loyalty" (432); and the Colonel himself betrays the very organization that employs him.

In the literature and film of Vietnam, this sense of a nation at war with itself and confused about its mission overseas is conveyed through a surreal sense of ontological otherness. It was Michael Herr who first depicted

Vietnam as another "world" with different rules. After the Tet offensive, Herr notes, "the Mission council joined hands and passed together through the Looking Glass" (*Dispatches,* 69). Tim O'Brien would develop this idea in *Going After Cacciato* (1978), which is loosely based on *Alice in Wonderland.* As the novel's protagonist, Paul Berlin, fantasizes about walking away from the war to Paris, he falls into a surreal Vietnamese tunnel complex. There he is greeted by Major Li Van Hgoc of the Forty-eighth Vietcong Battalion.

> How, he asked Li Van Hgoc, did they hide themselves? How did they maintain such quiet? Where did they sleep, how did they melt into the land? Who were they? What motivated them—ideology, history, tradition, religion, politics, fear, discipline? What were the sects of Quang Ngai? Why did the earth glow red? Was there meaning in the way the night seemed to move? Illusion or truth? How did they wiggle through wire? Could they fly, could they pass through rock like ghosts? Was it true they didn't value human life? Did their women really carry razor blades in their vaginas, booby traps for dumb GIs? Did he know anything about the time of silence along the Song Tra Bong? Was it really a Psy-Ops operation? ... Why was the land so scary—criss-crossed with paddies, the tunnels and burial mounds, thick hedges and poverty and fear.[59]

This passage is part of a literary and filmic tradition that understands the jungle as a figure for the North Vietnamese. In response to Berlin, Li Van Hgoc replies: "The soldier is but the representative of the land. The land is your true enemy" (*Going After Cacciato,* 77). Denis Johnson appropriates this racialized geography when he has James Houston imagine Vietcong tunnels full of "hospitals and brothels, and horrible things, piles of offal from VC atrocities, dead babies, assassinated priests" (*Tree of Smoke,* 259).

Johnson's novel is thus part of a much larger U.S. mythos about Vietnam, a kind of self-perpetuating narrative that continues to define U.S. perceptions of the war. This tradition figures the internal divisions and public incoherence of U.S. policy through a surreal aesthetic that re-creates the U.S. soldier's sense of confusion and terror. Surrealism is, of course, a modernist movement, but it is the one that most typifies the postmodern penchant for ontological dislocation. In the Vietnam narrative, surreality seems less a modernist exploration of the psyche than a vehicle for representing the

U.S. sense of a fundamentally unknowable conflict. It converts the frontiers of U.S. empire into a site of epistemological confusion. With its atmosphere of psychedelic horror and lunacy, Coppola's *Apocalypse Now* is the apotheosis of the tradition. Coppola's Vietnam is a place where marines surf under the cover of helicopter fire, Playboy bunnies perform in the jungle, and a covert-operations assassin takes a hallucinatory journey after the renegade philosopher king Colonel Kurtz, who, like Johnson's Colonel Sands, has achieved mythic status among his followers.

In converting Joseph Conrad's *Heart of Darkness* into a tale of Southeast Asian covert operations, Coppola, like Johnson, took his cue from Herr. Herr's *Dispatches* is in fact the foundational work from which all of these other narratives derive their echoes of Conrad and Antonin Artaud and their sense of Vietnam as a zone of unknowability. "Sean Flynn," writes Herr of his fellow war correspondent, "could look more incredibly beautiful than even his father, Errol, had thirty years before as Captain Blood, but sometimes he looked more like Artaud coming out of some heavy heart-of-darkness trip, overloaded on information, the input! The input!" (*Dispatches,* 17). In *Tree of Smoke,* Skip Sands becomes lost in the writings of Artaud and Georges Bataille as he awaits orders in the jungle. At a

Figure 8. Francis Ford Coppola's *Apocalypse Now* (1979) is the ultimate portrayal of Vietnam as a surreal nightmare in which U.S. soldiers can no longer distinguish themselves from a racialized enemy and landscape. Here, amid a ritualistic animal sacrifice, Captain Willard (Martin Sheen) emerges from a river in camouflage to assassinate the rogue U.S. colonel Kurtz.

crucial moment in the novel (when James Houston decides to "frag those [Green Beret] mother fuckers into dead red meat"), a soldier named "Conrad appeared among them as silently as a thought" (508). Two of Johnson's other grunts—Joker and Cowboy—are now clichés of the great American Vietnam film. Joker is the central figure in Kubrick's *Full Metal Jacket.* A war correspondent whose helmet reads "Born to Kill," he is an emblem of the inability to separate the functions of reporter and soldier, objectivity and partisanship. If Johnson's Joker is derived from Kubrick's, then both seem to come straight from Herr's account of "haunted" young men who inscribe their helmets with "their war names" and "their fantasies (BORN TO LOSE, BORN TO RAISE HELL, BORN TO KILL, BORN TO DIE)" (71). Vietnam fiction always seems to run backward to Michael Herr, the journalist whose nonfiction dispatches themselves read as if *they* had been written by "Artaud coming out of some heavy heart-of-darkness trip" (*Dispatches,* 17).

This entire tradition of representation reflects the epistemology of the covert sphere: the secret nature of the war; the incomprehensibility of the mission, the enemy, and the land; the hypermasculine camaraderie and eroticized violence; and the "postmodern" confusion of fact and fiction. In all of these ways, Herr's account is crucial, for its blurring of fact and fiction is shaped by a pervasive sense of secrecy and unknowability. "Hiding low under the fact-figure crossfire there was a secret history, and not a lot of people felt like running in there to bring it out" (51). Herr, of course, did run "in there to bring it out," but what he brought out reads a lot like literary fiction. Herr himself repeatedly suggests that the surreal and fictional qualities of the war stem from its origins in covert-intelligence operations. "It was a spookwar," he writes, a campaign run by "not exactly soldiers, not even advisors yet, but Irregulars, working in remote places under little direct authority, acting out their fantasies with more freedom than most men ever know…, elevated crazies of older adventures who'd burst from their tents and bungalows to rub up hard against the natives, hot on the sex-and-death trail, 'lost to headquarters'" (51).

This account associates the covert origins of the war with not only male fantasy and irrationality but also the blurring of journalism and fiction. In a superb illustration of the covert sphere as a cultural imaginary, Herr explains how the mystified nature of the conflict privileges *fiction* as a way of understanding it:

You couldn't find two people who agreed about when it began, how could you say when it began going off? Mission intellectuals like 1954 as the reference date; if you saw as far back as War II and the Japanese occupation you were practically a historical visionary. "Realists" said that it began for us in 1961, and the common run of Mission flack insisted on 1965, post-Tonkin Resolution, as though all the killing that had gone before wasn't really war. Anyway, you couldn't use the standard methods to date the doom; might as well say that Vietnam was where the Trail of Tears was headed all along, the turnaround point where it would touch and come back to form a containing perimeter; might just as well lay it on the proto-Gringos who found the New England woods too raw and empty for their peace and filled them up with their own imported devils. Maybe it was already over for us in Indochina when Alden Pyle's body washed up under the bridge at Dakao, his lungs all full of mud; maybe it caved in with Dien Bien Phu. But the first happened in a novel, and while the second happened on the ground it happened to the French, and Washington gave it no more substance than if Graham Greene had made it up, too. (51)

The problem in dating the war is that—like every other "hot" element of the Cold War—it began in secret. Herr offers two possible markers of its beginning—one historical (the French defeat at Dien Bien Phu in 1954) and the other fictional (the death of Graham Greene's "quiet American"). The point here is not simply that Washington treats French colonial history as if it were mere fiction, but rather that, from a U.S. perspective, *everything* in Vietnam has the status of fiction. Vietnam is a place where "things got mixed, the war itself with those parts of the war that were just like the movies, just like *The Quiet American* or *Catch-22*" (184). For an American who has seen "too many movies," battles first seem like "a jungle play with giant helicopters and fantastic special effects" (183). Combat troops exposed to "seventeen years of war movies" end up "making war movies in their heads." At every turn, *fiction* shapes the conception, prosecution, and Western experience of the war.

Perhaps this is why even Herr's journalistic account must be "considered postmodern," as Fredric Jameson puts it. "The extraordinary linguistic innovations of the book," Jameson notes, are "dictated by problems of content" (*Postmodernism*, 44). That is, they are not stylistic choices—not merely "one (optional) style among many available" (45–46)—but rather expressions of a "postmodernist war" itself (44). While it is perhaps too easy to locate aesthetic qualities (modernist fragmentation, postmodern heterotopia) in calamitous social events, Jameson's comments suggest that the conditions of knowledge in Vietnam shaped Herr's exhilarating mixture of speculation, imagination, and reporting.

That *this* text would then become a basis for the most influential fictional accounts of the era tells us something vitally important about the representation of Cold War foreign affairs. The essence of Herr's *Dispatches* is its relentless expression of confusion, fictionality, and incomprehensibility. In a "spookwar" shaped by the dictates of state secrecy and official obfuscation, even the correspondent struggles to sort the smoldering remains of the war's false documents.

4

The Work of Art in the Age of Plausible Deniability

Narrative Dysfunction

The defense of imaginative writing against the claims of history and other "serious" discourses dates back at least to Philip Sidney's late sixteenth-century *Defence of Poesy*. But when did the defense of poetry begin to invoke the deceptions of the state? When, that is, did novelists begin to trumpet the value of fiction over history and nonfictional discourse as a corrective to state secrecy?

The answer seems to be during the 1960s.[1] Consider, for instance, Norman Mailer's groundbreaking narrative of the 1967 anti-Vietnam march on the Pentagon, *Armies of the Night*. Trying to narrate the event first as fiction and then as history, Mailer eventually decides that "the mystery of the events at the Pentagon cannot be developed by the methods of history—only by the instincts of the novelist."[2] To some extent, this assertion rests on the familiar notion that the novel can render the "interior experience" (i.e., the individual human experience) of events in a way traditional historical narrative cannot. But Mailer also finds traditional history blocked by new features of the Cold War public sphere: "Journalistic information available from both sides is so incoherent, inaccurate, contradictory, malicious, even based on error that no accurate history is conceivable" (*Armies of the Night*, 284). This critique echoes Habermas's account of the mass cultural transformation of the public sphere. But it also links the transformation of the public sphere to Cold War state deception. The march on the Pentagon, Mailer asserts, was a protest against "the authority, because the authority lied. It lied through the teeth of corporation executives and Cabinet officials and police enforcement officers and newspaper editors and advertising agencies, and in its mass magazines" (104). The "authority" and the "corporation" are Mailer's shorthand for a vast apparatus of media structures, corporate interests, and state institutions whose headquarters is the Pentagon but which also includes the CIA, the FBI, and even "the Warren Commission" (104). The chief effect of this apparatus is a national "state of suppressed schizophrenia"—a contradiction between religious fervor and technological rationality—which makes "the average good Christian American secretly [love] the war in Vietnam" (212). In a dysfunctional public sphere, Mailer suggests, "misinformation in systematic form tends to create mass schizophrenia" (161).

Mailer's account of this problem is among the most influential historiographic experiments of the postwar era. As Linda Hutcheon points out, it illustrates that the "basic postmodernist stance—of a questioning of authority—obviously is a result of the ethos of the 1960s."[3] The wave of postmodern historiographic metafiction that followed *The Armies of the Night* has similarly asserted the value of fiction over history—not only the sense that fiction offers something history cannot but also the sense that history is at some level indistinguishable from fiction.[4] This shift itself is not primarily a result the Cold War. It is part of a larger, twentieth-century attack on the empiricist historiography of the nineteenth century, a critique that has troubled the notion of "facts," stressed the creative power of the historian, and emphasized the literary qualities of historical narrative.[5] As history has come to seem more like fiction and canonical history has been critiqued as an ideological vehicle, many novelists have argued that the truth-value of fiction sometimes trumps that of narrative history.

It is nonetheless striking how many U.S. authors understand the postmodern historiographic crisis as a specific consequence of the National

Security State. For the novelist Charles Baxter, state deception transformed the nature of U.S. narrative, making it "dysfunctional." "The greatest influence on American fiction for the last twenty years," Baxter writes, is Richard Nixon, "the inventor, for our purposes and for our time, of the concept of *deniability*":

> What difference does it make to writers of stories if public figures are denying their responsibility for their own actions? ... Well, to make an obvious point, they create a climate in which social narratives are designed to be deliberately incoherent and misleading. Such narratives humiliate the act of storytelling [for] only a coherent narrative can manage to explain public events.... Every story is a history ... and when there is no comprehensible story, there is, in some sense, no history; the past, under those circumstances, becomes an unreadable mess.[6]

Baxter here finds the narratives of an entire society transformed by the official duplicity of the Cold War state. The covert operations of Ronald Reagan and George Bush, for instance—particularly their "efforts to acquire deniability on the arms-for-hostages deal with Iran"—produced "public befuddlement about facts, forgetfulness under oath, and constant disavowals of political error and criminality" ("Dysfunctional Narratives," 396). While Baxter lays this problem at Nixon's feet, it is in fact an institutional feature of the Cold War. Richard Nixon may still be the most enduring public face of deniability, but he was certainly not its "inventor," as Baxter claims. If deniability can be said to have an author, then it was George Kennan, whose 1948 National Security Council memorandum NSC-10/2 gave the CIA its charter to covert actions so long as "the U.S. government can plausibly disclaim any responsibility for them."[7] This concept anchored other major secret policy documents long before Richard Nixon ever took office. In National Security Action Memorandum 273, for instance, the Kennedy administration laid out its plan for a secret war in Vietnam, Laos, and Cambodia that could be conducted only if the president were assured "plausibility of denial."[8]

The real problem, then, is an *institutionally* supported "culture of disavowal" that Baxter believes has trickled down from presidents to every corner of U.S. culture, from the lurid blame game of the afternoon talk-show circuit to prizewinning novels by Jane Smiley and Don DeLillo. The major quality of "narrative dysfunction," as Baxter describes it, is a lack of causal explanation. In a dysfunctional narrative, the narrator uses the passive voice and "gathers around herself a cloak of unreliability" ("Dysfunctional Narratives," 398). Such narratives fail to identify "the agent of the action" or "why it was done" (397). "One of the signs of a dysfunctional narrative is that we cannot leave it behind, and we cannot put it to rest, because it does not, finally, give us the explanation we need to enclose it" (397). In all of these ways, Baxter describes features scholars commonly associate with postmodern narrative. According to Marie-Laure Ryan, postmodern "antinarrative" sometimes resembles a sketch under constant revision, "where represented events never gel into 'facts' and never fit into…a stable and comprehensible narrative." Brian McHale describes a similar strategy called "weak narrativity," which involves "telling stories 'poorly,' distractedly, with much irrelevance and indeterminacy, in such a way as to *evoke* narrative coherence while at the same time withholding commitment to it and undermining confidence in it."[9]

Significantly, however, while Ryan and McHale describe the *deliberate* construction of a "poor," weak, or (to return to Baxter's term) "dysfunctional" narrative, Baxter views narrative dysfunction as a symptom, and not a critique, of official obfuscation. For instance, while he calls the Kennedy assassination "*the* narratively dysfunctional event of our era" (because "no one really knows who's responsible for it"), he also singles out DeLillo's *Libra* as one of his major examples of dysfunctional narrative ("Dysfunctional Narratives," 397). This seems misguided to me. What *Libra* so brilliantly reveals about the Kennedy case is the dysfunction of *the public sphere itself.* While the novel undoubtedly depicts the historical record as "an unreadable mess," to use Baxter's phrase, it does so to critique the conditions of knowledge produced by the Cold War security apparatus. Its historiographic skepticism is both a symptom of state secrecy and a powerful commentary on it.

Narrative dysfunction is a central paradox of covert-sphere postmodernism. On the one hand, narratives in which "events never gel into 'facts'" seem to reproduce the effects of deniability and ahistoricism that Baxter and others find so problematic. On the other hand, deliberately "weak" or dysfunctional narrativity is a powerful way to reveal the conditions of knowledge in a regime of state secrecy. Hence, DeLillo locates the value of his novel *Libra* in its use of invention over traditional historiography.

"In a case in which rumors, facts, suspicions, official subterfuge, conflicting sets of evidence, and a dozen labyrinthine theories all mingle," he explains, *Libra* offers readers "a way of thinking about the [Kennedy] assassination without being constrained by half-facts or overwhelmed by possibilities." DeLillo calls his novel a "refuge" and an asset precisely because it "makes no claim to literal truth," but is a "work of imagination" in which the author has "altered and embellished reality." What DeLillo specifically needed to "invent," moreover, was "officers of intelligence agencies and...organized crime figures."[10] In other words, the work of the fiction writer seems most urgently needed at the interface of public history and the covert state.

Works like *Libra* balance narrative invention with expressions of historical skepticism to suggest the limits of knowledge in a dysfunctional public sphere. While the novel offers two richly detailed explanations of Kennedy's assassination, it intermeshes them, refusing to resolve the popular "lone-gunman versus conspiracy" debate. *Libra* also imagines the endless frustrations of the CIA historian Nicholas Branch, suggesting that even access to the secret archive of the state cannot produce a clear causal narrative.

Many novels of covert action are characterized by a similar postmodern epistemological skepticism. Margaret Atwood's *Bodily Harm* (1981) contains two mutually incompatible endings because its protagonist is "disappeared" after cavorting with a CIA agent during a revolution on a Caribbean island.[11] *The Handmaid's Tale* (1985) ends with similar ambivalence just when the repressive theocracy of Gilead is linked to projects of the CIA. According to the novel's faux-historical epilogue, the commander to whom the protagonist is enslaved is probably one of two men who participated in "top-secret Sons of Jacob Think Tanks, at which the philosophy and social structure of Gilead was hammered out." Both men may have become infertile by contact with "a virus that was developed by secret pre-Gilead gene-splicing experiments with mumps, and which was intended for insertion into the supply of caviar used by top officials in Moscow."[12] One of the two men, moreover, developed Gilead's revolutionary strategy from "an obscure 'CIA' pamphlet on the destabilization of foreign governments" (*Handmaid's Tale,* 307). On the basis of these plans, he carried out assassinations, orchestrated the violent overthrow of Congress, and initiated several genocidal projects.

Like *Libra,* then, *The Handmaid's Tale* is a "work of imagination" that begins with the premise of a CIA project gone awry. While Atwood takes much more imaginative liberty than DeLillo, her novel refers to recogniz-able historical events. Gilead is loosely modeled on the Islamic theocracy born in the 1979 Iranian Revolution, which, initially supported by Iranian women, eventually led to an extraordinary suppression of women's rights. By mapping this social horror onto the United States of the Reagan-Bush era and recasting the Iranian clerics as U.S. fundamentalist Christians, At-wood imagines what U.S. policy on Iran might have looked like had it played out on U.S. soil. After all, the Iranian Revolution was long-delayed blowback from the CIA's 1953 "Operation Ajax," which replaced the dem-ocratically elected Mohammad Mossadeq with an autocratic puppet, Mo-hammad Reza Shah Pahlavi. Thirty years later, as Atwood was finishing *The Handmaid's Tale,* members of the Reagan administration were secretly collaborating with the new Iranian theocracy in order to finance the over-throw of another popularly elected government—this one in Nicaragua.[13]

Atwood works hard to show how such events become invisible to west-erners. The novel's epilogue, ostensibly the transcript of a "Gileadean Stud-ies" conference in the year 2195, is a tour-de-force critique of academic detachment and so-called postmodern relativism. The keynote speaker of the conference is James Pieixoto, a patronizing Cambridge historian who mocks Offred's education, jests about "the Underground Frailroad," and wishes Offred had provided a great-man history of her master instead of a social history of female experience (*Handmaid's Tale,* 310). Significantly, Pieixoto is a liberal whose ironic detachment is a result of his comfort-able academic position in a society much like the United States of 1985. He receives enthusiastic applause when he warns against "passing moral judgment upon the Gileadeans" because "such judgments are of necessity culture-specific." "Gileadean society," he adds, "was subject to factors from which we ourselves are happily more free. Our job is not to censure but to understand" (302). Coming after Offred's grisly narrative about the decline of an industrial democracy into a genocidal theocracy, these sentiments satirize moral relativism and American exceptionalism. Atwood wants readers to shake off the presumption that this tale is "mere" fiction—that nothing dystopian could ever happen *here.*

Such assumptions, it is crucial to note, are possible only when the im-perial activity of the state is clandestine. It is easy, Atwood suggests, for U.S. citizens to view Iran with a sense of cultural chauvinism and ironic detachment when they do not understand their own government's role in the creation of Iran's authoritarian nightmare. Even if we dispense with such allegorical implications and take Gilead on its own terms, Pieixoto's historiographical position is shaped by the problem of state secrecy. "As all historians know," he remarks in the closing lines of the novel, "the past is a great darkness, and filled with echoes. Voices may reach us from it; but what they say to us is imbued with the obscurity of the matrix out of which they come; and, try as we may, we cannot always decipher them precisely in the clearer light of our own day" (311). This is a familiar statement of postmodern historiographic skepticism, but here it is a direct consequence of state secrecy in a regime that emerged from the Cold War CIA.

But there is more to say, for historical uncertainty in this epilogue is not simply a result of state secrecy. It is also a direct consequence of Gilead's hyperdomestic sphere, which forbids women knowledge of state affairs. Much to the frustration of Pieixoto and company, the best extant source on Gilead, the handmaid's tale, provides only furtive glimpses into the secret male world of state policy. What Pieixoto laments, then, is *his own* "feminization"—which is to say, his confinement to the limited perspective of the handmaid. By restricting a male historian to Offred's position and associating him with Cold War American exceptionalism, Atwood provides a superb illustration of how the Cold War security state feminizes the public and lays a basis for the emergence of postmodernism. Ultimately, it is Pieixoto's inability to gain access to the inside perspective of the commander that inspires his postmodern attitude toward historiographic "obscurity," "darkness," and uncertainty—and his acceptance of what Baxter calls "narrative dysfunction."

Calculated Ellipsis

With the possible exception of DeLillo and Mailer, Joan Didion is the most important U.S. novelist of the National Security State. She is also a master of "narrative dysfunction" as a vehicle for understanding the feminization of the Cold War public sphere. Beginning in the mid-1970s, as her journalism took her in and out of the developing world, Didion wrote a series of novels designed to explore the effect of Cold War secrecy on democracy: *A Book of Common Prayer* (1977), *Democracy* (1984), and *The Last Thing He Wanted* (1996).[14] These novels are eerily similar. All are about the plight of a privileged, naive, and forgetful U.S. woman in a colonial setting where the United States is secretly orchestrating local affairs. The novels share several features: the female protagonist is torn between relationships with a public figure and a covert agent; a parent loses a rebellious daughter, who is subsequently aided by the covert agent; and the story is narrated by a more savvy and cynical woman, who is always a female journalist in the mold of Didion herself. The narrator of *Democracy* is, in fact, "Joan Didion." While each narrator dedicates herself to explaining the demise of her hapless foil, she inevitably fails and instead narrates her own failure to tell the story she meant to tell. Each novel, in other words, uses narrative dysfunction to reveal the dysfunction of the Cold War public sphere.

Allegory is Didion's primary vehicle for this critique. *Democracy* exposes the internal contradictions of the Cold War state through the story of a wealthy family's self-destruction. The novel's protagonist, Inez (Christian) Victor, is married to a liberal U.S. senator from Hawaii, Harry Victor, but she is in love with Jack Lovett, a CIA officer specializing in Southeast Asia and the Pacific. The narrative chronicles the decline of the Christian family when Inez's father murders Inez's sister and her lover, who is a U.S. congressman. A second family crisis occurs when Jessie Victor, the drug-addled daughter of Harry and Inez, runs off to Vietnam. At nearly the same time, Inez leaves Harry Victor for Jack Lovett, and it is Jack, rather than Harry, who recovers Jessie from Vietnam.

In his brilliant reading of *Democracy,* Alan Nadel argues that this allegory charts the breakdown of Cold War consensus ideology: "Inez Victor represents Americans facing the dissolution of their patriarchal, hegemonic conception of themselves. Their protocol, manners, status, and Christian morality have been reduced to a series of photo opportunities, euphemisms, and captions—a collage of images that mask a history of infidelity.... Faced with this hypocrisy, the American (Inez) remains a Victor in name only—as she and her father had been Christians in name only—refusing any of the other associations connected with her husband or nation."[15] By the end of the Vietnam War, the Cold War narrative of "democracy" is at odds with the facts of U.S. empire. Didion echoes the breakdown of this ideological consensus in her narrator's own "failed" narrative, which ultimately cannot tell the story the narrator sets out to write. To borrow Baxter's language, Didion's intentionally dysfunctional narrative is an emblem of the crumbling edifice of Cold War containment.

It is, Nadel writes "overburdened by 'facts' that cannot be legitimized within the governing fiction and fictions that cannot be legitimized by the facts."[16]

But why does *Democracy* relate this breakdown through such an elaborate rhetoric of secrecy and publicity? Following Nadel's lead, I want to pursue the more specific way in which Didion's allegory addresses the relation of democracy to covert action. It is no accident that Inez Victor is *publicly* married to an emblem of representative democracy (Senator Harry Victor) and *secretly* in love with his covert counterpart (CIA officer Jack Lovett). Inez is a public figure on the model of Jackie Kennedy—highly feminized, frequently seen and photographed, but resolutely apolitical in her public appearances. Her husband, Senator Victor, is the public face of the purported U.S. commitment to democracy and human rights. Senator Victor repeatedly descends on tropical capitals to obtain "official assurance that human rights remained inviolate in the developing (USAID Recipient) nation" (*Democracy,* 93). His organization—the Alliance for Democratic Institutions (ADI)—in fact seems deliberately indistinguishable from the U.S. Agency for International Development (USAID), a Kennedy-era vehicle of U.S. foreign influence. As Harry Victor does the state's public work, Jack Lovett runs the Kennedy administration's secret war, which he calls "the assistance effort" in Vietnam (71). Like the U.S. public, Inez both knows and does not know Jack's work: "He's running a little coup somewhere," she speculates. "I just bet" (34).

In this allegory, family problems are inseparable from national problems, and Didion goes to great lengths to coordinate the public implosion of the Christians with the disintegration of the U.S. adventure in Southeast Asia. Jessie Victor runs off to Saigon on the very night in 1975 when the U.S. evacuation of Da Nang devolves into rioting. Jack recovers her while also bringing home other U.S. national "assets," including "the cash reserves of the Saigon branches of the Bank of America" (195), the contents of a nuclear reactor (186), and "twenty years of American contacts" (196). Although Jack is "a man who for more than twenty years had maintained a great attraction to a woman whose every move was photographed" (41), his relationship with Inez is completely secret until he recovers Jessie from Vietnam. Only then, when the public begins to discover other covert aspects of the U.S. war, does Jack become a public figure: "Jack Lovett's name was just beginning to leak out of the various investigations

into arms and currency and technology dealings on the part of certain former or perhaps even current overt and covert agents of the United States
government" (217).

Democracy thus develops an elaborate framework for thinking about the
relation of publicity and secrecy in Cold War democracy. Didion insistently
points to the failure of public institutions to provide the knowledge necessary for real democracy. Didion's figure for the U.S. public, Inez, is notably
forgetful. In an important interview, Inez tells a reporter that "the major
cost" of publicity is "memory." Being constantly in public, she explains, has
the effect of "shock treatments"—it causes one to conflate the present with
previous "clips" (50–53). What Inez seems to mean here is that her private
memories have become contaminated by mass-mediated representations,
and it is no longer clear which memories are real and which are not. If Inez
represents the public, then her comment makes the Habermasian point
that public memory is falsified by the regime of publicity. But Jack Lovett
connects this point to the related problem of state secrecy when he chas-
tises Senator Victor and his aide, saying, "You people...don't actually see
what's happening in front of you. You don't see it unless you...read it in
the New York *Times*, then you start talking about it. Give the speech. Call
for an investigation" (100–101). The irony of this critique is that Harry
cannot see the love affair developing in front of him between Jack and
Inez. Yet Jack's comment also suggests that the most important institution
of the public sphere—the newspaper of record—misrepresents the world
to both the public and its democratic representative, in part by "not seeing"
covert state action.

The novel's dialectic of publicity and secrecy is integral to its purposeful
narrative dysfunction. Like all of Didion's work, *Democracy* is preoccu-
pied with the difficulty of telling a story. From the beginning, the narrator expresses hesitation and doubt. She compulsively emphasizes her
own authorial perspective and suggests alternative ways in which the story
could be told. "Call me the author," the second chapter begins. "*Let the
reader be introduced to Joan Didion, upon whose character and doings much
will depend.*... So Trollope might begin this novel." Didion, however, is no
Trollope (or Melville), and hence she begins over and over again because
she has "no unequivocal way of beginning" (16). Chapter 3 is yet another
abortive start, this one consisting of the narrator's abandoned original
draft: "Inez imagined her mother dancing." After a detailed recounting

of this memory, however, comes a stunning retraction: "Inez remembered no such thing" (21). Similar reversals, equivocations, and narrative breakdowns punctuate *Democracy*. The problem is partly that Inez Victor's story "is a hard story to tell," and partly that the narrator, Joan Didion, began the story "at a point in my life when I lacked certainty, lacked even that minimum level of ego which all writers recognize as essential to the writing of novels" (15–17).

If the first problem is a result of the Cold War covert sphere, the second would at first seem more personal. After all, Didion describes a nearly identical crisis in her 1979 autobiographical essay, "The White Album," which was composed and published in pieces between 1968 and 1978. In that essay, Didion recounts her overwhelming sense that she lived "in a world of people moved by strange, conflicted, poorly comprehended, and, above all, devious motivations." She suddenly begins "to doubt the premises of all the stories I had ever told" and struggles to place events in "a narrative line."[17] In what would become a defining feature of her work, Didion here expresses a profound struggle with motive, causality, and narrative coherence. In a line essentially lifted from "The White Album," the narrator of *A Book of Common Prayer* laments, "I did not know why I did or did not do anything at all," and yet she also notes that a story depends on a clear sense of the narrator's motives: "We are uneasy about a story until we know who is telling it. In no other sense does it matter who 'I' am: 'the narrator' plays no motive role in this narrative, nor would I want to" (10). Didion's stylistic signature—the unexplained juxtaposition of striking "images"—is partly an effort to resist the projection of motive onto the narrative. Her narrators decline to provide certain details they "could give you" (*Democracy,* 161); they cancel others with a "strike that"; they refer to the "shards" of abandoned versions; they are haunted by Prufrock's "hundred indecisions./A hundred visions and revisions" (*Democracy,* 73; *Last Thing He Wanted,* 226); and they repeatedly proclaim, "I am resisting narrative here" (*Democracy,* 113).

If "The White Album" links narrative dysfunction to a sense that public events no longer made sense in the long, hot summer of 1968, then *Democracy* specifically links narrative dysfunction to U.S. covert action. Didion makes this point most powerfully in a brief anecdote about teaching a Berkeley course on concepts of democracy in George Orwell, Henry Adams, Ernest Hemingway, and Norman Mailer. The "hypothesis" of the class is that style reflects a writer's "ideas of democracy" (71). The obvious implication of this anecdote is that it also applies to *Democracy,* whose halting, elliptical, ironic style clearly reflects Didion's vision of dysfunctional Cold War democracy. It is no accident that *Democracy's* narrator lectures at Berkeley on "the same short-term basis on which Harry Victor had lectured there," or that she does so just as the United States is withdrawing from Vietnam (71). By connecting her own teaching with the failure of the U.S. war and its liberal apologist, Harry Victor, Didion suggests the role of the writer in a democracy. In case we miss the point, she includes the essay prompts she gave her students: "Consider the political implications of both the reliance on and the distrust of abstract words, consider the social organization implicit in the use of the autobiographical third person. *Consider, too, Didion's own involvement in the setting: an atmosphere results. How?*" (72). The italicized section here, Didion reveals earlier in the novel, comes from an English composition textbook containing one of Didion's essays. By adding it to her own questions, Didion invites us to join her students in assessing the meaning of her own style. The "autobiographical third person" is ostensibly a reference to *The Education of Henry Adams,* yet Adams was also the anonymous author of a hugely popular 1880 romantic novel called, not coincidentally, *Democracy.* Adams thus helps make the questions here reflexive. The "abstract word" in question is "democracy," and the political question is how the writer fosters public "reliance on" or "distrust of" this idea of democracy.[18]

This passage is crucial. It is the dual nature of the Cold War state—and not some individual neurosis—that inspires the elliptical and hesitant style of Didion's novel, its juxtaposition of images in place of continuous, explanatory narrative. As a writer, Didion seems most committed to the idea that explanatory narrative is possible, but usually misleading. "I know the conventions and how to observe them, how to fill in the canvas I have already stretched," she explains, as she declines to do precisely these things. Instead, she elects to leave the canvas unfinished: "The heart of the narrative is a certain calculated ellipsis, a tacit contract between writer and reader to surprise and be surprised, how not to tell you what you do not yet want to know" (*Democracy,* 162). This remarkable statement captures the basic social contract of the Cold War security state, which is a tacit agreement to tolerate certain abrogations of democracy so long as they are not discussed in public. The "style" of the National Security State is understatement, public deception, pretended innocence, and deniability. It is a regime rooted in calculated ellipsis. Thus it is true not only that "Didion uses style as argument," as Barbara Grizzuti Harrison remarks, but also that Didion's style *imitates* the logic of Cold War democracy in order to critique it.[19] It is the narrative embodiment of the dysfunctional covert sphere.

The Feminization of the Public Sphere

In her account of the relation between publicity and secrecy in contemporary culture, Jodi Dean updates Jeremy Bentham's classification of public knowledge. In order to address the problem of an ignorant demos, Bentham separates those who use evidence to make independent judgments from those who follow the thinking of others or have little interest in public affairs.[20] Borrowing Žižek's terminology, Dean calls these two groups, respectively, "the public-supposed-to-know" and "the public-supposed-to-believe." While the latter, less-informed group poses a potential problem for democracy, Bentham argues that democracy is protected by the informed, stable judgment of the "public-supposed-to-know." Publicity underpins this system by persuading "the public-supposed-to-believe to believe that someone knows," Hence, for Dean, publicity is the "ideology of technoculture," the relentless drive to uncover the secrets that will hold together the fantasy of the public.[21]

But what happens when public-supposed-to-*know* starts to publicize its own unknowing? This is the basic question of Didion's entire corpus. She repeatedly allegorizes Bentham's two aspects of the public in the figures of the journalist-narrator (the public-supposed-to-know) and the naive protagonist (the public-supposed-to-believe). Didion does so, moreover, to ask what happens to democracy when the guarantors of the public sphere decide that they have been reduced from a public-supposed-to-know to a public-supposed-to-believe. This question is central to *Democracy,* but it is even clearer in Didion's earlier novel, *A Book of Common Prayer.*

A Book of Common Prayer is the story of Charlotte Douglas, an attractive American of forty who dies in a revolution on the tiny Caribbean island of Boca Grande. The novel is narrated by Charlotte's foil, Grace Strasser-Mendana, an anthropologist and longtime inhabitant of the tropics, and the largest landowner on Boca Grande. Grace is the widow of Edgar Strasser, whose father, Victor (the connection to the Victors of *Democracy* is not accidental), colonized Boca Grande and whose brothers—Luis, Victor Jr., and Antonio—have since struggled (often violently) to be its dictator.

The two women at first seem strikingly different. Grace is ironic, laconic, and brilliant. Charlotte, by contrast, is shockingly optimistic, innocent, and amnesic. "I'm not 'political' in the least," says Charlotte (151). Divorced from an irascible professor, she has remarried a left-wing lawyer and international arms trafficker, Leonard Douglas—who may, or may not, also have ties to U.S. intelligence. While Grace sees through the deceptive and deadly political theater of Boca Grande, Charlotte lives in a "fiction" of her own making (151). "Charlotte," says Grace, "seemed not to listen. Charlotte seemed not to see" (185). Charlotte views Boca Grande as a "miniature capital where nothing need be real," except the trappings of U.S. power—such as the embassy and the airport (151).

As in *Democracy,* then, the allegorical figure for the U.S. public is a liberal woman who is unaware of the corruption in the developing world, stunningly optimistic, "apolitical," and convinced of her immunity from violence: "She understood that something was always going on in the world but believed that it would turn out all right. She believed the world was peopled with others like herself. She associated the word 'revolution' with the Boston Tea Party, one of the few events in the history of the United States prior to the westward expansion to have come to her attention" (*Book of Common Prayer,* 40). Charlotte's naive, bourgeois optimism often manifests itself as repression or historical amnesia. While Charlotte's childhood school attempted to cultivate "'the development of a realistic but optimistic attitude' it was characteristic of Charlotte that she unconsciously amended this phrase to 'realistic and optimistic'" (46). Charlotte repeatedly tells Grace "that she could not remember" (122, 135). "I am so tired of remembering things," she tells her husband, Leonard (99). "Someone had shuffled her memory," Grace tells us. "Certain cards were lost" (118). What Charlotte "forgets" in particular is conflict, whether familial or social. She is deeply nostalgic for the days before her daughter, Marin, became a subversive. When the FBI informs Charlotte that Marin has hijacked an L-1011, Charlotte concludes that "Marin could not fly an L-1011 so Marin must be skiing at Squaw Valley" (49). On Boca Grande, when a vicious colonel steals vaccine in order to extort money from Charlotte, "within a week she had revised the incident to coincide with her own view of human behavior"—which, Grace repeatedly reminds us, is ludicrously optimistic. In a stunning moment, Charlotte fails to see that two "decorators" she has hired are using her phone to order weapons for a revolution (169).

Like Inez Victor, then, Charlotte Douglas is a stand-in for the U.S. public-supposed-to-believe. She is the liberal face of American exceptionalism. Grace, by contrast, sees herself as part of the public-supposed-to-know. "I know for months before the fact when there is about to be a 'transition' in Boca Grande," she explains, because such upheavals "have a sound the attentive ear can detect," like the sound of "oil wells about to come in," or the "harmonic tremor" of an earthquake or volcano (146). In this regard, Grace is just like the ultrasensitive narrator of *Democracy,* who "as the grandchild of a geologist…learned early to anticipate the absolute mutability of hills and waterfalls and even islands" (*Democracy,* 18). This extraordinary sensitivity, combined with a heightened sense of impermanence, is part of what Grace calls "the equatorial view"—the sense that "everything here changes and nothing appears to" (*Book of Common Prayer,* 118). It is Grace's ability to perceive subtle changes beneath the apparent permanence of her world that distinguishes her from Charlotte, who, Grace informs us, "did not take the equatorial view" (118). Grace understands Boca Grande as a "game" with "certain ritual moves." The winner is always "the player who lands his marker in the Ministry of Defense." To do so, he "must first get the *guerrilleros* into the game. The *guerrilleros* seem always to believe that they are playing on their own, but they are actually a diversion, a disruptive element placed on the board only to be 'quelled' by 'stronger leadership.' …*El Presidente,* whoever is playing *El Presidente* at the moment, falls ill, and is urged to convalesce at Bariloche, in Argentina," and the minister of defense becomes the new president (146–47). This "equatorial view" of regime change differs strikingly from what is reported in the U.S. press. As Grace remarks, "The events in Boca Grande are inflexibly reported on the outside as signs of a popular uprising, but they are not. 'NEW LEASE ON DEMOCRACY IN BOCA GRANDE' is one headline I recall from the *New York Times*" (147). Grace here sounds like a young Daniel Ellsberg mocking the readers of the *Times* as "rubes" and "yokels."[22] She has positioned herself as the ultimate insider, one whose suspicion penetrates the veneer of democracy's trappings.

But crucially, *A Book of Common Prayer* hinges on the ironic collapse of the radical distinction between Charlotte and Grace. For it turns out that the arch and brilliant Grace has failed to realize that her own husband, Victor, was also an arms trafficker who worked with Charlotte's husband, Leonard Douglas.[23] In fact, the large emerald in Charlotte Douglas's wedding ring was a gift from Victor Strasser to Leonard Douglas when the two men met secretly in Bogotá, Colombia, to arrange funding for the Tupamaros, a leftist guerrilla group in Uruguay. This wedding ring, a traditional patriarchal symbol of possession, is thus additionally a symbol of the covert relations between men, given by one husband to the other as part of a secret exchange of weapons in a Cold War proxy battle. Leonard Douglas reveals this information to Grace on the eve of a coup d'état in Boca Grande only because he needs Grace's help getting Charlotte out of the country. He also informs Grace that the guerrillas have received far more weapons than usual. The "script" Grace has assumed for this coup is incorrect.

These revelations turn the opposition between Grace and Charlotte on its head. Even though Grace owns most of Boca Grande, she ultimately doesn't know who is planning to overthrow it. "I had no idea," Grace eventually confesses. "I prided myself on listening and seeing and I had never even heard or seen that Edgar played the same games Gerardo played" (188). In fact, Grace is eventually forced to admit, "I am more like Charlotte than I thought I was" (210). Both women are married to clandestine Cold War power brokers. Both have suffered the "loss" of a rebellious child. If Charlotte seems a deluded and forgetful revisionist, these qualities soon infect Grace's narrative. Grace begins to tell us things she "remembers," only to correct herself: "I only think that. I never knew that. Empirically" (161–62). By the end of the novel, she is "less and less certain that this story has been one of delusion. Unless the delusion was mine" (213).

This sudden collapse of the narrator's radical distinction between naïveté and suspicion is ultimately the source of dysfunction that comes to haunt the narrative. The novel begins, "I will be her witness. That would translate *seré su testigo,* and will not appear in your travelers' phrasebook because it is not a useful phrase for the prudent traveler" (2). Crucially, Grace begins her narrative by interpolating the reader as a tourist, placing us in the role of Charlotte Douglas. By the end of the narrative, however, Grace is forced to admit, "I have not been the witness I wanted to be" (213).

The problem is not a moral failure; rather, an epistemological barrier has confined Grace to an outsider's position. "I no longer know what the real points are," she confesses (210). She is forced to "recognize the equivocal nature of even the most empirical evidence" (212).

So, too, is the reader. In perhaps the strongest indication of narrative dysfunction, the reader never understands Leonard's or Victor's real motives or affiliations. Leonard's support for the leftist Tupamaros seems consistent with his public work defending left-wing radicals, but it seems inconsistent with his frequent meetings with foreign military officials. In this novel, moreover, as in the Cold War, *funding* guerrillas is not the same as *supporting* guerrillas. In Boca Grande, supplying the *guerrilleros* is usually a feint of power brokers. In the end, Grace reminds us, "the *guerrilleros* would all be shot and the true players would be revealed" (161). Thus, Leonard's supplying the Tupamaros is as likely to be a CIA plot as the work of a revolutionary leftist. Because secrecy makes anything seem possible, explanatory narrative is compromised.

If Grace is a figure for the public-supposed-to-know, then this novel tells the story of how the public-supposed-to-know became the public-supposed-to-believe. Crucially, it relates this story through an allegory in which *both* aspects of the public are figured as women "out of the know." It is the particular status of Grace and Charlotte as women that bars them from knowledge of the male sphere in which covert deals happen. "All I know empirically," Grace concludes, "is *I am told*. I am told, and so she said. I heard later. According to her passport. It was reported. Apparently" (212). Inside knowledge is possessed by men. Women, even journalists, anthropologists, and historians, no matter how smart or sensitive, are at a remove from the clandestine events that shape the political world. Their relation to the covert world is like that of Offred to the commander: they cannot enter the world of male power but must rather intuit it by reading between the lines. The allegorical connection between the amnesic U.S. public and the marginalized woman is captured perfectly in Antonio Strasser's misogynistic epithet for Charlotte—"*norteamericana cunt*" (198). In case we miss the relation between the individual female body and the geopolitical, Grace tells us that Charlotte, in moving to Boca Grande, "believed she had located herself at the very cervix of the world, the place through which a child lost to history must eventually pass" (149).

At the allegorical level, radical children in these novels represent a "lost generation" in the United States. It is no accident that both of the rebellious daughters in *The Book of Common Prayer* and *Democracy* recall Patty Hearst, who was kidnapped and purportedly brainwashed into carrying out terrorist acts for the Symbionese Liberation Army in 1974.[24] Together, in fact, Jessie Victor and Marin Douglas embody the Janus-faced conundrum of Patty Hearst: on the one hand, Hearst seemed a drug-addled victim of her own privilege, like Jessie Victor; on the other, she seemed a zealous and hard-hearted revolutionary, like Marin Douglas. Hearst symbolized a generational rejection of mass publicity, for which the media empire of her father, William Randolph Hearst, was arguably the dominant U.S. symbol. If there was ever a single maker of the public-supposed-to-believe, the Hearst Corporation would be it. And hence it is significant that the family narratives in these novels include not only amnesic mothers but daughters whose rebellion implies a rejection of the public sphere's central institution.

In the Cold War, the public-supposed-to-know *cannot* know the details of covert government. Hence, the public-supposed-to-know is converted increasingly into a public-supposed-to-believe. Its original role is assumed by government institutions, which "enable the public-suppose-to-believe to believe that *someone* knows."[25] Didion's fiction figures this transformation through female bafflement over the flows of international power. In doing so, it reveals how the security state feminizes the public, shuttling it toward the putatively "apolitical" but "safe" space of the nineteenth-century domestic sphere.

The Journalist as Patsy

"In Bogotá," the 1974 essay that would become one basis for *A Book of Common Prayer,* begins with the problem that perpetually haunts Didion: "Of the time I spent in Bogotá I remember mainly images, indelible but difficult to connect."[26] This statement registers a hallmark of Didion's style. Explanatory narrative seems difficult and must be implied by striking but disconnected images. What makes the images so hard to connect in this case are the two distinct identities assumed by Didion—one as *"una turista norteamericana,"* the other as a reporter with an interest in revealing the violent history of Colombia to a U.S. audience. Not coincidentally, these are precisely the identities at the core of both *Democracy* and *The Book of Common Prayer.*

"In Bogotá" is structured to move the reader quietly from the perspective of a tourist to that of a journalist. Early in the essay, Didion paints an otherworldly picture of life in the "cool dining rooms" of elite Bogotá hotels, of soirees among U.S. diplomats and stylish Colombian artists and models. Later, as she moves into the rural countryside, she begins to note Bogotá's violent past—not only the distant European invasion but the 1953 coup of General Gustavo Rojas Pinilla, who was himself ousted in 1957 and was, at the time of Didion's visit, attempting a comeback on a Peronist platform.[27] The countryside is also dotted with signs of the Cold War— "crude representations of the hammer and sickle and admonitions to vote *Communista*" ("In Bogotá," 194). Eventually, Didion arrives at a massive salt mine built by the Banco de la República in 1954, when the Rojas Pinilla regime was beginning to flounder in its efforts to repress *La Violencia.* In this gargantuan mine, capable of supplying salt to all of South America, the Banco de la República carved a cathedral large enough for ten thousand worshippers. As Didion eats lunch in the hotel above this subterranean cathedral, she notes the absurd formality of the waiters, "as if this small inn on an Andean precipice were Vienna under the Hapsburgs" (196).

"In Bogotá" thus anticipates the architecture of *A Book of Common Prayer.* Didion first assumes the jet-setting posture of a Charlotte Douglas before moving to the more critical stance of a Grace Strasser. The essay's initial "images" explicitly evoke Charlotte. A Bogotá newspaper reports that Didion "resembles an American tourist" ("In Bogotá," 191). An airport worker tells Didion that her bags "smell American"—a comment repeated in *A Book of Common Prayer* when Gerardo tells Charlotte, "You smell American" (*Book of Common Prayer,* 152). The initial tone of "In Bogotá," moreover, evokes Charlotte's dream of selling the *New Yorker* a "letter from Boca Grande"—a naive tourist portrait of the "land of contrasts," the "economic fulcrum of the Americas" (*Book of Common Prayer,* 4–5). In Bogotá, Didion gazes at "the emeralds in shop windows"—an act that anticipates the novel's major symbol of male exchange and female unknowing. As Didion journeys away from the tourist section of "In Bogotá," her attention shifts from emeralds to salt—from a symbol of elite patriarchal display to a symbol of basic bodily need and human labor. The cathedral of

salt turns out not to be a remnant of European colonialism but a rare public works project of the Rojas Pinilla regime. Yet here, of all places, there
is another tourist locale—the hotel restaurant whose pleasant European
trappings evoke the history of Western empire atop the site of a salt mine
that supplies all of South America.

The unexplained juxtaposition of the essay's two major images—the
tourist paradise and the cathedral of salt—is signature Didion. What explains this laconic and brilliant arrangement, and why are the images so
"indelible but difficult to connect"? The answer lies in the "calculated
ellipsis" between these sites. The essay insinuates that its major images
are connected by certain features of the Cold War, U.S. empire, and the
relation of these things to *La Violencia*. But Didion suppresses any clear
narrative explanation of such relations, leaving only a single, telling clue.
Just before Didion departs the tourist zone for the Colombian countryside, she runs into members of the local "American presence," including
an impeccably mannered young "information officer" widely believed to
be with the CIA. "We had nothing in common," she notes of this man,
"except the eagles on our passports, but those eagles made us, in some
way I did not entirely understand, co-conspirators, two strangers heavy
with responsibility for seeing that the eagle should not offend" ("In Bogotá," 191). This is an important comment. Didion understands herself
here as an unwitting agent of the state. Although she does not "entirely
understand" her role, she knows it requires diplomacy, an ability to present the United States in the best light. For a journalist, this sort of diplomacy requires a capacity for repression or invention—a willingness
to offer "tourist" journalism in place of political reporting, or perhaps
a considered reluctance to explore the relation of a CIA presence to the
tourist trade, the export of natural resources, or *La Violencia*. The question raised by Didion's unsettling reflection, in other words, is whether a
journalist abroad is indeed a "co-conspirator" of the U.S. National Security State. After all, the covert nature of covert action is often determined
by the press.

The unexpected collusion of the journalist and the CIA agent here
resonates throughout Didion's fiction. The narrator of *Democracy,* for example, notes that CIA officers like Jack Lovett "view other people as wild-
cards…and they gravitate to occupations in which they can deal their own
hand" (*Democracy,* 36). But it is *Democracy*'s narrator who later calls Jessie

"the crazy eight in this narrative" (164), and it is the narrator who shares Jack Lovett's belief that

> all behavior was purposeful, and the purpose could be divined by whoever attracted the best information and read it most correctly. A Laotian village indicated on one map and omitted on another suggested not a reconnaissance oversight but a population annihilated.... A shipment of laser mirrors from Long Beach to a firm in Hong Kong that did no laser work suggested not a wrong invoice but a transshipment, reexport, the diversion of technology to unfriendly actors. All nations, to Jack Lovett, were "actors," specifically "state actors" ("nonstate actors" were the real wildcards here, but in Jack Lovett's extensive experience the average nonstate actor was less interested in the laser mirrors than in M-16s, AK-47s, FN-FALs). (36–37)

Democracy relies fundamentally on the narrator's assumption that the apparent "unpredictability of human behavior" is really "a higher predictability..., a more complex pattern discernible only after the fact" (215). This form of suspicion is in fact the basis of Didion's entire oeuvre. Like the "before" and "after" maps of the Laotian village, her writings present disparate images without explaining their connection—how the village disappeared, who supplied the mirrors to whom, how the Boca Grande rebels got their weapons, or who really supplied the Tupamaros. Didion wants to train her readers to read "calculated ellipses" as *apparent* accidents that must be suspected of having an underlying connection.

The question, then, is how to fill such gaps and who best to do it. Is it the work of the journalist or the novelist? This is a crucial question in all of the texts I have examined thus far, but it is especially pressing in Didion's 1996 novel, *The Last Thing He Wanted*.[28] Like Didion's earlier novels, this tale of arms dealing and assassination, based loosely on the Iran-Contra affair, is about a journalist's attempt to tell the story of another naive American woman who finds herself "over her head" in an international conflict (*Last Thing He Wanted,* 12). In this case, however, both women are journalists. The narrator is writing a *New York Times Magazine* article on Treat Morrison, a distinguished diplomat who, in his own words, became involved "in 1984 in the matter of what later became known as the lethal, as opposed to the humanitarian, resupply" of Nicaraguan rebels (44).[29] But through Morrison the narrator eventually stumbles onto the story of Elena McMahon, a reporter who was covering the 1984 U.S. presidential elections when she became the patsy in a U.S. intelligence plot designed to aid the Nicaraguan Contras. Like "In Bogotá," where Didion becomes the "co-conspirator" of a CIA agent, this novel asks us to consider how foreign correspondents, including the narrator, might become "patsies" for U.S. intelligence.

The Last Thing He Wanted is strikingly similar to *Democracy* and *A Book of Common Prayer.* Like Jack Lovett and Leonard Douglas, Treat Morrison is a keen reader of apparently inconsequential detail: he "had built an entire career on remembering the details that might turn out to be *wild cards,* using them, playing them" (*Last Thing He Wanted,* 155, emphasis added). The novel's narrator, like Grace Strasser and the "Joan Didion" of *Democracy,* shares this capacity for close reading, whereas the novel's protagonist, Elena McMahon, lacks it. Like Didion's other narrators, the "not quite omniscient author" (5) of *The Last Thing He Wanted* wishes to "come at this [story] straight," but she is also full of doubt about her own "reconstruction" of events (13). Elena McMahon, meanwhile, is a version of Inez Victor and Charlotte Douglas. She becomes briefly involved with one savvy navigator of the covert sector, Treat Morrison, and her father, Dick McMahon, is a Kennedy-era intelligence agent turned mercenary gunrunner. The story begins when Dick McMahon falls seriously ill and Elena agrees to be his courier in a million-dollar arms deal that will set him up for retirement. But after she is flown to a secret base in Costa Rica, her passport is stolen and she is whisked away to a Caribbean island, where she becomes a pawn in a CIA plot.

The centerpiece of this operation is a bogus assassination attempt against the island's U.S. ambassador, Alex Brokaw, who has been advocating a major U.S. military buildup in the area. After the attempt on the ambassador's life, Treat Morrison begins to suspect the attack is a false flag operation of U.S. intelligence: the Honduran gunmen suddenly disappear; a potential witness turns up dead; the timing of the attack seems conveniently tied to legislative sessions on aid to the Contras; and lots of serious-looking U.S. men have been flooding the island following numerous "fact finding" missions conducted by a brash, young senatorial aide. In short, a host of clues imply to Morrison "that Alex Brokaw, in an effort to lay the foundation for a full-scale covert buildup on the island, had himself put the assassination into play and was now lending credibility to the report with further suggestions of American personnel under siege" (174). When Morrison flies to the island to conduct his own investigation, he finds that Elena

McMahon has been set up to take the blame. When he attempts to get her back to the United States, both he and Elena are shot, and Elena is killed.

These events are totally misrepresented by the press. After Morrison is evacuated for medical treatment, the Associated Press (AP) labels Elena McMahon the "suspected assassin" (220). The next day, officials discover Sandinista literature that has been planted in Elena's room, and the U.S. embassy reports the "capture" of a phony arms shipment. The AP then completes the government's work with a follow-up story reporting that rumors of Elena "supplying arms and other aid to the Sandinista government in Nicaragua" have been "incontrovertibly corroborated" (220). Elena McMahon is thus made a patsy, but she is not the only one. The entire press corps has been converted from guarantors of the public sphere to unwitting tools of U.S. intelligence.

Here Didion suggests that the journalist's impulse to fill a gap can lead to a dysfunctional history. Despite six hundred stories on Elena McMahon, the newspaper reporting on the case is "less than fruitful" (11). The problem is not simply that information has been suppressed. "There are documents, more than you might think," says the narrator. "Depositions, testimony, cable traffic, some of it not yet declassified but much in the public record" (10). As with the Kennedy assassination, part of the problem is the sheer magnitude of potentially relevant data, which includes "ten volumes, two thousand five hundred and seven pages, sixty-three days of testimony":

> There was for example the airline that operated out of St. Lucia but had its headquarters in Frankfurt (Volume VII, Chapter 4, "Implementing the Decision to Take Policy Underground") and either was or was not (conflicting testimony on this) ninety-nine percent owned by a former Air West flight attendant who either did or did not live on St. Lucia. There was for example the team of unidentified men (Volume X, Chapter 2, "Supplemental Material on the Diversion") who either did or did not (more conflicting testimony) arrive on the northern Costa Rican border to burn the bodies of the crew of the unmarked DC-3 that at the time it crashed appeared to be registered to the airline that was or was not ninety-nine percent owned by the former Sky West flight attendant who did or did not live on St. Lucia. (10–11)

The epistemological problem here is not simply secrecy but also a proliferation of facts—some accurate, some fabricated, and all "indelible but difficult to connect" ("In Bogotá," 193). The year 1984, according to the narrator of *The Last Thing He Wanted,* "was a period during which a significant minority among the population at large appears to have understood how government funds earmarked for humanitarian aid might be diverted, even as the General Accounting Office monitored the accounts, to more pressing needs" (54–55). Yet even the savvy historian of such a project faces a version of the historical sublime in which the sheer volume of potentially relevant data makes a coherent explanatory narrative exceptionally difficult.[30]

Didion explicitly attributes vexed historiography under these conditions to the "daunting structural obstacles" of the state: "entire layers of bureaucracy dedicated to the principle that self-perpetuation depended on the ability not to elucidate but to obscure" (169). The structural obfuscation of the clandestine state requires the astute observer to employ the analytic habit of a Treat Morrison, Jack Lovett, Grace Strasser, or "Joan Didion." The keen observer, for instance, may notice minor wire stories on the chartered aircraft of "spectral companies with high concept names (*Amalgamated Commercial Enterprises Inc., Defex S.A., Energy Resources International*)" that failed to leave an airport or crashed or were discovered to be carrying military weapons (67). But when such connections are discerned, they are hard to confirm in accordance with standard journalistic practice. "Some people in Washington said that [such] flights *could not be* occurring, or *could only be* occurring, *if indeed they were* occurring, outside the range of possible knowledge" (68). The public record here is a record of both unknowing and public knowledge of this unknowing.

The result is profound historical skepticism and amnesia. News reports like the one on Elena McMahon's connection to the Sandinistas, the narrator sardonically notes, are "history's rough draft. We used to say. When we believed that history merited a second look" (11). The accusation in these lines—that we have forgotten the events of the 1980s and we have forgotten to be critical of what is presented as news—is directed at both the press and the reader. Like Grace Strasser, the narrator of *The Last Thing He Wanted* assumes the novel's reader is part of the public-supposed-to-believe, a forgetful tourist like Charlotte Douglas. She deliberately conceals the name of the island so that our memories of

Caribbean travel—"the metallic taste of tinned juice in rum punches," "the Jet Ski misunderstanding," the "coconut oil"—do not "get in the way" (89).[31] "If you remember 1984, which I notice fewer and fewer of us care to do," she jabs, then perhaps you can understand Elena's story. "Cast your mind back," she encourages us. "Refresh your memory if necessary: go to Nexis, go to microfiche" (67). Ultimately, however, such efforts cannot produce a traditional history. "I still believe in history," she says before one of her many revisions. "Let me amend that. I still believe in history to the extent that I believe history to be made exclusively and at random by people like Dick McMahon. There are still more people like Dick McMahon around than you might think" (33).

This assumption explains the appeal of fiction to a journalist like Didion. If the Cold War security state is the arbiter of public discourse, then explanation is difficult not only for *la turista* but also for the reporter. One can speculate; one can juxtapose interesting and disturbing facts; but one struggles to *report* the connection between these facts under the protocols of the correspondent. As Alan Nadel points out, "Whereas the journalist depends on received information, the novelist depends on invented information," and yet "the journalist is always already one more fictional frame," for without "the impulse of the fiction writer … a journalist would be *dysfunctional*" and "could not render a coherent version of events."[32] Indeed, in *The Last Thing He Wanted,* the shooting of Elena McMahon and Treat Morrison must ultimately be invented. "Imagine how this went down," writes the narrator, implying that she must fill in documentary narrative with fiction (*Last Thing He Wanted,* 221). Invention is the mode of choice here because it allows the narrative to proceed. But Didion also makes an ethical choice *not* to smooth the gaps in the record. By pointing up her own speculation and allowing ellipses to disrupt a satisfying narrative, she teaches the reader how to identify the obscure traces of the covert sector.

Even working under this self-imposed injunction, Didion worries that she has adopted the methods of the intelligence operative. This is why she casts herself as a "co-conspirator" of the CIA in "In Bogotá"; it is why her narrators are so much like Jack Lovett, Treat Morrison, and Leonard Douglas; and it is why her fiction compulsively depicts a brilliant female journalist agonizing over the possibility that her own "reconstruction" of events will not only fail to explain but will mask the real movement of chess pieces, wild cards, and tokens of power on the international game board.

Metafiction in Wartime

It is one thing to claim that postmodernism reflects the National Security State when one's examples come from fictions about covert action. But what about texts that have little explicit relation to foreign affairs? I want to close this chapter by suggesting that Cold War institutions may have shaped postmodernism in ways that have been overlooked. My example is a landmark in the history of postmodern narrative, John Barth's 1967 metafictional story "Lost in the Funhouse."[33] Published just before the Tet offensive, the story is both a coming-of-age tale and an intensely self-conscious parable about fiction writing itself. It is the story of Ambrose, a sensitive and artistic thirteen-year-old boy, who goes with his family to an amusement park in Ocean City during World War II to celebrate the Fourth of July. Ostensibly, the story relates Ambrose's awkward and ultimately abortive attempt to traverse the funhouse with a fourteen-year-old girl named Magda. In Baxter's terms, the text is profoundly "dysfunctional." The narrator avoids causal explanation, constantly interrupting the story's forward progress to comment on its rhetorical elements. These comments reveal the funhouse as a symbol of both sexual knowledge and narrative itself. The narrator halts the story to present the classic model of literary plot, "Freitag's triangle," and notes that "in a perfect funhouse you'd be able to go only one way" (85). But Ambrose can no more find a linear path through the funhouse than the narrator can through the story. Long after the moment when "we should have passed the apex of Freitag's triangle and made brief work of the *dénouement,*" Ambrose has missed the climax, lost track of Magda, and become stuck in the funhouse. Although he "wishes he had never entered," he consoles himself that "he will construct funhouses for others and be their secret operator" (97).

Just prior to this conclusion, the narrator asks abruptly and inexplicably, "What relevance does the war have for the story? Should there be fireworks outside or not?" (96). This is an important question, for it concerns the narrative's twinning of sex and narrative and its own historical context just after Vietnam shifted from a secret to a public war. In his foreword to the 1987 edition, Barth notes that the collection was written and assembled between 1966 and 1968,

> a time of more than unusual ferment in American social, political, and artistic life. Our unpopular war in Vietnam, political assassinations, race riots, the hippie counterculture, pop art, mass poetry readings, street theater, vigorous avant-gardes as in all the arts, together with dire predictions not only of the death of the novel but of the moribundity of the print medium in the electronic global village—those flavored the air we breathed then, along with occasional tear gas and other contaminants. One may sniff traces of that air in the *Funhouse*. (vii–viii)

What relevance, then, does the war have for "Lost in the Funhouse"? The story is set during World War II, but the conflict seems distant. Its only signs are the spoiling of the Ocean City surf by a sunken oil tanker and the cancellation of the traditional fireworks because of enemy U-boats. But the cancellation of the fireworks is more important than it might initially seem. Fireworks are a symbol of climax, and their cancellation ties the story's endless deferral of sexual and narrative knowledge to the distant war. Barth explicitly stresses both meanings of fireworks, which function as an analogue to "going all the way" through the funhouse (80). When Uncle Carl asks suggestively "if they were going to have fireworks that night," Ambrose's mother replies that "she could do without fireworks: they reminded her too much of the real thing," to which Ambrose's father replies, "All the more reason to shoot off a few now and then" (81). But in this dysfunctional narrative, there are no fireworks. The war has made them impossible. This is its "relevance...for the story." If the story is about the difficulty of attaining knowledge—sexual and narrative—then war is the source of its dysfunction.

Perhaps this is why the epiphany in the story—the intellectual revelation that substitutes for the traditional climax—is Ambrose's sudden and overwhelming vision of his own unknowing: "Nothing was what it looked like. Every instant, under the surface of the Atlantic Ocean, millions of living animals devoured one another. Pilots were falling in flames over Europe; women were being forcibly raped in the South Pacific.... If you knew all the stories behind all the people on the boardwalk, you'd see that *nothing* was what it looked like" (90–91). If this story is about the difficulty of obtaining traditional forms of knowledge, what it supplies in their place is an awareness of how hard it is to know. Ambrose's difficulty with knowing "in the biblical sense" (it is no accident that the other young characters are named Peter and Magdalene) is a result of his sensitivity, tolerance for ambiguity, and interest in the "nonserious" business of fiction writing. If leaving the funhouse with this knowledge would be the equivalent of completing a conventional linear narrative, then this deliberately dysfunctional metafiction instead conveys a sense that, in a time of war, it is hard to know what things really "look like" and hard to tell traditional stories.

What may seem a strikingly ahistorical and playful metafiction thus turns out to be substantially influenced by the problem of Cold War public knowledge. It is no accident that Barth returned twenty years later to this context, reinfusing the aesthetic experiment of "Lost in the Funhouse" with a sense of historical context. If Vietnam "flavored the air" in which this story was written, then might it have influenced the construction of a narrative that everywhere investigates its own claims to knowledge? The answer is yes—not because postmodern narrative is fundamentally *about* the Cold War, but because it is about knowing, and questions of public knowing could not go far in the acrid climate of the late 1960s without entering the problematic space of the covert sphere.

5

Postmodern Amnesia

Assassins of Memory

Poor David Webb. Webb—aka Jason Bourne, the CIA assassin created by Robert Ludlum and catapulted to Hollywood fame by the directors Doug Liman and Paul Greengrass—cannot remember who he is or what he has done. What he does know is that his work has not been nice. He possesses astonishing physical and mental skills. He is a preternaturally keen observer, a master of strategy, and a lethal human weapon. He is also deeply unhappy and dangerous to everyone he likes.[1]

Like many late twentieth-century literary amnesiacs, Bourne turns out to be a casualty of U.S. intelligence. His memories were disappeared as part of the CIA's secret "Treadstone" program, a latter-day version of Korean War–era brainwashing. But if the assassin of Richard Condon's 1959 *Manchurian Candidate* was the unwitting pawn of an enemy mind-control program, then the post–Cold War situation has changed radically. Bourne is a pawn of the *U.S.* security state. In the late twentieth-century cultural imaginary, the state has cynically embraced brainwashing as just one more tool for producing assets who will do "whatever it takes" to save U.S. lives. "No red tape," explains Treadstone's director. "No more getting bad guys in our sights and then watching them escape while we wait for some bureaucrat to issue the order." More important still, Treadstone allows both the U.S. public and the state's agents to live guilt free, untroubled by disturbing memories of foul (but "necessary") deeds. If the Cold War public "can't handle the truth," as Colonel Jessup scornfully shouts in *A Few Good Men,* neither, apparently, can the agents of the state. What, then, could be better than a program of covert operations that *no one* remembered, not even its perpetrators?[2]

This fantasy is not new. Bourne comes from a long line of unwitting fictional assassins. James Bond was a brainwashed amnesiac in *The Man with the Golden Gun* (1965). Philip K. Dick's iconic 1966 story, "We Can Remember It for You Wholesale" (later adapted by Paul Verhoeven into *Total Recall* [1990]), is about the uncanny deletion and reimplantation of a secret agent's memories of covert action. Similarly forgetful state servants have surfaced with increasing frequency over the past fifty years, featuring in visual productions including *Codename Icarus* (1981), *Jacob's Ladder* (1990), *The Long Kiss Goodnight* (1996), *Conspiracy Theory* (1997), *Menno's Mind* (1997), *The Sleep Room* (1998), *Time Lapse* (2001), *Alias* (2001–06), *Blind Horizon* (2003), *Paycheck* (2003), *Second Nature* (2003), *The Manchurian Candidate* (1962 and 2004), *Torture Room* (2007), *My Own Worst Enemy* (2008), *XIII: The Conspiracy* (2008), *Dollhouse* (2009), *Salt* (2010), *Homeland* (2011), and even the video game *Call of Duty: Black Ops* (2010).[3]

Not all covert sphere narratives explain amnesia through the implausible mechanism of mind control. Jess Walter's brilliant post-9/11 novel, *The Zero,* is the Kafkaesque tale of a New York City police officer, Brian Remy, whose traumatic amnesia prevents him from understanding how his work for a top secret security agency is producing some of the very threats he is investigating. Steven Gahgan's 2005 film, *Syriana*—based mainly on Robert Baer's scathing indictment of the CIA, *See No Evil* (2002)—explains unwitting assassination much more prosaically. The CIA veteran Bob Barnes (a fictional version of Baer) plans the assassination of a Middle Eastern prince because his Langley superiors tell him the prince is a terrorist funder and a "bad guy." In fact, however, the prince is a liberal reformer in the style of Mohammed Mossadeq (the Iranian prime minister overthrown by the CIA's "Operation Ajax" in 1953); his only crime is trying to help his country benefit more from the sale of oil rights. In Baer's world, robust amnesia is not necessary to ensure that the assassin "sees no evil" in his work; bureaucratic compartmentalization does the trick. As the Washington insider Dean Whiting later tells Barnes, "Your entire career you've been used and probably never even known what for."[4]

Nonetheless, covert action and faulty memory are repeatedly linked—and not only in fiction. As I noted in chapter 2, the political scientist Michael Rogin sees public "amnesia" as a necessary precondition of covert U.S. foreign policy. Rogin has in mind not a state program of memory control like the ones imagined by Condon, Ludlum, or Dick, but an ideological system of "easily forgettable...movies, television series, political shows." For Rogin, paradoxically, the incessant *revelation* of covert action in such "surface entertainments" allows the public "both to have the experience and not to retain it in memory." The result is both "motivated forgetting"—a concept similar to Freudian repression—and a tendency to conflate actual and fictional images of the past. When democracy relies on "entertainments" to provide public knowledge of its secret affairs, the contradictions of empire are "normalized to invisibility" through a blurring of fictional and real operations.[5]

Why the repeated association of covert action and amnesia? Why do so many writers understand clandestine foreign policy through themes of *forgetting*—psychic repression, traumatic amnesia, and recovered memory—instead of concealment, deception, and secrecy? One reason is that psychic repression helps theorize public *half*-knowledge of postwar U.S. empire. The radical self-division of Jason Bourne, for instance, represents the public's simultaneous knowing and unknowing. Bourne is at once an innocent, patriotic American (Matt Damon was cast perfectly in the role) and a ruthless assassin. Although he loathes his work and fights his former agency, it turns out that he volunteered for covert duty. "You *chose* the program," his CIA trainer reminds him.[6] It is only long after he has requested this patriotic assignment that the state's dirty work begins to trouble him in the form of intrusive, if sketchy, memories of horrible deeds.

In all of these regards, then, Jason Bourne is remarkably like the U.S. public, which accedes to the abrogation of democracy on principle and is later shocked when the details of official subterfuge and violence surface in the press. Like the public, Bourne knows he has done unspeakable things, but he does not quite know what they are. Like Bourne, the public toler-ates covert actions by "forgetting" them, and the state assists in this dis-avowal by classifying the details of such actions. Bourne thus allegorizes public knowledge in the covert sphere. The state's erasure of his memories conceptualizes the effects of state secrecy through a fantasy in which not even a state assassin can remember his defense of the realm.

Like most spy melodramas, the Bourne trilogy is conflicted in its stance on covert action. On the one hand, the plot critiques state secrecy, depicting the CIA as a menace whose defeat is among the pleasures of the drama. On the other hand, the film locates narrative pleasure in the astonishing skills of the covert agent, which are not only placed in the service of the public but are also absolutely necessary in combating the state's perverse use of secrecy for undemocratic goals. Like most amnesia plots, the Bourne story is ultimately more about remembering than forgetting. While it depicts the security state as a black hole of secrets, it eventually reveals these secrets to public scrutiny, "healing" the wounded public sphere with the light of publicity. Yet this fantasy of democracy restored comes in the "nonserious" vehicle of melodrama, which has the paradoxical effect of inviting its view-ers to dismiss covert action as an exaggeration that can, in any case, be cor-rected by the restoration of the democratic public sphere.

Amnesia is thus a prominent trope of the covert sphere, a way of ad-dressing the problem of democracy in an era of covert foreign policy. But that is only part of the story. Amnesia is also a major trope of postmodern

Figure 9. After breaking into a top secret training facility, David Webb (aka Jason Bourne, played by Matt Damon, right) finally recalls that he willfully executed a prisoner to complete his CIA training.

aesthetics and theory, particularly the view that the difficulty of grounding historical narratives has led to dangerous forms of collective forgetting. Fredric Jameson, David Harvey, and Jean Baudrillard all suggest that postmodernity is characterized by an ahistorical nostalgia and diminished historical consciousness. For Jameson, postmodernism is a mode in which "the past as 'referent' finds itself gradually bracketed, and then effaced altogether, leaving us with nothing but texts" and condemning us "to seek History by way of our own pop images and simulacra of that history, which itself remains forever out of reach." Baudrillard finds historical referentiality so crippled that he has called the Vietnam War a series of simulations that "sealed the end of history." One of Harvey's chief examples of postmodernism is the 1988 film *Blade Runner*—an adaptation of *Do Androids Dream of Electric Sheep?* by the amnesia-obsessed, sci-fi giant Philip K. Dick—in which a group of humanoid "replicants" is controlled by fabricated memories of their nonexistent childhoods. And a favorite example of "postmodern relativism" is Holocaust denial—whose perpetrators are, in the words of Pierre Vidal-Naquet, "assassins of memory."[7] Such representations of the postmodern suggest that the recent surge of stories about traumatic amnesia is an expression of vexed historiography.

Far from being simply a reflection of the covert sphere, then, amnesia has become a cultural obsession. Mnemonic aids have come back into fashion. The "Memory Olympics" has gained in popularity. A new literary culture has shaped itself around the memoir. Innumerable critics have asserted that we live in "an age of forgetting" and suffer from some variety of "historical amnesia."[8] At the turn of the twenty-first century a major press published an "amnesia anthology," and full-blown amnesia has become an organizing feature of both innovative fiction (by writers such as Steven Erikson, Lydia Davis, Kathy Acker, Douglas Cooper, Jonathan Lethem, and Jess Walter) and popular cinema (*Memento, Eternal Sunshine of the Spotless Mind, Mulholland Drive,* and *The Adjustment Bureau* are the least forgettable). At the same time, an increasingly familiar array of traumatic amnesias—the results of everything from brain injury and brainwashing to multiple personality disorder and satanic ritual abuse—have become cultural obsessions.[9] Ongoing debate over failures of memory—such as multiple personality disorder and "recovered memory syndrome"—reveals the necessity but also the difficulty of relying on individual memory as a record of the past. The inability of individuals to access their own traumatic pasts in turn suggests the inability of historians to "re-member" the past. Such difficulties reflect the postmodern condition: the fragmentation of the self into parts not available to consciousness or memory; the inability to distinguish between authentic memories and simulations; and the difficulty of finding sound correspondences between past events and the narratives that purport to describe those events.

On the one hand, then, amnesia is a pervasive trope for the historiographical dilemma of postmodernism, a way of articulating the conditions of knowledge in postwar society through the psychoanalytic framework of repression, disavowal, and forgetting. On the other hand, amnesia is a prominent trope of the covert sphere, a way of addressing the problem of democracy in an era of covert foreign policy. The coincidence of these two matters is no accident, for as I have been arguing, U.S. postmodernism was substantially shaped by the institutions of the Cold War. Rogin's linking of covert foreign policy to amnesia, for instance, is explicitly an account of "postmodern American empire." Yet the popular thrillers with which I began this discussion are not postmodern in any aesthetic sense. Whereas postmodern narrative emphasizes the difficulty of knowing, the espionage thriller confidently supplies "secrets" of the covert world in the form of melodramatic fantasy.

How, then, does postmodern narrative represent the "amnesia" produced by the National Security State? In what follows, I turn to Tim O'Brien's remarkable 1994 novel *In the Lake of the Woods,* which recounts the My Lai massacre through a disturbing tale of posttraumatic amnesia. Before I come to this example, however, I need to sketch more fully how the concept of postmodernism reflects the problem of public knowledge in an era of state secrecy. Not only has postmodernism persistently addressed "historical amnesia," but its engagement with the politics of memory explicitly evolved around the dialectics of spectacle and secrecy structuring the covert sphere.

The Dialectics of Spectacle and Secrecy

There is nothing particularly new about the notion that mass media and late capitalism produce a passive and forgetful citizenry. This view was crucial to the Frankfurt School and it later received perhaps its most influential articulation in Guy Debord's 1967 *Society of the Spectacle,* which portrays late twentieth-century Western society as a network of images that mediate all social relationships, foster apathy, and ultimately falsify our knowledge of the world. The theme of amnesia runs through *The Society of the Spectacle.* The spectacle, Debord argues, fulfills Napoleon's dream of "monarchically directing the energy of memories":

> The pseudo-events that vie for attention in the spectacle's dramatizations...are quickly forgotten, thanks to the precipitation with which the spectacle's pulsing machinery replaces one with the next. At the same time, everything really lived has no relation to society's official version....And it is misunderstood and forgotten to the benefit of the spectacle's false memory of the unmemorable. The spectacle, being the reigning social organization of a paralyzed history, of a paralyzed memory, of an abandonment of any history founded in historical time, is in effect a *false consciousness of time.*[10]

Less extravagant, but similar, claims about postmodern nostalgia and ahistoricism run through other influential critiques, most notably those of Baudrillard and Jameson. Indeed, an entire line of thinking about postmodernism is indebted to *The Society of the Spectacle,* particularly its emphasis on how cultural institutions enforce the ideology of late capitalism. This line of thinking, which is the basis of Rogin's understanding of postmodernism, reflects the late Cold War era in which it was developed. Toward the end of the Reagan-Bush era, for instance, the televised Gulf War spectacularly ratified accounts of postmodernism as a depthless veneer of simulacra shielding the foreign operations of U.S. empire.

By the end of the Cold War, however, a new model of postmodernism had begun to displace the one focused on commodity culture, spectacle, and global capitalism. The new approach tended to see postmodern skepticism as a more positive expression of historiographic complexity. Interestingly, this model also placed forgetting front and center, but it emphasized the role of trauma as a model for the recovery of lost, forgotten, or "secret" histories. Scholars such as Linda Hutcheon, Diane Elam, and Amy Elias found benefits in historiographical skepticism and parody, and they observed that postmodernists had updated the historical romance to critique the ideological process by which history is constructed. Many of their central literary examples concerned traumatic events repressed from popular historical consciousness. As Amy Elias argues, much postmodern narrative rests on a "posttraumatic imaginary."[11]

In other words, if postmodern *spectacle* seemed to Michael Rogin "the cultural form for amnesic representation" during the Reagan-Bush era, then by the turn of the century *trauma* had taken its place. Scholars of postmodern narrative increasingly emphasized the discursive construction of history, especially the exclusion of certain painful events from canonical, orthodox, public histories. It is worth noting the influence of the Cold War on this process. As a number of scholars have demonstrated, a substantial ideological apparatus has long managed the production of U.S. history textbooks as a vehicle of mandatory education.[12] This institutional effect contributed to the growing sense that the work of the writer was to make visible the "secret" or "repressed" content of the collective unconscious—particularly traumatic histories of marginalized subjects—in a form that explained how dominant histories could have repressed this material in the first place. Historiographic metafiction and posttraumatic narrative became major vehicles of this impulse at the end of the twentieth century.[13]

While trauma replaced spectacle as a primary subject of discourse on postmodernism, it retained a focus on the problem of vexed historical reference. As Cathy Caruth explains in her influential 1996 account, trauma is both a model of "historical witness" and a kind of "unclaimed experience." The central feature of trauma for Caruth is not "the direct experience of the threat, but precisely the *missing* of the experience, the fact that...it has not yet been fully known."[14] To put this claim in Rogin's terms, traumatized persons tend "both to have the experience and not to retain it in memory."[15] But Caruth goes a step further. For her, traumatized persons so excise their experience from consciousness that they never truly experience it in the first place: "The historical power of the trauma is not just that the experience is repeated after forgetting, but that it is only in and through its inherent forgetting that it is first experienced at all." It is this notion of secondhand experience that makes trauma a powerful model of history. The patient's struggle to recover a "missed" trauma is like the historian's struggle to recover an impersonal past—a past that cannot simply be "remembered." The meaning of trauma is for Caruth so historiographic that even Freud's major study of traumatic neurosis is in the end a study of history: "*Beyond the Pleasure Principle,*" she writes, "ultimately asks what it would mean to understand history as the history of trauma."[16] The answer suggested by much late twentieth-century scholarship is that it would mean understanding the crucial elements of history to be inaccessible to collective consciousness—repressed, invisible, or "secret."

Spectacle and trauma are thus emblems of the two dominant scholarly approaches to postmodernism: on the one hand, the postmodernism of Jameson, Baudrillard, Mark Poster, and Hal Foster, with its emphasis on commodity culture and simulacra (Warhol's "Diamond Dust Shoes," the Bonaventure Hotel, the Gulf War); and, on the other hand, the postmodernism of Hutcheon, Elam, and Elias, with its more sanguine view that historiographic metafiction issues a progressive challenge to orthodox histories by recovering repressed sources of collective pain (as in the fiction of Leslie Marmon Silko, Toni Morrison, Pat Barker, E. L. Doctorow, and many others). Crucially, although critics began to shift emphasis from spectacle to trauma, the emphasis on cultural repression and forgetting stayed the same. Both approaches express concern about forgetting and other aberrations of memory: déjà vu, selective memorialization, collective "screen memories," "collective repression," "social amnesia," "motivated forgetting," "organized forgetting," and repressed memory.[17]

What do these two general approaches to postmodernism have to do with the covert sphere? First, their objects—public spectacles and traumatic secrets—jointly articulate the major conceptual opposition of the covert sphere. Second, each approach itself addresses how the public could miss, misrecognize, disavow, or forget important recent events. In brief, postmodern theory is centrally concerned with epistemological problems like those generated within the covert sphere. Yet postmodernism is obviously not limited to the matter of the Cold War. Its objects of study are much more diverse. How, then, does "collective amnesia" about covert action relate to collective amnesia about other traumatic historical episodes, such as American slavery, Native American genocide, immigrant and minority experience, and other national shames?[18] It is helpful to distinguish three separate problems of knowledge entangled in the discourse on cultural memory. First, there is the general historiographic problem of narrating events that one did not witness, a problem opened up by modernist perspectivism and taken to its limits in poststructuralist and postmodernist skepticism. Second, there are the ideological screens of political spectacle and canonical history that tend to obscure painful or shameful events. Third, there is the deliberate state suppression of publicly relevant information. State secrecy produces public unknowing that augments, but exceeds, the unknowing generated by the first two problems. The state keeps some major policy actions from public view for more than a generation. This practice has crucial political and cultural effects. Yet state secrecy has its greatest effect by encouraging the disavowal of contradictions within democracy. In other words, while we should not discount the repressive effects of state secrecy (in the sense of Foucault's "repressive hypothesis"), the most powerful effects of state repression are ideological in nature.

Secret History

I turn now to a novel that links the problems of state secrecy and amnesia in an unusually sophisticated way, Tim O'Brien's *In the Lake of the Woods*.[19] O'Brien's novel depicts a traumatic event that cannot be remembered by anyone—including its narrator, its author, and its protagonist. The latter is John Wade, a career Minnesota politician and Vietnam veteran once known to his comrades as "Sorcerer." As the novel opens, Wade, a Democrat running for U.S. Senate in Minnesota, has just lost the primary after revelations that he participated in the slaughter of several hundred Vietnamese civilians in the hamlet of Thuan Yen, an event commonly known in the United States as the My Lai massacre. After his crushing political defeat, Wade and his wife, Kathy, retreat to an isolated cabin in the northern Minnesota lake country where, one night, Kathy mysteriously disappears. Wade may—or may not—have murdered her. He cannot remember. What he does remember of that night is boiling a kettle of water and pouring it on all the houseplants while muttering "Kill Jesus"—the most hateful expression he could conjure. And he recalls, shortly thereafter, boiling another kettle and bringing it to the bedroom, where he watched Kathy sleep. But he cannot recall whether he poured the boiling water on her face and then sank her deep in the lake, along with their motorboat, or whether he simply went to sleep and awoke to find that she had deserted him. In the morning, he is surprised and worried that she is missing. Over the next weeks he searches loyally for her, despite a constant "burn of guilt" that his "faulty memory" has erased a horrible truth (192). The mystery of Kathy's disappearance continues right up to the end of the novel, when Wade, too, "disappears," taking a boat north to Canada. We never find out what has become of either John or Kathy Wade.

O'Brien's novel is about the relation between secrecy and amnesia. In some ways, the narrative resembles postwar noir tales in which an amnesic detective begins to suspect himself. But *In the Lake of the Woods* is much more unconventional in the way it interweaves Wade's struggle to remember Kathy's disappearance with his memories of the massacre at Thuan Yen, and eventually with other historical genocides. O'Brien, in other words, makes it clear that Wade's individual case of amnesia is inseparable from more serious collective-memory failures. By offering no final explanation—only a vast historical apparatus that cannot explain its central trauma—the narrative's radical ambiguity indicts the amnesia of the public and the dysfunction of the public sphere. And yet the novel warns *against* this collective historical amnesia through a tale of profound individual amnesia.

This contradiction explains the multiple oddities of O'Brien's novel. First, *In the Lake of the Woods* has an unusually self-negating plot structure. It contains both the story of John Wade's traumatic life and a frame story about another veteran's attempt to unravel Wade's mystery. This second figure, the novel's narrator, is an obsessive researcher who tries—but ultimately fails—to get to the bottom of Kathy's disappearance. In place of a final explanation, he offers eight different hypotheses about Kathy's disappearance: she was murdered, committed suicide, got lost in the woods, ran away from John, and so on. Each hypothesis is a chapter-long imaginative reconstruction that sometimes enters Kathy's point of view, but only after the narrator has warned us that he is merely speculating. In addition to his speculations, the narrator provides seven chapters of "evidence," which consist entirely of short quotations from those who knew the Wades and from various historical documents and texts. These statements are arranged so as to offer provocative commentary on the novel's primary story.

O'Brien takes great pains to simulate the facticity of his narrator's research. The narrator provides 136 often elaborate citations, some of which refer to real texts, others of which are spurious (for example, "transcript, Court-Martial of Lieutenant William Calley, U.S. National Archives, box 4, folder 8, p. 1735" [264n107]).[20] Increasingly, the notes become confessional descriptions of the narrator's "four years of hard labor" (30n21) researching the book. As the Wade mystery lingers, the narrator claims to "lose sleep over mute facts and frayed ends" (269n120) and even quotes the Wades' exasperated relatives telling him that his obsession with the case is irritating them (194, 266, 269). Like the most scrupulous of biographers, he warns us that "much of what might appear to be fact in this narrative— action, word, thought—must ultimately be viewed as a diligent but still imaginative reconstruction of events" (30n21). By the end of the novel, he has thrown up his hands, saying, "Who will ever know? It's all hypothesis, beginning to end" (303). In short, our intrepid narrator's own skepticism has undone him. He is like Nicholas Branch, the endlessly frustrated CIA historian in Don DeLillo's *Libra,* who, despite years of research, can never bring himself to write the agency's official history of the Kennedy assassination.

When it comes to historical blockage, however, *In the Lake of the Woods* takes a radical bound past *Libra.* DeLillo's novel confines much of its skepticism to brief sections about Nicholas Branch while its primary narrative offers a clearly dramatized, fictional account of the Kennedy assassination. O'Brien's novel, on the other hand, extends historiographic uncertainty into its primary narrative by refusing to solve the mystery of Kathy Wade's disappearance. In this regard it exceeds even Didion's most elliptical productions, for not even the man *present* at the novel's central event can recall what happened. On the night of Kathy's disappearance, we are told,

> a ribbon of time went by, which [John Wade] would not remember, then later he found himself crouched at the side of the bed...watching Kathy sleep....He would remember smoothing back her hair. He would remember pulling a blanket to her chin and then returning to the living room, where for a long while he lost track of his whereabouts....The unities of time and space had unraveled. There were manifold uncertainties, and in the days and weeks to come, memory would play devilish little tricks on him....At one point during the night he stood waist-deep in the lake. At another point he found himself completely submerged, lungs like stone, an underwater rush in his ears. (*Lake of the Woods,* 50–52)

Whereas historical uncertainty haunts Didion's narrators and DeLillo's historian, it haunts O'Brien's protagonist himself, who suffers profound traumatic amnesia.

But there is another oddity to Wade's amnesia. While he cannot recall his actions on the night of Kathy's disappearance, he *does* remember the intensely traumatic events at Thuan Yen, where he ran and hid from the butchery of his comrades, and then, in two separate moments of panic, shot an elderly Vietnamese man and a member of his own unit, PFC Weatherby. Wade's troubled memories of these acts and the horrific slaughter directed by his commander, Lieutenant William Calley, return repeatedly, despite Wade's intense efforts to erase them from his mind and from the historical record. Wade also remembers, in vivid detail, the traumas of his childhood—particularly his alcoholic father's suicide. His experience thus reverses the classic psychoanalytic model of traumatic repetition, and the more recent phenomenon of "repressed memory syndrome," in which an *early* event is repressed only to return through later unconscious repetition or neurosis. Here, it is the ultimate event that is forgotten only after the earlier ones have come more fully to mind. This is a case not only of "robust repression"—to use the term of the recovered-memory movement critics Richard Ofshe and Margaret Thaler Singer—but of *instantaneous* robust repression.[21]

The question, then, is why O'Brien has marshaled the concept of traumatic amnesia in such an unusual fashion. Why has he allowed historiographic skepticism to haunt *both* segments of his novel, transforming the problem of historical representation into a problem of *individual* memory? And why has he chosen to account for collective, historical violence in the context of individual, domestic violence?

The answers to these questions lie partly in the allegorical potential of the novel. Like Jason Bourne, John Wade is an emblem of the bifurcated security state. In public, Wade is literally a representative of democracy: a brilliant state senator, "an idealist in many ways—a Humphrey progressive, a believer in the fundamental human equities" (*Lake of the Woods*, 151). Underneath, he is "Sorcerer": the boy who practiced magic to forget his father's "secret drinking that was not a secret"; the "college spy" who stalked his future wife; the politician who secretly perfected "his posture, his gestures, his trademark style"; and the U.S. marine who once assembled Vietnamese villagers on a beach, performed a set of "card tricks and rope tricks," then whispered into a military radio "and made their village disappear" in a blaze of white phosphorus (156, 152, 65). When Wade tries to tell his wife that, as Sorcerer, he has "*done* things," "ugly things," she dismisses him, suggesting they see a movie. Like the Cold War public, Kathy Wade knows but does not want to know. She knows John spies on her, but she tries to ignore it, despite admitting that John occasionally scares her and gives her "this creepy feeling" (72). O'Brien's novel thus shares the allegorical architecture of Didion's *Democracy,* where Senator Harry Victor and the CIA agent Jack Lovett represent the public and secret faces of the Cold War state, respectively, and the woman who loves both of them, Inez, represents the forgetful U.S. public. O'Brien's novel, however, consolidates the two faces of the state in the single, tormented figure of Wade, whose remarkable capacity for amnesia far exceeds that of Inez.

This is so because Wade's forgetting stems from trauma. Whereas Inez forgets because of her immersion in the public sector, Wade forgets because he struggles to balance his public persona with his traumatic knowledge of state violence. Hence, *In the Lake of the Woods* is at times almost a treatise on trauma. The novel's "Evidence" chapters, for instance, include excerpts from a founding text of the recovered-memory movement, Judith Herman's 1992 *Trauma and Recovery.* Herman asserts that trauma brings us "face to face . . . with the capacity for evil in human nature," and that "the violation of a human connection, and consequently the risk of a post-traumatic stress disorder, is highest of all when the survivor has been not merely a passive witness but also an active participant in violent death or atrocity."[22] Similar citations from psychological texts, veteran recovery manuals, and Wade's relatives suggest that the mature John Wade is still suffering from the war and particularly from the holocaust at Thuan Yen. Crucially, however, and very much in the spirit of Herman's work, O'Brien traces Wade's posttraumatic stress not simply to Vietnam but to the events of his childhood—and particularly to the pressures of masculinization. "More than anything else," the narrator tells us, "John Wade wanted to be loved, and to make his father proud" (212). But Mr. Wade is an abusive alcoholic who refers to his son as "Jiggling John . . . even though he wasn't fat" (212). His incessant ridicule turns homophobic when John takes up magic and begins to spend hours practicing alone in the basement. "That pansy magic crap," says his father. "'What's wrong with baseball, some regular exercise?' He'd shake his head. 'Blubby little pansy'" (67). When Mr. Wade finally hangs himself in the garage, John is left, at fourteen, with no way to obtain his father's approval.

The psychodrama of masculinization is central to all of O'Brien's fiction, which presents going to war as an act rooted not in courage but in dread fear of not living up to a masculine ideal. As the narrator of "On the Rainy River" says, "I would go to the war—I would kill and maybe die—because I was embarrassed not to."[23] Or as Paul Berlin puts it in *Going After Cacciato* (1978), "I fear being thought of as a coward, I fear that even more than cowardice itself" (286). In 1994, O'Brien himself admitted, "I have written some of this before, but I must write it again. I was a coward. I went to Vietnam."[24] More frightening than the terror of battle is the imagined shame of avoiding war and its certification of masculinity. O'Brien's characters thus worry profoundly about how their fathers will view their service, and they fantasize elaborately about the praise their service might eventually win them. Paul Berlin envisions that "he would shake his father's hand and look him in the eye. 'I did okay,' he would say. 'I won some medals.' And his father would nod" (*Going After Cacciato,* 44). Such fantasies are particularly fraught for John Wade, who, unlike Berlin, is a survivor of paternal abuse and abandonment, and whose need for fatherly approval is thus exceptionally strong.[25] "It was in the nature of love that John Wade went to the war," explains the narrator. "Only to be loved. He imagined his father, who was dead, saying to him, 'Well, you did it, you hung in there, and I'm so proud, just so incredibly goddamn proud'" (*Lake of the Woods,* 59–60).

In such fantasies, O'Brien illuminates how a masculinist cultural imaginary underpins the work of the security state. The need for fatherly approval is so strong that it becomes the deepest source of trauma in O'Brien's work, deeper even than battlefield trauma, because it is what motivates young men to go into battle in the first place. *In the Lake of the Woods* develops this insight more fully than O'Brien's other work by insisting on the childhood origins of Wade's sorcery. It is the trauma of his father's suicide, as much as his own war experience, that shapes Wade's potential for violence. "What John felt that night [the night of his father's suicide], and for many nights afterward, was the desire to kill" (14). O'Brien so tightly interweaves this early trauma with the trauma of war that they soon become inseparable. On the night Wade returns from Vietnam, for instance, he lies curled up in the dark, pleading with his dead father:

> But his father wouldn't listen and wouldn't stop, he just kept dying. "God, I *love* you," John said, and then he . . . found himself at his father's funeral—fourteen years old, a new black necktie pinching tight—except the funeral was being conducted in bright sunlight along an irrigation ditch at Thuan

Yen—mourners squatting on their heels and wailing and clawing at their eyes—John's mother and many other mothers—a minister crying "Sin!"—an organist playing music—and John wanted to kill everybody who was weeping and everybody who wasn't...he wanted to grab a hammer and scramble down into the ditch and kill his father for dying. (42)

Here, as elsewhere, it is not only the ceaseless repetition of memories, but also the inseparability of discrete traumas, that stimulates Wade's fury. He feels the same "killing rage" after losing the election: "He wanted to hurt things. Grab a knife and start cutting and slashing and never stop" (5). As he stands by Kathy's bed with the boiling kettle in his hand, he sees images from Thuan Yen: "a wooden hoe and a vanishing village and PFC Weatherby and hot white steam" (51). In a key narrative strategy, O'Brien enmeshes the distinct traumas of John Wade's life until each seems both a cause of the next and a result of the former.

This strategy permits O'Brien to undertake the novel's central theoretical task: the extension of Wade's story into an exploration of U.S. history. First, as I will explain in detail later, O'Brien weaves Wade's traumas not only with each other but with an increasingly wide circle of collective, historical traumas. Second, through the uncanny and incessant repetition of traumatic memories, O'Brien recontextualizes historical events to suggest the power of narrative context to produce historical meaning. The first time we see Wade shoot his smiling comrade Weatherby, for instance, the act seems cold-blooded and thoughtless (64). During a later, more detailed memory, we learn that Wade has been surprised by Weatherby while cowering in a ditch full of dead bodies so that he can stop watching Weatherby gleefully slaughter innocent villagers (111, 220). Such retellings imitate the repetitive nature of traumatic memory and illustrate the power of context in shaping historical interpretation.

Third, and most important, O'Brien uses the inseparability of Wade's traumatic memories to develop a thesis about the widespread relation between secrecy and forgetting. Like all of the historiographic commentary of this novel, O'Brien's critique of historical amnesia is embodied in John Wade. And like Wade's capacity for violence, his astonishing ability to forget is born in the wake of his father's suicide, for it is to cope with the suicide that John develops his most defining mental habit: "He tried to pretend that his father was not truly dead. He would talk to him in his imagination, carrying on whole conversations about baseball and school and girls.... John would sometimes invent elaborate stories about how he could've saved his father.... He imagined yelling in his father's ear, begging him to please stop dying. Once or twice it almost worked. 'Okay,' his father would say, 'I'll stop, I'll stop,' but he never did" (14–15). Here, confronted with the ceaseless repetition of traumatic memory—"the fucker kept hanging himself. Over and over" (286)—Wade learns to manage trauma through fantasy and confabulation.

O'Brien's central figure for this creative mental habit is the mirror in front of which John practices magic.

> In the mirror, where miracles happened, John was no longer a lonely little kid. He had sovereignty over the world....
>
> In the mirror, where John Wade mostly lived, he could read his father's mind. Simple affection, for instance. "Love you, cowboy," his father would think.
>
> Or his father would think, "Hey, report cards aren't everything." (65)

Magic gives Wade a sense of control and accomplishment. But more important, it begins to *assimilate functions of fiction making*—the narrative practice of simulating reality through illusion. O'Brien explicitly associates these techniques both with secrecy and with the functioning of the traumatized mind. Young John Wade internalizes the image of the mirror in which he witnesses his own capacity for deception and control, until eventually he conceives of his memory as a creative, fictional power rather than a faithful record of events. His head becomes a "hall of mirrors" that hides emotional pain behind more comforting fictions.

> The mirror made this possible, and so John would sometimes carry it to school with him, or to baseball games, or to bed at night. Which was another trick: how he secretly kept the old stand-up mirror in his head. Pretending, of course—he understood that—but...
>
> The mirror made things better.
>
> The mirror made his father smile at him all the time. (66)

Once he transforms his memory into a fictive tool, it allows him to replace painful events with more pleasant ones. His head becomes "a box of mirrors...a place to hide" from emotional pain (212–13).

It is worth stressing the close association O'Brien develops here between secrecy and spying, on the one hand, and fantasy or fiction making, on the other, particularly given the importance of this association in Cold War intelligence (see chapter 3). John Wade's dual interests in magic and spying stem from his attempt to understand secrets—especially his father's "secret drinking that wasn't secret" (66) and the mystery of "why his father hated him" (208). John's magic tricks, like the "mirror trick" of fantasizing his father's responses, are explicitly related to his capacity for spying: "The spying was like an elaborate detective game, a way of crawling into his father's mind. Nothing ever got solved—no answers at all—but still the spying made things better. It brought him closer to his father. It was a bond" (209–10). When Kathy becomes the object of John Wade's desire, he begins to spy on her to ensure that she will not abandon him in a repeat of his father's vanishing act.

It is through the connection between these three things—magic, secrecy, and espionage—that Wade develops the central fantasy of his adult identity: that as "Sorcerer," he can control the chaos around him and receive the love and approval his father never gave him. Amid the holocaust at Thuan Yen—as his comrades slaughter anything that breathes—Wade is mute with horror until finally he declares, "Go away." Suddenly, with this "most majestic trick of all," "the little village [begins] to vanish inside its own rosy glow" (110–11). "Over time," Wade's "most profound memory" of the massacre becomes its "impossibility": "This could not have happened. Therefore it did not. Already he felt better" (111). As he flees the butchery, shooting an old man whose hoe he mistakes for a rifle, he feels "only the faintest sense of culpability. The forgetting trick mostly worked" (111).

The "mirror trick" is thus a version of the paradoxical half-knowledge that allows the public to disavow the contradiction between the rhetoric of democracy and the nature of covert warfare. In Wade's case, this sleight of mind is a way of surviving Vietnam and managing his knowledge of a national shame so that no one—especially Kathy—can find out the truth. But the mirror trick begins to create confusions of identity and reality. After pressuring Kathy to have an abortion Wade finds that his mental "box of mirrors" creates disturbing "fun-house reflections: deformations and odd angles," turning him "inside out and upside down" (159). When Kathy finally disappears, he realizes "his whole life had been managed with mirrors and now he was totally baffled and totally turned around and had no idea how to work his way out" (242).

The figure of the internal mirror marries the themes of secrecy and trauma to the aesthetics of postmodernism. O'Brien carefully weaves these connections into every aspect of the novel. Lake of the Woods sounds eerily like Vietnam—a place of "secret channels and...tangled forests" where "the wilderness was all one thing, a great curving *mirror*" (1, emphasis added). Like the other mirrors in which Wade performs, Lake of the Woods is the source of a magic trick, the great vanishing act in which both John and Kathy slip into thin air. The town of Angle Inlet, the tiny village from which Kathy Wade disappears, is a real place—the northernmost spot in the continental United States, part of the Northwest Angle, a little spit of land that shoots up into Canada where the border snakes its way down the Rainy River. This is an area of mythic power for O'Brien, the setting for his brilliant story "On the Rainy River," which relates a young man's near flight to Canada to dodge the draft. All of O'Brien's fiction has a trapdoor like this one, where the protagonist can escape the war in the manner of Paul Berlin, who in *Going After Cacciato* simply walks out of Vietnam all the way to Paris. Lake of the Woods is a similar escape hatch, a place that offers a magical way out of the horror of Vietnam. And this is why the lake is a "great curving mirror" that reflects the theme of magic and fabulation in the novel. The "angle" eventually becomes one of the narrator's metaphors for the array of perspectives and voices that make up the novel. "The angle shapes reality," he notes. "Partly window, partly mirror, the angle is where memory dissolves" (*Lake of the Woods,* 288). Angle Inlet, in other words, is literally a "wilderness of mirrors"—the term the CIA counterintelligence master James Jesus Angleton used for the epistemological chaos of the spy world.[26]

Wade's ritual self-deception and mnemonic erasure become so elaborate that he emerges as a latter-day Jay Gatsby, someone who believes it is possible to "repeat the past," "to remake himself, to vanish what was past and replace it with things good and new."[27] Not only does he modify the rosters linking him to My Lai but, like Gatsby, he generates a Franklinian "self-improvement list" (*Lake of the Woods,* 79) and awards himself a medal. Because his comrades know him only as "Sorcerer," he trusts that "over time...memory itself would be erased" (272). These forms of deception are linked to Wade's concept of secrecy. Wade sees Vietnam as "a secret," and he believes that everyone, including himself, is defined and controlled by "incredible secrets":

> History was a secret. The land was a secret. There were secret caches, secret trails, secret codes, secret missions, secret terrors and appetites and longings and regrets. Secrecy was paramount. Secrecy *was* the war....
>   Sorcerer had his own secrets.
>   PFC Weatherby, that was one. Another was how much he loved the place—Vietnam—how it felt like home. And there was the deepest secret of all, which was the secret of Thuan Yen, so secret that he sometimes kept it secret from himself. (73)

The concept of a secret inner life has always been essential to liberal, and especially masculine, subjectivity, and the notion that one keeps secrets from oneself became culturally viable with the rise of psychoanalysis. But *In the Lake of the Woods* extends self-deception well beyond Freudian ground and into the postmodern territory of robust repression and multiple personality, where one can forget one's own recent actions wholesale. The novel does so specifically by using the divided self as a figure for the divided state and its prosecution of the Vietnam War—which it brought out of secrecy through a fictional event in the Gulf of Tonkin and repeatedly misrepresented to both the U.S. public and U.S. troops. This is why Wade connects his own self-deception to historiographic skepticism ("History was a secret") and covert warfare ("secrecy *was* the war"). If we cannot trust even our own testimony, then what hope is there for a valid history of events? This is the question Wade's amnesia is designed to provoke. His forgetting is not simply an individual anomaly. It is a way of representing the status of collective memory in the Cold War security state. Wade is a postmodern hall of mirrors because he is an emblem of the covert sphere, a place in which the truth of events is always out of reach, obscured by failures of memory, falsified documents, and misleading testimony.

This allegory explains O'Brien's emphasis on trauma as a source of forgetting. As Herman puts it, in a line cited by O'Brien's narrator, "The ordinary response to atrocities is to banish them from consciousness." Elsewhere Herman is quoted observing that "the risk of a post-traumatic stress disorder...is highest of all when the survivor has been not merely a passive witness but also an active participant in violent death or atrocity."[28] When

Senator Bob Kerrey admitted, some thirty years after the fact, his participation in the slaughter of thirteen unarmed Vietnamese women and children, he was unable to avoid speaking in apparent contradictions: "Part
of living with the memory, some of those memories, is to forget them....I
carry memories of what I did, and I survive and live based upon lots of
different mechanisms....It's entirely possible that I'm blacking a lot of
it out."[29]

O'Brien shows how this logic operates at a cultural, as well as an individual, level. The narrator presents a litany of actual testimony suggesting
as much. "Look, I don't remember," says one My Lai participant. "I can't
specifically recall," claims another. "I am struck," says a senior army in-
vestigator, "by how little of these events I can or even wish to remember"
(*Lake of the Woods,* 139). By combining such remarks, O'Brien depicts an
entire society committed to the forms of forgetting and "deniability" that
have defined U.S. political leadership since the presidency of Ronald Reagan, who, in the words of Charles Baxter, established "the proving ground
of historical amnesia."[30] O'Brien himself observed on the eve of his novel's
publication:

> Now, more than 25 years later, the villainy of that Saturday morning in 1968
> has been pushed off to the margins of memory. In the colleges and high
> schools I sometimes visit, the mention of My Lai brings on null stares, a sort
> of puzzlement, disbelief mixed with utter ignorance. Evil has no place, it
> seems, in our national mythology. We erase it. We use ellipses. We salute
> ourselves and take pride in America the White Knight, America the Lone
> Ranger, America's sleek laser-guided weaponry beating up on Saddam and
> his legion of devils.[31]

John Wade's amnesia, in short, is an expression of dismay about the ahistoricity of the present generation. It is a version of the critique offered by
Jameson, Harvey, Baudrillard, and others, but it is even more specifically
focused on U.S. public ignorance about U.S. foreign policy.

The Magic Show

This critique of public amnesia explains why O'Brien eventually places
Wade's experience on a much broader historical canvas. As "evidence"

in the case of Kathy Wade's disappearance, his narrator begins to include material drawn from the biographies of Presidents Wilson, Johnson, and Nixon—unhappy children who, like Wade, satisfied their longing for love and approval through politics. O'Brien cites other politicians on the traumatic shock of losing an election and the tendency to conceal things from their families. He includes accounts of magic that locate its appeal in the longing for supernatural power and control. Soon he begins to build in actual testimony about the My Lai incident, in which dumbstruck veterans try to excuse their appalling savagery or claim to forget it altogether. He cites novels and psychiatric manuals, newspapers and military records—all of this alongside fictional testimony from his own characters. Eventually, he confronts us with much older historical events: General Sherman's call for the extermination of Sioux "men, women and children" (260); the U.S. slaughter of three hundred Cheyenne; the last words of General Custer ("John! Oh John!" [145, 260], a common term for Indians that also seems eerily to address John Wade); and both American and British soldiers describing the "savage" slaughter of innocents in the American War of Independence (262–63).

In the Lake of the Woods thus charts a cycle of violation and murder in the United States that stems from both the experience of war and the much more ordinary experience of masculinization. O'Brien does not articulate this notion as such, but instead presents a suggestive collage of historical and fictional echoes that are, like the experience of trauma itself, fragmented and repetitive. Yet what is so striking about these fragments is that they are presented as evidence in the case of Kathy Wade. If they tell a story at all, it is one that must be pieced together and seems unrelated to Kathy, about whose fate, the narrator finally admits, "nothing is solved" (304n136). It is, rather, about the collective atrocities that have punctuated all the armed conflicts of the United States—how they can be forgotten by their perpetrators and remain inaccessible to their historians. By calling this national history "evidence" in the case of Kathy Wade, O'Brien invites us to see her allegorically, as a figure for the public that threatens to disappear amid the contradictions between the public rhetoric of democracy and the sorcery of foreign adventures. Yet while O'Brien relates the events at Thuan Yen in horrifying detail, he interweaves this national shame with a story of individual grief and amnesia, a story that is unresolved from all of its widely divergent points of view. What is the meaning of a story that

our Sorcerer-author has made to look like a true crime mystery, but rigged
to be fundamentally insoluble and ambiguous? How can a *fictional* plot be
a mystery to its own (amnesic?) author? "My feeling," O'Brien explained
in an interview, "is that John Wade didn't kill her. But that's just what I
think."[32] And why is this story ultimately a Vietnam story? How did we
get from individual violence to collective, Cold War trauma?

The answer to these questions lies in a final puzzling feature of *In the
Lake of the Woods*. It turns out that, in composing this novel, O'Brien bor-
rowed key sections of two earlier (1991) autobiographical essays. The first
of these, "The Magic Show," describes how O'Brien came to believe that
"fiction writing involves a desire to enter the mystery of things." It begins
this way:

> As a kid, through grade school and into high school, my hobby was magic. I
> enjoyed the power; I liked making miracles happen. In the basement, where
> I practiced in front of a stand-up mirror, I caused my mother's silk scarves
> to change color. I used a scissors to cut my father's best tie in half, display-
> ing the pieces, and then restored it whole. I placed a penny in the palm of
> my hand, made my hand into a fist, made the penny into a white mouse.
> This was not true magic. It was trickery. But I sometimes pretended oth-
> erwise, because I was a kid then, and because pretending was the thrill of
> magic, and because for a time what seemed to happen became a happen-
> ing itself. I was a dreamer. I liked watching my hands in the mirror, imag-
> ining how someday I might perform much grander magic, tigers becoming
> giraffes, beautiful girls levitating like angels in the high yellow spotlights,
> naked maybe, no wires and strings, just floating.[33]

The bulk of this passage also appears in *Lake of the Woods* (31), where, converted to the third person, it is used to describe young John Wade.

I draw attention to this source not simply to show that O'Brien is au-
tobiographically related to young John Wade, but because "The Magic
Show" is a theoretical blueprint for *In the Lake of the Woods*. The central
claim of the essay is that storytellers are "sorcerers." Both magic and fiction, O'Brien claims, are "solitary endeavors" in which one aims "for tension and suspense, a sense of drama," and that satisfy a basic human "desire
to enter the mystery of things," "to know what cannot be known" ("Magic
Show," 379). This "interpenetration of magic and stories" (380) obviously
shapes the character of John Wade, whose confabulations are inseparable

from his interest in magic. "If the writer is a *sorcerer,*" write Deleuze and
Guattari, "it is because writing is a becoming."[34] Being a writer, O'Brien
explains, is like being a healer or miracle worker—one who controls the
world: "The shaman or witch doctor was believed to have access to an
unseen world, a world of demons and gods," not only through magic but
through "stories *about* those spirits" (380). Even the "personage of Jesus,"
O'Brien points out, was both "a doer of...miracles" and "a teller of miraculous stories" (380). The possession of these godlike powers was a compelling childhood fantasy for O'Brien. "I liked the aloneness" of magic,
he declares, "as God and other miracle makers must also like it...I liked
shaping the universe around me. I liked the power" (379). This fantasy
is visible in the displaced Oedipal struggles of O'Brien's novel, where a
nascent storyteller, deprived of a father with whom to compete, suddenly
wishes to kill the Father above. Both the furious John Wade and Alexandre
Dumas (whose case is cited by our narrator) respond to the deaths of their
fathers by wishing to "Kill Jesus" or "kill God" (*Lake of the Woods,* 200).

"The Magic Show" expresses a more constructive vision of divine activity than the novel. But if the essay begins with the profound hope that
"as writers we might discover that which cannot be known through empirical means" ("Magic Show," 381), it eventually converts this hope into
a radical antiempiricism. We may want magic to plumb the secrets of the
world, O'Brien argues, but we also crave uncertainty and mystery; thus
"there is something both false and trivial about a story that arrives at absolute closure" (383). O'Brien ultimately rejects the idea that we can unravel
"the mysteries of the human spirit" (384). "We 'know' human character—
maybe even our own—," he writes, "in the same way we know black holes;
by their effects on the external world" (384). This view of human inef-
fability is echoed by the novel's narrator, whose remarks are repeatedly
lifted from "The Magic Show": "Our lovers, our husbands, our wives,
our fathers, our gods—," he says in one such passage, "they are all beyond
us."[35] Later he quotes Freud making a similar point: "Whoever under-
takes to write a biography binds himself to lying, to concealment, to flummery.... Truth is not accessible."[36]

It is worth stressing how much O'Brien links these expressions of unknowability to global conflict. A similar sense of mystery and confusion
haunted the Cold War public during the Vietnam War. As the narrator
explains in *The Things They Carried,* "The very facts were shrouded in

uncertainty. Was it a civil war? A war of national liberation or simple aggression? Who started it, and when, and why? What really happened to the USS *Maddox* on that dark night in the Gulf of Tonkin?"[37] The proposition that individuals are inscrutable must thus be understood within the collective, historical dimension of this novel—as a statement partly about the unknowability of cold warfare.

More important still, a narrative rooted in the concept of magic, mystery, and flummery has adopted the very qualities of the covert state. That is, if "sorcery" is the stock-in-trade of intelligence agencies, it is also the stock-in-trade of the fiction writer attempting to make visible the work of the state.

But the use of sorcery exists in tension with the moral injunction that impelled the writer to take up sorcery in the first place. This conflict becomes evident in the second source for *In the Lake of the Woods*. This is the 1994 autobiographical essay "The Vietnam in Me," a confessional piece published on the eve of the novel's publication, in which O'Brien admits he was once a "chubby and friendless" child whose cowardice and "desperate love craving" led him to fight a war he believed was "mistaken, probably evil."[38] This essay differs radically from "The Magic Show" in its depiction of writing. It relates O'Brien's journey to Thuan Yen in February of 1994 during a period in which he is barely in control of his life, profoundly depressed, anxious, suicidal—suffering not only the aftereffects of his combat experience but also its painful repetition in his own writing. Unlike the fantasy of controlling the world through the magic of fiction, this essay reveals the nightmare of posttraumatic stress in which writing about Vietnam is a haunting compulsion that wreaks havoc in O'Brien's life. As he puts it, "You don't have to be in Nam to be in Nam." If "The Magic Show" is a literary manifesto for the imaginative power to transcend a painful reality, "The Vietnam in Me" is a classic expression of trauma's power to create endless human suffering. Just as important, while "The Magic Show" is an expression of radical historiographic skepticism, "The Vietnam in Me" laments historical forgetting and moral unaccountability. In this second essay O'Brien regrets that "the villainy of that Saturday morning in 1968 has been pushed off to the margins of memory" and clearly states that while he can understand the butchery of Thuan Yen, his own unit never crossed the "conspicuous line between rage and homicide."

O'Brien's two source essays thus correspond to the divided structure of his novel and the rival impulses of its protagonist and its narrator. They also correspond to two distinct, but connected, responses to trauma—one geared toward repression and erasure, the other toward acknowledgment and documentation. While John Wade's habit of confabulation is at odds with the narrator's desire to unearth the truth, these two authorial impulses are nonetheless linked through the experiences of O'Brien himself. "The Magic Show" celebrates manipulation, erasure, and fiction; "The Vietnam in Me" champions openness, publicity, and history. If Wade's narrative depicts posttraumatic *repression,* the battle to convert shame, guilt, and uncontrollable repetition into something more tolerable, then the narrator's story represents the equally frustrating attempt to *recover* the traumatic experience, to convert it from trauma to history. Insofar as fiction can be distinguished from history, the two narrative strands of the novel represent the fictional and the historical, respectively.[39] On one hand, we have the sorcerer's desire to fictionalize, to perform the priestly rite of transforming the painful past into a wondrous illusion; on the other hand, we have the historian's desire to unearth, to confess the truth, to document the past, to solve the mystery. On one hand, the expression of historiographic skepticism; on the other, the realist impulse.

These rival impulses correspond to the division between the covert and public spheres. The primary narrative of John Wade is driven by historiographic skepticism, vanishing tricks, the healing of pain through misdirection, illusion, and fantasy. The novel's historical narrative, by contrast, expresses a realist desire to terminate the experience of trauma by putting it into perspective—perhaps on the basis of Herman's view that one escapes trauma by offering public testimony.[40] But in the precincts of the covert sphere, this proves impossible. No matter how much the narrator wants to critique the society that has forgotten these events, he must admit that he, too, has no purchase on them. His footnotes (often lifted from "The Magic Show") become more frequent, intimate, and confessional. By the end of the novel, he admits that his platoon, too, committed "atrocities—the dirty secrets that live forever inside all of us. I have my own PFC Weatherby. My own old man with a hoe" (*Lake of the Woods,* 301n130). He, too, has learned to forget. "I can understand," he admits, "how [Wade] kept things buried, how he could never face or even recall the butchery at Thuan Yen. For me after a quarter century nothing much remains of that ugly war. A handful of splotchy images" (301n130).

Here, in a sort of traumatic infectiousness, the narrator's experience begins to blend uneasily with Wade's—and with O'Brien's. As Mark Heberle has observed, "Wade spends the last several months of his service as a clerk, which gives him the opportunity to change his identity by altering military records, rewriting himself out of Charlie Company and into Alpha Company—O'Brien's own company. Thus, not only does O'Brien rewrite himself as Wade, but Wade tries to rewrite himself as O'Brien."[41] By the end of the novel, Wade, the narrator, and O'Brien have all begun to morph into one another as the narrator's memories of combat come to seem untrustworthy, *less real* than his dramatic renderings of John Wade's life. "In a peculiar way," the narrator notes, "the ordeal of John Wade...has a vivid, living clarity that seems far more authentic than my own faraway experience. Maybe that's what this book is for. To remind me. To give me back my vanished life" (301n130). This is more than a simple salute to the imaginative power of fiction, for in the end the narrator admits that there is something oddly *amnesic* about his own memory. "On occasion," he confesses, "I find myself wondering if these old tattered memories weren't lifted from someone else's life, or from a piece of fiction I once read or once heard about" (301n130). This unsettling suspicion is actually experienced by a surprising number of Vietnam veterans, who report "they have forgotten where some of their memories came from—their own experience, documentary photographs, or Hollywood movies."[42] So powerful is narrative fiction, in fact, that even nonveterans have written themselves into the war—as, for instance, when the distinguished historian Joseph Ellis admitted fabricating Vietnam war stories for his students.[43] Such phenomena verge on the contentious territory of recovered memory syndrome and its evil twin, false memory syndrome. They are artifacts of a covert sphere dominated by narrative fictions.

The strange epistemology of this imaginary is what ultimately blurs the lines between Wade and O'Brien's narrator-historian. The narrator's sense that his own memories may be false is only another version of John Wade's inability to recall what he has done (or not done) to his wife. This is one way of understanding why the narrator believes that writing the "history" of John Wade might "give him his life back," provide the clarity to help him recover his own "vanished" past. Yet the narrator cannot shake the suspicion that his own memories are products of this narrative rather than his own life. This sensation is akin to the traumatic effect that Caruth calls "unclaimed experience." In both cases, the traumatized subject has, to use her terms, *"missed"* the traumatic experience and must now approach it *as a historian.* The paradox, however, is that, conceived this way, traumatic events can be historicized only via an "amnesic" experience, which destabilizes the authority of the memory to provide testimony.

In the end, then, we are not much further than when we started: the real and the fictional—history and fantasy—are hopelessly intertwined. The epistemology of the covert sphere has fractured the novel's conflicting missions: on the one hand, to unmask the repressed nightmares of U.S. history; on the other, to display an awesome capacity for storytelling, fiction, and magic that is uncomfortably akin to deception, confabulation, and trickery. At every turn our narrator seems to maintain a scrupulous skepticism about his difficulty in depicting the past, and yet the novel's uneasy blending of Wade, narrator, and O'Brien—its linking of trauma and fantasy—leaves open the possibility that our sorcerer-author has staged everything, even his own skepticism. O'Brien himself has done much to heighten this suspicion. He is well-known for telling audiences a purportedly autobiographical tale before impishly revealing that "none of it is true. Or very little of it. It's—invented." He explains this stunt in paradoxical terms that sound almost like a defense of John Wade's duplicity. Fiction, even in the guise of autobiography, O'Brien tells his audiences, is "for getting at the truth when the truth isn't sufficient for the truth."[44]

This problem—the need to document the truth of events *and* the sense that only narrative "magic" can simulate the intensity of those events—reflects the conditions of knowledge in the covert sphere and ultimately brings O'Brien's narrative to a halt. Just as the original trauma of the soldier can only be reapproached as history, so the narrative of John Wade gives way to the narrative of historical reconstruction. But the latter narrative can only ever document the profound difficulty of narrating history. If telling the story is what allows the sufferer to transcend trauma, as Judith Herman claims, then O'Brien's narrative seems to document the need to repeat that trauma compulsively, not only as memory, but as historical fiction too.

6

The Geopolitical Melodrama

Ground Zero

Two responses dominated early American attempts to comprehend the bombings of the World Trade Center and the Pentagon on September 11, 2001. The first was a widespread sense of disbelief and confusion about the possible motives for such an attack. Americans repeatedly asked why anyone would perpetrate such acts. What had the United States or its citizens done to warrant such a vicious assault?

The second response came from government officials struggling to provide answers to this question. Only hours after the attacks, President Bush declared that "freedom itself was attacked this morning by a faceless coward and freedom will be defended."[1] This view was widely circulated by the mass media and eventually became the Bush administration's official explanation. Ten days after the attacks, President Bush fleshed it out by explaining the terrorists' motives to a joint session of Congress:

> Americans are asking "Why do they hate us?" They hate what they see right here in this chamber: a democratically elected government. Their leaders are self-appointed. They hate our freedoms: our freedom of religion, our freedom of speech, our freedom to vote and assemble and disagree with each other.[2]

Faced with a broad public desire to understand whether U.S. behavior had provoked a daring act of war, the administration offered a strikingly narcissistic theory. The attacks, it argued, were motivated by jealousy over the magnificence of our democratic institutions. This assertion not only dismissed the possibility that U.S. policy or privilege had motivated the terrorists but also shored up the national ego with a reassertion of American exceptionalism.

Such rhetoric is, of course, nothing new in the United States, which Christopher Lasch famously described as ground zero of "the culture of narcissism."[3] It is nonetheless striking how swiftly Bush's explanation caught on. Dan Rather echoed it when he declared that terrorists "are losers...and...losers sometimes develop a deep and abiding hatred for...winners."[4] Robert Kaplan, the diplomatic history insider, managed to put it more elegantly: "Western technological capitalism and U.S. popular culture is egalitarian, opulent, and successful in ways Communism never was. Resentment, fear and envy of this success inspires hatred for the U.S. dynamic culture among fundamentalist Muslims."[5] This explanation fostered a widespread reassertion of national pride and dramatically curtailed the critical review of U.S. foreign policy that might have followed the attacks of 2001. It also underwrote two wars and sweeping new forms of domestic hypervigilance. How can we explain the appeal of this response? What social and cultural forces supported its extraordinary popularity?

The first thing to recognize is that the Bush administration immediately and reactively redeployed both a rhetoric and a security strategy rooted in the protocols of the Cold War. Despite the extraordinary transformations of the post–Cold War world, the administration overtly articulated its intention to defend the nation through covert initiatives. The administration made this case for a new state of exception through a rearticulation of Cold War exceptionalism. As Donald Pease explains, exceptionalism was a state fantasy that "defined America as the fulfillment of the world's dream of an ideal nation." In so doing, "it eradicated the difference between the national ideal U.S. citizens wanted and the faulty nation they had, by representing America as having already achieved all that a nation could be.... The state fantasy of exceptionalism thereby introduced the disavowal of imperialism as the unacknowledged mediator in between the state's policies and the practicable life worlds of U.S. citizens."[6]

I have been arguing throughout this book that the ideological disavowal of imperialism was dramatically assisted by the segregation of state policy into overt and covert sectors. Through this bifurcation, the state institutionalized "deniability" as both a government policy and a model of citizenship (a model in which the good citizen declares, "I can't know and I don't really want to know"). The state thus provided an infrastructure that helped it "disappear" the dirty work of empire and preserve the fantasy of exceptionalism from challenges that could (and occasionally did) arise when the public learned of certain imperial practices.

These structures did not waste away in the decade between the fall of the Berlin Wall and the attacks of 9/11/2001. Instead, the state continued to deploy extraordinary covert resources in pursuit of a more nebulous, distant, mobile enemy said to be capable of penetrating the domestic United States for a range of horrifying purposes. Hence, a continuous structure for the regulation of knowledge about foreign policy persisted during the interregnum between the end of the Cold War and the rise of George W. Bush's "Homeland Security State."[7]

But this institutional account is only part of the story, for state fantasy is structured primarily through public discourse. What, then, were the specific vehicles of the "new American exceptionalism" of the post-9/11 moment?[8] Which explanatory narratives were most publicly available to help U.S. citizens imagine (or fantasize) their nation in a global context? During George W. Bush's first term, scholarly, diplomatic, and legal accounts of anti-American terrorism and U.S. antiterror policy were notably scarce. In fact, the most influential vehicles for "understanding" terrorism were popular fictions. Among these, the most important was a specific form I call "the geopolitical melodrama."

The geopolitical melodrama is defined by its yoking of two distinct but related nightmares. First, an external enemy of state—usually a cell of terrorists—takes aim at the U.S. population and security infrastructure, which is depicted as a technologically miraculous apparatus that is nonetheless vulnerable to external attacks. Second, this massive system itself goes awry, threatening the democracy it was designed to prevent. Through a melodramatic contest between these twin dangers, geopolitical melodramas adjudicate the proper balance between national security and individual freedom.[9]

The geopolitical melodrama is a legacy of Cold War fictions designed to interrogate the nature and cost of state security. In the years surrounding 9/11/2001, major film versions include *Patriot Games* (1992), *Clear and Present Danger* (1994), *True Lies* (1994), *Outbreak* (1995), *Broken Arrow* (1996), *The Peacemaker* (1997), *Enemy of the State* (1998), *The Siege* (1998), *Collateral Damage* (2002), *The Sum of All Fears* (2002), *Syriana* (2005), *The Kingdom* (2007), *Rendition* (2007), *Body of Lies* (2008), and *Traitor* (2008). A host of related films—the *Die Hard* series (1988–2007), *Executive Decision* (1996), *Independence Day* (1996), *The Rock* (1996), *Air Force One* (1997), *Face/Off* (1997), *Swordfish* (2001), and *Munich* (2005), to name only a few—share many features of the form, including the use, or threatened use, of massive weapons on U.S. soil and the deployment of a technologically sophisticated U.S. defense apparatus against these threats. Geopolitical melodrama has become increasingly important in television series such as *The Agency* (2001–03), *Alias* (2001–06), *24* (2001–10), *Threat Matrix* (2003–04), *The Grid* (2004), *Sleeper Cell* (2005–06), *The Unit* (2006–09), *The Company* (2007), *Strike Back* (2010–), and *Homeland* (2011–), all of which depict espionage and counterterrorism forces heading off dire national threats.[10]

Since 9/11/2001, such narratives have also served as a major forum for debate about the efficacy of torture—a subject to which I will return—but on the whole the genre has been remarkably stable since the last decade of the twentieth century. Its most important quality is its narcissism—by which I mean its tendency to address global conflict by obliterating foreign perspectives in a self-aggrandizing focus on U.S. "victimization."[11] While the geopolitical melodrama begins by dramatizing a serious external threat, it eventually turns inward. Its victims, agents, and even villains usually turn out to be westerners associated with clandestine government. In the rare case that they come from abroad they are trumped by the bigger danger of the National Security State, which the narrative's hero must battle in order to save the nation. In this way, I argue, the geopolitical melodrama becomes a powerful vehicle for American exceptionalism. While it begins with an eye to those who might actually be targets of the National Security State, it ends up "disappearing" these external enemies in a narcissistic fantasy of domestic danger and heroic self-defense. This tendency is encouraged by the epistemology of the covert sphere, which grants popular fiction an unusually powerful role in shaping public attitudes about U.S. national security. Indeed, despite its "unserious" nature, the geopolitical melodrama informs a surprising number of "serious" explanations of U.S. antiterrorism policy, and it thus helps explain U.S. responses to the events of 9/11.

Enemies, Foreign and Domestic

The plot of the geopolitical melodrama develops when an innocent—often an agent of the U.S. government—becomes enmeshed in the national security apparatus. In Edward Zwick's *The Siege,* for instance, Anthony Hubbard, a high-ranking FBI agent (played by Denzel Washington), pursues a cell of Islamic terrorists who have committed suicide bombings of a loaded New York City bus, a crowded Broadway theater, and an elementary school. As Hubbard struggles to stop these attacks, the film introduces the even more sinister threat of a repressive occupation of the city by U.S. forces. After the president places New York under martial law, General William Devereaux (Bruce Willis) floods the city with troops, cordons off an Arabic section of Brooklyn, interns young Arab American men in a concentration camp, and personally tortures a suspected terrorist to death. Hubbard complains that Devereaux is playing into the terrorists' hands, shouting, "What if what they want is for us to...shred the Constitution?" In response, Devereaux declares, "I *am* the law," and turns the vast resources of the military on Hubbard and his agents. In this way, the film weds a sense of panic about Islamist terror with a familiar critique of an overbearing U.S. security structure. Indeed, the initial terrorist attacks turn out to be motivated by Devereaux's secret kidnapping and imprisonment of a militant sheikh, and the bombers turn out to be Shiite Iraqis who were taught terrorist techniques by their CIA handler (Annette Bening).

The same pattern unfolds in Philip Alden Robinson's *Sum of All Fears*— a post-9/11 film in which a nuclear explosion kills tens of thousands at a Baltimore Ravens football game. The overanxious U.S. response to this attack, however, soon becomes a much bigger threat: President Fowler, circling in Air Force One, angrily initiates a retaliatory nuclear strike against

Figure 10. In the geopolitical melodrama, external threats are always trumped by the nightmare of the security state run amok. In *The Siege*, the law-abiding FBI agents Anthony Hubbard (Denzel Washington) and Frank Haddad (Tony Shalhoub) are attacked by a U.S. Army helicopter and arrested on the order of U.S. Army General William Devereaux (Bruce Willis).

Russia, which is wrongly suspected of the first bombing. Only the individual efforts of the rookie CIA analyst Jack Ryan (Ben Affleck) avert a disaster. In the second season of the Fox television series *24*, the detonation of a nuclear device on U.S. soil produces virtually the same error: the vast state security apparatus urges the president to strike immediately—but mistakenly—at a suspected Middle Eastern nation. When he balks, he is removed from power by an emergency vote of his cabinet and vice president. Here again the narrative converts an external threat into a nightmare of democracy overturned, civil liberties suspended, the rule of law supplanted by state sovereignty. Virtually the same plot is served up over the 193 episodes of the show's eight seasons.

Tony Scott's *Enemy of the State* is exemplary in this regard. Leaving only a vestigial fear of the foreign enemy, it shows how U.S. citizens skeptical about the security state may themselves become subject to its powers. When a National Security Agency supervisor murders a congressman opposed to sweeping new spy legislation, an unwitting ecologist captures the incident on videotape. The tape is then ruthlessly pursued by NSA agents, until it ends up, accidentally, in the hands of Robert Clayton Dean (Will Smith). Dean's legal career and family life are turned upside down by NSA agents employing powerful satellite and bugging equipment. The film's anxieties about an out-of-control National Security State are part of a Cold War tradition that runs from *Dr. Strangelove* and *Fail-Safe* in 1964, through *War Games* and *The Day After* in 1983, up through *Eagle Eye* in 2008 and *Echelon Conspiracy* in 2009.

The geopolitical melodrama invests extraordinary resources in its depiction of the terrifying and miraculous U.S. security apparatus. Satellites roar overhead, locating individual targets with implausible dexterity and precision. With a few keyboard clicks of their remote operators, they scan the gridded landscape, whisking us across continents and zooming in on fleeing suspects. Their astonishing responsiveness makes them a sort of narrator—able to map the relation between the global and the local while simultaneously offering a fantasy of U.S. technical superiority. In *Patriot Games,* the analyst Jack Ryan (Harrison Ford) watches a Special Forces raid from the comfort of a secret room in CIA headquarters. A live satellite feed beams back infrared heat signatures of U.S. troops destroying a terrorist camp in northern Africa. As the silent monitor shows a U.S. ranger slip into a tent to shoot two sleeping men, a CIA analyst sips coffee and declares impassively, "That is a kill." In *24* and *Alias,* agents retask satellites, beam data to handheld computers, and deploy software with extraordinary powers. In *The Siege,* officers use high-tech imaging not only to capture a militant in the desert but also to watch a CIA officer have sex with a suspected terrorist. *Enemy of the State* is an ecstasy of surveillance and countersurveillance, a vision of the National Security State as a quasi-divine power.

The listening and imaging capacities of the state, these narratives suggest, have begun to literalize the system of "nerves and rays" by which Freud's famous patient Schreber understood God to be watching him everywhere and all the time.[12] The paranoid sense of surveillance that Freud attributed to a narcissistic projection of superego may now be materialized as an institutional feature of the state. It is worth recalling that Schreber's deepest fear was that God wished to make him his "bride," for it points to a similar anxiety in the cultural imaginary through which U.S. citizens confront the covert state. The terror of an omnipotent but feminizing security apparatus invites compensatory fantasies of heroic male agency and national superiority. If American exceptionalism is a projection of national superego, as Donald Pease argues in his psychoanalytics of state fantasy, then the fantasy of a supernaturally powerful surveillance apparatus is a locus of exceptionalism.[13] After all, it is the security apparatus that purports to preserve U.S. democracy—making it "invincible," "exempt" from

Figure 11. *Enemy of the State* fantasizes a supremely powerful surveillance apparatus. In this sequence, NSA agents easily commandeer a satellite to track a fleeing citizen across Manhattan rooftops.

history, a beacon of "freedom," and so on. But because the security state accomplishes this task in secret, it also becomes an object of fascination, anxiety, and paranoia. In a society where state policy hides the mechanisms of empire, exceptionalism and narcissism become two sides of the same American coin.

The geopolitical melodrama balances these rival visions of the state through a plot in which the hero must master the surveillance apparatus, turning it from threat to tool. In the central opposition between the lone agent and the system, the agent is both a victim of the system—subject to bugging, surveillance, and manipulation—and utterly reliant on it. This plot structure validates the depiction of the security technology as both terrifying and necessary. In *The Sum of All Fears,* for instance, Ryan eventually averts disaster by barging into the Pentagon and commandeering a special communication technology to send messages directly to the Russian president. Hubbard of *The Siege* steals army surveillance equipment to locate the final terrorist. The agents of *24* and *Alias* routinely deceive their superiors and commandeer intelligence equipment in pursuit of their own hunches. *Enemy of the State* takes this logic to the extreme by putting its protagonist, Robert Clayton Dean (Will Smith), in the hands of a paranoid, ex-intelligence officer living in his own surveillance-proof facility— itself a miniature, rival version of the state's vast security system. This man, Brill (Gene Hackman)—essentially a reprise of Hackman's role in Francis Ford Coppola's classic surveillance film, *The Conversation* (1974)—uses advanced surveillance equipment to help Dean fight off the NSA. Thus, while the film warns against invasive surveillance (it opens with the NSA's murder of a U.S. senator opposed to an invasive new spy law), it nonetheless suggests that sophisticated spy technology is the only reasonable solution to the problem.

This pattern is not confined to narratives about terrorism proper. In Wolfgang Petersen's *Outbreak,* the foreign terror is a deadly hemorrhagic virus that has been imported to a small U.S. city by way of a contraband African monkey. Drawing on journalist Richard Preston's *The Hot Zone* (1995), which fantasized the spread of Ebola virus to Washington, DC, *Outbreak* thus registers anxiety about global trade and immigration. The racism underlying these worries is articulated in a single, horrifying shot in which Petersen dissolves the face of an African monkey into that of an African man whose village has been decimated by the disease. As in all the films addressed here, though, the Third World threat is eventually displaced by the internal danger of a sovereign, clandestine security state. As a Centers for Disease Control team headed by Colonel Sam Daniels (Dustin Hoffman) heads off to confront the illness, the town falls under an increasingly repressive military quarantine. Eventually, suspecting that General Donald McClintock (Donald Sutherland) is using the outbreak to obtain a biological weapon, Hoffman goes AWOL and does battle with the U.S. Army, traces the virus to its source, and develops an antibody only moments before the president incinerates the town in a U.S. airstrike.

Whatever It Takes

Repeatedly on display in the geopolitical melodrama, then, is not simply anxiety about foreign invasion but anxiety about the power of complex U.S. technological and military systems. If the plot begins by speculating about what might happen to the state without a vast defensive apparatus, it concludes, equally melodramatically, by imagining what might happen if this apparatus came unhinged from the democratic values it is supposed to protect. This conflict between external invasion and internal repression has the ostensible function of interrogating the relation between civil rights and state security. Yet beneath this important question lies a more familiar postwar fear about anonymous systems, agencies, and institutions. The genre's portrayal of surveillance technology places it in the postwar "paranoid" tradition, which has a primary investment in defending a traditional model of liberal individualism against the apparent dangers of large postwar agencies.[14]

The protagonist of the geopolitical melodrama is thus the classic "rugged" male individualist of the western or the noir detective tale: a clearheaded maverick with a penchant for breaking social rules and an abiding disgust for the political infighting, inertia, and rule-bound strictures of bureaucracy.[15] The celebration of individual agency in the geopolitical melodrama is a masculinist fantasy that compensates for the dread terror of becoming a feminized ward of the security state. Jack Ryan repeatedly bucks his superiors in *The Sum of All Fears* and *Patriot Games*. Anthony Hubbard of *The Siege* cannot resume his manhunt until he does battle with General Devereaux, whose troops follow, detain, and shoot at him. In *24,* the nation lies in the hands of the rogue antiterrorist agent Jack Bauer (Kiefer Sutherland), who is forever pursued by both foreign terrorists *and* U.S. government officials as he attempts to thwart a devastating attack on U.S. citizens. Protagonists of this sort permit the narrative to resolve the twin threats of external invasion and internal repression through a fantasy of heroic male agency. If the security system seems threatening, then perhaps the lone agent can usurp its functions to protect the nation, all the while reassuring us that there is still room for individual agency within the vast and terrifying network we have erected to protect ourselves from the world.

This is a familiar story, but it is not the whole story, for the agents in these dramas are not quite *lone* agents. In a departure from other male genre fictions, the agents of the geopolitical melodrama must balance threats to the *nation* against threats to their families—for in the geopolitical melodrama terrorism may threaten the general population, but eventually, "it gets personal." In *True Lies,* terrorists put Harry Tasker's marriage on the line and kidnap his daughter. They use John McClane's estranged wife as a pawn in *Die Hard.* They invade the Ryan home in *Patriot Games* and seriously wound his wife and daughter during a failed murder attempt. In season 1 of *24,* Jack Bauer's wife is murdered by terrorists; in others, his girlfriends and daughter are held hostage. *Alias* so intertwines family dynamics and spy games that its hero, Sidney Bristow, goes on joint missions with her mother and father, who each work for opposing intelligence services (except when their double or triple agency makes the issue of their motives too difficult to track).

The family drama is crucial to the cultural work of the geopolitical melodrama, because it generates a motive for the hero to override the law in a *reasonable* attempt to save his family. Can we really blame Jack Bauer for stealing a suitcase nuke, or Harry Tasker for borrowing a Harrier jet, when they're only trying to save their children? As Joel Surnow, cocreator of *24* puts it: "They say torture doesn't work. But I don't believe that. I don't think it's honest to say that if someone you love was being held, and you had five minutes to save them, you wouldn't do it. Tell me, what would you do? If someone had one of my children, or my wife, I would *hope* I'd do it. There is nothing—nothing—I wouldn't do."[16] In such instances maverick behavior is not mere individualism but *selfless* individualism in the service of a greater good. And yet, significantly, this greater good is *only* that of the family, not that of the social body as a whole. In fact, the interests of the distressed family are almost always opposed to those of the nation, since the latter is precisely what is protected by the procedural rules that the hero violates. Thus the geopolitical melodrama constructs heroism as the *successful* risk of the many to protect the few, and it succeeds in this reversal of the concept of social good only through a fantasy in which both goals can be accomplished in one astonishing stroke.

More important still, the narrative articulates a defense of pragmatic *illegal* action. The agent can overcome the twin threats of foreign terror and an overbearing security system only by violating procedure or breaking the law. Indeed, bad procedure and illegality amount to the same thing here because the rules of the security bureaucracy stand in for the rule of law itself, and the narrative paints rules as potentially dangerous abstractions insufficiently flexible to guarantee public safety. This is why the genre pits abstract democratic values against the security of specific family members. The conflict generates a motive for the protagonist to override the law in a completely *reasonable* attempt to save his family and, in so doing, to prove superior to the law at serving the collective good.

The political implications of this structure lie in its allegory of the nation-state. Although the hero has an adversarial relation to government, the central dramatic decisions of the plot place the hero in the position of government officials. In such moments, the hero is a figure for the government; bureaucratic rules represent U.S. law; and family members are representative citizens who seem ill served by such rules. If the hero must do "whatever it takes" to protect his family, then by extension the government should do the same to protect its citizens. *Patriot Games,* for instance, is an allegory of the "special relationship" between the United States and the United Kingdom. Its Irish American protagonist, Jack Ryan, is a figure for the U.S. government. Ryan is a retired CIA analyst who is ambivalent about the use of covert methods. At the opening of the film, he heroically thwarts the murder of Queen Elizabeth's cousin by an Irish Republican Army splinter group. This assistance to the Crown then provokes the IRA to threaten Ryan and his family. When CIA officials subsequently ask Ryan to rejoin the agency, embracing covert methods to hunt down the IRA cell, Ryan's wife Cathy (Anne Archer) rejects this proposal, saying, "I can't go back to that life." But her dismissal of Cold War methods ("that life") does not last long. When the terrorist cell attacks the Ryans on

Figure 12. In the bowels of a subterranean command center in Langley, Virginia, CIA analyst Jack Ryan (Harrison Ford) of *Patriot Games* reluctantly watches satellite imagery of U.S. Special Forces slaughtering men and women he identified as terrorists.

U.S. soil—nearly killing Cathy and gravely wounding the Ryans' daughter—Cathy insists that Jack return to the CIA. "You get 'em, Jack," she tells her husband angrily, "I don't care what you have to do. Just get 'em."

Cathy Ryan is thus a figure for the U.S. public. Through her dramatic change, *Patriot Games* represents the shifting demands of a citizenry that despises covert methods but then demands *and disavows* such methods when threatened. "I don't care what you have to do" not only means "use any necessary measures"; it also means "I don't want to know about these measures." It is the essence of public half-knowledge in the covert sphere.

By constructing dramas around this logic, the plot of the geopolitical melodrama offers a powerful defense of extralegal government action. Alongside its dread of government surveillance and intrusion, the narrative critiques the rule of law itself. Like cumbersome bureaucratic regulations, this critique suggests, law cannot encompass the "exceptional circumstances" generated by antistate terrorism. The best policy on terror, in other words, is actually *two* policies—one public and idealistic, the other covert and pragmatic. This argument is part of the originary crisis of democracy that Giorgio Agamben calls "the state of exception." The periodic crises that cause nations to suspend democratic rule, Agamben suggests, are not anomalies but permanent, self-negating features of democracy. "If exceptional measures," he explains, are only "the result of periods of political crisis then they find themselves in the paradoxical position of being juridical measures that cannot be understood in legal terms, and the state of exception appears as the legal form of what cannot have legal form."[17] The "legal form of what cannot have legal form" is the paradoxical logic of the covert sector, which itself is the institutional sedimentation of the "state of exception" in a set of permanent governmental structures. The geopolitical melodrama—with its fantasy of maverick pragmatism or "whatever it takes"—is the fictional articulation of this logic.

It is for this reason that the issue of torture has taken such a prominent place in the genre. While older films like *The Siege* depict torture as brutal and ineffective, certain post-9/11 scripts like *24* present it as effective and moral, increasingly the work of heroes rather than villains. In season 1 of *Sleeper Cell,* for instance, the FBI undercover agent Darwyn Al-Sayeed shoots a suspect in the head in order to maintain his undercover role within a Los Angeles cell of Al Qaeda. His report of the murder horrifies his superiors, who initiate disciplinary proceedings against him. Yet the show's dramatic rendering of Al-Sayeed's act makes it seem unavoidable and heroic: the victim, a loose-lipped member of the terror cell, is being slowly tortured to death, so Al-Sayeed steals the cell leader's gun and puts the man out of his misery. The Fox drama *24* so frequently depicts torture that it came to the center of a national debate on the subject.[18] Roughly every other episode (the National Parents Council counted sixty-seven incidents in 125 episodes), Jack Bauer beats, drugs, electrocutes, shoots, or threatens to kill the families of those with information about a "ticking bomb."[19] These acts are miraculously efficacious, producing the sort of intelligence gems that expert interrogators dismiss as fantasy.

Central to the fantasy of efficacious torture is the "ticking bomb scenario" itself, which originated in the 1960 Jean Lartéguy novel *Les centurions,* still a favorite among U.S. military leaders.[20] The much-celebrated visual innovations of *24* are aesthetic expressions of the putative ticking bomb. Each season of *24* unfolds in "real time," over twenty-four episodes that together depict a day in the life of Bauer and company. This fidelity to the ticking bomb requires the occasional use of split screens to show events unfolding simultaneously in up to four different locations. The viewer is constantly reminded that the clock is ticking. Each dramatic segment begins with a digital clock devouring the precious milliseconds before catastrophe will rip the nation asunder. This nick-of-time aesthetic

Figure 13. The signature split-screen images of the Fox drama *24* capture its allegory in miniature. Here, at the beginning of season 2 (2002), the ticking clock is framed by a terrorist threat, a representative of democracy (Dennis Haysbert as President David Palmer), the rogue state agent (Kiefer Sutherland as Jack Bauer), and the family Bauer will protect at any cost.

transformed the cultural fantasy through which state policy was imagined, and as I will illustrate below, it transformed state policy itself.

Because *24* was endorsed by Bush administration officials and was closely aligned with its policies (the show's conservative writers were "like a Hollywood television annex to the [Bush] White House," joked Joel Surnow's friend, Roger Director), it has been seen as the ultimate post-9/11 drama.[21] Yet while its embrace of hard-line tactics and its depiction of terrorist acts grew more alarming after September 11, 2001, it is important to remember that *24* was conceived before 9/11. Its pilot episode was shot in 2000. While the show's writers used depictions of torture in support of the Bush administration's post-9/11 antiterror policies, the major features of *24* are those of the geopolitical melodrama—especially its extreme anxiety about the military industrial complex, which it depicts as a monstrous and shadowy threat to democracy and human rights. Thus, despite being the neoconservative melodrama par excellence, *24* shares a lot with liberal versions of the geopolitical melodrama, including those that critique torture (*The Siege, Traitor, Rendition*). One of the most overlooked aspects of *24*, for example, is how frequently it depicts torture of *innocent* U.S. agents and civilians. I make this observation not to suggest that *24* is "fair and balanced" on the subject of torture. On the contrary, the speed with which mistakenly tortured government agents put aside their bitterness and return to service only trivializes torture more. I make the observation, however, because it points to the most unappreciated feature of the series: in each season, several U.S. counterterrorism agents and public representatives *actually are* in league with the enemy.

This is perhaps *the* crucial element of the geopolitical melodrama: not only are its victims upper-middle-class U.S. citizens; *so are its villains*. The terrorist threats traced through eight seasons of *24* turn out, in the end, to be organized, financed, or somehow supported by a cabal of U.S. corporate military suppliers. Similarly, the ultimate perpetrators in *Alias, Sum of All Fears, Collateral Damage, The Siege, Clear and Present Danger, Enemy of the State, True Lies, The Rock, Broken Arrow, Outbreak, Face/Off, Body of Lies, Syriana,* and the *Die Hard* series are *not* Third World figures, as first seems the case, but disgruntled U.S. military personnel, CIA agents, sophisticated European criminals, or corporate figures lurking in the shadows of the military-industrial complex. This logic is so powerful that under the relentless pressure for melodrama to keep "upping the ante," it took only three seasons for *24* to make its archvillain none other than the president of the United States.

The geopolitical melodrama, in other words, gestures toward global political struggle, but it obsessively returns to the matter of "American liberty." It sets out to find the sources of anti-American terror but, like Cold War narrative, it ends up fighting domestic threats on domestic turf. It rarely depicts the grievances of anti-American terrorists, tends to avoid the history of U.S. foreign policy, and often conceives of terror as a problem without political motives. In all of these ways, the geopolitical melodrama provides a fantasy in which the covert apparatus of the post–Cold War state is understood not as a tool of empire but as a threat to U.S. citizens.

Demonology

Here, then, are the cultural functions of the geopolitical melodrama. First, it heightens the fear of a devastating external attack through the depiction of worst-case scenarios. Second, it offers a counterthreat: the hypertrophied and undemocratic security apparatus. This counterthreat allows the drama to enact a familiar debate about the proper balance between individual freedom and state power—a debate that hinges on the hero's ability to outwit his own security apparatus, break protocol to save his family, and finally bring the apparatus itself back into the service of his own selfless, antiterrorist crusade. Third, and consequently, the plot legitimates the logic of the "state of exception" and the covert sphere. And fourth, it does so within a paranoid narcissism that explains terrorism primarily as a product of, and a problem for, U.S. citizens.

But there is still more to say, for in its shift from external to internal threats, the geopolitical melodrama momentarily aligns the activities of the terrorist with those of the hero-agent, *both* of whom must combat the U.S. security state. The most basic requirement of the plot is that the hero must personally fight the very state security apparatus that is *also* the nemesis and often the target of the terrorist. Like much Cold War literature and film, then, the geopolitical melodrama engages in an odd dance of attraction to and repulsion from the enemy, momentarily aligning the objectives of its own hero with those of the terrorist. After establishing a sharp distinction between terrorists and U.S. citizens, it undermines this distinction by allowing U.S. citizens to occupy the position of rebellion and fear experienced by typical targets of the system. In so doing, it recognizes— but disavows—the terror of the security apparatus for those outside the "homeland" who become subject to its methods.

This latent recognition of the Other should not be entirely surprising to those familiar with the U.S. political tradition of countersubversion that Michael Rogin calls "demonology." Rogin identifies three major historical targets of that tradition—the red and black "savages" of the frontier era, the immigrant working classes of the late nineteenth century, and Cold War Communists. To this list we can now add the post–Cold War jihadist. The racialized demonization of such figures stems not only from a desire to define the nation against its putative enemies, but also from a need to assert the nature of the ideal liberal subject. Rogin explains:

American history in each countersubversive moment has constituted itself in binary opposition to the subversive force that threatened it. Demonology begins as a rigid insistence on difference. That insistence has strategic propaganda purposes, but it also derives from fears of and forbidden desires for identity with the excluded object. In countersubversive discourse, therefore, the opposition breaks down. Its cultural and political productions register the collapse of demonological polarization in a return of the politically and psychologically repressed.[22]

In counterterrorist discourse, as in anti-Communist discourse, a paradoxical demonizing *and* mirroring of the enemy occurs. Similarities between the terrorist and archetypal U.S. heroes (such as the colonial guerrilla or the outgunned freedom fighter) are dismissed in favor of the demonized image of a depraved and envious "coward." At the same time, this external threat is met with a limitation of civil liberties strikingly akin to the repressive authoritarianism associated with the terrorist. "They hate our freedoms.... Their leaders are self-appointed," said President Bush, as his administration curtailed civil liberties and demanded an unprecedented shift of power to the executive branch.

In such pronouncements, demonology and American exceptionalism come together in a single formulation that *recognizes* but then *disavows* the way state policy has begun to mirror the behavior attributed to the enemy. "In the face of an authoritarian, paranoid enemy that envies the magnificence of our democratic institutions, we must use covert and sovereign countermeasures"—or so the argument goes. What the geopolitical melodrama recognizes, in its substitution of hero for terrorist, is that the state has erected a potentially dangerous system of clandestine institutions. The disavowal comes in the genre's almost total erasure of the history and claims of those who are the real targets of the state's clandestine apparatus. In this way, covert-sphere fictions take a step beyond those typically attributed to demonology and exceptionalism. Donald Pease notes that Cold War state fantasy invited citizens to act out "the state's surveillance practices" against minoritized populations "rather than considering themselves targets."[23] But the geopolitical melodrama *does* invite U.S. citizens to imagine themselves targets of the security state—not in an expression of solidarity with minoritized targets, but rather in a narcissistic fantasy that "disappears" populations with grievances about U.S. policy.

How does the fear of catastrophe visited upon the U.S. from without become so swiftly converted into paranoia about the state's own defenses? Writing only days after the 9/11 attacks, Slavoj Žižek brilliantly observed that Westerners had long contemplated similar events in late twentieth-century catastrophe films: "Not only were the media bombarding us all the time with the talk about the terrorist threat; this threat was also obviously libidinally invested—just recall the series of movies from *Escape From New York* to *Independence Day*. That is the rationale of the often-mentioned association of the attacks with Hollywood disaster movies: the unthinkable which happened was the object of fantasy, so that, in a way, America got what it fantasized about, and this was the biggest surprise."[24]

Interestingly, however, Žižek devotes more of his analysis to a related, but somewhat different, narrative tradition. This second tradition— exemplified by the stories of Philip K. Dick and films like *The Matrix* (1999) and *The Truman Show* (1998)—allegorizes ideological control through the concept of a bubble or sphere that insulates U.S. citizens from knowledge of the "real world." As Žižek explains, "The ultimate American paranoiac fantasy is that of an individual living in a small idyllic Californian city, a consumerist paradise, who suddenly starts to suspect that the world he is living in is a fake, a spectacle staged to convince him that he lives in a real world, while all the people around him are in fact actors and extras in a gigantic show."[25] This second narrative tradition is related to the catastrophe tradition. "It is the awareness that we live in an insulated artificial universe which generates the notion that some ominous agent is threatening us all the time with total destruction."[26] The fantasy of solipsistic enclosure is not only a representation of U.S. privilege but also of U.S. half-knowledge. It represents the ideological system that keeps U.S. citizens from confronting the facts of U.S. empire and its attendant privileges. The recognition *and disavowal* of this system is what inspires the fantasy of self-destruction. The catastrophe fantasy is a return of the repressed knowledge that U.S. citizens are sheltered—physically and epistemologically—from the horrors that occur in so many other places in the world.

The geopolitical melodrama combines *both* of these fantasies internally. It expresses anxiety about an ominous external threat, but then turns inward, aligning its hero with the original enemy. In doing so, it offers a momentary vision of the U.S. security apparatus from without. This knowledge is swiftly disavowed, however, when the hero regains control of the security apparatus and uses it as a tool to preserve the nation.

Through this dynamic, the most influential representations of terrorism and antiterrorism of the late Clinton and early George W. Bush presidencies rendered contemporary anti-Western terrorism incomprehensible. It became an abstraction on which to project familiar anxieties about individual autonomy and social control. This way of "knowing" about terrorism reflects the epistemology of the covert sphere. When the state engages secretly with a distant and inscrutable enemy, it alters the way in which citizens understand both their enemies and the state's countermeasures.

Melodrama as Policy

The institutions of the covert sector thus give *fiction* an outsize role in the cultural construction of terrorism. Where else can Americans go to understand the nature of the War on Terror? An obvious answer is traditional news sources. So it seems instructive to consider ABC's January 2006 broadcast entitled "What Can the NSA Do Anyway?" Standing outside the NSA building in Washington, a young reporter asks, "Can the National Security Agency listen to your cell phone calls? You bet," he answers, breathlessly listing the agency's astonishing resources. With "satellites 22,000 miles in space, submarines tapping into fiber-optic cables at the bottom of the ocean, enormous Boeing 707s packed with eavesdropping gear, and major listening centers, the NSA is 'Big Brother's Big Ear.'" And how does the report illustrate these purported NSA capabilities? With film clips from—what else?—the geopolitical melodrama. NSA analysts use computers as "a starting point," says the reporter, "like in *Enemy of the State,* a movie about an NSA agent gone bad." As the reporter describes the plot, ABC shows a clip of computers scanning thousands of phone calls, driver's licenses, bank records, and phone logs to identify a suspect. "An enormous eye miles up," continues the reporter, the NSA is "able to see details in inches, like in last season's *24*"—and here the video segues to a clip of *24*'s tech specialist Chloe O'Brian using her keyboard to zoom from a satellite image of Los Angeles to the details of an automobile license plate.[27]

In such moments, the blurring of fiction and journalism is historically determined by the logic of the covert sphere. Because the War on Terror belongs to a class of events that the public is officially barred from knowing in ways that it can know about other government programs, imaginary representations become an exceptionally powerful source of "information" about government action. Where else could ABC News have gone for confirmation about the operations of the NSA? The strange relation between the reality and representation of covert government runs the other way too, for government agencies often tap the entertainment industry for assistance with secret work. According to the International Spy Museum, CIA officials watched *Mission Impossible* to help brainstorm new spy gadgets.[28] By October 2001, writes Žižek, "a group of Hollywood scenarists and directors, specialists in catastrophe movies, had been established at the instigation of the Pentagon, with the aim of imagining possible scenarios for terrorist attacks and how to fight them."[29] In September 2002, the Interrogation Control Element of the Defense Intelligence Agency gathered intelligence officials, psychologists, and SERE (survival, evasion, resistance, escape) experts to brainstorm more effective modes of interrogation. One of the major ideas generated at the session, according to its coordinator, Diane Beaver, was to mine the show *24* for new approaches. "Bauer had many friends at Guantánamo," Beaver notes, and "he gave people lots of ideas."[30] Perhaps this is why Michael Chertoff, George W. Bush's chief of Homeland Security, would later declare that *24* "reflects real life" and also that the heroic action depicted in *24* "is what we do every day in the government."[31] It is also why U.S. Army Brigadier General Patrick Finnegan, dean of the U.S. Military Academy at West Point, personally visited *24* creator Joel Surnow to warn him that "soldiers in Iraq were being influenced by the uninhibited—and unrepentant—use of torture on the series."[32]

The point here is not simply that visual fictions influence viewers. It is rather that the *structure* of the covert sphere limits such influence to little *but* fiction—and that, as a result, national policy is frequently understood, debated, and even shaped in relation to melodramatic fantasy. As the syndicated talk show host Laura Ingraham put it in her defense of violent interrogation: "The average American loves *24*, okay? They love Jack Bauer. They love *24*. In my mind, that's as close as we're going to get to a national referendum that it's okay to use tough tactics against high-level al Qaeda operatives."[33] In its inane suggestion that the Nielsen ratings are a referendum on state policy, this comment nonetheless correctly discerns the powerful link between the geopolitical melodrama and foreign policy. On the one hand, the geopolitical melodrama allows public contemplation of U.S. policy—albeit in the nonserious space of fictional entertainment; on the other hand, it suggests that such matters are best adjudicated outside the public sphere.

But why take the word of a conservative talk show host? What of our leaders themselves? "No one else seems to notice," observed David Foster Wallace in October 2001, "that some of [Bush's] lines sound almost plagiaristically identical to statements made by Bruce Willis [General William Devereaux] in *The Siege* a couple years back."[34] In his 2006 book, *War by Other Means,* the Bush administration legal counsel John Yoo defended his memorandums authorizing torture by asking, "What if, as the popular Fox television program '24' recently portrayed, a high-level terrorist leader is caught who knows the location of a nuclear weapon? Should it be illegal for the President to use harsh interrogation short of torture to elicit this information? ... Unfortunately, these are no longer hypothetical scenarios."[35]

Yoo's assertion that "ticking bomb" scenarios are "no longer hypothetical" makes visible the surreal way in which the most melodramatic fictions have, for a certain group of policymakers, ceased to seem fictional. In June 2007, for example, while speaking to a panel of senior judges from North America and Europe, U.S. Supreme Court Justice Antonin Scalia defended U.S. antiterrorist policy by citing season 2 of *24.* Rebuffing a Canadian judge's remark that, "thankfully, security agencies ... do not subscribe to the mantra 'What would Jack Bauer do?'" Scalia struck back: "Jack Bauer saved Los Angeles. ... He saved hundreds of thousands of lives. ... Are you going to convict Jack Bauer? Say that criminal law is against him? 'You have the right to a jury trial.' Is any jury going to convict Jack Bauer? I don't think so."[36] Even John McCain, who has repeatedly repudiated torture, had the following response when *Newsweek* asked him in 2005 about a hypothetical "ticking bomb scenario." "If al Qaeda had hidden a nuclear bomb in New York and a suspect involved in the plot had been captured," McCain replied, "you do what you have to do. But you take responsibility for it. Abraham Lincoln suspended *habeas corpus* in the Civil War, and FDR violated the Neutrality Acts before World War II."[37]

Lest these examples suggest that only conservatives craft U.S. foreign policy within the melodramatic fantasy of the ticking bomb scenario, consider the comments Bill Clinton offered in 2007 to NBC's *Meet the Press:*

> I think America's policy should be to oppose torture, to honor the Geneva Conventions for several reasons. One is, it's almost always counterproductive. If you beat somebody up, they'll tell you what they want to hear [*sic*].

Two is, it... really hurts us in the rest of the world and helps to recruit other terrorists. And thirdly, it makes our own people vulnerable to torture. You know, there's a one in a million chance that you might be alone somewhere, and you're Jack Bauer on "24." That's the Jack Bauer example, right? It happens every season with Jack Bauer, but to—in the real world it doesn't happen very much. If you have a policy which legitimizes this, it's a slippery slope and you get in the kind of trouble we've been in here with Abu Ghraib, with Guantánamo, with lots of other examples.... I think what our policy ought to be is to be uncompromisingly opposed to terror—I mean to torture, and that if you're the Jack Bauer person, you'll do whatever you do and you should be prepared to take the consequences. And I think the consequences will be imposed based on what turns out to be the truth.... But... if you... actually had the Jack Bauer moment, we call it, I think you should be prepared to live with the consequences. And yet, ironically, if you look at the show, every time they get the president to approve something, the president gets in trouble, the country gets in trouble. And when Bauer goes out there on his own and is prepared to live with the consequences, it always seems to work better.[38]

What could better explain the logic of the covert sphere? Our *public* policy must be *"uncompromisingly* opposed... to torture"—with the exception of a single compromise: that we expect *covert* agents to act outside the law so long as we don't know about it and they can "live with the consequences." What consequences? Probably none, because as Scalia suggests, no jury will "convict Jack Bauer."

Bill Clinton knows better than almost anyone alive what it feels like for the president to enact counterterror policy, but despite this knowledge, the "don't ask, don't tell" approach he takes here warns against presidential action and presidential knowledge—both of which can lead to "trouble." Since at least the Iran-Contra hearings of the 1980s, fear of such domestic legal "trouble" has strengthened the Cold War strategy of presidential deniability, further severing the operational aspects of the covert sphere from the public supervision of the president. It is precisely because of this severing that even Clinton can conceptualize U.S. antiterror policy through a *fictional* scenario with melodramatic stakes, convenient solutions, and a grandiose vision of U.S. intelligence. Despite all the national intelligence estimates and daily briefings, even the president must rely on fiction to conjure the *operational details* of covert action.

This fact lays bare the relation between the covert sphere and the popular fictions of terror. The geopolitical melodrama articulates a rationale for the covert sector even as it expresses profound anxiety about the undemocratic underpinnings of the state security structure. This contradiction between democratic values ("honor the Geneva Conventions") and covert action ("do whatever you do") is tolerable only because of the genre's structural narcissism, its tendency to erase the effects of empire outside the homeland. Once the narrative rules out representation of non-U.S. perspectives, it not only champions renegade individualism as a desirable interruption of democratic rule, but it even makes this fantasy seem a defense of civil liberties.

The framework of the geopolitical melodrama thus echoes the logic by which President Bush so swiftly deemed "our freedom" the obvious target of the 9/11 attacks. It helps explain why Americans were so well prepared, after 9/11, to debate the proper relation between security and liberty but so perplexed about the motives of the attackers, which were variously identified as zealotry, jealousy, insanity, brainwashing, religious intolerance, the desire for virgins, and so on. A decade later, U.S. citizens still lack a clear sense of their enemy. Given the nature of Western discourse on terror, is it surprising that Americans continue to understand terrorism through psychological, rather than historico-political, frameworks, or that the United States is still in a "war" despite little public consensus about the nature, goals, or grievances of its enemies?[39]

These problems are reflected in the popular U.S. fictions of terror, which in 2001 constituted the dominant national discourse on the subject. What is finally most revealing about these fictions is the system of contradictions that defines them: their dread of external assault is trumped by their fear of government repression; their disgust for the terrorist is tempered by sympathy for those combating the security apparatus; and their anxiety about the suspension of law is undercut by their celebration of maverick pragmatism. All of these contradictions reflect the public secret at the heart of U.S. democracy: we have institutionalized undemocratic means of preserving our democracy.

NOTES

Preface

1. Corey Flintoff, "Afghan TV Show Aims to Burnish Police Reputation," *Morning Edition*, National Public Radio, December 7, 2010, http://www.npr.org/2010/12/07/131857237/afghan-tv-show-aims-to-burnish-police-reputation.

Introduction

1. Jane Mayer, *The Dark Side: The Inside Story of How the War on Terror Turned into a War on American Ideals* (New York: Doubleday, 2008), 39.
2. Ibid.
3. Quoted ibid., 10.
4. George W. Bush, "Transcript of President Bush's Address to a Joint Session of Congress on Thursday Night, September 20, 2001," CNN, September 20, 2001, http://archives.cnn.com/2001/US/09/20/gen.bush.transcript/.
5. "By 'the public sphere,'" writes Habermas, "we mean first of all a realm of our social life in which something approaching public opinion can be formed. Access is guaranteed to all citizens. A portion of the public sphere comes into being in every conversation in which private individuals assemble to form a public body," a process now accomplished through "the media of the public sphere." Jürgen Habermas, "The Public Sphere: An Encyclopedia Article," *New German Critique* 3 (1974): 49. See also Habermas, *The Structural Transformation of the Public Sphere: An Inquiry into*

a Category of Bourgeois Society, trans. Thomas Burger with Frederick Lawrence (Cambridge, MA: MIT Press, 1989).

6. Mayer, *Dark Side,* 48.

7. In stressing the persistence of Cold War security institutions into the twenty-first-century War on Terror, I do not mean to suggest that the two periods are fundamentally alike. For an ingenious account of the way post–Cold War U.S. political culture transformed the Cold War discourse of "American exceptionalism," see Donald Pease, *The New American Exceptionalism* (Minneapolis: University of Minnesota Press, 2009). Pease argues that the post–Cold War period has been characterized by a "breakdown of the encompassing state fantasy called American exceptionalism that had regulated U.S. citizens' relationship to the political order for the preceding half century" (1). Pease details the transformation of the Cold War National Security State into the Homeland Security State through a post–Cold War interregnum during which a plague of short-lived state fantasies competed to replace the overarching fantasy of Cold War exceptionalism. This interregnum began with George Herbert Walker Bush's notion of a "New World Order," but it was George W. Bush's Homeland Security State that, unfortunately, "was most successful in establishing a state fantasy...as encompassing and inclusive as the cold war state fantasy" (204). Pease thus sees September 11, 2001, as a crucial historical marker, one that "supplied a conclusive ending to the cold war even as it permitted the state to inaugurate an utterly different configuration" (154). Similarly, Phillip Wegner argues that 9/11 marked a distinctive end to the Cold War (*Life between Two Deaths, 1989–2001: U.S. Culture in the Long Nineties* [Durham: Duke University Press, 2009]). While I find these periodizing arguments persuasive, my point is that neither 9/11 nor the new state configuration it inaugurated displaced covert action as the heart of U.S. foreign policy. This continuity is the basis on which I treat the two periods together. As Pease himself notes, the War on Terror's "powers of governance surpassed even the reach of the cold war" (*New American Exceptionalism,* 154).

It is worth adding here that the Cold War itself is hardly a monolithic period and must be understood partly as a cluster of smaller movements and dynamics. The same is true of its representations. The culture of the 1950s seems strikingly serious, patriotic, and nervous when compared with that of the 1960s (which produced satires like *Catch-22, Dr. Strangelove,* and *The Russians Are Coming! The Russians Are Coming!*). Along with the war in Southeast Asia, the scandals, investigations, and exposé journalism of the late 1960s and '70s (Daniel Ellsberg, Seymour Hersh, Woodward and Bernstein) resulted in heightened cynicism about government, a more aggressive press, and some institutional reforms. The Reagan-Bush era saw a revival of American exceptionalism, complete with nostalgia for the 1950s and amnesic accounts of U.S. empire. Beginning in the 1990s terrorism became a dominant focus of fiction about state security. The period directly after 9/11 was characterized by a revival of anxiety akin to that of the early 1950s, but leftist disgust at the George W. Bush administration eventually led to more cynical and satiric representations of the covert state. On cultural dynamics of the Cold War, see Alan Nadel, *Containment Culture: American Narratives, Postmodernism, and the Atomic Age* (Durham: Duke University Press, 1995). Nadel shows persuasively how the "containment culture" of the 1950s dissolved amid the rise of postmodernism, Cold War satire, and growing public unease about the Cold War security state.

8. National Security Council, "NSC 10 4-A, 17 December, 1947," document 35, in *CIA Cold War Records: The CIA under Harry Truman,* ed. Michael Warner (Washington, DC: CIA History Staff/Center for the Study of Intelligence, 1994), 173.

9. Kenneth Osgood, *Total Cold War: Eisenhower's Secret Propaganda Battle at Home and Abroad* (Lawrence: University Press of Kansas, 2006), 38. Other important histories of the period include Martin Walker, *The Cold War* (New York: Henry Holt, 1994); Walter LaFeber, *America, Russia, and the Cold War, 1945–2000* (New York: McGraw Hill, 2002).

10. National Security Council, "NSC 10/2, 18 June 1948," document 43, *CIA Cold War Records: The CIA under Harry Truman,* ed. Michael Warner (Washington, DC: CIA History Staff/Center for the Study of Intelligence, 1994), 215–16; emphasis added.

11. Over the next decade and a half, to take a few obvious examples, White House officials would solemnly declare that "there was absolutely no—N-O—no deliberate attempt to violate Soviet airspace" with U-2 aircraft, that the United States had absolutely no intention of "intervening in Cuba," that our policy in Indonesia was "one of careful neutrality," that we were not involved in Guatemala, and so on. See David Wise and Thomas B. Ross, *The Invisible Government* (New York: Random House, 1964), 356.

12. Gregory Mitrovich, *Undermining the Kremlin: America's Strategy to Subvert the Soviet Bloc, 1947–1956* (Ithaca, NY: Cornell University Press, 2000), 58.

13. Osgood, *Total Cold War,* 97. Osgood shows that Eisenhower radically transformed the U.S. military into an institution dedicated to managing public opinion at home and abroad (see 39–40). See also Frances Stonor Saunders, *The Cultural Cold War: The CIA and the World of Arts and Letters* (New York: New Press, 1999), 41.

14. Wise and Ross, *Invisible Government,* 4.

15. Harry S. Truman, "Limit CIA Role to Intelligence," *Washington Post,* December 22, 1963, A11.

16. Fareed Zakaria, "What America Has Lost," *Newsweek,* September 13, 2010, 18. With the exception of one earlier year, the total national intelligence budget became public only in fiscal year 2007. Because the distribution of funds among intelligence agencies is still secret and because much intelligence work is overseen by the Department of Defense, the public figure potentially understates total expenditures. Even if the public figure is accurate, intelligence claims more resources than all domestic sectors of government except Health and Human Services ($78.7B in 2010) and Transportation ($72.5B in 2010). But even these domestic agencies spend heavily on national security. The Preparedness and Response unit of Health and Human Services, for instance, funds Project BioShield, a domestic response to chemical, biological, and radiological attack; and the Interstate Highway System was developed under Eisenhower partly to speed evacuation of cities in the event of nuclear attack.

17. Statistical data here come from articles by Dana Priest and William Arkin: "A Hidden World, Growing beyond Control," *Washington Post,* July 19, 2010; "National Security Inc.," *Washington Post,* July 20, 2010; and "The Secrets Next Door," *Washington Post,* July 21, 2010; all available at http://projects.washingtonpost.com/top-secret-america/articles/#article-index. In offering these figures, I do not mean to suggest that covert action is the predominant function of intelligence agencies. Although such information is hard to obtain, the former CIA director William Colby is on record saying that by 1978 "propaganda, political action, and paramilitary activities" consumed 40–50% of agency resources (Osgood, *Total Cold War,* 97).

18. The so-called Moynihan Commission report is officially titled *Report of the Commission on Protecting and Reducing Government Secrecy, 1997, Senate Document 105–2, Pursuant to Public Law 236,* 103rd Congress (Washington, DC: U.S. Government Printing Office, 1997), http://www.fas.org/sgp/library/moynihan/index.html. Moynihan's own compelling critique of state secrecy is best expressed in Daniel Patrick Moynihan, *Secrecy: The American Experience* (New Haven, CT: Yale University Press, 1999).

19. Giorgio Agamben, *State of Exception,* trans. Kevin Attell (Chicago: University of Chicago Press, 2005).

20. Nancy Fraser, "Rethinking the Public Sphere: A Contribution to the Critique of Actually Existing Democracy," in *Habermas and the Public Sphere,* ed. Craig Calhoun, 109–42 (Cambridge, MA: MIT Press, 1992).

21. Michael Warner, *Publics and Counterpublics* (Cambridge, MA: Zone/MIT, 1992).

22. Drawing on Jacqueline Rose's *States of Fantasy* (Oxford: Clarendon, 1996), Donald Pease offers a brilliant psychoanalytics of national identity in which "state fantasy" becomes the ideological mechanism that covers the gap between national ideals and state practice. A "state fantasy" is not a collective delusion or false consciousness; it is a socially salient "structure of desire"

that reorganizes the way citizens "want to participate in the state's imperial will," and in so doing produces an even *stronger* desire to form the anti-imperial nation of their fantasy (*New American Exceptionalism,* 1, 21). The primary state fantasy of the Cold War, "American exceptionalism," functioned by eradicating "the difference between the national ideal U.S. citizens wanted and the faulty nation they had, by representing America as having already achieved all that a nation could be" (22).

23. See Bonnie Honig, *Emergency Politics: Paradox, Law, Democracy* (Princeton, NJ: Princeton University Press, 2009).

24. In *Critique and Crisis: Enlightenment and the Pathogenesis of Modern Society* (1959; repr., Cambridge, MA: MIT, 1988), Reinhart Koselleck argues that secret societies such as the Illuminati were the mechanism that permitted the emergence of democracy. Habermas has been criticized by even admiring readers for idealizing the bourgeois public sphere and painting too dim a view of the contemporary public sphere; neglecting serious barriers to participation by women, minorities, and the lower classes; too strictly separating the state from the public; presuming there can be a universal "public good"; frowning on the idea of multiple publics; and viewing the public sphere as a forum where social differences can be set aside. For excellent critical essays on these subjects by Keith Michael Baker, Seyla Benhabib, Craig Calhoun, Geoff Eley, Nancy Fraser, and others, see Craig Calhoun, ed., *Habermas and the Public Sphere* (Cambridge, MA: MIT Press, 1993). I am also indebted to Warner, *Publics and Counterpublics,* and Douglas Kellner, "Habermas, the Public Sphere, and Democracy: A Critical Intervention" (unpublished essay), http://www.gseis.ucla.edu/faculty/kellner/. For an excellent account of Habermas's relation to postmodernism, see Andreas Huyssen, *After the Great Divide: Modernism, Mass Culture, Postmodernism* (Bloomington: Indiana University Press, 1986), esp. 199–206. For an insightful discussion of privacy and literature in relation to the Cold War public sphere, see Deborah Nelson, *Pursuing Privacy in Cold War America* (New York: Columbia University Press, 2002).

25. Such "secrets" often concern the history of marginalized groups, and interestingly, narratives of marginalization often employ a rhetoric of secrecy and covert action. It is no accident, for instance, that the central crisis of Ralph Ellison's *Invisible Man* is the deathbed confession of the narrator's grandfather that he has been "a traitor" all his born days, and "a spy in the enemy's country." The novel is deeply invested in the clandestine, depicting its protagonist as an unwitting victim of subterfuge who eventually commits himself to "covert preparation for a more overt action." Moreover, the covert methodology of the novel—what Alan Nadel calls its "invisible criticism"—operates not unlike the so-called Aesopian language sometimes attributed to Cold War Communists: "Who knows," Ellison's narrator concludes, "but that, on the lower frequencies, I speak for you?" Ralph Ellison, *Invisible Man* (New York: Viking, 1952), 16, 13, 581. Similar links between espionage and identity are central to novels like Chang-Rae Lee's *Native Speaker* (New York: Riverhead, 1996) and Susan Choi's *A Person of Interest* (New York: Penguin, 2008). Gloria Anzaldúa's "Enemy of the State" even more explicitly understands mestiza consciousness as a form of espionage, a "ferreting in the dark/psyches of a people/uncovering secrets." Anzaldúa virtually paraphrases the Invisible Man's grandfather when she asks, "Who'd ever think her/a spy/betraying her country/unmasking her country" (Gloria E. Anzaldúa, *The Gloria Anzaldúa Reader,* ed. AnaLouise Keating [Durham: Duke University Press, 2009], 97–98). On "Aesopian language," see Ellen Schrecker, *Many Are the Crimes: McCarthyism in America* (Boston: Little Brown, 1998), 194. Alan Nadel's *Invisible Criticism: Ralph Ellison and the American Canon* (Iowa City: University of Iowa Press, 1988) is a fascinating study of Ellison's subterranean commentary on the canon of U.S. literature. For an outstanding discussion of Ellison's novel in relation to the rhetoric of the public sphere, the politics of visibility and invisibility, and the history of racialization in U.S. literature and culture, see Robyn Wiegman's *American Anatomies: Theorizing Race and Gender* (Durham: Duke University Press, 1995).

26. Wise and Ross, *Invisible Government,* 4.

27. Saunders, *Cultural Cold War,* 38

28. For a fuller version of this argument, see Timothy Melley, *Empire of Conspiracy: The Culture of Paranoia in Postwar America* (Ithaca, NY: Cornell University Press, 2000). The following are excellent accounts of the subject: Patrick O'Donnell, *Latent Destinies: Cultural Paranoia and Contemporary U.S. Narrative* (Durham: Duke University Press, 2000); Peter Knight, *Conspiracy Culture: From Kennedy to "The X-Files"* (New York: Routledge, 2000); and Mark Fenster, *Conspiracy Theories: Secrecy and Power in American Culture* (Minneapolis: University of Minnesota Press, 2001).

29. Michel Foucault, *The History of Sexuality,* trans. Robert Hurley (New York: Vintage, 1978), 1:78–80.

30. Michael Taussig, *Defacement: Public Secrecy and the Labor of the Negative* (Stanford: Stanford University Press, 1999), 5, 2, 7, 6; original emphasis removed from some passages.

31. Leaks come in many forms. Most involve a covert source protected by a visible journalist and press. Some, however, come in the form of tell-all memoirs or other publications, including spy novels. According to J. Ransom Clark—a former CIA officer who now keeps a bibliography of intelligence materials (http://intellit.muskingum.edu)—such books, once rare, have become increasingly popular since the 1997 memoir of Duane R. Clarridge, *A Spy for All Seasons: My Life in the CIA* (New York: Scribner, 1997). See Scott Shane, "Ex-Spies Tell It All," *New York Times,* March 15, 2005, http://www.nytimes.com/2005/03/15/books/15spyb.html?_r=1.

32. I am indebted here to a talk by Joseph Masco on "the secrecy-publicity matrix" given at the Duke University workshop on "Security, Suspicion, and Intelligence," Durham, NC, October 17, 2008.

33. Rory Carroll, "Kathryn Bigelow Given Information on Unit That Killed Osama bin Laden," *Guardian,* May 23, 2012, http://www.guardian.co.uk/world/2012/may/24/kathryn-bigelow-bin-laden-intelligence. "Zero Dark Thirty" is a working title. The Internet Movie Database indicates a release date of December 12, 2012, for Bigelow's "Untitled Project" (http://pro.imdb.com/title/tt1790885/).

34. Paglen is a geographer and artist who has developed a number of fascinating projects about the "black world" of U.S. intelligence agencies. These include the photography of top secret government sites and the mapping of classified spacecraft in orbit with data from amateur astronomers. See Trevor Paglen, *Invisible: Covert Operations and Classified Landscapes* (New York: Aperture, 2010), and *Blank Spots on the Map: The Dark Geography of the Pentagon's Secret World* (New York: NAL, 2010).

35. According to Philip Caputo, Ken Lopez's catalog of Vietnam literature alone contains 3,500 titles. Philip Caputo, "Casualties of War," *New York Times Book Review,* June 20, 2010, 1.

36. It is worth recalling here Annabel Patterson's argument that in early modern England, fiction was a primary vehicle for political opinions potentially threatening to the state. See Annabel Patterson, *Censorship and Interpretation: The Conditions of Writing and Reading in Early Modern England* (Madison: University of Wisconsin Press, 1984).

37. Joseph Wilson, "What I Didn't Find in Africa," *New York Times,* July 6, 2003, http://www.nytimes.com/2003/07/06/opinion/what-i-didn-t-find-in-africa.html?src=pm.

38. Julie Bosman, "In Novels, an Ex-Spy Returns to the Fold," *New York Times,* March 19, 2011, B1, B4. The Plame affair is notable for several other reasons: first, it is a reverse-gendered form of the allegorical narrative that Joan Didion, among others, has so insistently used to address the problem of covert action. In Didion's version, a woman is in love with a public official and a spy (see chapter 4). In this case, the woman is the spy and she is married to a public official. The marriage is almost splintered when the ambassador fights the administration in public and the covert operative maintains her vow of secrecy. Eventually, however, she elects to testify to Congress and tell the story of her exposure for political purposes. *Fair Game* was dropped by its initial publisher, Crown, and when it was eventually published by Simon & Schuster it was heavily redacted

by the CIA. Plame Wilson's new line of novels will still need to be vetted by the CIA, but presumably much less aggressively. See Valerie Plame Wilson, *Fair Game: My Life as a Spy, My Betrayal by the White House* (New York: Simon & Schuster, 2007). The film *Fair Game* (DVD, directed by Doug Liman [2010; Santa Monica, CA: Summit Entertainment, 2011]) is also based on Joseph Wilson's *The Politics of Truth: Inside the Lies That Led to War and Betrayed My Wife's CIA Identity: A Diplomat's Memoir* (New York: Carroll and Graf, 2004).

39. Daniel Ellsberg, *Secrets: A Memoir of Vietnam and the Pentagon Papers* (New York: Viking, 2002), 237–38.

40. In the context of Habermas's work, my association of fiction with the covert sphere may seem problematic, for fiction was crucial to the emergence of the bourgeois *public* sphere. The novel, Habermas explains, "fashioned for the first time the kind of realism that allowed anyone to enter into the literary action as…substitute relationships for reality." The novel not only permitted empathic readers to imitate the private relationships described in fiction but allowed the growth of a new discourse in which readers "reflected critically and in public" on such texts. Yet the novel itself does not epitomize reason for Habermas. Indeed, for Habermas, the novel places a "final veil over the difference between reality and illusion. The reality as illusion that the genre created received its proper name in English, 'fiction': it shed the character of the *merely* fictitious" and "allowed anyone to enter into the literary action as a substitute…for reality" (*Structural Transformation,* 50). Fiction, in other words, *mystifies* the relation between reality and discourse. What makes fiction such an important part of the growth of public reason is not its essential blurring of "reality and illusion" but its positioning in a much larger apparatus of critical discourses and institutions—the *Tischgesellschaften* (table societies), literary societies, salons, and coffeehouses; the concert halls, theaters, and museums; the pamphlets, journals, book clubs, libraries, and subscription services. For Habermas, the emergence of the literary public sphere comes with the institutionalization of "art *criticism* as conversation" (40). As critics became "spokesmen for the public" (41), an entire culture of critical discussion came to define the rational public sphere: "On the one hand, philosophy was no longer possible except as critical philosophy, literature and art no longer except in connection with literary and art criticism. What the works of art themselves criticized simply reached its proper end in the 'critical journals.' On the other hand, it was only through the critical absorption of philosophy, literature, and art that the public attained enlightenment" (42). The novel became an instrument of enlightenment, in other words, because it was situated amid a welter of critical discourses.

Whereas the novel originally contributed to public reason by communicating a vision of *private life,* the primary cultural work of covert sphere narrative is to communicate to the public a vision of *secret state work.* As state secrecy increases, it hinders the privileged forms of modern narrative knowledge—history and journalism—that insist on the correspondence of narrative to events. Such correspondences are difficult to trace when it is hard (or illegal) to obtain documents, official confirmation, and other traditional forms of evidence. In certain areas of critical importance to democracy, fiction thus begins to supplant the social functions of narrative discourses rooted in the modern ideal of truth as a correspondence between statements and evidence. At the same time, putatively nonfiction discourse comes to resemble fiction, for it lacks the evidence that distinguishes it from fiction. A widespread historiographic crisis develops, a sense that it is difficult to narrate important events in the form of history. This blurring of the distinction between fiction and history is a central feature of postmodernism.

41. Jeremy Bentham dealt with this problem by concentrating on the small sector of the public that thinks independently on the basis of public information. Jeremy Bentham, "Essay on Political Tactics," chapter 2, "Of Publicity," in *The Works of Jeremy Bentham,* vol. 2, ed. John Bowring (1821; repr., New York: Russell and Russell, 1962), 312–13.

42. Warner, *Publics and Counterpublics,* 72. A public, Warner explains, "exists *by virtue of being addressed*" and "in this sense is as much notional as empirical" (67). Habermas refers to the

"fiction of the *one* public," clearly acknowledging the ideological status of the concept of the public (*Structural Transformation*, 56).

43. Noam Chomsky, *Toward a New Cold War: U.S. Foreign Policy from Vietnam to Reagan*, rev. ed. (1982; repr., New York: New Press, 2003), 88.

44. John Lewis Gaddis, *We Now Know: Rethinking Cold War History* (Oxford: Oxford University Press, 1998).

45. Arguing in 1978 against a "repressive model" of power emblematized by the absolutist state, Foucault famously declared, "We still have not cut off the head of the king" (Foucault, *History of Sexuality*, 1:188). I have no intention of reanimating the sovereign, but the role of the state cannot be ignored. I am indebted to Andrew Hebard's careful overview of how American studies has tended to "dismiss the concept of the state as an ideological fiction" or to "reify it as an object … whose representations are only read symptomatically as ideology" *The Poetics of Sovereignty in American Literature, 1885–1910* [Cambridge: Cambridge University Press, forthcoming].

46. On this concept, see Donald Pease, "New Americanists: Revisionist Interventions into the Canon," *boundary 2* 17, no. 1 (Spring 1990): 1–38.

47. Slavoj Žižek, *Looking Awry: An Introduction to Jacques Lacan through Popular Culture* (Cambridge, MA: MIT Press, 1992), 27–35, 70, 168. Žižek offers multiple alternative versions of this formula throughout his work, which I am greatly simplifying for concision. For Žižek, belief is "radically exterior," embodied in *action*, not knowledge. Hence belief and knowledge are usually in contradiction and must be managed by fantasy. Žižek describes three primary ways in which we avoid a confrontation with the real: first, fetishistic disavowal (I know very well, but just the same…); second, obsessive activity (a compulsion to take the problem seriously that converts it into a source of trauma); and finally, psychotic projection of meaning onto the real (seeing it as "a message" of some kind) (ibid., 35).

48. William Gibson, *Spook Country* (New York: Putnam, 2007), 79–80. This NSA policy was first reported by James Risen and Eric Lichtblau, "Bush Lets U.S. Spy on Callers without Courts," *New York Times*, December 16, 2005, http://www.nytimes.com/2005/12/16/politics/16program.html?pagewanted=all.

49. *A Few Good Men*, DVD, directed by Rob Reiner (1992; Burbank: Culver City, CA: Columbia, 1997).

50. Slavoj Žižek, "Welcome to the Desert of the Real!" *South Atlantic Quarterly* 101, no. 2 (Spring 2002): 385–89. Reprinted, substantially modified, in *Welcome to the Desert of the Real: Five Essays on September 11 and Related Dates* (London: Verso, 2002).

51. Taussig, *Defacement*, 6.

52. John R. Searle, "The Logical Status of Fictional Discourse," *New Literary History* 6, no.2 (1975): 320. Searle is developing a point from J. L. Austin's essential study, *How to Do Things with Words* (Oxford: Oxford University Press, 1962), 22.

53. Joseph Burkholder Smith, *Portrait of a Cold Warrior: Second Thoughts of a Top CIA Agent* (New York: Ballantine, 1976), 316.

54. Harry Mathews, *My Life in CIA* (Normal, IL: Dalkey Archive Press, 2005).

55. CIA, "Clandestine Service History, Overthrow of Premier Mossadeq of Iran, November 1952–August 1953," http://www.nytimes.com/library/world/mideast/041600iran-cia-index.html. As Mark Gasiorowski notes, "The most general conclusion that can be drawn from these documents is that the CIA extensively stage-managed the entire coup, not only carrying it out but also preparing the groundwork for it by subordinating various important Iranian political actors and using propaganda and other instruments to influence public opinion against Mossadeq" ("What's New on the Iran 1953 Coup in the *New York Times* Article [April 16, 2000, front page] and the Documents Posted on the Web," Electronic Briefing Book no. 28, National Security Archive, April 19, 2000, http://www.gwu.edu/~nsarchiv/NSAEBB/NSAEBB28/). For excellent histories of this episode, see Tim Weiner, *Legacy of Ashes: The History of the CIA* (New York: Anchor,

2007), 92–105, and Stephen Kinzer, *All the Shah's Men: An American Coup and the Roots of Middle East Terror* (New York: John Wiley and Sons, 2003).

56. Dwight D. Eisenhower, *Mandate for Change, 1953–1956: The White House Years* (Garden City, NY: Doubleday, 1963), 164.

57. U.S. Department of State, "Diplomacy and Defense: A Test of National Maturity," *Department of State Bulletin,* December 4, 1961. See *Encyclopedia Britannica Profiles: The American Presidency,* s.v. "John F. Kennedy: A Long Twilight Struggle," http://www.britannica.com/presidents/article-9116921.

58. David C. Martin, *Wilderness of Mirrors: Intrigue, Deception, and the Secrets That Destroyed Two of the Cold War's Most Important Agents* (New York: HarperCollins, 1981), 124–25. The Kennedys were well aware that many plots were being developed to topple Castro. My point is that even with such knowledge there was a simultaneous tendency toward disavowal. For more on the Kennedys' attempts to remove Castro, see Seymour Hersh, *The Dark Side of Camelot* (Boston: Little Brown, 1997).

59. Martin, *Wilderness of Mirrors,* 128–29.

60. The White House, "First Lady Michelle Obama to Surprise Visitors on White House Tour at 10:45 AM ET," press release, White House Press Office, January 20, 2010, http://www.whitehouse.gov/the-press-office/first-lady-michelle-obama-surprise-visitors-white-house-tour-1045-am-et-livestream-.

61. "International Spy Museum in Washington, D.C.," *Voice of America News,* http://www.youtube.com/watch?v=vAPtgEtr3BE&feature=related.

62. International Spy Museum, http://www.spymuseum.org.

63. Ibid.

64. Central Intelligence Agency, CIA Museum, https://www.cia.gov/about-cia/cia-museum/. Since the end of the Cold War, the agency has granted increasing public access (punctuated by occasional retrenchment) to formerly classified documents. In 1995, for example, the CIA acknowledged and permitted publication of key papers from its once secret academic journal, *Studies in Intelligence.* The volume's editor, a Yale political scientist, notes that the CIA judged that "releasing most of this material would further its institutional interests" and particularly wanted the "special visibility that could come from publication by a major university press" (especially the one that provided the early agency most of its top brass) (H. Bradford Westerfield, *Inside CIA's Private World: Declassified Articles from the Agency's Internal Journal, 1955–1992* (New Haven, CT: Yale University Press), xiv.

65. "Rare Look at In-House CIA Museum," *Voice of America Television,* June 13, 2008, http://www.youtube.com/watch?v=hgBRvrEb_a4.

66. Central Intelligence Agency, "The CIA Museum: The People behind the Magic," https://www.cia.gov/news-information/featured-story-archive/cia-museum-the-people.html.

67. CIA Museum, https://www.cia.gov/about-cia/cia-museum/.

68. On the postmodern synthesis of "high" and mass cultural forms, see Ihab Hassan, "POSTmodernISM: A Paracritical Bibliography," in *The Postmodern Turn: Essays in Postmodern Theory and Culture* (1971; repr., Columbus: Ohio State University Press, 1987), 25–45; Huyssen, *After the Great Divide;* and Fredric Jameson, *Postmodernism; or, The Cultural Logic of Late Capitalism* (Durham: Duke University Press, 1989).

69. Nadel, *Containment Culture,* esp. 13–37; Ellen Tyler May, *Homeward Bound: American Families in the Cold War Era,* rev. ed. (New York: Basic Books, 1999).

70. Michael Davidson, *Guys Like Us: Citing Masculinity in Cold War Poetics* (Chicago: University of Chicago Press, 2004); Robert J. Corber, *Homosexuality in Cold War America: Resistance and the Crisis of Masculinity* (Durham: Duke University Press, 1997).

71. Amy Kaplan, *The Anarchy of Empire in the Making of U.S. Culture* (Cambridge, MA: Harvard University Press, 2002). Donald Pease describes how the "domestic" has been refigured, since

9/11, from "Virgin Land" to "Ground Zero" and "Homeland." Through the latter terms, Pease argues, the Bush administration transformed the "governing metaphor that has anchored the people to a relationship to the national territory" (*New American Exceptionalism,* 155).

72. For a study of gendered constructs in George Kennan's early conception of cold warfare, see Frank Costigliola, "'Unceasing Pressure for Penetration': Gender, Pathology, and Emotion in George Kennan's Formation of the Cold War," *Journal of American History* 83, no. 4 (1997): 1309–39. Books on the cult of masculinity among early cold warriors include Robert D. Dean, *Imperial Brotherhood: Gender and the Making of Cold War Foreign Policy* (Amherst: University of Massachusetts Press, 2003); and K. A. Cuordileone, *Manhood and American Political Culture in the Cold War* (New York: Routledge, 2004).

73. The notion of a "boy gang"—a Beat generation dream of artistic community—is one form of the elite, male "compulsory homosociality" that Davidson locates throughout the Cold War United States. See Davidson, *Guys Like Us,* 13–19. As Saunders (*Cultural Cold War*) and others have shown, the CIA was an elite, literary community.

74. I am not suggesting that the domestic sphere was in fact a place of female passivity. I am describing an ideology of womanhood. This ideology undoubtedly affected female civic participation, but in practice, of course, many individuals resisted expectations.

75. Michael Buckley, *NERDS: National Espionage, Rescue, and Defense Society* (New York: Amulet, 2010).

76. Tim Ingham, "*Call of Duty* Series Tops 55 Million Sales," *MCV: The Market for Computer and Video Games,* November 27, 2009, http://www.mcvuk.com/news/read/call-of-duty-series-tops-55-million-sales. See also Shane Richmond, "Call of Duty: Modern Warfare 3 Breaks Sales Records," *Telegraph,* November 11, 2011, http://www.telegraph.co.uk/technology/video-games/video-game-news/8884726/Call-of-Duty-Modern-Warfare-3-breaks-sales-records.html.

77. "*Call of Duty: Black Ops*—Official Single Player Trailer [HD]," YouTube, http://www.youtube.com/watch?v=41gr0IF91eg; "*Call of Duty: Black Ops*—World Premiere Uncut Trailer," YouTube, http://www.youtube.com/watch?v=OtRnpC7ddv8.

78. Susan Jeffords, *The Remasculinization of America: Gender and the Vietnam War* (Bloomington: Indiana University Press, 1989); Ann Douglas, *The Feminization of American Culture* (New York: Knopf, 1977). Andreas Huyssen links the split between high art and mass culture with the birth of a feminized consumer culture. See *After the Great Divide,* 44–62.

79. In fact, Bush never actually used the phrase "go shopping," though he was widely cited as doing so and has since admitted meaning as much. What Bush said at O'Hare Airport in Chicago, on September 27, 2001, was, "When they struck, they wanted to create an atmosphere of fear. And one of the great goals of this nation's war is to restore public confidence in the airline industry. It's to tell the traveling public: Get on board. Do your business around the country. Fly and enjoy America's great destination spots. Get down to Disney World in Florida. Take your families and enjoy life, the way we want it to be enjoyed." Of those remarks Bush more recently observed, "I would be mocked and criticized for telling Americans to 'go shopping' after 9/11. I never actually used that phrase, but that's beside the point. In the threat-filled months after 9/11, traveling on airplanes, visiting tourist destinations, and, yes, going shopping, were acts of defiance and patriotism" (*Decision Points* [New York: Crown, 2010], 443–44).

80. On the history of this tendency, including its effect on the discipline of American studies, see Amy Kaplan, "'Left Alone with America': The Absence of Empire in the Study of American Culture," in *Cultures of American Imperialism,* ed. Amy Kaplan and Donald Pease, 3–21 (Durham: Duke University Press, 1993); and also Amy Kaplan, *Anarchy of Empire.*

81. As Michael Bérubé observes, the most important distinction in postwar fiction is not between modernism and postmodernism but between literature written here and literature written abroad. Bérubé, "Teaching Postmodern Fiction without Being Sure That the Genre Exists,"

Chronicle of Higher Education, May 19, 2000, http://chronicle.com/article/Teaching-Postmodern-Fiction/10227. There is indeed a striking difference between U.S. representations of the covert sphere and work written by expatriates of nations subject to Cold War covert action (notable examples include Junot Díaz, *The Brief and Wondrous Life of Oscar Wao* [New York: Riverhead, 2007]; Moshin Hamid, *The Reluctant Fundamentalist* [New York: Harcourt, 2007]; and Salman Rushdie, *Shalimar the Clown* [New York: Random House, 2005]). Ann Douglas, likewise, argues that the division between postmodern and postcolonial literature reflects the division between U.S. and non-U.S. perspectives on the Cold War. Ann Douglas, "Periodizing the American Century: Modernism, Postmodernism, and Postcolonialism in the Cold War Context," *Modernism/Modernity* 5, no. 3 (1998): 71–98.

82. Tobin Siebers, *Cold War Criticism and the Politics of Skepticism* (Oxford: Oxford University Press, 1993), 29–30, 112, 34.

83. *The Package,* DVD, directed by Andrew Davis (1989; Beverly Hills, CA: MGM, 2000).

84. Osgood, *Total Cold War,* 147, 408n74; Weiner, *Legacy of Ashes,* 106–19.

85. James Bamford, *Body of Secrets: Anatomy of the Ultra-Secret National Security Agency* (New York: Anchor, 2002), 78–91.

86. Saunders, *Cultural Cold War,* 129.

87. Ibid., 234–51, esp. 245.

88. Andreas Huyssen gives an excellent account of the way postmodernism responds to the solidification of a modernist canon as a Cold War weapon against Soviet realism. This public dynamic in fact was supported deliberately and secretly by the cultural wing of the CIA—a fact that emerged after Huyssen's *After the Great Divide* was published in 1986. On *Four Quartets,* see Saunders, *Cultural Cold War,* 248.

89. Habermas, *Structural Transformation,* 53–54.

90. Ibid., 35.

91. Ibid., 27.

92. Ibid., 195. Part of the interest and difficulty of Habermas's concept, as Keith Michael Baker points out, is that the public sphere can be understood either as "a normative ideal or as an actually existing social reality" ("Defining the Public Sphere in Eighteenth-Century France: Variations on a Theme by Habermas," in Calhoun, *Habermas and the Public Sphere,* 183). Even if we read the bourgeois public sphere as an ideal, as Craig Calhoun points out, Habermas tends to assess the eighteenth century through its most celebrated thinkers (Locke and Kant) and the contemporary public sphere through popular mass culture. As a result, he tends to overestimate contemporary degeneration of the public sphere. Indeed, Habermas's idealized portrait of the eighteenth-century public sphere must be understood in part as a strategy for setting up the story of the public sphere's tragic decline amid the forces of public relations, advertising, and spectacle. Whereas publicity once purportedly "guaranteed the connection between rational-critical public debate and the legislative foundation of domination," Habermas claims, it now "serves the manipulation *of* the public" (*Structural Transformation,* 177–78). The growth of public relations in the mid-twentieth-century United States, in particular, helped transform public discourse into "acts of individuated reception" and the public sphere into "a public sphere in appearance only" (171, 161).

93. Ibid., 201, 140. The quoted passage is from M. L. Goldschmidt, "Publicity, Privacy, and Secrecy," *Western Political Quarterly* 7 (1954): 401; my emphasis.

94. Saunders, *Cultural Cold War,* 360. I discuss this figure, C. D. Jackson, more fully in chapter 2. Important intelligence officials often had private-sector positions, and many private-sector organizations were fronts for the CIA. Some of its companies made tidy profits. Other forms of crossover are too detailed to summarize here. To give a few examples: the well-known Fodor travel guides were begun by the former Office of Strategic Services (OSS) lieutenant Eugene Fodor and were routinely written by active CIA personnel; Lyman Kirkpatrick, the executive assistant to the director of the CIA, wrote the annual "Armies of the World" article for *Encyclopedia*

Britannica, which was itself owned by a former assistant secretary of state, William Benton; and CIA-contracted reviews appeared in the *New York Times* and other major papers. And so on. See Saunders, *Cultural Cold War,* esp. 232–51.

95. Gibson, *Spook Country,* 108.

96. On these distinctions and their history, see Osgood, *Total Cold War,* 29–30, 76–150, esp. 77–78. White propaganda is attributed to a source, whereas gray propaganda is not. Black propaganda is "secret, subversive propaganda that deliberately lied and slandered, purporting to come from enemy sources rather than the American government" (30).

97. The crucial account of this effect is Peter Sloterdijk, *Critique of Cynical Reason,* trans. Michael Eldred (1983; repr., Minneapolis: University of Minnesota, 1987).

98. Jean-François Lyotard, *The Postmodern Condition: A Report on Knowledge,* trans. Geoff Bennington and Brian Massumi (Minneapolis: University of Minnesota Press, 1984).

99. Habermas and Lyotard see the results of these changes quite differently. For an account of these differences, see Martin Jay, "Habermas and Modernism," *Praxis International* 4, no. 1 (1984): 1–14.

100. George Kennan, "Planning of Foreign Policy," in *Measures Short of War: The George F. Kennan Lectures at the National War College 1946–47,* ed. Giles D. Harlow and George C. Maerz (June 18, 1947; repr., Washington, DC: National Defense University Press, 1991), 212; emphasis added. Saunders mistakenly reports this passage as a December 1947 address to the National War College (*Cultural Cold War,* 433, note 13).

101. In a compelling discussion of this dynamic, Jodi Dean notes that secrecy still constitutes the phantom "public" by providing it with a categorical boundary *and* an object of desire: "The secret promises that a democratic public is within reach—as soon as everything is known." Dean, *Publicity's Secret: How Technoculture Capitalizes on Democracy* (Ithaca, NY: Cornell University Press, 2002), 10.

102. Quoted in Victor Marchetti and John D. Marks, *The CIA and the Cult of Intelligence* (New York: Laurel/Dell, 1980), 3.

103. I have elsewhere called this phenomenon "postmodern transference." See Melley, *Empire of Conspiracy,* esp. 13, 37–41. The classic description of the early modern worldview is E. M. W. Tillyard, *The Elizabethan World Picture* (New York: Vintage, 1959).

104. Marchetti and Marks, *CIA and the Cult of Intelligence,* 3.

105. Don DeLillo, *Libra* (New York: Viking, 1988), 317.

106. On this concept and its relation to Max Weber's argument about the modern "disenchantment of the world," see Morris Berman, *The Reenchantment of the World* (Ithaca, NY: Cornell University Press, 1981).

107. See Nadel, *Containment Culture,* esp. 1–37 and 157–203. Nadel argues that "postmodern narratives" often "make legible the failure of containment," which itself "requires straight narratives" (34). Marilyn Dekoven argues that postmodernism "was emergent" in the 1960s— not that the 1960s themselves were postmodern but that "the shift or pivot to the postmodern" occurred in that decade (*Utopia Limited: The Sixties and the Emergence of the Postmodern* [Durham: Duke University Press, 2004], 8, 18.) Ann Douglas makes a strong case for the Cold War origins of postmodernism ("Periodizing the American Century").

108. Huyssen, *After the Great Divide,* 190, 197.

109. Nadel, *Containment Culture,* 35. Nadel shows, for instance, how Cold War epistemology manifested itself through an obsession with truthfulness and phoniness in Salinger's *Catcher in the Rye.* He later associates the incipient postmodernism of *Catch-22* with the public revelation of duplicity in the Bay of Pigs incident.

110. Jean Baudrillard, "The Precession of Simulacra," trans. Paul Foss and Paul Patton, in *Art After Modernism: Rethinking Representation,* ed. Brian Wallis, 253–81 (New York: New Museum of Contemporary Art, 1984).

111. Douglas, "Periodizing the American Century," 76.

112. My significant debts on this subject are indicated widely throughout this introduction. As Michael Bérubé observes, it is remarkably difficult to specify literary postmodernism because its aesthetic markers are present in modernist, romantic, and even eighteenth-century fiction. The typical rejoinder to this problem, Bérubé notes, is that "modernist fiction is fragmentary, experimental, and self-reflexive, but that postmodern fiction is, um, well, more so" ("Teaching Postmodernist Fiction"). Most postwar fiction, moreover, including much influential literature, is essentially realist. A useful approach here is that of Amy Elias, who views postmodernism as a historically specific renewal of an old fabulist tendency in literature (*Sublime Desire: History and Post-1960s Fiction* [Baltimore: Johns Hopkins University Press, 2001]). This makes postmodernism, as Bérubé notes, a matter of degree or emphasis—but there is nothing wrong with that. Lyotard, for instance, conceives of postmodernism as the leading edge of the avant-garde, a "sublime" aesthetic resistant to decoding because it is so cutting edge. In my view, it is less important to draw a hard and fast line between modernism and postmodernism than to recognize that these movements have significant overlaps and are primarily reactions against realism and modernity. For an interesting study of "unknowing" in modernism and postmodernism, see Philip Weinstein, *Unknowing: The Work of Modernist Fiction* (Ithaca, NY: Cornell University Press, 2005).

113. Brian McHale, *Postmodernist Fiction* (New York: Methuen, 1987). McHale extends this account in *Constructing Postmodernism* (New York: Routledge, 1992).

114. Jameson, *Postmodernism,* 413.

115. Ibid., 27. Jameson's example comes from Marguerite Séchehaye's, *Autobiography of a Schizophrenic Girl,* trans. Grace Rubin-Rabson (1951; repr., New York: Grune and Stratton, 1968), 19.

116. Linda Hutcheon, *The Poetics of Postmodernism: History, Theory, Fiction* (New York: Routledge, 1988), 5.

117. McHale, *Postmodernist Fiction,* 11.

118. Jameson, *Postmodernism,* 43.

119. Ibid., 44, 412–13, 44.

120. Ibid., 413.

121. John Le Carré, *The Looking Glass War* (London: Coward McCann, 1965).

122. Robert Littell, *The Company* (New York: Overlook, 2002), 550. It is stranger still that Littell almost shares the surname of Alice Liddell, the purported inspiration for Carroll's Alice.

123. DeLillo, *Libra,* 13, 47, 153, 277.

1. Brainwashed!

1. "Clarke Wants Terrorists Treated Like Victims of Cult Brainwashing," *Daily Telegraph,* October 2, 2005, http://www.telegraph.co.uk/news/uknews/1499694/Clarke-wants-terrorists-treated-like-victims-of-cult-brainwashing.html. The U.S. Senate overwhelmingly approved the Detainee Treatment Act on October 5, 2005. The act prohibits U.S. personnel from exceeding the *Army Field Manual*'s limits on coercive interrogation. On December 30, 2005, however, President George W. Bush used a "signing statement" to avoid enforcing the law. Mayer, *Dark Side,* 320–21.

2. Mayer first reported this and other related news in Jane Mayer, "The Black Sites: A Rare Look inside the C.I.A.'s Secret Interrogation Program," *New Yorker,* August 13, 2007, http://www.newyorker.com/reporting/2007/08/13/070813fa_fact_mayer; and Mayer, "The Experiment: The Military Trains People to Withstand Interrogation; Are Those Methods Being Misused at Guantánamo?" *New Yorker,* July 11, 2005, http://www.newyorker.com/archive/2005/07/11/050711fa_fact4?currentPage=1.

3. Mayer, *Dark Side,* 156.

4. Ibid., 139–81. In his trial transcript, Zubaydah freely confesses to being an enemy of the United States and to organizing terrorist events directed at military targets. But he also claims

to dislike the targeting of civilians and claims never to have been a member of Al Qaeda. He reports profound mental health consequences from his treatment. "Verbatim Transcript of Combatant Status Review Tribunal Hearing for ISN 10016 [Zayn Al Abidin Muhammad Husayn, aka Abu Zubaydah]," C05403111, Tribunal at U.S. Naval Base, Guantánamo Bay, Cuba, March 27, 2007, 1–30, American Civil Liberties Union, http://www.aclu.org/national-security/verbatim-transcript-combatant-status-review-tribunal-csrt-hearing-abu-zubaydah. U.S. officials progressively downgraded his status from a top member of Al Qaeda to a mere "travel agent." See also Joby Warrick and Peter Finn, "Internal Rifts on Road to Torment," *Washington Post,* July 19, 2009, http://www.washingtonpost.com/wp-dyn/content/article/2009/07/18/AR2009071802065.html.

5. Mayer, *Dark Side,* 157. The military advertises SERE as a "Resistance Training Laboratory" where completion of training is a badge of honor among elite U.S. forces. See David J. Morris, "Empires of the Mind: SERE, Guantánamo, and the Legacies of Torture," *Virginia Quarterly Review* (Winter 2009): 211–21, http://www.vqronline.org/articles/2009/winter/morris-sere/.

6. Stephen Whitfield, *The Culture of the Cold War,* 2nd ed. (Baltimore: Johns Hopkins University Press, 1996), 15.

7. Eugene Dennis and eleven other Communist Party leaders were charged with conspiring to overthrow the government when they attempted to meet and organize for their group. In 1951, their conviction was upheld by the U.S. Supreme Court. See Ellen Schrecker, *Many Are the Crimes: McCarthyism in America* (Boston: Little, Brown, 1998), 198; and Whitfield, *Culture of the Cold War,* 48–49.

8. Edward Hunter, "'Brain-Washing' Tactics Force Chinese into Ranks of Communist Party," *Miami News,* September 24, 1950; *Brain-Washing in Red China: The Calculated Destruction of Men's Minds* (New York: Vanguard, 1951); and *Brainwashing: The Story of Men Who Defied It* (New York: Farrar, Straus, and Cudahy, 1956).

9. Hunter, *Brain-Washing* (1951), 302, 223.

10. Osgood, *Total Cold War,* 53–54.

11. Letter from Eisenhower to Harry S. Truman, December 16, 1950, quoted ibid., 51–52.

12. "If one of our high government officials shows signs of a changed personality," warned the board in a memo to the director of Central Intelligence, "steps should be taken to have him 'confined to quarters' for at least 24 hours." CIA, "Briefing for the Psychological Strategy Board," memorandum to the director of Central Intelligence, May 13, 1953, The Black Vault, CIA MK-ULTRA documents, 4 CD-ROMs, disk 2, MORI ID no. 146086, http://documents.theblackvault.com/documents/mkultra/MKULTRA1/DOC_0000146086/0000146086_0001.TIF.

13. Hunter, *Brainwashing* (1956), 12, 3–4.

14. Ibid., 12–13, 24, 309.

15. George Kennan, 861.00/2—2246: Telegram, The Charge in the Soviet Union, Kennan to the Secretary of State, SECRET, Moscow, February 22, 1946—9 p.m., National Security Archive, http://www.gwu.edu/~nsarchiv/coldwar/documents/episode-1/kennan.htm; Edward Hunter, *The Black Book on Red China* (New York: Bookmailer, 1961), 134.

16. J. Edgar Hoover, *Masters of Deceit* (New York: Pocket, 1958), 75. See also Schrecker, *Many Are the Crimes,* esp. 161.

17. David Riesman, Nathan Glazer, and Reuel Denney, *The Lonely Crowd: A Study of the Changing American Character* (New Haven, CT: Yale University Press, 1950); William Whyte, *The Organization Man* (New York: Simon and Schuster, 1956); and Vance Packard, *The Hidden Persuaders* (New York: Pocket Books, 1957). I discuss these texts extensively in *Empire of Conspiracy.* For an account that connects Riesman (and Cold War visual culture) to brainwashing, see Alan Nadel, "Cold War Television and the Technology of Brainwashing," in *American Cold War Culture,* ed. Douglas Field, 146–63 (Edinburgh: Edinburgh University Press, 2005).

18. H. H. Wubben, "American Prisoners of War in Korea: A Second Look at the 'Something New in History' Theme," *American Quarterly* 22, no. 1 (1970): 3–19.

19. Senate Subcommittee to Investigate the Administration of the Internal Security Act and Other Internal Security Laws of the Committee of the Judiciary, *The Effect of Red China Communes on the United States,* testimony of Edward Hunter, 86th Cong., 1st sess., March 24, 1959, 24.

20. Joost A. M. Meerloo, *Rape of the Mind: The Psychology of Thought Control, Menticide, and Brainwashing* (Cleveland: World Publishing, 1956); hereafter cited parenthetically. See also Meerloo, "The Crime of Menticide," *American Journal of Psychiatry* 107 (1951): 594–98; and Meerloo, "Suicide, Menticide, and Psychic Homicide," *AMA Arch Neurological Psychiatry* 81, no. 3 (1959): 360–62.

21. Robert Jay Lifton, *Thought Reform and the Psychology of Totalism: A Study of "Brainwashing" in China* (1961; repr., Chapel Hill: University of North Carolina Press, 1989), 45.

22. *Invasion of the Body Snatchers,* DVD, directed by Don Siegel (1956; Hollywood: Republic, 1998).

23. I call this expression "agency panic." For a fuller description of this response and its role in postwar U.S. culture, see Melley, *Empire of Conspiracy.*

24. William Sargant, *Battle for the Mind: A Physiology of Conversion and Brain-Washing* (London: Heinemann, 1957), xiii.

25. Cabling the State Department in 1946, Kennan offered a strikingly psychoanalytic account that painted the Kremlin worldview as "neurotic," insecure, "fanatically" committed to the destruction of "our traditional way of life," and "impervious to the logic of reason" but "highly sensitive to logic of force" (Kennan, "861.00/2–2246: Telegram"). When Kennan went on to publish a version of this analysis in *Foreign Affairs* under the name Mr. X, its ideas were then widely circulated in the popular press. When an enemy is distant and apparently inscrutable, a relatively small number of observers have extraordinary power to shape public opinion about it.

26. David Seed, *Brainwashing: The Fictions of Mind Control; A Study of Novels and Films since World War II* (Kent, OH: Kent State University Press, 2004), 48. I am indebted to Seed's thorough and interesting book.

27. For more detail, see ibid.; and Melley, *Empire of Conspiracy.* In addition to the Bourne films, discussed in chapter 5, the list includes *Codename Icarus* (1981), *Jacob's Ladder* (1990), *Total Recall* (1990), *The Long Kiss Goodnight* (1996), *Conspiracy Theory* (1997), *Menno's Mind* (1997), *The Sleep Room* (1998), *Time Lapse* (2001), *Alias* (2001–06), *Blind Horizon* (2003), *Second Nature* (2003), *The Manchurian Candidate* (Demme, 2004), *Torture Room* (2007), *My Own Worst Enemy* (2008), *Dollhouse* (2009), and *XIII: The Conspiracy* (2008).

28. Norman Mailer, *The Armies of the Night: History as a Novel, the Novel as History* (New York: Signet, 1968), 103, 281.

29. This diagnosis remains in the current DSM-IV. See American Psychiatric Association, "Dissociative Disorder Not Specified," *Diagnostic and Statistical Manual of Mental Disorders,* 4th ed. (Washington, DC: American Psychiatric Association, 2000), 532. For an overview of this diagnosis in relation to so-called cults, see Dick Anthony, "Pseudoscience and Minority Religions: An Evaluation of the Brainwashing Theories of Jean-Marie Abgrall," *Social Justice Research* 12 (1999): 421–56.

30. Jerrold M. Post, "Terrorist Psycho-Logic," in *Origins of Terrorism: Psychologies, Ideologies, Theories, States of Mind,* ed. Walter Reich (Washington, DC: Woodrow Wilson Center Press, 1990), 34. Other studies based on interviews with jihadists have dismissed the "brainwashing hypothesis." See Marc Sageman, *Understanding Terrorist Networks* (Philadelphia: University of Pennsylvania, 2004); and Robert A. Pape, "The Strategic Logic of Suicide Terrorism," *American Political Science Review* 97, no. 3 (2003): 343–61.

31. Dominic Streatfeild, interview with Steve Hassan, in *Brainwash: The Secret History of Mind Control* (New York: Thomas Dunne, 2007), 276.

32. *Homeland,* TV series, directed by Michael Cuesta, Alex Gansa, and Howard Gordon (Burbank, CA: Showtime, October 2, 2011–December 18, 2011).

33. Post, "Terrorist Psycho-Logic," 36.

34. Kathleen Taylor, "Thought Crime," *Guardian,* October 8, 2005, http://www.guardian. co.uk/world/2005/oct/08/terrorism.booksonhealth.

35. John Marks, *The Search for the "Manchurian Candidate": The CIA and Mind Control* (1979; repr., New York: Norton, 1991), 133–34.

36. Marks, *Search,* 24, 31, 23, 25. In his 1951 study, Hunter attributes his discovery of brainwashing in part to the impression the Mindszenty trial made on him. See Hunter, *Brain-Washing in Red China,* 10–11.

37. CIA, "Narrative Description of the Overt and Covert Activities of [Redacted]," January 1, 1950 [estimated], The Black Vault, CIA MK-ULTRA documents, disk 2, MORI ID no. 190882, 3, http:// documents.theblackvault.com/documents/mkultra/MKULTRA2/DOC_0000190882/0000190882_ 0003.TIF. In an earlier version of this chapter (Melley, "Brain Warfare: The Covert Sphere, Terrorism, and the Legacy of Cold War," *Grey Room* 45 [2011]: 26–27), I dated this memorandum "January 1950" because the CIA's MORI Index for its declassified MK-ULTRA documents lists its estimated publication as "01/01/1950." A more thorough study of related documents suggests that the document was probably written between 1951 and 1953. It is appendix C of a detailed plan for the covert study of various techniques on an overseas population. The full document projects completion of the study in 1954 and claims that researchers have already established methods for some of their protocols. It thus seems unlikely that the proposal was written as early as 1950.

38. Marks, *Search,* 25; Michael Rogin, *"Ronald Reagan," the Movie: And Other Episodes in Political Demonology* (Berkeley: University of California Press, 1987), esp. 44–80, 272–300.

39. On "the prevalent CIA notion of a 'mind-control gap,'" see Marks, *Search,* 25.

40. Allen W. Dulles, "Brain Warfare, Summary of Remarks by Mr. Allen W. Dulles at the National Alumni Conference of the Graduate Council of Princeton University, Hot Springs, VA, April 10, 1953," The Black Vault, CIA MK-ULTRA documents, disk 1, MORI ID no. 14, 3, 12, http://docu ments.theblackvault.com/documents/mkultra/MKULTRA1/DOC_0000146077/0000146077_0003. TIF.

41. Marks, *Search,* 139.

42. Alfred W. McCoy, *A Question of Torture: CIA Interrogation from the Cold War to the War on Terror* (New York: Holt, 2006), 7.

43. Marks, *Search,* 138. Hinkle and Wolff's official CIA report, which Dulles forwarded to J. Edgar Hoover in 1956, concludes that "there is nothing mysterious about personality changes resulting from the brainwashing process," which is distinct from "thought-control or mass indoctrination" primarily insofar as it relies on "physiological deprivation." See Allen W. Dulles, "A Report on Communist Brainwashing," memorandum to J. Edgar Hoover, April 25, 1956, TOTSE, http://www.zoklet.net/totse/en/conspiracy/mind_control/165615.html. See also L. E. Hinkle Jr. and H. G. Wolff, "Communist Interrogation and Indoctrination of 'Enemies of the State': Analysis of Methods Used by the Communist State Police (a special report)." *Archives of Neurology and Psychiatry* 76 (1956): 115–74.

44. Albert D. Biderman, "The Image of 'Brainwashing,'" *Public Opinion Quarterly* 26, no. 4 (1962): 547–63; Edgar H. Schein, *Coercive Persuasion: A Socio-Psychological Analysis of the "Brainwashing" of American Civilian Prisoners by the Chinese Government,* with Inge Schneier and Curtis H. Barker (New York: Norton, 1961); and Lifton, *Thought Reform.* For a helpful overview of all these works, see Anthony, "Pseudoscience," esp. 424–34.

45. Lifton, *Thought Reform,* 13, 15; emphasis in original.

46. CIA, *KUBARK Counterintelligence Interrogation,* July 1963, 1, National Security Archive, http://www.gwu.edu/~nsarchiv/NSAEBB/NSAEBB27/01–01.htm. For Hinkle and Wolff's findings, see Dulles, "Report on Communist Brainwashing."

47. McCoy, *Question of Torture,* 51.

48. For a superb inside account of this issue, see Smith, *Portrait of a Cold Warrior.*

49. According to Air Force Reserve Colonel Steve Kleinman, a senior intelligence officer for survival training in the Department of Defense, no SERE instructors at JPRA (Fairchild Air Force Base in Spokane, WA) had "real life experience questioning foreign prisoners."

50. Scott Lucas, *Freedom's War: The American Crusade against the Soviet Union* (New York: New York University Press, 1999), 84.

51. Richard Condon, *The Manchurian Candidate* (New York: McGraw-Hill, 1959).

52. Hoover, *Masters of Deceit,* 256–57.

53. Ibid., 255.

54. See Whitfield, *Culture of the Cold War;* Nadel, *Containment Culture;* Corber, *Homosexuality in Cold War America;* Davidson, *Guys Like Us;* May, *Homeward Bound;* and Michael Rogin, "Kiss Me Deadly: Communism, Motherhood, and Cold War Movies," *Representations* 6 (Spring 1984): 1–36.

55. See Phillip Wylie, *A Generation of Vipers* (New York: Farrar and Rhinehart, 1942).

56. Allen Ginsberg, *Deliberate Prose* (Harmondsworth: Penguin, 2000), 12.

57. William S. Burroughs, "The Limits of Control," in *The Adding Machine: Selected Essays* (New York: Arcade, 1985), 117.

58. Sylvia Plath, *The Bell Jar* (1963; repr., New York: Perennial, 1999), 85; Betty Friedan, *The Feminine Mystique* (New York: Dell, 1963), 275. As Peter Knight notes, "*The Feminine Mystique* offers an account of what would come to be known as patriarchy *as if* it were a conspiracy" (Knight, *Conspiracy Culture,* 124). See also Ellison, *Invisible Man;* E. L. Doctorow, *The Book of Daniel* (New York: Random House, 1971); and Ken Kesey, *One Flew Over the Cuckoo's Nest* (New York: Viking, 1962).

59. Hunter, *Brain-Washing* (1951), 11–12.

60. Lifton, *Thought Reform,* 4.

61. Thomas Hill Schaub shows how "psychological terms of social analysis" played a vital role in Cold War culture by shifting attention away from "economics and class consciousness" (*American Fiction in the Cold War* [Madison: University of Wisconsin Press, 1991], 91).

62. Joost Meerloo, "Pavlovian Strategy as a Weapon of Menticide," *American Journal of Psychiatry* 110 (1954): 809–13.

63. Meerloo, *Rape of the Mind,* 28–29. Mayo quoted in Meerloo, *Rape of the Mind,* 20.

64. Edward Hunter, quoted in Marks, *Search,* 134.

65. House Committee on Un-American Activities, *Communist Psychological Warfare (Brainwashing),* consultation with Edward Hunter, author and foreign correspondent, 85th Cong., 2nd sess., March 13, 1958, http://www.crossroad.to/Quotes/globalism/Congress.htm.

66. McCoy, *Question of Torture,* 10.

67. Ibid., 51.

68. Dulles, "Report on Communist Brainwashing."

69. Joseph Margulies, "Abu Zubaydah's Suffering," *Los Angeles Times,* April 30, 2009, http://articles.latimes.com/2009/apr/30/opinion/oe-margulies30.

2. Spectacles of Secrecy

1. *Angels in America* extends far beyond the Rosenberg case but connects repeatedly to the case through its depiction of Ethel Rosenberg and the prosecutor Roy Cohn. The Kennedy assassination is the subject of notable novels by D. M. Thomas, Don DeLillo, and Norman Mailer. The attacks of 9/11 and their aftermath are at the center of fiction by DeLillo, Jess Walter, and Jonathan Safran Foer. Like slavery, the Vietnam War is more than a singular event, and according to John Newman et al., an astonishing 666 novels had been written about Vietnam as of 1995. Among the most notable are works by Michael Herr, Philip Caputo, Tim O'Brien, Bobby Ann Mason, Thom Jones, Larry Heinemann, Robert Olen Butler, Graham Greene, Eugene Burdick

and William J. Lederer, Robert Stone, John Crowther, Gustav Hasford, and David Halberstam. John Newman et al., *Vietnam War Literature,* 3rd ed. (New York: Scarecrow, 1996).

2. On the VENONA decrypts, see Ronald Radosh and Joyce Milton, *The Rosenberg File,* 2nd ed. (1983; New Haven, CT: Yale University Press, 1997).

3. Alice Jardine, "Flash Back, Flash Forward: The Fifties, the Nineties, and the Transformed Politics of Remote Control," in *Secret Agents: The Rosenbergs, McCarthyism, and Fifties America,* ed. Marjorie Garber and Rebecca L. Walkowitz (New York: Routledge, 1995), 114. I have been at pains throughout this study to separate postmodern aesthetic experiments (which are conscious literary strategies) from what Amy Elias calls "the ahistorical postmodernism of the streets" (*Sublime Desire,* xvii). The latter is usually a conflation of fiction and history, or simulation and reality, in social life itself.

4. Walter Schneir and Miriam Schneir, *Invitation to an Inquest,* 4th ed. (1965; New York: Doubleday, 1983), 73.

5. Ibid., 477–78.

6. Ibid., 106.

7. Gold was exceptionally sheltered by his mother and never became comfortable around other women. See Allen M. Hornblum, *The Invisible Harry Gold: The Man Who Gave the Soviets the Atom Bomb* (New Haven, CT: Yale University Press, 2011). On the representation of Ethel Rosenberg, see Marjorie Garber and Rebecca L. Walkowitz, eds., *Secret Agents: The Rosenbergs, McCarthyism, and Fifties America* (New York: Routledge, 1995).

8. Quoted in Schneir and Schneir, *Invitation to an Inquest,* 136. Jardine notes that the Jell-O box was, "at the very least, a double imitation," since Jell-O advertises itself as an "imitation" of real food ("Flash Back," 115). *United States of America v. Julius Rosenberg, Ethel Rosenberg, Anatoli A. Yakovlev, also known as "John," David Greenglass and Morton Sobell,* transcript of trial, New York, March 6–April 6, 1951, University of Missouri–Kansas City School of Law, http://law2.umkc.edu/faculty/projects/ftrials/rosenb/ROS_TRIA.HTM.

9. Schneir and Schneir, *Invitation to an Inquest,* 138. See also Jardine, "Flash Back," 115.

10. Schneir and Schneir, *Invitation to an Inquest,* 127, 268. There is ongoing disagreement about how much Greenglass's drawing may have helped the Soviets. At the time of the trial, the Associated Press science editor Howard Blakeslee opined that the idea of using lenses to cause an implosion may have been useful even in the absence of any technical specifications for how to do so. The Schneirs present extensive evidence refuting the sometimes-contradictory trial testimony of John Derry, an electrical engineer, that the stolen information was useful (270–82). Ralph Radosh and Joyce Milton maintain that the information was useful, citing several former Soviet intelligence figures trumpeting the importance of Julius Rosenberg's contributions to the Soviet bomb. See Radosh and Milton, *Rosenberg File,* xxii–xxx.

11. Jardine, "Flash Back," 116.

12. Michael Rogin, "'Make My Day!': Spectacle as Amnesia in Imperial Politics," *Representations* 29 (Winter 1990): 106, 105, 103.

13. Ibid., 117, 105.

14. Ibid., 114, 116.

15. Larry McCaffrey, "As Guilty as the Rest of Them: An Interview with Robert Coover," *Critique* 41, no. 1 (2000): 116.

16. Schneir and Schneir, *Invitation to an Inquest,* 72; emphasis added to final quotation. The Schneirs' work stands out among a number of similar critiques of the government's case. These include Virginia Gardner, *The Rosenberg Story (New York: Masses and Mainstream, 1954);* Alvin H. Goldstein, *The Unquiet Death of Julius and Ethel Rosenberg* (New York: Lawrence Hill, 1975); Robert Meeropol and Michael Meeropol, *We Are Your Sons: The Legacy of Julius and Ethel Rosenberg* (Boston: Houghton Mifflin, 1975); Louis Nizer, *The Implosion Conspiracy* (Garden City, NY: Doubleday, 1973); William A. Reuben, *The Atom Spy Hoax* (New York: Action Books, 1954);

Malcolm Pitman Sharpe, *Was Justice Done? The Rosenberg-Sobell Case* (New York: Monthly Review Press, 1956); Donald Freed, *Inquest* (New York: Hill and Wang, 1970); Jonathan Root, *The Betrayers* (New York: Coward McCann, 1963); John Wexley, *The Judgment of Julius and Ethel Rosenberg* (New York: Cameron and Kahn, 1955); and Ilene Philipson, *Ethel Rosenberg: Beyond the Myths* (New York: Franklin Watts, 1988). One of the best histories of the case is Virginia Carmichael's *Framing History: The Rosenberg Stories and the Cold War* (Minneapolis: University of Minnesota Press, 1993).

17. Radosh and Milton, *Rosenberg File,* esp. ix–xxx. Some critics of Radosh and Milton's position point out that KGB officers were financially incented to produce confirmation of the case against Julius and that a great deal of NSA analysis must be taken on faith to conclude that "Liberal" was indeed Julius Rosenberg. A more plausible objection is that the secrets gathered by Greenglass and Rosenberg had marginal worth, a position disputed by Radosh and Milton among others. There is relatively little dispute that Ethel had a negligible role in the espionage and that the government acted unethically in the Rosenberg trial.

18. Robert Coover, *The Public Burning* (New York: Viking, 1977), 4; hereafter cited parenthetically.

19. Geoffrey Wolff, "An American Epic," *New Times,* August 19, 1977, 54.

20. The following accounts offer interesting perspectives on the novel's postmodernism: Molly Hite, "'A Parody of Martyrdom': The Rosenbergs, Cold War Theology, and Robert Coover's *The Public Burning,*" *Novel* 27, no. 1 (1993): 85–101; Hutcheon, *Poetics of Postmodernism,* 193–94; Raymond Mazurek, "Metafiction, the Historical Novel, and Coover's *The Public Burning,*" *Critique* 23, no. 3 (1982): 29–41; Paul A. Orlov, "A Fiction of Politically Fantastic 'Facts': Robert Coover's *The Public Burning,*" in *Politics and the Muse: Studies in the Politics of Recent American Literature,* ed. Adam J. Sorkin, 111–23 (Bowling Green, OH: Bowling Green State University Press, 1989); Tom LeClair, "Robert Coover, *The Public Burning,* and the Art of Excess," *Critique* 23, no. 3 (1982): 5–28; Bernhard Reitz, "The Reconstruction of the Fifties in E. L. Doctorow's *The Book of Daniel* and Robert Coover's *The Public Burning,*" in *Historiographic Metafiction in Modern American and Canadian Literature,* ed. Bernd Engler and Kurt Müller, 223–40 (Paderborn, Ger.: Ferdinand Schoningh, 1994); Kathryn Hume, *American Dream, American Nightmare: Fiction since 1960* (Urbana: University of Illinois Press, 2000).

21. Baudrillard, "Precession of Simulacra." For Baudrillard, the contemporary regime of simulation disables the reality principle.

22. Doctorow, *Book of Daniel,* 288.

23. Hoover, *Masters of Deceit.* On this subject, see Tom Dumm, "The Trial of J. Edgar Hoover," in Garber and Walkowitz, *Secret Agents,* 77–92. See also Richard Gid Powers, *Secrecy and Power: The Life of J. Edgar Hoover* (New York: Free Press, 1987).

24. It was Henry James who warned against the "fatal futility of Fact" in his preface to *The Spoils of Poynton* (1908; repr., New York: Scribners, 1908), vii. The "fatal futility of Fact" is a way of suggesting the writer's need to invent in the face of "clumsy life"—a point later taken up by Tim O'Brien (see chapter 4).

25. See, most centrally, Judith Butler, *Gender Trouble: Feminism and the Subversion of Identity* (London: Routledge, 1989).

26. The classic example of this argument concerns money. Currency is valuable only if we all *act* as though it has value.

27. Robert Coover, "The Babysitter," in *Pricksongs and Descants,* 206–39 (New York: Dutton, 1969).

28. Oana Godeanu-Kenworthy, "The Political Other in Nineteenth-Century British North America: The Satire of Thomas Chandler Haliburton," *Early American Studies* (Spring 2009): 205–34. Haliburton's satire was originally published in *The Novascotian* before appearing in a three-part series (in 1836, 1838, and 1840) as *Sam Slick, the Clockmaker, His Sayings and Doings* (repr., Toronto: Musson Book Company, 1935).

29. "Our brethren are already in the field! Why stand we here idle?" (Patrick Henry, "Give Me Liberty or Give Me Death"). "The world must be familiarized with the idea of considering our proper domination to be the continent of North America. From the time when we became an independent people it was as much a law of nature that this become our pretension as that the Mississippi should flow to the sea. Spain has possessions upon our southern and Great Britain upon our northern borders, but it is impossible that centuries should elapse without finding them annexed to the United States" (John Quincy Adams, address to president's cabinet, 1819). "Time is money" (Ben Franklin, "Advice to a Young Tradesman," 1748). "Damn the torpedoes and full steam ahead" (Admiral David G. Farragut, 1864). "No pent-up Utica contracts our powers" (William Howard Taft, 1913). "Fear is the foundation of most governments" (John Adams, letter to George Wythe, April 1776). "It is our manifest destiny to overspread the continent allotted by Providence for the free development of our yearly multiplying millions" (John L. O'Sullivan, "Annexation," *Democratic Review,* 1845). "We cannot escape history" (Abraham Lincoln, "Annual Message to Congress," 1862). "Let us therefore animate and encourage each other, and shew the whole world, that a Freeman contending for Liberty on his own ground is superior to any slavish mercenary on earth" (George Washington, general orders to troops, July 2, 1776). "Our cause is just. Our union is perfect" (John Dickinson, *Declaration of Causes and Necessity of Taking Up Arms,* 1775).

30. Whitfield, *Culture of the Cold War,* 56.

31. Frances Fitzgerald, *America Revised: History Schoolbooks in the Twentieth Century* (New York: Random House, 1979), 10.

32. Jean-Paul Sartre, *Libération,* June 20, 1953, quoted in Schneir and Schneir, *Invitation to an Inquest,* 254, and Coover, *Public Burning,* 466.

33. Arthur Miller, quoted on the back cover of Schneir and Schneir, *Invitation to an Inquest.*

34. Linda Hutcheon, *The Politics of Postmodernism* (New York: Routledge, 1989), 9, et passim.

35. Jameson is particularly helpful here. Although Doctorow is "the epic poet of the disappearance of the American radical past," his "splendid novels" must nonetheless "convey this great theme formally...by way of that very cultural logic of the postmodern which is itself the mark and symptom of his dilemma" (*Postmodernism,* 24–25). The "great theme" to which Jameson refers is the loss of history as a referent. Although Doctorow is himself distressed about this loss, his narrative approach echoes the problem itself. That is, rather than returning to realism (trying "to gaze directly on some putative real world"), Doctorow embraces pastiche and other techniques, essentially accepting the notion that we "can only 'represent' our ideas and stereotypes about the past,... which itself remains forever out of reach" (25).

36. Hayden White, "Historical Text as Literary Artifact," in *Tropics of Discourse* (Baltimore: Johns Hopkins University Press, 1978), 87.

37. Ibid.

38. Don DeLillo, "The Power of History," *New York Times Magazine,* September 7, 1997, 60. The headlines in question appeared on the front page of the *New York Times* on October 4, 1951. In this essay DeLillo cites *The Public Burning* as an example of how fiction ("a kind of religious fanaticism, with elements of obsession, superstition and awe") will "sooner or later" enter an "adversarial relationship with history" (62). It is striking that both Coover and DeLillo have built novels on the strange relation of baseball to cold war, traced this relation to the nation's newspaper of record, and troubled the idea of the newspaper as an objective account of real events.

39. Brian McHale's two narratological studies (*Postmodernist Fiction* and *Constructing Postmodernism*) powerfully suggest that this is *the* primary quality of postmodern fiction.

40. The second ellipsis in this passage is in the original. The first and third are mine.

41. The references here include "Danger of Atom Bomb Attack Is Greatest in Period Up to This Fall, Expert Asserts," *New York Times,* March 28, 1951, A1; and Bob Considine, "Fearfully

Destructive Power of Atomic Bomb," *Deseret News,* January 8, 1951, 3B. Considine was a Hearst columnist; his article was syndicated by International News Service and ran widely.

42. In April 1949, before Joseph McCarthy's grandstanding, Henry Luce personally supervised a two-page *Life* photo spread of U.S. Communist "dupes," including Dorothy Parker, Norman Mailer, Leonard Bernstein, Lillian Hellman, Aaron Copland, Langston Hughes, Clifford Odets, Arthur Miller, Charlie Chaplin, Frank Lloyd Wright, Marlon Brando, and Henry Wallace. The magazine had published an admiring issue on Stalin only six years earlier. "Dupes and Fellow Travelers Dress Up Communist Front," *Life,* April 4, 1949, 42–43. The spread is part of a larger section titled "Red Visitors Cause Rumpus."

43. Henry Luce, "A Prospectus for a New Magazine: Confidential," 1936, New York Times Archive, http://artsbeat.blogs.nytimes.com/2010/04/23/the-show-book-of-the-world-henry-luces-life-magazine-prospectus/; John Stomberg, *"Life Magazine,"* in *Encyclopedia of Twentieth-Century Photography,* ed. Lynne Warren (New York: Routledge, 2006), 952.

44. Luce, "Prospectus."

45. See ibid., and Stomberg, *"Life Magazine."*

46. Michael Wood, "The New Journalism," review of *The New Journalism,* by Tom Wolfe, ed. Tom Wolfe and E. W. Johnson, *New York Times,* July 22, 1973, http://www.nytimes.com/books/98/11/08/specials/wolfe-journalism.html.

47. Tim O'Brien, *The Things They Carried* (New York: Penguin, 1990), 89.

48. Blanche Wiesen Cook, *The Declassified Eisenhower: A Divided Legacy of Peace and Political Warfare* (New York: Doubleday, 1981), 121.

49. Saunders, *Cultural Cold War,* 146, 360.

50. Ibid., 149.

51. Osgood, *Total Cold War,* 82.

52. Saunders, *Cultural Cold War,* 146–51. See also Osgood, *Total Cold War,* 76–83.

53. Schneir and Schneir, *Invitation to an Inquest,* 363–66.

54. Ibid., 412.

55. Ibid., 413n1.

56. Robert Coover, *The Universal Baseball Association, Inc., J. Henry Waugh, Prop.* (New York: Plume, 1968). A similar interest in religious myth is at the heart of Coover's first novel, *The Origin of the Brunists* (New York: Putnam, 1966).

57. Coover, *Universal Baseball Association,* 224.

58. Coover's language is strikingly similar to the Schneirs' account of Gold's pretrial statement. "At the time of his arrest, Harry Gold had 'completely forgotten' his visit to David Greenglass five years before. He had 'forgotten' the vital meeting with Yakovlev in New York, where he had received a sheet of onionskin paper with instructions for his half of the jello box side; he had 'forgotten' his three separate trips to the Greenglass apartment on June 2 and 3 and the password 'I come from Julius'; and he had 'forgotten' turning over Greenglass's data to Yakovlev on his return to New York. Then, more than a week later, Harry Gold 'remembered' that he had met someone in Albuquerque and recalled various details about the meeting" (Schneir and Schneir, *Invitation to an Inquest,* 368–69).

3. False Documents

1. Adam Liptak, "Truth, Fiction and the Rosenbergs," *New York Times,* January 21, 2006, B1.

2. E. L. Doctorow, "False Documents," in *Jack London, Hemingway, and the Constitution: Selected Essays, 1977–1992,* 149–64 (New York: Random House, 1993); hereafter cited parenthetically. On this essay and on Doctorow's narrative technique, see Geoffrey Galt Harpham's excellent essay "E. L. Doctorow and the Technology of Narrative," *PMLA* 100, no. 1 (1985): 81–95.

3. *True Lies,* DVD, directed by James Cameron (1994; Los Angeles: Twentieth Century Fox, 1998). Like most such films, *True Lies* uses the family as an allegory of the nation. Tasker's

deception of his own family is a metaphor for the covert state's deception of the public. The presumption of the film is that the real work of the state, and its heroic secret agents, can never be appreciated by the public. As a corollary, of course, the nation's history is often deceptive, masking a truer "secret history" of such agents and their acts. The film is notable for its recognition and ultimate reinforcement of the gender dynamics of the covert sphere. Tasker's wife (Jamie Lee Curtis) accidentally stumbles into the spy world, where she learns the true nature of Harry's work, and even helps him, though ultimately he must save the day. See chapter 6 for a discussion of similar narratives.

4. O'Brien, *Things They Carried,* 203; hereafter cited parenthetically.

5. For an excellent summary of Habermas's view of modernity in relation to postmodernism, see David Harvey, *The Condition of Postmodernity: An Enquiry into the Origins of Cultural Change* (Oxford: Basil Blackwell, 1989).

6. Lyotard, *Postmodern Condition;* hereafter cited parenthetically.

7. The protagonist of Doctorow's *City of God* (2000; repr., New York: Plume, 2001), a figure much like Doctorow, has his work described as "fiction about nonfiction" (89)—an apt description of Doctorow's work. The opening lines of *Ragtime* (New York: Random House, 1975), the novel published just prior to "False Documents," mocks the falsifications of canonical U.S. history by taking them seriously: "There seemed to be no entertainment that did not involve great swarms of people…. There were no Negroes. There were no immigrants" (3–4).

8. Hayden White, "The Fictions of Factual Representation," in *Tropics of Discourse,* 122.

9. White, "Historical Text as Literary Artifact," in *Tropics of Discourse,* 98–99.

10. Searle, "Logical Status of Fictional Discourse," 320.

11. Norman Mailer, *Harlot's Ghost* (New York: Random House, 1991), 30; hereafter cited parenthetically.

12. As Joseph Tabbi explains in his excellent reading of Mailer's entire oeuvre, the dualism of Alpha and Omega was part of Mailer's ambitious attempt to develop a model of "psychic division, conflict, and conciliation promising to rival Freud's." In earlier work, Mailer called this system "Alpha and Bravo." In *Harlot's Ghost* he makes it a feature of Kittredge Montague, whose "dualistic psychology," Tabbi explains, "represent[s] conflicting aspects of the human psyche, like separate personalities living in a single person, whose peculiar tensions are thought to embody contradictions and differential relationships within society at large." *Postmodern Sublime: Technology and American Writing from Mailer to Cyberpunk* (Ithaca, NY: Cornell University Press, 1996), 47, 52.

13. Thomas Schaub observes that Cold War authors routinely attempted to think of the social order through the figure of consciousness (*American Fiction,* esp. 91). One of Tabbi's most interesting insights is that the "postmodern sublime" results not only from the attempt to represent a vast technological system but also from the attempt to think of the social order as a "mind" or "consciousness." The "imagination of the state"—as a description of Hubbard's work and Mailer's—is clearly an attempt to think along these lines. See Tabbi, *Postmodern Sublime,* esp. 1–4, 51–55, 62–64.

14. Another form of this relation involves what Shawn Rosenheim calls "the cryptographic imagination"—the interrelation of literary study and the analysis of secret messages (*The Cryptographic Imagination: Secret Writings from Edgar Allan Poe to the Internet* [Baltimore: Johns Hopkins University Press, 1996]).

15. "Profile: Dame Stella Rimington," *BBC News,* February 17, 2009, http://news.bbc.co.uk/2/hi/uk_news/7894348.stm.

16. Celia McGee, "The Burgeoning Rebirth of a Bygone Literary Star," *New York Times Book Review,* January 13, 2007, http://www.nytimes.com/2007/01/13/books/13hume.html?_r=1.

17. Saunders, *Cultural Cold War,* 237–40; Martin, *Wilderness of Mirrors,* 12–13, 17.

18. DeLillo, *Libra,* 260, 258; hereafter cited parenthetically.

19. Don DeLillo, *The Names* (New York: Knopf, 1982), 317, 201–3.

20. Don DeLillo, *White Noise* (New York: Viking, 1985), 213. The notion of a CIA literary analyst is the basis of Sydney Pollack's film *Three Days of the Condor* (1975; Los Angeles, Paramount, 1999), adapted from James Grady's *Six Days of the Condor* (New York: Norton, 1974). The name of Jack's wife, Tweedy Browner, is eerily similar to that of the CIA deputy director Bronson Tweedy. A former Vienna Station chief and head of the Eastern European Division, Tweedy was a European history major at Princeton who arrived at a Freiburg study-abroad program the day Hitler became chancellor. I am tempted to suggest that he was the United States' first "Hitler studies" major ("Bronson Tweedy, CIA Agent," *Washington Post,* October 9, 2004, B7).

21. Tabbi, *Postmodern Sublime,* esp. 1–29.

22. As Kathryn Hume notes, "*Libra* mixes fiction with fact, insofar as anything about the Kennedy assassination can be called fact" (*American Dream,* 151).

23. On the concept of cultural history, see Mark Poster's excellent book *Cultural History and Postmodernity: Disciplinary Readings and Challenges* (New York: Columbia University Press, 1997). On the relation of agency, subjectivity, and postmodernism in *Libra,* see O'Donnell, *Latent Destinies,* 45–76; and Melley, *Empire of Conspiracy,* 133–60.

24. DeLillo, *White Noise,* 291–92.

25. Nina Baym, "Melodramas of Beset Manhood: How Theories of American Fiction Exclude Women Authors," *American Quarterly* 33, no. 2 (1981): 123–39.

26. Don DeLillo, *Mao II* (New York: Viking, 1992), 41; hereafter cited parenthetically.

27. Kathleen Fitzpatrick, *The Anxiety of Obsolescence: The American Novel in the Age of Television* (Nashville: Vanderbilt University Press, 2006).

28. Saunders, *Cultural Cold War,* 39–40. OPC, for example, would go on to conduct brutal experiments in mind control, overthrow democratically elected governments in Iran and Guatemala, and supervise the notorious "Project Phoenix" in Vietnam.

29. Truman, "Limit CIA Role to Intelligence."

30. House Select Committee on Intelligence, *The CIA and the Media,* 95th Cong., 1st and 2nd sess., 1978, quoted in Osgood, *Total Cold War,* 97.

31. In describing these functions, I am not just referring to the major compartments, or "directorates," of the CIA or any other intelligence organization. The modern CIA has four institutional components: the Directorate of Intelligence, the National Clandestine Service, the Directorate of Science and Technology, and the Directorate of Support. While my comments distinguish between the Intelligence and Clandestine services, these functions are not so easy to separate. Covert action, for instance, contributes to intelligence gathering. Nonetheless, the functional division between intelligence analysis and covert action was explicitly articulated by the architects of the Cold War security state and is important to Denis Johnson's *Tree of Smoke,* which I discuss next.

32. Harlow and Maerz, *Measures Short of War,* 212; Saunders, *Cultural Cold War,* 38.

33. While covert action is most often associated with paramilitary efforts, psychological warfare was in fact the primary mode of engagement with the enemy. The Cold War was a "struggle for men's minds," as Dwight Eisenhower put it during his run for president in 1952, and Eisenhower made substantial policy changes based on this notion. Truman had already created a Psychological Strategy Board (PSB) in 1951 to coordinate simultaneous, frantic efforts in the departments of Defense and State, the CIA, the Technical Cooperation Administration, and the Economic Cooperation Administration. Staffed with both advertising and public relations executives and covert operators, the PSB redefined propaganda along lines laid out by Edward Bernays: it was not simply a strategic description of policy; it *was* policy—a set of actions, a way to "make events happen," according to one PSB consultant. "Many people think 'psychological warfare' means just the use of propaganda," said Eisenhower shortly before the 1952 election, but in fact the United States needed a "psychological effort...on a national scale" using "every psychological weapon that is available to us." So important was psychological warfare

to Eisenhower that he established his Jackson Committee on the subject before his inauguration. "The most significant conclusion of the Jackson Committee," writes Kenneth Osgood, was "its finding that psychological warfare could not be separated from other aspects of U.S. foreign policy" but "should intrude on the very policy-making process itself" (*Total Cold War,* 80). This view prompted a host of policy changes, including NSC 5412/2, which added "deception plans and operations" to the CIA's arsenal and mandated that the CIA manipulate popular opinion in non-Communist states. This work was carried out both through the sponsorship of literature, art, and intellectual work and through the development of "media control" agencies such as the International Information Administration (IIA), Voice of America (VOA), U.S. Information Agency (USIA), U.S. Information Service (USIS), Foreign Operations Administration (FOA), and Agency for International Development (USAID). By 1959, U.S. agencies were spending half a billion dollars a year to influence world opinion, not including the massive (but secret) expenditures of the CIA for the same purpose. The total figure is thus over .5% of all federal spending for the year ($93.5 B), but when secret funds are factored in, it is significantly closer to 1% (Osgood, *Total Cold War,* 90).

34. Denis Johnson, *Tree of Smoke* (New York: Farrar, Straus, and Giroux, 2007); hereafter cited parenthetically.

35. The influence of policymakers on intelligence has long been a concern within the intelligence community. But influential experts have often taken a view opposite to that of Colonel Sands. In his landmark 1949 work, *Strategic Intelligence for American World Policy,* Sherman Kent suggested that "of the two dangers—that of intelligence being too far from the users and that of being too close—the greater danger is the one of being too far" (1949; repr., Hamden, CT: Archon Books, 1965), 1182. In 1989, the secretary of defense Robert Gates wrote: "Contrary to the view of those who are apprehensive over a close relationship between policymakers and intelligence, it is not close enough. More interaction, feedback and direction as to strategies, priorities, and requirements are critical to better performance" ("An Opportunity Unfulfilled: The Use and Perceptions of Intelligence in the White House," *Washington Quarterly* [Winter 1989]: 40).

36. William J. Lederer, *A Nation of Sheep* (New York: Norton, 1961), 93.

37. Eugene Burdick and William J. Lederer, *The Ugly American* (1958; New York: Norton, 1999). The book was originally contracted as nonfiction and then changed to fiction at the suggestion of an editor. "What we have written," the authors note in the introduction, "is not just an angry dream but rather the rendering of fact into fiction" (7). *The Ugly American* makes an argument similar to that of Edward Lansdale, the spy who advocated ethnographic knowledge of local customs as a basis of Third World counterinsurgency. Lansdale, who looms large in Johnson's novel and bears a resemblance to Colonel Sands, appears in *The Ugly American* as Colonel Hillendale. It is worth noting that Johnson's Colonel lionizes John F. Kennedy, who was so powerfully impressed by Burdick and Lederer's novel that he sent it to all of his fellow senators. See Cuordileone, *Manhood and American Political Culture,* 220.

38. Rebecca Leung, "Bush Sought 'Way' to Invade Iraq? O'Neill Tells *60 Minutes* Iraq Was 'Topic A' 8 Months before 9-11," *Sixty Minutes,* CBS News, January 4, 2011, http://www.cbsnews.com/stories/2004/01/09/60minutes/main592330.shtml. For a fuller account and more supporting documents, see also Ron Suskind, *The One Percent Doctrine: Deep Inside America's Pursuit of Its Enemies since 9/11* (New York: Simon and Schuster, 2006). A secret "Downing Street memo," prepared for a July 23, 2002, meeting between the British prime minister Tony Blair and President George W. Bush, reported that "Bush wanted to remove Saddam, through military action, justified by the conjunction of terrorism and WMD. But the intelligence and facts were being fixed around the policy" ("The Secret Downing Street Memo," *Times [London],* May 1, 2005, http://www.timesonline.co.uk/tol/news/uk/article387374.ece).

39. Seymour Hersh, "The Stovepipe: How Conflicts between the Bush Administration and the Intelligence Community Marred the Reporting on Iraq's Weapons," *New Yorker,* October 27, 2003, http://www.newyorker.com/archive/2003/10/27/031027fa_fact.

40. Condoleezza Rice, interview by Wolf Blitzer, *CNN Late Edition with Wolf Blitzer,* September 8, 2002, http://transcripts.cnn.com/TRANSCRIPTS/0209/08/le.00.html.

41. See Baudrillard, "Precession of Simulacra," 275–81.

42. The operations arm of the CIA has had many names over the years. The original Office of Policy Coordination (OPC) was subsumed in 1952 by the Directorate of Plans, which in 1973 became the Directorate of Operations. In 2005, the DO was renamed the National Clandestine Service. See John Ranelagh, *The Agency: The Rise and Decline of the CIA* (New York: Simon and Schuster, 1986); and "Offices of the CIA," Central Intelligence Agency, https://www.cia.gov/offices-of-cia/index.html.

43. For a concise and readable history of these ventures, see Weiner, *Legacy of Ashes.* See also Rhodri Jeffreys, *The CIA and American Democracy* (New Haven, CT: Yale University Press, 1989); and Christopher Andrew, *For the President's Eyes Only: Secret Intelligence and the American Presidency from Washington to Bush* (New York: Harper Collins, 1995).

44. Westerfield, *Inside CIA's Private World,* viii. The division between scientific and "human" approaches to intelligence, notes Westerfield, appears in part a generational split: "Those being newly recruited out of American Ph.D. programs" are likely to bring a "social-science orientation into the agency," where "old timers at CIA are unlikely to find [social science] appeals persuasive" (xx).

45. Fredric Jameson, foreword to Lyotard, *Postmodern Condition,* xi–xii.

46. Burdick and Lederer, *Ugly American;* Frances Fitzgerald, *Fire in the Lake: The Vietnamese and the Americans in Vietnam* (New York: Little Brown, 1972); Song of Solomon 3:6; Joel 2:30–31; Exodus 33:9–10.

47. Saunders, *Cultural Cold War.*

48. John P. Dimmer Jr., "Observations on the Double Agent," 1962, in Westerfield, *Inside CIA's Private World,* 437.

49. Martin, *Wilderness of Mirrors,* 128. Lansdale demurred, saying that William King Harvey, the creator of the Berlin Tunnel and eventual point man on secret Cuba policy, was the United States' real 007. Contrary to Voss's claim, the term "eyes only" does appear in CIA documents.

50. Later, Kathy Jones gives Skip the complete reference: "First Corinthians 12:5–6 etc. 'And there are differences of administrations but the same Lord. And there are diversities of operations, but it is the same God which worketh in all'" (153).

51. McHale, *Postmodernist Fiction,* esp. 26–59.

52. John Barth, "Lost in the Funhouse," in *Lost in the Funhouse: Fiction for Print, Tape, Live Voice,* 72–97 (1967; repr., New York: Anchor, 1988).

53. Peter L. Berger and Thomas Luckmann, *The Social Construction of Reality: A Treatise in the Sociology of Knowledge* (New York: Anchor, 1966), 21.

54. Michel Foucault, *The Order of Things: An Archaeology of the Human Sciences,* trans. A. M. Sheridan Smith (New York: Pantheon, 1970), xviii.

55. Michael Herr, *Dispatches* (New York: Knopf, 1977), 69, 87; hereafter cited parenthetically.

56. See Rogin, *"Ronald Reagan," the Movie.*

57. O'Brien, "The Ghost Soldiers," in *Things They Carried,* 228–29.

58. *Apocalypse Now* is the story of a covert-operations assassin sent to kill a highly decorated but renegade U.S. colonel. *Platoon* pits two sergeants against each other—the vicious Barnes and the more sympathetic Grodin—and forces other marines to choose sides. The first part of *Full Metal Jacket* ends with a marine recruit killing his drill instructor and himself. *Apocalypse Now,* DVD, directed by Francis Ford Coppola (1979; Santa Monica, CA: Lions Gate, 2010); *Platoon,* DVD, directed by Oliver Stone (1986; Beverly Hills, CA: MGM, 2001); *Full Metal Jacket,* DVD, directed by Stanley Kubrick (1987; Burbank, CA: Warner, 2007).

59. Tim O'Brien, *Going After Cacciato* (1978; repr., New York: Delta, 1979), 77; hereafter cited parenthetically.

4. The Work of Art in the Age of Plausible Deniability

1. The defense of "secret history" as a form of authorial protection dates at least to 560. In *The Secret History,* Procopius defends omitting "the real explanation of many matters...during the life of certain persons" who "would have put me to a most horrible death." Procopius, *The Secret History,* trans. Richard Atwater (Chicago: P. Covici, 1927), http://www.fordham.edu/halsall/basis/procop-anec.html. In *Censorship and Interpretation,* Annabel Patterson persuasively argues that early modern dramatic fiction facilitated oblique criticism of the sovereign or state policy.

2. Mailer, *Armies of the Night,* 284; hereafter cited parenthetically.

3. Hutcheon, *Poetics of Postmodernism,* 202. Hutcheon does not view Mailer's novel as historiographic metafiction in the strict sense but sees it as one of several notable "non-fictional novels...which come very close to historiographic metafiction in their form and content" (117). On the periodization of postmodernism in the 1960s, see Dekoven, *Utopia Limited.*

4. Compelling accounts of this resurgence include Hutcheon, *Politics of Postmodernism* and *Poetics of Postmodernism;* and Elias, *Sublime Desire.*

5. Key thinkers in the shift toward a less positivist, more narratological account of history include Friedrich Nietzsche, Carl Becker, Benedetto Croce, and Robin Collingwood. Since the mid-twentieth century, the list has grown far too long, running through the Annales school, the social history movement, and into cultural studies. Hayden White is still the most prominent thinker arguing that history is difficult to distinguish from fiction. See White, *Tropics of Discourse,* and *The Content of the Form: Narrative Discourse and Historical Representation* (Baltimore: Johns Hopkins University Press, 1987).

6. Charles Baxter, "Dysfunctional Narratives, or 'Mistakes Were Made,'" in *Crafting Fiction: In Theory, in Practice,* ed. Marvin Diogenes and Clyde Moneyhun (London: Mayfield, 2001), 396–97; hereafter cited parenthetically. Baxter borrows the concept "narrative dysfunction" from the poet C. K. Williams, who uses it to describe the breakdown of stories that give us a sense of identity and moral purpose. Baxter, however, sees this tendency as widespread and he lays it at the feet of the Cold War state.

7. National Security Council, "NSC 10/2," 215–16.

8. The White House, "National Security Action Memorandum 273," November 26, 1963, John McAdams, The Kennedy Assassination, Marquette University, http://mcadams.posc.mu.edu/viet16.htm. The phrase "plausibility of denial" was inserted between the memo's draft date (November 21, 1963) and its issue date, five days later. There is no evidence that the phrase was inserted as a result of President Kennedy's assassination on November 22, 1963.

9. Marie-Laure Ryan, "The Modes of Narrativity and Their Visual Metaphors," *Style* 26, no. 3 (1992): 9–10; Brian McHale, "Weak Narrativity: The Case of Avant-Garde Narrative Poetry," *Narrative* 9, no. 2 (2001): 165.

10. DeLillo, author's note, *Libra,* 458.

11. Margaret Atwood, *Bodily Harm* (Toronto: McClelland and Stewart, 1981).

12. Margaret Atwood, *The Handmaid's Tale* (1985; New York: Anchor, 1998), 306, 307, 309; hereafter cited parenthetically.

13. I am not suggesting Atwood knew of Iranian arms sales, which mostly took place after publication of *The Handmaid's Tale,* but she was certainly aware of rumors about an arms-for-hostages deal in the fall of 1979 to help unseat President Carter. See Gary Sick, "The Election Story of the Decade," *New York Times,* April 15, 1991, http://www.nytimes.com/1991/04/15/opinion/the-election-story-of-the-decade.html.

14. Joan Didion, *A Book of Common Prayer* (New York: Simon and Schuster, 1977); *Democracy* (New York: Simon and Schuster, 1984); *The Last Thing He Wanted* (New York: Knopf, 1996); all cited parenthetically hereafter.

15. Nadel, *Containment Culture,* 276.

16. Ibid., 277.

17. Joan Didion, "The White Album," in *The White Album* (New York: Simon and Schuster, 1979), 15, 11. When she first published "The White Album" as a whole in 1979, Didion dated the essay "1968–78." However, sections 3, 5, and 9 of the "The White Album" were separately published in *The Saturday Evening Post* between March 1968 and January 1969.

18. It was Didion's husband, John Gregory Dunne, who suggested that Didion call the novel "Democracy." See Joan Didion, *The Year of Magical Thinking* (New York: Knopf, 2005), 221.

19. Barbara Grizzuti Harrison, "Joan Didion: Only Disconnect," in *Off Center: Essays by Barbara Grizzuti Harrison* (New York: Dial, 1980), 119.

20. Bentham, "Essay on Political Tactics," 312–13.

21. Dean, *Publicity's Secret,* 20–22, 4. On the notion of a "subject supposed to know," see Slavoj Žižek, *The Plague of Fantasies* (London: Verso, 1997). On "the subject supposed to believe," see Rastko Mocnik, "Ideology and Fantasy," in *The Althusserian Legacy,* ed. E. Ann Kaplan and Michael Sprinkler, 139–60 (New York: Verso, 1993).

22. Ellsberg, *Secrets,* 237.

23. See A. J. Langguth, *Hidden Terrors* (New York: Pantheon, 1978) on how U.S. intelligence used USAID and the Office of Public Safety to train Uruguayan police in the use of torture. In July 1970, the Tupamaros kidnapped and killed Dan Mitrione, a USAID official who had earlier trained Brazilian security forces in the use of interrogation tactics.

24. Joan Didion, "Girl of the Golden West," which originally appeared in the *New York Review of Books* (1982), is reprinted in *After Henry,* 95–109 (New York: Vintage, 1993).

25. Dean, *Publicity's Secret,* 20; emphasis added.

26. Joan Didion, "In Bogotá," in *The White Album* (New York: Simon and Schuster, 1979), 193; hereafter cited parenthetically.

27. The 1948 assassination of populist liberal presidential candidate Jorge Eliécer Gaitán set off the wave of rioting known as *El Bogotazo* and the long period of unrest known as *La Violencia.* The unrest was viewed with alarm by Washington, which feared a Communist uprising. In 1953, Rojas Pinilla took power in a bloodless coup widely supported by both conservative and liberal Colombians and by the United States. His initial efforts stemmed *La Violencia,* but ultimately his repressive rule failed to end the violence and he was replaced in 1957 by a new civilian coalition government. Rojas Pinilla was the only Latin American leader to commit a battalion of troops to the U.S.-led force in Korea, which gained him considerable U.S. support and weaponry. See Stephen J. Randall, *Colombia and the United States: Hegemony and Independence* (Athens: University of Georgia Press, 1992); and Walter LaFeber, *Inevitable Revolutions: The United States in Central America* (New York: Norton, 1983).

28. Didion, *Last Thing He Wanted,* 10.

29. This so-called resupply is a fictional incident imagined to constitute part of the larger Iran-Contra scandal, during which elements of the Reagan administration illegally redirected funds to the Contras, right-wing Nicaraguan "freedom fighters" attempting to overthrow the socialist Sandinista government.

30. As Samuel Cohen notes, Didion's interweaving of fact and fiction at such moments complicates the picture further: "When readers can't know what is real, when real and not-real are cheek-by-jowl, what sort of conclusions are they supposed to draw about these stories and the real world?" (*After the End of History: American Fiction in the 1990s* [Iowa City: University of Iowa Press, 2009], 146).

31. A number of clues suggest that the island is in the Bahamas and probably San Salvador Island. San Salvador Island has an airport and a "view of Rum Cay." It is also the island Columbus

landed on after "the long voyage from the Cape Verdes." Other elements of Didion's fictional island, however—especially the fading embassy and the medical school—suggest that the location is a larger island such as Nassau.

32. Nadel, *Containment Culture,* 281; emphasis added.

33. Barth, "Lost in the Funhouse"; hereafter cited parenthetically.

5. Postmodern Amnesia

1. Robert Ludlum, *The Bourne Identity* (New York: Turtleback, 1988); *The Bourne Supremacy* (New York: Turtleback, 1989); and *The Bourne Ultimatum* (New York: Turtleback, 1991). *The Bourne Identity,* DVD, directed by Doug Liman (2002; Universal City, CA: Universal, 2004); *The Bourne Supremacy,* DVD, directed by Paul Greengrass (2004; Universal City, CA: Universal, 2005); *The Bourne Ultimatum,* DVD, directed by Paul Greengrass (2007; Universal City, CA: Universal, 2008).

2. Tony Gilroy, Scott Z. Burns, and George Nolfi, "The Bourne Ultimatum," final shooting script, June 20, 2007, 53, Internet Movie Script Database (IMSDb), http://www.imsdb.com/scripts/Bourne-Ultimatum,-The.html; *A Few Good Men.*

3. Ian Fleming, *The Man with the Golden Gun* (London: Jonathan Cape, 1965); Philip K. Dick, "We Can Remember It for You Wholesale," 1966; repr. in *We Can Remember It for You Wholesale and Other Classic Stories,* 35–52 (New York: Citadel, 2002); *Codename Icarus,* TV series, DVD, directed by Marilyn Fox (1981; Chatsworth, CA: Homevision, 2006); *Jacob's Ladder,* DVD, directed by Adrian Lyne (1990; Santa Monica: Lions Gate, 1998); *The Long Kiss Goodnight,* DVD, directed by Renny Harlin (1996; Los Angeles: New Line, 1997); *Conspiracy Theory,* DVD, directed by Richard Donner (1997; Burbank, CA: Warner Brothers, 1997); *Menno's Mind,* DVD, directed by Jon Kroll (1997; Los Angeles: Showtime, 2000); *The Sleep Room,* TV miniseries, DVD, directed by Anne Wheeler (1998; Toronto: CBC, 1998); *Time Lapse,* DVD, directed by David Worth (2001; Santa Monica, CA: Lions Gate, 2001); *Alias,* TV series, created by J. J. Abrams (Burbank, CA: ABC, September 30, 2001–May 22, 2006); *Blind Horizon,* DVD, directed by Michael Hausmann (2003; Santa Monica, CA: Lions Gate, 2005); *Paycheck,* DVD, directed by John Woo (2003; Los Angeles: Paramount, 2003); *Second Nature,* DVD, directed by Ben Bolt (2003; Burbank, CA: TNT, 2003); *The Manchurian Candidate,* DVD, directed by Jonathan Demme (2004; Los Angeles: Paramount, 2004); *Torture Room,* DVD, directed by Eric Forsberg (2007; La Crosse, WI, Platinum Disc/Echo Bridge, 2010); *My Own Worst Enemy,* TV series, created by Jason Smilovic (Burbank, CA: NBC, 2008); *XIII: The Conspiracy,* TV miniseries, DVD, directed by Duane Clark (2008; Toronto, Canada: Phase 4, 2010); *Dollhouse,* TV series, DVD, created by Joss Whedon (Los Angeles: Fox, 2009–10); *Salt,* DVD, directed by Phillip Noyce (2010; Culver City, CA: Columbia, 2010); *Homeland,* TV series. A trailer for *Call of Duty: Black Ops* places the viewer in the position of a warrior who has forgotten his actions and is supplied with imagery of horrifying combat ("*Call of Duty Black Ops* Official Teaser Trailer," YouTube, http://www.youtube.com/watch?v=LeSRdMhGx_g).

4. *Syriana,* directed by Stephen Gaghan (2005; Burbank, CA: Warner Brothers, 2006); Robert Baer, *See No Evil: The Story of a Ground Soldier in the CIA's War on Terrorism* (New York: Crown, 2002); Robert Siegel, "Ex-CIA Agent Robert Baer, Inspiration for *Syriana,*" *All Things Considered,* National Public Radio, December 6, 2005, http://www.npr.org/templates/story/story.php?storyId = 5041385.

5. Rogin, "Make My Day!" 105–6, 103.

6. Gilroy, Burns, and Nolfi, "Bourne Ultimatum," 100. The script here reads, "You chose to come here! You chose to stay! And no matter how much you want to forget it...eventually you're going to have to face how you chose...to become Jason Bourne!"

7. Jameson, *Postmodernism,* 18, 25; Baudrillard, "Precession of Simulacra," 278; Harvey, *Condition of Postmodernity,* 308–14; Pierre Vidal-Naquet, *Assassins of Memory: Essays on the Denial of the Holocaust,* trans. Jeffrey Mehlman (New York: Columbia University Press, 1992).

8. The phrase "age of forgetting" comes from Charles Baxter, "Shame and Forgetting in the Information Age," in *The Business of Memory: The Art of Remembering in an Age of Forgetting,* ed. Charles Baxter (St. Paul, MN: Graywolf Press, 1999), 148. The term "culture of amnesia" comes from Andreas Huyssen, *Twilight Memories: Marking Time in a Culture of Amnesia* (New York: Routledge, 1995). Huyssen's outstanding work on cultural memory also includes *Present Pasts: Urban Palimpsests and the Politics of Memory* (Stanford: Stanford University Press, 2003).

9. Jonathan Lethem, ed., *The Vintage Book of Amnesia: An Anthology of Writing on the Subject of Memory Loss* (New York: Vintage, 2000); Steven Erikson, *Rubicon Beach* (New York: Simon and Schuster, 1986); Lydia Davis, *Almost No Memory* (New York: Farrar, Straus, and Giroux, 2001); Kathy Acker, *In Memoriam to Identity* (New York: Grove, 1998); Douglas Cooper, *Amnesia* (New York: Hyperion, 1994); Jonathan Lethem, *Amnesia Moon* (New York: Houghton Mifflin Harcourt, 2005); Jess Walter, *The Zero* (New York: Harper, 2006); *Memento,* DVD, directed by Christopher Nolan (2000; Culver City, CA: Sony, 2004); *Eternal Sunshine of the Spotless Mind,* DVD, directed by Michael Gondry (2004; Universal City, CA: Universal, 2004); *Mulholland Drive,* DVD, directed by David Lynch (2000; Universal City, CA: Universal, 2001); *The Adjustment Bureau,* DVD, directed by George Nolfi (2011; Universal City, CA: Universal, 2011).

10. Guy Debord, *The Society of the Spectacle,* trans. Donald Nicholson-Smith (1967; New York: Zone, 1995), 76, 114.

11. Elias, *Sublime Desire,* 49.

12. See Fitzgerald, *America Revised;* Whitfield, *Culture of the Cold War,* 56; and James Loewen, *Lies My Teacher Told Me: Everything Your American History Textbook Got Wrong* (New York: New Press, 1995).

13. See especially Kirby Farrell, *Post-Traumatic Culture: Injury and Interpretation in the Nineties* (Baltimore: Johns Hopkins University Press, 1998); Hutcheon, *Poetics of Postmodernism* and *Politics of Postmodernism;* Diane Elam, *Romancing the Postmodern* (London: Routledge, 1992); Elias, *Sublime Desire;* and Fredric Jameson, *The Political Unconscious: Narrative as a Socially Symbolic Act* (Ithaca, NY: Cornell University Press, 1982).

14. Cathy Caruth, *Unclaimed Experience: Trauma, Narrative, and History* (Baltimore: Johns Hopkins University Press, 1996), 8, 62.

15. Rogin, "Make My Day!" 105.

16. Caruth, *Unclaimed Experience,* 17, 60.

17. Powerful accounts of these subjects include the work of Huyssen; Peter Krapp, *Déjà Vu: Aberrations of Cultural Memory* (Minneapolis: University of Minnesota Press, 2004); Marita Sturken, *Tangled Memories: The Vietnam War, the AIDS Epidemic, and the Politics of Remembering* (Berkeley: University of California Press, 1997); and Ian Hacking, *Rewriting the Soul: Multiple Personality and the Sciences of Memory* (Princeton, NJ: Princeton University Press, 1995).

18. In thinking about this question, it is instructive to consider Toni Morrison's *Beloved* (New York: Knopf, 1987), which is, among other things, the story of an amnesiac. Murdered by her mother, Sethe—a runaway slave desperately trying to prevent her family's reenslavement—Beloved returns to haunt her family, first as a ghost, then as a mysterious young woman with few memories and an overwhelming desire for stories of the past. Beloved's amnesia is partly a narrative strategy for the recovery of a traumatic history. It gives Sethe, Denver, and Paul D. a reason to overcome the "work of beating back the past" and begin talking about the violence of slavery (*Beloved,* 73). Amnesia and trauma are thus linked to Morrison's historiographical project, which takes as its starting point the paradoxical difficulty but necessity of confronting the "unspeakable things unspoken" in the experience of slavery. As the narrator finishes passing on her tale she repeats that "it was not a story to pass on" (*Beloved,* 275)—suggesting both that the experience of slavery can never be conveyed (passed *on*) but also that the story could not be ignored (*passed* on). This paradox is partly a result of traumatic repression, but it also relates to epistemological barriers like those present in a regime of state secrecy. Historical sources about the African American

experience of slavery are relatively scarce. Not only did slave owners attempt to keep their slaves illiterate but, as a character notes in Gayl Jones's posttraumatic novel of slavery, *Corregidora,* "they burned all the papers, so there wouldn't be no evidence" (*Corregidora* [New York: Beacon, 1975], 14). It is partly for this reason that both Jones and Morrison develop innovative conceptions of collective memory to dramatize an elusive past. Morrison's version is "rememory," the recall of an ancestor's experience as if it were one's own memory (*Beloved,* 36). This concept is a figure for historical fiction itself—for the artistic license to imagine details that cannot be confirmed in a traditional written record of "primary sources." This postmodern fictional strategy blurs traditional ontological boundaries such as the lines between discreet persons and time. As in many covert-sphere fictions, such postmodern aesthetics seem less an end in themselves than a response to a fundamental epistemological barrier.

19. Tim O'Brien, *In the Lake of the Woods* (Boston: Houghton Mifflin, 1994); hereafter cited parenthetically. Samuel Cohen's critical response to an earlier version of this argument helped me rethink the implications of O'Brien's unresolved narrative, and I am grateful to him. See Cohen, *After the End of History,* 125–28.

20. The 1995 Penguin paperback edition of the novel contains only 133 notes. O'Brien appears to have removed from this edition several short excerpts of testimony from *The Court-Martial of Lt. Calley,* by Richard Hammer, which is cited extensively in both versions. The changes do not significantly alter the novel.

21. Richard J. Ofshe and Margaret Thaler Singer, "Recovered-Memory Therapy and Robust Repression: Influence and Pseudomemories," *International Journal of Clinical and Experimental Hypnosis* 24, no. 4 (1994): 391–410.

22. Judith Lewis Herman, *Trauma and Recovery* (New York: Basic Books, 1992), quoted in O'Brien, *Lake of the Woods,* 27n13, 144n55.

23. O'Brien, "On the Rainy River," in *Things They Carried,* 62.

24. Tim O'Brien, "The Vietnam in Me," *New York Times Magazine,* October 2, 1994, http://www.nytimes.com/books/98/09/20/specials/obrien-vietnam.html.

25. Indeed, for all its apparently endless horror, *In the Lake of the Woods* is the one novel of O'Brien's that actually realizes the central fantasy of all the others: the flight to Canada, the disappearing act, the escape from the social pressures of reputation and manhood. In *The Things They Carried,* this notion is depicted realistically; in *Going After Cacciato* it becomes an elaborately imagined fantasy that Paul Berlin must finally bring to a close because, while he wishes to run away, he is also "afraid of running away . . . afraid of what might be thought of me by those I love. . . . The loss of their respect. . . . The loss of my own reputation (286). At the end of *Going After Cacciato,* Paul Berlin realizes that it is only "social power, the threat of social consequences, that stops [him] from making a full and complete break" (286). But John Wade no longer faces such a threat. He has already been disgraced and the only person he loves is now missing. There is nothing left for him to do but to flee responsibility by disappearing forever.

26. Martin, *Wilderness of Mirrors.* It seems merely an ironic coincidence that Angle Inlet could have been called "Angleton."

27. The first quotation is from F. Scott Fitzgerald, *The Great Gatsby* (New York: Scribner's, 1925), 99. The second is from O'Brien, *Lake of the Woods,* 238.

28. Herman, *Trauma and Recovery,* quoted in O'Brien, *Lake of the Woods,* 138, 142.

29. Gregory L. Vistica, "What Happened in Thanh Phong," *New York Times Magazine,* April 25, 2001, http://www.nytimes.com/2001/04/25/magazine/25KERREY.html.

30. Baxter, "Shame and Forgetting," 148. Crucially, notes Michael Rogin, what Reagan specifically could not remember was his own administration's covert operations ("Make My Day!" 102).

31. O'Brien, "Vietnam in Me."

32. Dave Edelman, "The Things He Carried: Tim O'Brien on Love, Murder and Vietnam," *Baltimore City Paper,* October 19, 1994, http://www.dave-edelman.com/reviews/obrien.cfm.

33. Tim O'Brien, "The Magic Show," in *Crafting Fiction: In Theory, In Practice,* ed. Marvin Diogenes and Clyde Moneyhun (Mountain View, CA: Mayfield, 2001), 379; hereafter cited parenthetically.

34. Gilles Deleuze and Félix Guattari, *A Thousand Plateaus: Capitalism and Schizophrenia,* trans. Brian Massumi (Minneapolis: University of Minnesota Press, 1987), 265.

35. O'Brien, *Lake of the Woods,* 103n36. The other borrowings cited here appear at 269n120 and 298n127.

36. O'Brien, *Lake of the Woods,* 294.

37. O'Brien, *Things They Carried,* 44.

38. This is not to suggest that Wade is a mere stand-in for O'Brien. O'Brien clearly states in "The Vietnam in Me" that his own unit did not engage in the slaughter of civilians and he finds that there is "much to remember" about Vietnam.

39. As Hayden White has so persuasively demonstrated, these categories are difficult to separate and I do not mean to suggest otherwise; but even White distinguishes narratives of invented persons and events from narratives of actual persons and events.

40. Herman, *Trauma and Recovery,* 122.

41. Mark A. Heberle, *A Trauma Artist: Tim O'Brien and the Fiction of Vietnam* (Iowa City: University of Iowa Press, 2001), 250.

42. Sturken, *Tangled Memories,* 20.

43. Janny Scott, "Prominent Historian Admits He Misled Students into Believing He Served in Vietnam," *New York Times,* June 19, 2001, A19.

44. Tim O'Brien, "Writing Vietnam: Keynote Address" (lecture, Brown University, April 21, 1999), http://mama.stg.brown.edu/projects/WritingVietnam/obrien.html.

6. The Geopolitical Melodrama

1. Elisabeth Bumiller, "A Somber Bush Says Terrorism Cannot Prevail," with David E. Sanger, *New York Times,* September 12, 2001, A1.

2. George Bush, "Transcript of President Bush's Address to a Joint Session of Congress on Thursday Night, September 20, 2001," *CNN.com,* September 20, 2001, http://www.cnn.com/2001/US/09/20/gen.bush.transcript.

3. Christopher Lasch, *The Culture of Narcissism: American Life in an Age of Diminishing Expectations* (New York: Norton, 1979).

4. Dan Rather, interview by Larry King, *Larry King Live, CNN.com,* October 18, 2001, http://transcripts.cnn.com/TRANSCRIPTS/0110/18/lkl.00.html.

5. Robert Kaplan, interview by Liane Hansen, *Morning Edition,* National Public Radio, September 23, 2001.

6. Pease, *New American Exceptionalism,* 22–23. For a longer history of exceptionalism, see Deborah L. Madsen, *American Exceptionalism* (Edinburgh: Edinburgh University Press, 1998).

7. This is Donald Pease's phrase. See *New American Exceptionalism,* esp. 153.

8. Pease, *New American Exceptionalism.*

9. For an excellent treatment of melodrama and its history, see Peter Brooks, *The Melodramatic Imagination: Balzac, Henry James, Melodrama, and the Mode of Excess* (New Haven, CT: Yale University Press, 1995).

10. My primary interest here is the body of cultural representation that informed the Bush administration's response to the attacks of 9/11—that is, the body of visual representations from roughly 1990–2005. A number of films about terrorism and counterterrorism were subsequently released, some of which are visually and narratologically more sophisticated than earlier films. Notable in these later films is the increasing presence of foreign perspectives on the United States, particularly its foreign policy. Nonetheless, these films also share many of the structures I analyze here.

Die Hard, DVD, directed by John McTiernan (1988; Los Angeles: Twentieth-Century Fox, 2007); *Die Harder,* DVD, directed by Rennie Harlen (1990; Los Angeles: Twentieth-Century Fox, 2007); *Patriot Games,* DVD, directed by Phillip Noyce (1992; Los Angeles: Paramount, 2003); *Clear and Present Danger,* DVD, directed by Phillip Noyce (1994; Los Angeles: Paramount, 1998); *Die Hard with a Vengeance,* DVD, directed by John McTiernan (1995; Los Angeles: Twentieth-Century Fox, 2007); *Outbreak,* DVD, directed by Wolfgang Petersen (1995; Burbank, CA: Warner Brothers, 1997); *Broken Arrow,* DVD, directed by John Woo (1996; Los Angeles: Twentieth-Century Fox, 1999); *Independence Day,* DVD, directed by Roland Emmerich (1996; Los Angeles: Twentieth-Century Fox, 2003); *Air Force One,* DVD, directed by Wolfgang Peterson (1997; Culver City, CA: Sony, 1998); *The Rock,* DVD, directed by Michael Bay (1996; Burbank, CA: Disney, 1997); *Face/Off,* DVD, directed by John Woo (1997; Los Angeles: Paramount, 1998); *The Peacemaker,* DVD, directed by Mimi Leder (1997; Universal City, CA: Dreamworks, 1998); *Enemy of the State,* DVD, directed by Tony Scott (1998; Burbank, CA: Touchstone/Disney, 1999); *The Siege,* DVD, directed by Edward Zwick (1998; Los Angeles: Twentieth-Century Fox, 1999); *Swordfish,* DVD, directed by Dominic Sena (2001; Burbank, CA: Warner, 2004); *Collateral Damage,* DVD, directed by Andrew Davis (2002; Burbank, CA, Warner, 2004); *The Sum of All Fears,* DVD, directed by Philip Alden Robinson (2002; Los Angeles: Paramount, 2002); *Munich,* DVD, directed by Steven Spielberg (2005: Universal City, CA: Universal, 2006); *The Kingdom,* DVD, directed by Peter Berg (2007: Universal City, CA: Universal, 2007); *Live Free or Die Hard,* DVD, directed by Len Wiseman (2007; Los Angeles: Twentieth-Century Fox, 2007); *Rendition,* DVD, directed by Gavin Hood (2007; Los Angeles: New Line, 2008); *Body of Lies,* DVD, directed by Ridley Scott (2008; Los Angeles: Warner, 2009); *Traitor,* DVD, directed by Jeffrey Nachmanoff (2008; Troy, MI: Anchor Bay, 2008); *The Agency,* TV series, created by Michael Frost Beckner (Los Angeles: CBS, September 27, 2001–May 17, 2003); *Alias,* TV series, created by J. J. Abrams (Burbank, CA: ABC, September 30, 2001–May 22, 2006); *24,* TV series, created by Joel Surnow and Robert Cochran (Los Angeles: Fox TV, November 6, 2001–February 1, 2010); *Threat Matrix,* TV series, created by Daniel Voll (Burbank, CA: ABC, September 18, 2003–January 29, 2004); *The Grid,* TV miniseries, created by Mikael Salomon (Burbank, CA: TNT, September 7–8, 2004); *Sleeper Cell,* TV series, created by Ethan Rieff and Cyrus Voris (Los Angeles: Showtime, December 4, 2005–December 17, 2006); *The Unit,* TV series, created by David Mamet (Los Angeles: CBS, March 7, 2006–May 10, 2009); *The Company,* TV series, directed by Mikael Salomon (Burbank, CA: TNT, August 5, 2007–August 19, 2007); *Strike Back,* TV series, produced by Andy Harries and Elaine Pyke (Middlesex, UK: BBC, May 5, 2010–October 21, 2011).

11. The qualities of narcissism specified by the American Psychiatric Association's *Diagnostic and Statistical Manual of Mental Disorders,* 4th ed. (s.v. "Narcissistic Personality Disorder"), are virtually synonymous with the qualities of "American exceptionalism." They include a sense of grandiosity, fantasies of power, a belief in one's own specialness, a sense of entitlement, a lack of empathy, a need for admiration, and a tendency toward exploitation, arrogance, and selfishness. Narcissism is a useful category when construing American exceptionalism because it emphasizes both the inward-looking gaze that causes the disorder and the lack of empathy for others that is its worst consequence.

12. Sigmund Freud, "Psycho-Analytic Notes on an Autobiographical Account of a Case of Paranoia (Dementia Paranoides)," in *The Standard Edition of the Complete Psychological Works of Sigmund Freud,* ed. and trans. James Strachey, 12:3–82 (1911; London: Hogarth, 1953–74).

13. Pease, *New American Exceptionalism,* 23.

14. On this tradition, see Melley, *Empire of Conspiracy.*

15. *Alias* and *Homeland* both have unmarried female protagonists who exhibit much of the autonomy and skill of the traditional male hero. Neither has dependents that can be taken hostage.

16. Jane Mayer, "Whatever It Takes: The Politics of the Man behind *24,*" *New Yorker,* February 19, 2007, http://www.newyorker.com/reporting/2007/02/19/070219fa_fact_mayer.

17. Agamben, *State of Exception,* 1.

18. Useful accounts of this subject include Mark Bowden, "The Dark Art of Interrogation," *Atlantic,* October 2003, http://www.theatlantic.com/doc/200310/bowden; Sidney Blumenthal, "Fall of the House of Kitsch," *Salon,* November 8, 2006, http://www.salon.com/opinion/blumen thal/2006/11/08/election/; and Jacob Weisberg, "All the President's Accomplices: How the Country Acquiesced to Bush's Torture Policy," *Slate,* May 2, 2009, http://www.slate.com/id/2217359/.

19. Mayer, "Whatever It Takes."

20. The so-called ticking-bomb scenario seems to originate from Jean Lartéguy's, *Les centurions* (Paris: Presses de la Cité, 1960), a novel about the First Indochina War and later the French war in Algeria. According to Robert Kaplan, this work of fiction is essentially required reading for U.S. counterinsurgency warriors: "Lartéguy inhabits the very soul of the modern Western warrior, alienating some civilian readers in the process.... Some months back, Gen. David Petreaus—now commander of U.S. ground forces in Iraq—pulled *The Centurions* off a shelf at his home in Fort Leavenworth, Kansas, and gave me a disquisition about the small unit leadership principles exemplified by one of the characters. For half a decade now, Green Berets have been recommending Lartéguy's *The Centurions* and *The Praetorians* (1961) to me: books about French paratroopers in Vietnam and Algeria in the 1950s." Kaplan, "Rereading Vietnam," *Atlantic,* August 2007, http://www.theatlantic.com/doc/200708u/kaplan-vietnam/3.

21. Mayer, "Whatever It Takes."

22. Rogin, *"Ronald Reagan," the Movie,* 237.

23. Pease, *New American Exceptionalism,* 33.

24. Žižek, *Welcome to the Desert of the Real,* 15–16. Jean Baudrillard echoed this view in his 2002 essay "L'esprit du terrorisme" (*Le Monde,* February 11, 2001, http://www.egs.edu/faculty/ jean-baudrillard/articles/lesprit-du-terrorisme): "Que nous ayons rêvé de cet événement, que tout le monde sans exception en ait rêvé...cela est inacceptable pour la conscience morale occidentale, mais c'est pourtant un fait.... A la limite, c'est eux qui l'ont fait, mais c'est nous qui l'avons voulu." "The fact that we have dreamt of this event, that everyone without exception has dreamt of it...is unacceptable for Western moral conscience. Yet it is a fact.... At a pinch, we can say that they *did* it, but we *wished for* it" (in *The Spirit of Terrorism and Other Essays,* trans. Chris Turner [New York: Verso, 2002], 5). In place of Žižek's "fantasized," Baudrillard's unfortunate *"voulu"* ("wished for" or "wanted") reduces the notion of cultural fantasy, with its mix of desire and repulsion, to mere desire—as if Americans "wished" to be attacked. This simplification, however, does not alter the underlying similarity of the two accounts. Both suggest that popular representations of terror are a return of the repressed, a way in which U.S. citizens obliquely confront the global privilege and power of their nation.

25. Žižek, *Welcome to the Desert of the Real,* 12–13.

26. Žižek, "Welcome to the Desert of the Real!" 387.

27. ABC News, "What Can the N.S.A. Do Anyway? The National Security Agency Has Been Attracting Much Attention with Wiretaps," *Good Morning America,* January 25, 2006, http:// abcnews.go.com/GMA/story?id=1539078&CMP=OTC-RSSFeeds0312.

28. Amy Beth Graves, "Spy Museum Shows Off Espionage Tools," *InfoBeat* (Associated Press), January 15, 2001, http://fsbvg.homestead.com/files/spy_museum.txt.

29. Žižek, *Welcome to the Desert of the Real,* 16.

30. Philippe Sands, *Torture Team: Rumsfeld's Memo and the Betrayal of American Values* (New York: Palgrave MacMillan, 2008), 61–62.

31. Carol Costello, "The Politics of *24," The Situation Room,* CNN, January 16, 2007, http:// transcripts.cnn.com/TRANSCRIPTS/0701/16/sitroom.03.html. Chertoff spoke at a Heritage Foundation panel entitled "'24' and America's Image in Fighting Terrorism: Fact, Fiction or Does It Matter?" See Paul Farhi, "Calling On Hollywood's Terrorism 'Experts,'" *Washington Post,* June

24, 2006, http://www.washingtonpost.com/wp-dyn/content/article/2006/06/23/AR2006062301804. html.

32. Mayer, "Whatever It Takes." See also Edward Wyatt, "New Era in Politics, New Focus for '24,'" *New York Times,* January 8, 2009, C1.

33. Laura Ingraham, interview by Bill O'Reilly, *The O'Reilly Factor,* Fox, September 13, 2006, http://www.youtube.com/watch?v=LrsQPK. See also Andrew Ironside, "Conservatives Continue to Use Fox's *24* to Support Hawkish Policies," *Media Matters for America,* February 2, 2007, http://mediamatters.org/items/200702020015.

34. David Foster Wallace, "The View from Mrs. Thompson's," *Rolling Stone,* September 25, 2001, reprinted in *Consider the Lobster* (Boston: Little Brown, 2006), 140.

35. John Yoo, *War by Other Means* (Boston: Atlantic Monthly Press, 2006), 172–73.

36. Colin Freeze, "What Would Jack Bauer Do? Canadian Jurist Prompts International Justice Panel to Debate TV Drama *24*'s Use of Torture," *Globe and Mail (Toronto)*, June 16, 2007.

37. Evan Thomas and Michael Hirsh, "The Debate over Torture," *Newsweek,* November 21, 2005, 26.

38. William Jefferson Clinton, interview by Tim Russert, *Meet the Press,* NBC News, September 30, 2007, http://www.msnbc.msn.com/id/21065954/.

39. As the former counterterrorism chief Richard A. Clark pointed out almost immediately, the War on Terror is defined by a strategy (terrorism) and not a specific enemy with a particular history and set of objectives (*Against All Enemies: Inside America's War on Terror* [New York: Simon and Schuster, 2004]).

WORKS CITED

ABC News. "What Can the N.S.A. Do Anyway? The National Security Agency Has Been Attracting Much Attention with Wiretaps." *Good Morning America,* January 25, 2006. http://abcnews.go.com/GMA/story?id=1539078&CMP=OTC-RSSFeeds0312.

Acker, Kathy. *In Memoriam to Identity.* New York: Grove, 1998.

The Adjustment Bureau. DVD. Directed by George Nolfi. 2011; Universal City, CA: Universal, 2011.

Agamben, Giorgio. *State of Exception.* Translated by Kevin Attell. Chicago: University of Chicago Press, 2005.

The Agency. TV series. Created by Michael Frost Beckner. Los Angeles: CBS, September 27, 2001–May 17, 2003.

Air Force One. DVD. Directed by Wolfgang Peterson. 1997; Culver City, CA: Sony, 1998.

Alias. TV series. Created by J. J. Abrams. Burbank, CA: ABC, September 30, 2001– May 22, 2006.

American Psychiatric Association. *Diagnostic and Statistical Manual of Mental Disorders.* 4th ed. Washington, DC: American Psychiatric Association, 2000.

Andrew, Christopher. *For the President's Eyes Only: Secret Intelligence and the American Presidency from Washington to Bush.* New York: HarperCollins, 1995.

Anthony, Dick. "Pseudoscience and Minority Religions: An Evaluation of the Brainwashing Theories of Jean-Marie Abgrall." *Social Justice Research* 12 (1999): 421–56.

Anzaldúa, Gloria E. *The Gloria Anzaldúa Reader.* Edited by AnaLouise Keating. Durham: Duke University Press, 2009.

Apocalypse Now. DVD. Directed by Francis Ford Coppola. 1979; Santa Monica, CA: Lions Gate, 2010.

Atwood, Margaret. *Bodily Harm.* Toronto: McClelland and Stewart, 1981.

——. *The Handmaid's Tale.* 1985. Reprint, New York: Anchor, 1998.

Austin, J. L. *How to Do Things with Words.* Oxford: Oxford University Press, 1962.

Baer, Robert. *See No Evil: The Story of a Ground Soldier in the CIA's War on Terrorism.* New York: Crown, 2002.

Baker, Keith Michael. "Defining the Public Sphere in Eighteenth-Century France: Variations on a Theme by Habermas." In Calhoun, *Habermas and the Public Sphere*, 181–211.

Bamford, James. *Body of Secrets: Anatomy of the Ultra-Secret National Security Agency.* New York: Anchor, 2002.

Barth, John. "Lost in the Funhouse." 1967. In *Lost in the Funhouse: Fiction for Print, Tape, Live Voice*, 72–97. New York: Anchor, 1988.

Baudrillard, Jean. "L'esprit du terrorisme." *Le Monde*, February 11, 2001. http://www.egs.edu/faculty/jean-baudrillard/articles/lesprit-du-terrorisme.

——. "The Precession of Simulacra." Translated by Paul Foss and Paul Patton. In *Art after Modernism: Rethinking Representation,* edited by Brian Wallis, 253–81. New York: New Museum of Contemporary Art, 1984.

——. "The Spirit of Terrorism." In *The Spirit of Terrorism and Other Essays*, translated by Chris Turner, 3–34. New York: Verso, 2002.

Baxter, Charles. "Dysfunctional Narratives; or, 'Mistakes Were Made.'" In *Crafting Fiction: In Theory, in Practice,* edited by Marvin Diogenes and Clyde Moneyhun, 395–406. London: Mayfield, 2001.

——. "Shame and Forgetting in the Information Age." In *The Business of Memory: The Art of Remembering in an Age of Forgetting,* edited by Charles Baxter, 141–57. St. Paul, MN: Graywolf Press, 1999.

Baym, Nina. "Melodramas of Beset Manhood: How Theories of American Fiction Exclude Women Authors." *American Quarterly* 33, no. 2 (1981): 123–39.

Benhabib, Seyla. "Models of Public Space: Hannah Arendt, the Liberal Tradition, and Jürgen Habermas." In Calhoun, *Habermas and the Public Sphere,* 73–98.

Bentham, Jeremy. "Essay on Political Tactics." 1821. In *The Works of Jeremy Bentham,* vol. 2, *Of Publicity,* edited by John Bowring, 299–374. New York: Russell and Russell, 1962.

Berger, Peter L., and Thomas Luckmann. *The Social Construction of Reality: A Treatise in the Sociology of Knowledge.* New York: Anchor, 1966.

Berman, Morris. *The Reenchantment of the World.* Ithaca, NY: Cornell University Press, 1981.

Bérubé, Michael. "Teaching Postmodern Fiction without Being Sure That the Genre Exists." *Chronicle of Higher Education,* May 19, 2000. http://chronicle.com/article/Teaching-Postmodern-Fiction/10227.

Biderman, Albert D. "The Image of 'Brainwashing.'" *Public Opinion Quarterly* 26, no. 4 (1962): 547–63.

Blindfold. Directed by Philip Dunne. Burbank, CA: Universal, 1965.

Blind Horizon. DVD. Directed by Michael Hausmann. 2003; Santa Monica, CA: Lions Gate, 2005.

Blumenthal, Sidney. "Fall of the House of Kitsch." *Salon,* November 8, 2006. http://www.salon.com/opinion/blumenthal/2006/11/08/election/.

Body of Lies. Directed by Ridley Scott. 2008; Los Angeles: Warner, 2009.

Bosman, Julie. "In Novels, an Ex-Spy Returns to the Fold." *New York Times,* March 19, 2011, B1.

The Bourne Identity. DVD. Directed by Doug Liman. 2002; Universal City, CA: Universal, 2004.

The Bourne Supremacy. DVD. Directed by Paul Greengrass. 2004; Universal City, CA: Universal, 2005.

The Bourne Ultimatum. DVD. Directed by Paul Greengrass. 2007; Universal City, CA: Universal, 2008.

Bowden, Mark. "The Dark Art of Interrogation." *Atlantic,* October 2003. http://www.theatlantic.com/doc/200310/bowden.

Broken Arrow. DVD. Directed by John Woo. 1996; Los Angeles: Twentieth-Century Fox, 1999.

Brooks, Peter. *The Melodramatic Imagination: Balzac, Henry James, Melodrama, and the Mode of Excess.* New Haven, CT: Yale University Press, 1995.

Buckley, Michael. *NERDS: National Espionage, Rescue, and Defense Society.* New York: Amulet, 2010.

Bumiller, Elisabeth. "A Somber Bush Says Terrorism Cannot Prevail." With David E. Sanger. *New York Times,* September 12, 2001, A1.

Burdick, Eugene, and William J. Lederer. *The Ugly American.* 1958. Reprint, New York: Norton, 1999.

Burroughs, William S. "The Limits of Control." In *The Adding Machine: Selected Essays*, 117–21. New York: Arcade, 1985.

Bush, George W. *Decision Points.* New York: Crown, 2010.

——. "Transcript of President Bush's Address to a Joint Session of Congress on Thursday Night, September 20, 2001." *CNN.com*, September 20, 2001. http://archives.cnn.com/2001/US/09/20/gen.bush.transcript/.

Butler, Judith. *Gender Trouble: Feminism and the Subversion of Identity.* London: Routledge, 1989.

Calhoun, Craig, ed. *Habermas and the Public Sphere.* Cambridge, MA: MIT Press, 1993.

——. "Habermas and the Public Sphere." Introduction to Calhoun, *Habermas and the Public Sphere,* 1–50.

"*Call of Duty: Black Ops*; Official Single Player Trailer [HD]." YouTube. http://www.youtube.com/watch?v=41gr0IF91eg.

"*Call of Duty: Black Ops*; World Premiere Uncut Trailer." YouTube. http://www.youtube.com/watch?v=OtRnpC7ddv8.

Caputo, Philip. "Casualties of War." *New York Times Book Review,* June 20, 2010, 1.

Carmichael, Virginia. *Framing History: The Rosenberg Stories and the Cold War.* Minneapolis: University of Minnesota Press, 1993.

Carroll, Rory. "Kathryn Bigelow Given Information on Unit That Killed Osama bin Laden." *Guardian*, May 23, 2012. http://www.guardian.co.uk/world/2012/may/24/kathryn-bigelow-bin-laden-intelligence.

Caruth, Cathy. *Unclaimed Experience: Trauma, Narrative, and History.* Baltimore: Johns Hopkins University Press, 1996.

Central Intelligence Agency. "Briefing for the Psychological Strategy Board." Memorandum to the director of Central Intelligence. May 13, 1953. The Black Vault. CIA MK-ULTRA documents. 4 CD-ROMs. Disk 2. MORI ID no. 146086. http://documents.theblackvault.com/documents/mkultra/MKULTRA1/DOC_0000146086/0000146086_0001.TIF.

——. CIA Museum. Central Intelligence Agency. https://www.cia.gov/about-cia/cia-museum/.

——. "The CIA Museum: The People Behind the Magic." https://www.cia.gov/news-information/featured-story-archive/cia-museum-the-people.html.

——. "Clandestine Service History, Overthrow of Premier Mossadeq of Iran, November 1952–August 1953." March 1954. *New York Times on the Web*. http://www.nytimes.com/library/world/mideast/041600iran-cia-index.html.

——. *KUBARK Counterintelligence Interrogation*. July 1963. National Security Archive. http://www.gwu.edu/~nsarchiv/NSAEBB/NSAEBB27/01-01.htm.

——. "Narrative Description of the Overt and Covert Activities of [Redacted]." January 1, 1950 [estimated]. The Black Vault. CIA MK-ULTRA documents, disk 2, MORI ID no. 190882, 3. http://documents.theblackvault.com/documents/mkultra/MKULTRA2/DOC_0000190882/0000190882_0003.TIF.

——. "Offices of the CIA." https://www.cia.gov/offices-of-cia/index.html.

Choi, Susan. *A Person of Interest*. New York: Penguin, 2008.

Chomsky, Noam. *Toward a New Cold War: U.S. Foreign Policy from Vietnam to Reagan*. 1982. Revised edition, New York: New Press, 2003.

Clark, Richard A. *Against All Enemies: Inside America's War on Terror*. New York: Simon and Schuster, 2004.

"Clarke Wants Terrorists Treated Like Victims of Cult Brainwashing." *Daily Telegraph*, October 2, 2005. http://www.telegraph.co.uk/news/uknews/1499694/Clarke-wants-terrorists-treated-like-victims-of-cult-brainwashing.html.

Clarridge, Duane R. *A Spy for All Seasons: My Life in the CIA*. New York: Scribner, 1997.

Clear and Present Danger. DVD. Directed by Phillip Noyce. 1994; Los Angeles: Paramount, 1998.

Clinton, William Jefferson. Interview by Tim Russert. *Meet the Press,* NBC News, September 30, 2007. http://www.msnbc.msn.com/id/21065954/.

Codename Icarus. TV series. DVD. Directed by Marilyn Fox. 1981; Chatsworth, CA: Homevision, 2006.

Cohen, Samuel. *After the End of History: American Fiction in the 1990s*. Iowa City: University of Iowa Press, 2009.

Collateral Damage. DVD. Directed by Andrew Davis. 2002; Burbank, CA: Warner, 2004.

The Company. TV miniseries. Directed by Mikael Salomon. Burbank, CA: TNT, August 5, 2007–August 19, 2007.

Condon, Richard. *The Manchurian Candidate*. New York: McGraw-Hill, 1959.

Considine, Bob. "Fearfully Destructive Power of Atomic Bomb." *Deseret News,* January 8, 1951, 3B.

Conspiracy Theory. DVD. Directed by Richard Donner. 1997; Burbank, CA: Warner Brothers, 1997.

The Conversation. DVD. Directed by Francis Ford Coppola. 1974; Santa Monica, CA: Lions Gate, 2010.

Cook, Blanche Wiesen. *The Declassified Eisenhower: A Divided Legacy of Peace and Political Warfare.* New York: Doubleday, 1981.

Cooper, Douglas. *Amnesia.* New York: Hyperion, 1994.

Coover, Robert. "The Babysitter." In *Pricksongs and Descants*, 206–39. New York: Dutton, 1969.

———. *The Origin of the Brunists.* New York: Putnam, 1966.

———. *The Public Burning.* New York: Viking, 1977.

———. *The Universal Baseball Association, Inc., J. Henry Waugh, Prop.* New York: Plume, 1968.

Corber, Robert J. *Homosexuality in Cold War America: Resistance and the Crisis of Masculinity.* Durham: Duke University Press, 1997.

Costello, Carol. "The Politics of *24.*" *The Situation Room.* CNN, January 16, 2007. http://transcripts.cnn.com/TRANSCRIPTS/0701/16/sitroom.03.html.

Costigliola, Frank. "'Unceasing Pressure for Penetration': Gender, Pathology, and Emotion in George Kennan's Formation of the Cold War." *Journal of American History* 83, no. 4 (1997): 1309–39.

Cuordileone, K. A. *Manhood and American Political Culture in the Cold War.* New York: Routledge, 2004.

Davidson, Michael. *Guys Like Us: Citing Masculinity in Cold War Poetics.* Chicago: University of Chicago Press, 2004.

Davis, Lydia. *Almost No Memory.* New York: Farrar, Straus, and Giroux, 2001.

The Day After. DVD. Directed by Nicholas Meyer. 1983; Beverly Hills: MGM, 2004.

Dean, Jodi. *Publicity's Secret: How Technoculture Capitalizes on Democracy.* Ithaca, NY: Cornell University Press, 2002.

Dean, Robert D. *Imperial Brotherhood: Gender and the Making of Cold War Foreign Policy.* Amherst: University of Massachusetts Press, 2003.

Debord, Guy. *The Society of the Spectacle.* 1967. Translated by Donald Nicholson-Smith. New York: Zone, 1995.

Dekoven, Marilyn. *Utopia Limited: The Sixties and the Emergence of the Postmodern.* Durham: Duke University Press, 2004.

Deleuze, Gilles, and Félix Guattari. *A Thousand Plateaus: Capitalism and Schizophrenia.* Translated by Brian Massumi. Minneapolis: University of Minnesota Press, 1987.

DeLillo, Don. *Libra.* New York: Viking, 1988.

———. *Mao II.* New York: Viking, 1992.

———. *The Names.* New York: Knopf, 1982.

———. "The Power of History." *New York Times Magazine,* September 7, 1997. http://www.nytimes.com/library/books/090797article3.html.

———. *White Noise.* New York: Viking, 1985.

Diaz, Junot. *The Brief and Wondrous Life of Oscar Wao.* New York: Riverhead, 2007.

Dick, Philip K. "We Can Remember It for You Wholesale." 1966. Reprinted in *We Can Remember It for You Wholesale and Other Classic Stories*, 35–52. New York: Citadel, 2002.

Didion, Joan. *A Book of Common Prayer.* New York: Simon and Schuster, 1977.

———. *Democracy.* New York: Simon and Schuster, 1984.

———. "Girl of the Golden West." 1982. In *After Henry*, 95–109. New York: Vintage, 1993.

———. "In Bogotá." In *The White Album*, 187–97. New York: Simon and Schuster, 1979.

——. *The Last Thing He Wanted*. New York: Knopf, 1996.

——. "The White Album." 1968–1978. In *The White Album*, 11–48. New York: Simon and Schuster, 1979.

——. *The Year of Magical Thinking*. New York: Knopf, 2005.

Die Hard. DVD. Directed by John McTiernan. 1988; Los Angeles: Twentieth-Century Fox, 2007.

Die Harder. DVD. Directed by Rennie Harlen. 1990; Los Angeles: Twentieth-Century Fox, 2007.

Die Hard with a Vengeance. DVD. Directed by John McTiernan. 1995; Los Angeles: Twentieth-Century Fox, 2007.

Dimmer, John P., Jr. "Observations on the Double Agent." 1962. In *Inside CIA's Private World: Declassified Articles from the Agency's Internal Journal, 1955–1992*, edited by H. Bradford Westerfield, 437–49. New Haven, CT: Yale University Press.

Doctorow, E. L. *The Book of Daniel*. New York: Random House, 1971.

——. *City of God*. 2000. Reprint, New York: Plume, 2001.

——. "False Documents." In *Jack London, Hemingway, and the Constitution: Selected Essays, 1977–1992*, 149–64. New York: Random House, 1993.

——. *Ragtime*. New York: Random House, 1975.

Dollhouse. TV series. DVD. Created by Joss Whedon. 2009–10; Los Angeles: Fox, 2009–10.

Douglas, Ann. *The Feminization of American Culture*. New York: Knopf, 1977.

——. "Periodizing the American Century: Modernism, Postmodernism, and Postcolonialism in the Cold War Context." *Modernism/Modernity* 5, no. 3 (1998): 71–98.

Dr. Strangelove; or, How I Learned to Stop Worrying and Love the Bomb. DVD. Directed by Stanley Kubrick. 1964; Culver City, CA: Sony, 2001.

Dulles, Allen W. "Brain Warfare, Summary of Remarks by Mr. Allen W. Dulles at the National Alumni Conference of the Graduate Council of Princeton University, Hot Springs, VA, April 10, 1953." The Black Vault. CIA MK-ULTRA documents. Disk 1. MORI ID no. 14, 3, p. 12, http://documents.theblackvault.com/documents/mkultra/MKULTRA1/DOC_0000146077/0000146077_0003.TIF.

——. "A Report on Communist Brainwashing." Memorandum to J. Edgar Hoover, April 25, 1956. TOTSE. http://www.zoklet.net/totse/en/conspiracy/mind_control/165615.html.

Dumm, Tom. "The Trial of J. Edgar Hoover." *Secret Agents: The Rosenbergs, McCarthyism, and Fifties America*, edited by Marjorie Garber and Rebecca L. Walkowitz, 77–92. New York: Routledge, 1995.

Eagle Eye. Directed by D. J. Caruso. 2008; Universal City: Dreamworks, 2008.

Echelon Conspiracy. DVD. Directed by Greg Marcks. 2009; Los Angeles: Paramount, 2009.

Edelman, Dave. "The Things He Carried: Tim O'Brien on Love, Murder and Vietnam." *Baltimore City Paper*, October 19, 1994. http://www.dave-edelman.com/reviews/obrien.cfm.

Eisenhower, Dwight D. *Mandate for Change, 1953–1956: The White House Years*. Garden City, NY: Doubleday, 1963.

Elam, Diane. *Romancing the Postmodern*. London: Routledge, 1992.

Eley, Geoff. "Nations, Publics, and Political Cultures: Placing Habermas in the Nineteenth Century." In Calhoun, *Habermas and the Public Sphere,* 289–339.

Elias, Amy. *Sublime Desire: History and Post-1960s Fiction.* Baltimore: Johns Hopkins University Press, 2001.

Ellison, Ralph. *Invisible Man.* New York: Viking, 1952.

Ellsberg, Daniel. *Secrets: A Memoir of Vietnam and the Pentagon Papers.* New York: Viking, 2002.

Encyclopedia Britannica Profiles: The American Presidency, s.v. "John F. Kennedy: A Long Twilight Struggle." http://www.britannica.com/presidents/article-9116921.

Enemy of the State. DVD. Directed by Tony Scott. 1998; Burbank, CA: Touchstone/Disney, 1999.

Erikson, Steven. *Rubicon Beach.* New York: Simon and Schuster, 1986.

Eternal Sunshine of the Spotless Mind. DVD. Directed by Michael Gondry. 2004; Universal City, CA: Universal, 2004.

Executive Action. DVD. Directed by David Miller. 1973; Burbank, CA: Warner, 2007.

Executive Decision. DVD. Directed by Stuart Baird. 1996; Burbank, CA: Warner, 2010.

Face/Off. DVD. Directed by John Woo. 1997; Los Angeles: Paramount, 1998.

Fail-Safe. DVD. Directed by Sidney Lumet. 1964; Culver City, CA: Columbia, 2000.

Fair Game. DVD. Directed by Doug Liman. 2010; Santa Monica, CA: Summit, 2011.

Farhi, Paul. "Calling On Hollywood's Terrorism 'Experts.'" *Washington Post,* June 24, 2006. http://www.washingtonpost.com/wpdyn/content/article/2006/06/23/AR 2006062301804.html.

Farrell, Kirby. *Post-Traumatic Culture: Injury and Interpretation in the Nineties.* Baltimore: Johns Hopkins University Press, 1998.

Fenster, Mark. *Conspiracy Theories: Secrecy and Power in American Culture.* Minneapolis: University of Minnesota Press, 2001.

A Few Good Men. DVD. Directed by Rob Reiner. 1992; Culver City, CA: Columbia, 1997.

Fitzgerald, Frances. *America Revised: History Schoolbooks in the Twentieth Century.* New York: Random House, 1979.

———. *Fire in the Lake: The Vietnamese and the Americans in Vietnam.* New York: Little Brown, 1972.

Fitzgerald, F. Scott. *The Great Gatsby.* New York: Scribner's, 1925.

Fitzpatrick, Kathleen. *The Anxiety of Obsolescence: The American Novel in the Age of Television.* Nashville: Vanderbilt University Press, 2006.

Fleming, Ian. *The Man with the Golden Gun.* London: Jonathan Cape, 1965.

Flintoff, Corey. "Afghan TV Show Aims to Burnish Police Reputation." *Morning Edition.* National Public Radio, December 7, 2010. http://www.npr.org/2010/12/07/131857237/afghan-tv-show-aims-to-burnish-police-reputation.

Foucault, Michel. *The History of Sexuality: Vol. 1: An Introduction.* Translated by Robert Hurley. New York: Vintage, 1978.

———. *The Order of Things: An Archaeology of the Human Sciences.* Translated by A. M. Sheridan Smith. New York: Pantheon, 1970.

Fraser, Nancy. "Rethinking the Public Sphere: A Contribution to the Critique of Actually Existing Democracy." In Calhoun, *Habermas and the Public Sphere,* 109–142.

Freed, Donald. *Inquest.* New York: Hill and Wang, 1970.

Freeze, Colin. "What Would Jack Bauer Do? Canadian Jurist Prompts International Justice Panel to Debate TV Drama *24*'s Use of Torture." *Globe and Mail (Toronto)*, June 16, 2007, A9.

Freud, Sigmund. "Psycho-Analytic Notes on an Autobiographical Account of a Case of Paranoia (Dementia Paranoides)." In *The Standard Edition of the Complete Psychological Works of Sigmund Freud*, edited and translated by James Strachey, 12:3–82. 1911. London: Hogarth, 1953–74.

Friedan, Betty. *The Feminine Mystique*. New York: Dell, 1963.

Full Metal Jacket. DVD. Directed by Stanley Kubrick. 1987; Burbank, CA: Warner, 2007.

Gaddis, John Lewis. *We Now Know: Rethinking Cold War History*. Oxford: Oxford University Press, 1998.

Garber, Marjorie, and Rebecca L. Walkowitz, eds. *Secret Agents: The Rosenbergs, McCarthyism, and Fifties America*. New York: Routledge, 1995.

Gardner, Virginia. *The Rosenberg Story*. New York: Masses and Mainstream, 1954.

Gasiorowski, Mark. "What's New on the Iran 1953 Coup in the *New York Times* Article (April 16, 2000, front page) and the Documents Posted on the Web." Electronic Briefing Book no. 28. National Security Archive, April 19, 2000. http://www.gwu.edu/~nsarchiv/NSAEBB/NSAEBB28/.

Gates, Robert. "An Opportunity Unfulfilled: The Use and Perceptions of Intelligence in the White House." *Washington Quarterly* (Winter 1989): 35–44.

Gibson, William. *Spook Country*. New York: Putnam, 2007.

Gilroy, Tony, Scott Z. Burns, and George Nolfi. "The Bourne Ultimatum." Final shooting script. June 20, 2007. Internet Movie Script Database (IMSDb). http://www.imsdb.com/scripts/Bourne-Ultimatum,-The.html.

Ginsberg, Allen. *Deliberate Prose*. Harmondsworth: Penguin, 2000.

Godeanu-Kenworthy, Oana. "The Political Other in Nineteenth-Century British North America: The Satire of Thomas Chandler Haliburton." *Early American Studies* (Spring 2009): 205–34.

Goldschmidt, M. L. "Publicity, Privacy, and Secrecy." *Western Political Quarterly* 7 (1954): 401–16.

Goldstein, Alvin H. *The Unquiet Death of Julius and Ethel Rosenberg*. New York: Lawrence Hill, 1975.

The Good Shepherd. DVD. Directed by Robert De Niro. 2006; Universal City, CA: Universal, 2007.

Grady, James. *Six Days of the Condor*. New York: Norton, 1974.

Graves, Amy Beth. "Spy Museum Shows Off Espionage Tools." *InfoBeat* (Associated Press), January 15, 2001. http://fsbvg.homestead.com/files/spy_museum.txt.

Green Zone. DVD. Directed by Paul Greengrass. 2010; Universal City, CA: Universal, 2010.

The Grid. TV miniseries. Created by Mikael Salomon. Burbank, CA: TNT, September 7–8, 2004.

Habermas, Jürgen. "The Public Sphere: An Encyclopedia Article." *New German Critique* 3 (1974): 49–55.

———. *The Structural Transformation of the Public Sphere: An Inquiry into a Category of Bourgeois Society*. Translated by Thomas Burger, with Frederick Lawrence. Cambridge, MA: MIT Press, 1989.

Hacking, Ian. *Rewriting the Soul: Multiple Personality and the Sciences of Memory.* Princeton, NJ: Princeton University Press, 1995.

Hamid, Moshin. *The Reluctant Fundamentalist.* New York: Harcourt, 2007.

Hangmen. DVD. Directed by J. Christian Ingvordsen. 1987; Studio City, CA: Shapiro Entertainment, 2001.

Harpham, Geoffrey Galt. "E. L. Doctorow and the Technology of Narrative." *PMLA* 100, no. 1 (1985): 81–95.

Harrison, Barbara Grizzuti. "Joan Didion: Only Disconnect." In *Off Center: Essays*, 113–37. New York: Dial, 1980.

Harvey, David. *The Condition of Postmodernity: An Enquiry into the Origins of Cultural Change.* Oxford: Basil Blackwell, 1989.

Hassan, Ihab. "POSTmodernISM: A Paracritical Bibliography." In *The Postmodern Turn: Essays in Postmodern Theory and Culture*, 25–45. 1971. Reprint, Columbus: Ohio State University Press, 1987.

Hebard, Andrew. *The Poetics of Sovereignty in American Literature, 1885–1910.* Cambridge: Cambridge University Press, 2012.

Heberle, Mark A. *A Trauma Artist: Tim O'Brien and the Fiction of Vietnam.* Iowa City: University of Iowa Press, 2001.

Herman, Judith Lewis. *Trauma and Recovery.* New York: Basic Books, 1992.

Herr, Michael. *Dispatches.* New York: Knopf, 1977.

Hersh, Seymour. *The Dark Side of Camelot.* Boston: Little Brown, 1997.

——. "The Stovepipe: How Conflicts between the Bush Administration and the Intelligence Community Marred the Reporting on Iraq's Weapons." *New Yorker,* October 27, 2003. http://www.newyorker.com/archive/2003/10/27/031027fa_fact.

Hinkle, L. E., Jr., and Wolff, H. G. "Communist Interrogation and Indoctrination of 'Enemies of the State': Analysis of Methods Used by the Communist State Police." *Archives of Neurology and Psychiatry* 76 (1956): 115–74.

Hite, Molly. "'A Parody of Martyrdom': The Rosenbergs, Cold War Theology, and Robert Coover's *The Public Burning.*" *Novel* 27, no. 1 (1993): 85–101.

Homeland. TV series. Directed by Michael Cuesta, Alex Gansa, and Howard Gordon. Burbank, CA: Showtime, October 2, 2011–December 18, 2011.

Honig. Bonnie. *Emergency Politics: Paradox, Law, Democracy.* Princeton, NJ: Princeton University Press, 2009.

Hopscotch. DVD. Directed by Ronald Neame. 1980; New York: Criterion, 2002.

Hoover, J. Edgar. *Masters of Deceit.* New York: Pocket, 1958.

Hornblum, Allen M. *The Invisible Harry Gold: The Man Who Gave the Soviets the Atom Bomb.* New Haven, CT: Yale University Press, 2011.

Hume, Kathryn. *American Dream, American Nightmare: Fiction since 1960.* Urbana: University of Illinois Press, 2000.

Hunter, Edward. *The Black Book on Red China.* New York: Bookmailer, 1961.

——. *Brain-Washing in Red China: The Calculated Destruction of Men's Minds.* New York: Vanguard, 1951.

——. "'Brain-Washing' Tactics Force Chinese into Ranks of Communist Party." *Miami News,* September 24, 1950.

——. *Brainwashing: The Story of Men Who Defied It.* New York: Farrar, Straus, and Cudahy, 1956.

Hutcheon, Linda. *The Poetics of Postmodernism: History, Theory, Fiction.* New York: Routledge, 1988.

———. *The Politics of Postmodernism.* New York: Routledge, 1989.

Huyssen, Andreas. *After the Great Divide: Modernism, Mass Culture, Postmodernism.* Bloomington: Indiana University Press, 1986.

———. *Present Pasts: Urban Palimpsests and the Politics of Memory.* Stanford: Stanford University Press, 2003.

———. *Twilight Memories: Marking Time in a Culture of Amnesia.* New York: Routledge, 1995.

Independence Day. DVD. Directed by Roland Emmerich. 1996; Los Angeles: Twentieth-Century Fox, 2003.

Ingham, Tim. "*Call of Duty* Series Tops 55 Million Sales." *MCV: The Market for Computer and Video Games,* November 27, 2009. http://www.mcvuk.com/news/read/call-of-duty-series-tops-55-million-sales.

Ingraham, Laura. Interview by Bill O'Reilly. *The O'Reilly Factor,* Fox, September 13, 2006. http://www.youtube.com/watch?v=LrsQPK.

International Spy Museum. http://www.spymuseum.org.

"International Spy Museum in Washington, D.C." *Voice of America News.* http://www.youtube.com/watch?v=vAPtgEtr3BE&feature=related.

Invasion of the Body Snatchers. DVD. Directed by Don Siegel. 1956; Hollywood: Republic, 1998.

Ironside, Andrew. "Conservatives Continue to Use Fox's *24* to Support Hawkish Policies." *Media Matters for America,* February 2, 2007. http://mediamatters.org/items/200702020015.

Jacob's Ladder. DVD. Directed by Adrian Lyne. 1991; Santa Monica, CA: Lions Gate, 1998.

Jacoby, Russell. *Social Amnesia: A Critique of Social Psychology from Adler to Laing.* Boston: Beacon, 1975.

James, Henry. Preface to *The Spoils of Poynton,* v–xxiv. 1896. New York: Scribners, 1908.

Jameson, Fredric. Foreword to *The Postmodern Condition: A Report on Knowledge,* by Jean-François Lyotard, vii–xxi. Translated by Geoff Bennington and Brian Massumi. Minneapolis: University of Minnesota Press, 1984.

———. *The Political Unconscious: Narrative as a Socially Symbolic Act.* Ithaca, NY: Cornell University Press, 1982.

———. *Postmodernism; or, The Cultural Logic of Late Capitalism.* Durham: Duke University Press, 1989.

Jardine, Alice. "Flash Back, Flash Forward: The Fifties, the Nineties, and the Transformed Politics of Remote Control." In *Secret Agents: The Rosenbergs, McCarthyism, and Fifties America,* edited by Marjorie Garber and Rebecca L. Walkowitz, 107–23. New York: Routledge, 1995.

Jay, Martin. "Habermas and Modernism." *Praxis International* 4, no. 1 (1984): 1–14.

Jeffords, Susan. *The Remasculinization of America: Gender and the Vietnam War.* Bloomington: Indiana University Press, 1989.

Jeffreys, Rhodri. *The CIA and American Democracy.* New Haven, CT: Yale University Press, 1989.

Johnson, Denis. *Tree of Smoke*. New York: Farrar, Straus, and Giroux, 2007.

Jones, Gayl. *Corregidora*. New York: Beacon, 1975.

Kaplan, Amy. *The Anarchy of Empire in the Making of U.S. Culture*. Cambridge, MA: Harvard University Press, 2002.

——. "'Left Alone with America': The Absence of Empire in the Study of American Culture." In *Cultures of American Imperialism,* edited by Amy Kaplan and Donald Pease, 3–21. Durham: Duke University Press, 1993.

Kaplan, Robert. Interview by Liane Hansen. *Morning Edition*. National Public Radio, September 23, 2001.

——. "Rereading Vietnam." *Atlantic,* August 2007. http://www.theatlantic.com/doc/200708u/kaplan-vietnam/3.

Kellner, Douglas. "Habermas, the Public Sphere, and Democracy: A Critical Intervention." Unpublished essay, http://www.gseis.ucla.edu/faculty/kellner/.

Kennan, George. 861.00/2–2246: Telegram: The Charge in the Soviet Union. Kennan to the Secretary of State, SECRET, Moscow, February 22, 1946—9 p.m. National Security Archive, http://www.gwu.edu/~nsarchiv/coldwar/documents/episode-1/kennan.htm.

——. "Planning of Foreign Policy." In *Measures Short of War: The George F. Kennan Lectures at the National War College 1946–47*, edited by Giles D. Harlow and George C. Maerz, 207–18. June 18, 1947. Reprint, Washington, DC: National Defense University Press, 1991.

Kent, Sherman. *Strategic Intelligence for American World Policy*. 1949. Reprint, Hamden, CT: Archon Books, 1965.

Kesey, Ken. *One Flew Over the Cuckoo's Nest*. New York: Viking, 1962.

The Kingdom. DVD. Directed by Peter Berg. 2007: Universal City, CA: Universal, 2007.

Kinzer, Stephen. *All the Shah's Men: An American Coup and the Roots of Middle East Terror*. New York: John Wiley and Sons, 2003.

Knight, Peter. *Conspiracy Culture: From Kennedy to "The X-Files."* New York: Routledge, 2000.

Koselleck, Reinhart. *Critique and Crisis: Enlightenment and the Pathogenesis of Modern Society*. 1959. Reprint, Cambridge, MA: MIT Press, 1988.

Krapp, Peter. *Déjà Vu: Aberrations of Cultural Memory*. Minneapolis: University of Minnesota Press, 2004.

LaFeber, Walter. *America, Russia, and the Cold War, 1945–2000*. New York: McGraw Hill, 2002.

——. *Inevitable Revolutions: The United States in Central America*. New York: Norton, 1983.

Langguth, A. J. *Hidden Terrors*. New York: Pantheon, 1978.

Lartéguy, Jean. *Les centurions*. Paris: Presses de la Cité, 1960.

Lasch, Christopher. *The Culture of Narcissism: American Life in an Age of Diminishing Expectations*. New York: Norton, 1979.

Le Carré, John. *The Looking Glass War*. London: Coward McCann, 1965.

——. *The Spy Who Came in from the Cold*. London: Victor Gollancz, 1963.

LeClair, Tom. "Robert Coover, *The Public Burning,* and the Art of Excess." *Critique* 23, no. 3 (1982): 5–28.

Lederer, William J. *A Nation of Sheep.* New York: Norton, 1961.

Lee, Chang-Rae. *Native Speaker.* New York: Riverhead, 1996.

Lethem, Jonathan. *Amnesia Moon.* New York: Houghton Mifflin Harcourt, 2005.

———, ed. *The Vintage Book of Amnesia: An Anthology of Writing on the Subject of Memory Loss.* New York: Vintage, 2000.

Leung, Rebecca. "Bush Sought 'Way' to Invade Iraq? O'Neill Tells *60 Minutes* Iraq Was 'Topic A' 8 Months before 9-11." *Sixty Minutes.* CBS News, January 4, 2011. http://www.cbsnews.com/stories/2004/01/09/60minutes/main592330.shtml.

Leys, Ruth. *Trauma: A Genealogy.* Chicago: University of Chicago Press, 2000.

Lifton, Robert Jay. *Thought Reform and the Psychology of Totalism: A Study of "Brainwashing" in China.* 1961. Reprint, Chapel Hill: University of North Carolina Press, 1989.

Liptak, Adam. "Truth, Fiction and the Rosenbergs." *New York Times,* January 21, 2006, B1.

Littell, Robert. *The Company.* New York: Overlook, 2002.

Live Free or Die Hard. DVD. Directed by Len Wiseman. 2007; Los Angeles: Twentieth-Century Fox, 2007.

Loewen, James. *Lies My Teacher Told Me: Everything Your American History Textbook Got Wrong.* New York: New Press, 1995.

The Long Kiss Goodnight. DVD. Directed by Renny Harlin. 1996; Los Angeles: New Line, 1997.

Lucas, Scott. *Freedom's War: The American Crusade against the Soviet Union.* New York: New York University Press, 1999.

Luce, Henry. "A Prospectus for a New Magazine: Confidential." 1936. New York Times Archive. http://artsbeat.blogs.nytimes.com/2010/04/23/the-show-book-of-the-world-henry-luces-life-magazine-prospectus/.

Ludlum, Robert. *The Bourne Identity.* New York: Turtleback, 1988.

———. *The Bourne Supremacy.* New York: Turtleback, 1989.

———. *The Bourne Ultimatum.* New York: Turtleback, 1991.

Lustig, T. J. "'Moments of Punctuation': Metonymy and Ellipsis in Tim O'Brien." *Yearbook of English Studies* 31 (2001): 74–92.

Lyotard, Jean-François. *The Postmodern Condition: A Report on Knowledge.* Translated by Geoff Bennington and Brian Massumi. Minneapolis: University of Minnesota Press, 1984.

Madsen, Deborah L. *American Exceptionalism.* Edinburgh: Edinburgh University Press, 1998.

Mailer, Norman. *The Armies of the Night: History as a Novel, the Novel as History.* New York: Signet, 1968.

———. *Harlot's Ghost.* New York: Random House, 1991.

The Manchurian Candidate. DVD. Directed by John Frankenheimer. 1962. Beverly Hills: MMC Productions, 2004.

The Manchurian Candidate. DVD. Directed by Jonathan Demme. 2004; Los Angeles: Paramount, 2004.

Marchetti, Victor, and John D. Marks. *The CIA and the Cult of Intelligence.* New York: Laurel/Dell, 1980.

Margulies, Joseph. "Abu Zubaydah's Suffering." *Los Angeles Times,* April 30, 2009. http://articles.latimes.com/2009/apr/30/opinion/oe-margulies30.

Marks, John. *The Search for the "Manchurian Candidate": The CIA and Mind Control.* 1979. Reprint, New York: Norton, 1991.

Martin, David C. *Wilderness of Mirrors: Intrigue, Deception, and the Secrets That Destroyed Two of the Cold War's Most Important Agents.* New York: Harpercollins, 1981.

Mathews, Harry. *My Life in CIA.* Normal, IL: Dalkey Archive Press, 2005.

May, Ellen Tyler. *Homeward Bound: American Families in the Cold War Era.* Revised edition. New York: Basic Books, 1999.

Mayer, Jane. "The Black Sites: A Rare Look inside the C.I.A.'s Secret Interrogation Program." *New Yorker,* August 13, 2007. http://www.newyorker.com/reporting/2007/08/13/070813fa_fact_mayer.

——. *The Dark Side: The Inside Story of How the War on Terror Turned into a War on American Ideals.* New York: Doubleday, 2008.

——. "The Experiment: The Military Trains People to Withstand Interrogation; Are Those Methods Being Misused at Guantánamo?" *New Yorker,* July 11, 2005. http://www.newyorker.com/archive/2005/07/11/050711fa_fact4?currentPage=1.

——. "Whatever It Takes: The Politics of the Man behind *24.*" *New Yorker,* February 19, 2007. http://www.newyorker.com/reporting/2007/02/19/070219fa_fact_mayer.

Mazurek, Raymond. "Metafiction, the Historical Novel, and Coover's *The Public Burning.*" *Critique* 23, no. 3 (1982): 29–41.

McCaffrey, Larry. "As Guilty as the Rest of Them: An Interview with Robert Coover." *Critique* 41, no. 1 (2000): 115–25.

McCoy, Alfred W. *A Question of Torture: CIA Interrogation from the Cold War to the War on Terror.* New York: Holt, 2006.

McGee, Celia. "The Burgeoning Rebirth of a Bygone Literary Star." *New York Times Book Review,* January 13, 2007. http://www.nytimes.com/2007/01/13/books/13hume.html.

McHale, Brian. *Constructing Postmodernism.* New York: Routledge, 1992.

——. *Postmodernist Fiction.* New York: Methuen, 1987.

——. "Weak Narrativity: The Case of Avant-Garde Narrative Poetry." *Narrative* 9, no. 2 (2001): 161–67.

Meerloo, Joost A. M. "The Crime of Menticide." *American Journal of Psychiatry* 107 (1951): 594–98.

——. "Pavlovian Strategy as a Weapon of Menticide." *American Journal of Psychiatry* 110 (1954): 809–13.

——. *Rape of the Mind: The Psychology of Thought Control, Menticide, and Brainwashing.* Cleveland: World Publishing, 1956.

——. "Suicide, Menticide, and Psychic Homicide." *AMA Arch Neurological Psychiatry* 81, no. 3 (1959): 360–62.

Meeropol, Robert, and Michael Meeropol. *We Are Your Sons: The Legacy of Julius and Ethel Rosenberg.* Boston: Houghton Mifflin, 1975.

Melley, Timothy. "Brain Warfare: The Covert Sphere, Terrorism, and the Legacy of Cold War." *Grey Room* 45 (2011): 18–39.

——. *Empire of Conspiracy: The Culture of Paranoia in Postwar America.* Ithaca, NY: Cornell University Press, 2000.

Memento. DVD. Directed by Christopher Nolan. 2000; Culver City, CA: Sony, 2004.

Menno's Mind. DVD. Directed by Jon Kroll. 1997; Los Angeles: Showtime, 2000.

Mitrovich, Gregory. *Undermining the Kremlin: America's Strategy to Subvert the Soviet Bloc, 1947–1956.* Ithaca, NY: Cornell University Press, 2000.

Mocnik, Rastko. "Ideology and Fantasy." In *The Althusserian Legacy,* edited by E. Ann Kaplan and Michael Sprinkler, 139–60. New York: Verso, 1993.

Morris, David J. "Empires of the Mind: SERE, Guantánamo, and the Legacies of Torture." *Virginia Quarterly Review* (Winter 2009): 211–21. http://www.vqronline.org/articles/2009/winter/morris-sere/.

Morrison, Toni. *Beloved.* New York: Knopf, 1987.

Moynihan, Daniel Patrick. *Secrecy: The American Experience.* New Haven, CT: Yale University Press, 1999.

Mulholland Drive. DVD. Directed by David Lynch. 2000; Universal City, CA: Universal, 2001.

Munich. DVD. Directed by Steven Spielberg. 2005: Universal City, CA: Universal, 2006.

My Own Worst Enemy. TV series. DVD. Created by Jason Smilovic. Burbank, CA: NBC, 2008.

Nadel, Alan. "Cold War Television and the Technology of Brainwashing." In *American Cold War Culture,* edited by Douglas Field, 146–63. Edinburgh: Edinburgh University Press, 2005.

———. *Containment Culture: American Narratives, Postmodernism, and the Atomic Age.* Durham: Duke University Press, 1995.

———. *Invisible Criticism: Ralph Ellison and the American Canon.* Iowa City: University of Iowa Press, 1988.

"Narrative Description of the Overt and Covert Activities of [Redacted]." January 1, 1950. U.S. National Security Archive. CIA MK-ULTRA documents. 4 CD-ROMs. Disk 2. MORI ID no. 190882, http://documents.theblackvault.com/documents/mkultra/MKULTRA2/DOC_0000190882/0000190882_0003.TIF.

National Security Archive. George Washington University, Washington, DC. http://www.gwu.edu/~nsarchiv/.

National Security Council. "NSC 10 4-A, 17 December, 1947." Document 35. In *CIA Cold War Records: The CIA under Harry Truman,* edited by Michael Warner, 173. Washington, DC: CIA History Staff/Center for the Study of Intelligence, 1994.

———. "NSC 10/2, 18 June, 1948." Document 43. In *CIA Cold War Records: The CIA under Harry Truman,* edited by Michael Warner, 213–16. Washington, DC: CIA History Staff/Center for the Study of Intelligence, 1994.

Nelson, Deborah. *Pursuing Privacy in Cold War America.* New York: Columbia University Press, 2002.

Newman, John, David A. Willson, David J. DeRose, Stephen P. Hidalgo, and Nancy J. Kendall. *Vietnam War Literature.* 3rd ed. New York: Scarecrow, 1996.

Nizer, Louis. *The Implosion Conspiracy.* Garden City, NY: Doubleday, 1973.

O'Brien, Tim, *Going After Cacciato.* 1978. Reprint, New York: Delta, 1979.

———. *In the Lake of the Woods.* Boston: Houghton Mifflin, 1994.

———. "The Magic Show." 1991. In *Crafting Fiction: In Theory, In Practice,* edited by Marvin Diogenes and Clyde Moneyhun, 378–85. Mountain View, CA: Mayfield, 2001.

———. *The Things They Carried.* New York: Penguin, 1990.

———. "The Vietnam in Me." *New York Times Magazine,* October 2, 1994. http://www.nytimes.com/books/98/09/20/specials/obrien-vietnam.html.

———. "Writing Vietnam: Keynote Address." Lecture, Brown University, April 21, 1999. http://mama.stg.brown.edu/projects/WritingVietnam/obrien.html.

O'Donnell, Patrick. *Latent Destinies: Cultural Paranoia and Contemporary U.S. Narrative.* Durham: Duke University Press, 2000.

Ofshe, Richard J., and Margaret Thaler Singer. "Recovered-Memory Therapy and Robust Repression: Influence and Pseudomemories." *International Journal of Clinical and Experimental Hypnosis* 24, no. 4 (1994): 391–410.

Orlov, Paul A. "A Fiction of Politically Fantastic 'Facts': Robert Coover's *The Public Burning.*" In *Politics and the Muse: Studies in the Politics of Recent American Literature,* edited by Adam J. Sorkin, 111–23. Bowling Green, OH: Bowling Green State University Press, 1989.

Osgood, Kenneth. *Total Cold War: Eisenhower's Secret Propaganda Battle at Home and Abroad.* Lawrence: University Press of Kansas, 2006.

Outbreak. DVD. Directed by Wolfgang Petersen. Burbank, CA: Warner Brothers, 1997.

The Package. DVD. Directed by Andrew Davis. 1989; Beverly Hills: MGM, 2000.

Packard, Vance. *The Hidden Persuaders.* New York: Pocket Books, 1957.

Paglen, Trevor. *Blank Spots on the Map: The Dark Geography of the Pentagon's Secret World.* New York: NAL, 2010.

———. *Invisible: Covert Operations and Classified Landscapes.* New York: Aperture, 2010.

Pape, Robert A. "The Strategic Logic of Suicide Terrorism." *American Political Science Review* 97, no. 3 (2003): 343–61.

The Parallax View. Directed by Alan J. Pakula. 1974; Los Angeles: Paramount, 1999.

Patriot Games. DVD. Directed by Phillip Noyce. 1992; Los Angeles: Paramount, 2003.

Patterson, Annabel. *Censorship and Interpretation: The Conditions of Writing and Reading in Early Modern England.* Madison: University of Wisconsin Press, 1984.

Paycheck. DVD. Directed by John Woo. 2003; Los Angeles: Paramount, 2003.

The Peacemaker. DVD. Directed by Mimi Leder. 1997; Universal City, CA: Dreamworks, 1998.

Pease, Donald. *The New American Exceptionalism.* Minneapolis: University of Minnesota Press, 2009.

———. "New Americanists: Revisionist Interventions into the Canon." *boundary 2* 17, no. 1 (Spring 1990): 1–38.

Philipson, Ilene. *Ethel Rosenberg: Beyond the Myths.* New York: Franklin Watts, 1988.

Plame Wilson, Valerie. *Fair Game: My Life as a Spy, My Betrayal by the White House.* New York: Simon & Schuster, 2007.

Plath, Sylvia. *The Bell Jar.* 1963. Reprint, New York: Perennial, 1999.

Platoon. DVD. Directed by Oliver Stone. 1986; Beverly Hills: MGM, 2001.

Post, Jerrold M. "Terrorist Psycho-Logic." In *Origins of Terrorism: Psychologies, Ideologies, Theories, States of Mind,* edited by Walter Reich, 25–40. Washington, DC: Woodrow Wilson Center Press, 1990.

Poster, Mark. *Cultural History and Postmodernity: Disciplinary Readings and Challenges.* New York: Columbia University Press, 1997.

Powers, Richard Gid. *Secrecy and Power: The Life of J. Edgar Hoover.* New York: Free Press, 1987.

Priest, Dana, and William Arkin. "A Hidden World, Growing beyond Control." *Washington Post,* July 19, 2010. http://projects.washingtonpost.com/top-secret-america/articles/#article-index.

——. "National Security Inc." *Washington Post,* July 20, 2010. http://projects.washingtonpost.com/top-secret-america/articles/#article-index.

——. "The Secrets Next Door." *Washington Post,* July 21, 2010. http://projects.washingtonpost.com/top-secret-america/articles/#article-index.

Procopius. *The Secret History.* Translated by Richard Atwater. Chicago: P. Covici, 1927. http://www.fordham.edu/halsall/basis/procop-anec.html.

Radosh, Ronald, and Joyce Milton. *The Rosenberg File.* 1983. 2nd ed. New Haven, CT: Yale University Press, 1997.

Randall, Stephen J. *Colombia and the United States: Hegemony and Independence.* Athens: University of Georgia Press, 1992.

Ranelagh, John. *The Agency: The Rise and Decline of the CIA.* New York: Simon and Schuster, 1986.

"Rare Look at In-House CIA Museum." *Voice of America Television*, June 13, 2008. http://www.youtube.com/watch?v=hgBRvrEb_a4.

Rather, Dan. Interview by Larry King. *Larry King Live. CNN.com*, October 18, 2001, http://transcripts.cnn.com/TRANSCRIPTS/0110/18/lkl.00.html.

Reitz, Bernhard. "The Reconstruction of the Fifties in E. L. Doctorow's *The Book of Daniel* and Robert Coover's *The Public Burning.*" In *Historiographic Metafiction in Modern American and Canadian Literature,* edited by Bernd Engler and Kurt Müller, 223–40. Paderborn, Ger.: Ferdinand Schoningh, 1994.

Rendition. Directed by Gavin Hood. 2007; Los Angeles: New Line, 2008.

Report of the Commission on Protecting and Reducing Government Secrecy, 1997, Senate Document 105–2, Pursuant to Public Law 236. 103rd Congress. Washington, DC: U.S. Government Printing Office, 1997. http://www.fas.org/sgp/library/moynihan/index.html.

Reuben, William A. *The Atom Spy Hoax.* New York: Action Books, 1954.

Rice, Condoleezza. Interview by Wolf Blitzer. *CNN Late Edition with Wolf Blitzer*. September 8, 2002. http://transcripts.cnn.com/TRANSCRIPTS/0209/08/le.00.html.

Richmond, Shane. "*Call of Duty: Modern Warfare 3* Breaks Sales Records." *Telegraph,* November 11, 2011. http://www.telegraph.co.uk/technology/video-games/video-game-news/8884726/Call-of-Duty-Modern-Warfare-3-breaks-sales-records.html.

Riesman, David, Nathan Glazer, and Reuel Denney. *The Lonely Crowd: A Study of the Changing American Character.* New Haven, CT: Yale University Press, 1950.

Risen, James, and Eric Lichtblau. "Bush Lets U.S. Spy on Callers without Courts." *New York Times,* December 16, 2005. http://www.nytimes.com/2005/12/16/politics/16program.html?pagewanted=all.

The Rock. DVD. Directed by Michael Bay. 1996; Burbank, CA: Disney, 1997.

Rogin, Michael. "Kiss Me Deadly: Communism, Motherhood, and Cold War Movies." *Representations* 6 (Spring 1984): 1–36.

——. "'Make My Day!': Spectacle as Amnesia in Imperial Politics." *Representations* 29 (Winter 1990): 99–123.

——. *"Ronald Reagan," the Movie: And Other Episodes in Political Demonology.* Berkeley: University of California Press, 1987.

Root, Jonathan. *The Betrayers.* New York: Coward McCann, 1963.

Rose, Jacqueline. *States of Fantasy.* Oxford: Clarendon, 1996.

Rosenheim, Shawn. *The Cryptographic Imagination: Secret Writings from Edgar Allan Poe to the Internet.* Baltimore: Johns Hopkins University Press, 1996.

Rushdie, Salman. *Shalimar the Clown.* New York: Random House, 2005.

The Russians Are Coming! The Russians Are Coming! DVD. Directed by Norma Jewison. 1966; Beverly Hills: MGM, 2002.

Ryan, Marie-Laure. "The Modes of Narrativity and Their Visual Metaphors." *Style* 26, no. 3 (1992): 1–16.

Sageman, Marc. *Understanding Terrorist Networks.* Philadelphia: University of Pennsylvania, 2004.

Salt. DVD. Directed by Phillip Noyce. 2010; Culver City, CA: Sony, 2010.

Sands, Philippe. *Torture Team: Rumsfeld's Memo and the Betrayal of American Values.* New York: Palgrave MacMillan, 2008.

Sargant, William. *Battle for the Mind: A Physiology of Conversion and Brain-Washing.* London: Heinemann, 1957.

Saunders, Frances Stonor. *The Cultural Cold War: The CIA and the World of Arts and Letters.* New York: New Press, 1999.

Schaub, Thomas Hill. *American Fiction in the Cold War.* Madison: University of Wisconsin Press, 1991.

Schein, Edgar H. *Coercive Persuasion: A Socio-Psychological Analysis of the "Brainwashing" of American Civilian Prisoners by the Chinese Government.* With Inge Schneier and Curtis H. Barker. New York: Norton, 1961.

Schneir, Walter, and Miriam Schneir. *Invitation to an Inquest.* 1965. 4th ed. New York: Doubleday, 1983.

Schrecker, Ellen. *Many Are the Crimes: McCarthyism in America.* Boston: Little Brown, 1998.

Scott, Janny. "Prominent Historian Admits He Misled Students into Believing He Served in Vietnam." *New York Times,* June 19, 2001, A19.

Searle, John R. "The Logical Status of Fictional Discourse." *New Literary History* 6, no. 2 (1975): 319–32.

Séchehaye, Marguerite. *Autobiography of a Schizophrenic Girl.* Translated by Grace Rubin-Rabson. 1951. Reprint, New York: Grune and Stratton, 1968.

Second Nature. DVD. Directed by Ben Bolt. 2003; Burbank, CA: TNT, 2003.

"The Secret Downing Street Memo." *Times (London),* May 1, 2005. http://www.times online.co.uk/tol/news/uk/article387374.ece.

Seed, David. *Brainwashing: The Fictions of Mind Control; A Study of Novels and Films since World War II.* Kent, OH: Kent State University Press, 2004.

Seven Days in May. Directed by John Frankenheimer. 1964; Burbank, CA: Warner, 2000.

Shane, Scott. "Ex-Spies Tell It All." *New York Times,* March 15, 2005. http://www.ny times.com/2005/03/15/books/15spyb.html?_r=1.

Sharpe, Malcolm Pitman. *Was Justice Done? The Rosenberg-Sobell Case.* New York: Monthly Review Press, 1956.

Sick, Gary. "The Election Story of the Decade." *New York Times,* April 15, 1991. http://www.nytimes.com/1991/04/15/opinion/the-election-story-of-the-decade.html.

Siebers, Tobin. *Cold War Criticism and the Politics of Skepticism.* Oxford: Oxford University Press, 1993.

The Siege. DVD. Directed by Edward Zwick. 1998; Los Angeles: Twentieth-Century Fox, 1999.

Siegel, Robert. "Ex-CIA Agent Robert Baer, Inspiration for *Syriana.*" *All Things Considered.* National Public Radio, December 6, 2005. http://www.npr.org/templates/story/story.php?storyId=5041385.

The Sleep Room. TV miniseries. DVD. Directed by Anne Wheeler. 1998; Toronto: CBC, 1998.

Sleeper Cell. TV series. Created by Ethan Rieff and Cyrus Voris. Los Angeles: Showtime, December 4, 2005–December 17, 2006.

Sloterdijk, Peter. *Critique of Cynical Reason.* Translated by Michael Eldred. 1983. Reprint, Minneapolis: University of Minnesota, 1987.

Smith, Joseph Burkholder. *Portrait of a Cold Warrior: Second Thoughts of a Top CIA Agent.* New York: Ballantine, 1976.

Stomberg, John. "Life Magazine." In *Encyclopedia of Twentieth-Century Photography,* edited by Lynne Warren, 952–55. New York: Routledge, 2006.

Streatfeild, Dominic. *Brainwash: The Secret History of Mind Control.* New York: Thomas Dunne, 2007.

Strike Back. TV series. Produced by Andy Harries and Elaine Pyke. Middlesex, UK: BBC, May 5, 2010–October 21, 2011.

Sturken, Marita. *Tangled Memories: The Vietnam War, the AIDS Epidemic, and the Politics of Remembering.* Berkeley: University of California Press, 1997.

The Sum of All Fears. DVD. Directed by Philip Alden Robinson. 2002; Los Angeles: Paramount, 2002.

Suskind, Ron. *The One Percent Doctrine: Deep Inside America's Pursuit of Its Enemies since 9/11.* New York: Simon and Schuster, 2006.

Swordfish. Directed by Dominic Sena. 2001; Burbank, CA: Warner Brothers, 2004

Syriana. Directed by Stephen Gaghan. 2005; Burbank, CA: Warner Brothers, 2006.

Tabbi, Joseph. *Postmodern Sublime: Technology and American Writing from Mailer to Cyberpunk.* Ithaca, NY: Cornell University Press, 1996.

Taussig, Michael. *Defacement: Public Secrecy and the Labor of the Negative.* Stanford: Stanford University Press, 1999.

Taylor, Kathleen. "Thought Crime." *Guardian,* October 8, 2005. http://www.guardian.co.uk/world/2005/oct/08/terrorism.booksonhealth.

Thomas, Evan, and Michael Hirsh. "The Debate over Torture." *Newsweek,* November 21, 2005, 26.

Threat Matrix. TV series. Created by Daniel Voll. Burbank, CA: ABC, September 18, 2003–January 29, 2004.

Three Days of the Condor. Directed by Sydney Pollack. 1975; Los Angeles, Paramount, 1999.

Tillyard, E. M. W. *The Elizabethan World Picture.* New York: Vintage, 1959.

Time Lapse. DVD. Directed by David Worth. 2001; Santa Monica, CA: Lions Gate, 2001.

Torture Room. DVD. Directed by Eric Forsberg. 2007; La Crosse, WI, Platinum Disc/ Echo Bridge, 2010.

Traitor. Directed by Jeffrey Nachmanoff. 2008; Troy, MI: Anchor Bay, 2008.

True Lies. DVD. Directed by James Cameron. 1994; Los Angeles: Twentieth Century Fox, 1998.

Truman, Harry S. "Limit CIA Role to Intelligence." *Washington Post,* December 22, 1963, A11.

24. TV series. Created by Joel Surnow and Robert Cochran. Los Angeles: Fox TV, November 6, 2001–February 1, 2010.

The Unit. TV show. Created by David Mamet. Los Angeles: CBS, March 7, 2006–May 10, 2009.

United States of America v. Julius Rosenberg, Ethel Rosenberg, Anatoli A. Yakovlev, also known as "John," David Greenglass and Morton Sobell. Transcript of trial, New York, March 6–April 6, 1951. University of Missouri–Kansas City School of Law. http:// law2.umkc.edu/faculty/projects/ftrials/rosenb/ROS_TRIA.HTM.

U.S. Congress. House of Representatives. Committee on Un-American Activities. *Communist Psychological Warfare (Brainwashing).* Consultation with Edward Hunter, author and foreign correspondent. 85th Cong., 2nd sess., March 13, 1958. http://www. crossroad.to/Quotes/globalism/Congress.htm.

——. House of Representatives. Select Committee on Intelligence. *The CIA and the Media.* 95th Cong., 1st and 2nd sess., 1978.

——. Senate. Subcommittee to Investigate the Administration of the Internal Security Act and Other Internal Security Laws of the Committee of the Judiciary. *The Effect of Red China Communes on the United States.* Testimony of Edward Hunter. 86th Cong., 1st sess., March 24, 1959, 24.

U.S. Department of State. "Diplomacy and Defense: A Test of National Maturity." *Department of State Bulletin,* December 4, 1961.

van der Kolk, Bessel A., and Onno van der Hart. "The Intrusive Past: The Flexibility of Memory and the Engraving of Trauma." In *Trauma: Explorations in Memory,* edited by Cathy Caruth, 158–82. Baltimore: Johns Hopkins University Press, 1995.

van der Kolk, Bessel, Lars Weisaeth, and Onno van der Hart. "History of Trauma in Psychiatry." In *Traumatic Stress: The Effects of Overwhelming Experience on Mind, Body, and Society,* edited by Bessel A. van der Kolk, Alexander C. McFarlane, and Lars Weisaeth, 47–76. New York: Guilford, 1996.

"Verbatim Transcript of Combatant Status Review Tribunal Hearing for ISN 10016 [Zayn Al Abidin Muhammad Husayn, aka Abu Zubaydah]." C05403111, Tribunal at U.S. Naval Base, Guantánamo Bay, Cuba, March 27, 2007, 1–30. American Civil Liberties Union. http://www.aclu.org/national-security/verbatim-transcript-combatant-status-review-tribunal-csrt-hearing-abu-zubaydah.

Vidal-Naquet, Pierre. *Assassins of Memory: Essays on the Denial of the Holocaust.* Translated by Jeffrey Mehlman. New York: Columbia University Press, 1992.

Vistica, Gregory L. "What Happened in Thanh Phong." *New York Times Magazine,* April 25, 2001. http://www.nytimes.com/2001/04/25/magazine/25KERREY.html.

Walker, Martin. *The Cold War.* New York: Henry Holt, 1994.

Wallace, David Foster. "The View from Mrs. Thompson's." 2001. In *Consider the Lobster,* 128–40. Boston: Little Brown, 2006.

Walter, Jess. *The Zero*. New York: Harper, 2006.

War Games. DVD. Directed by John Badham. 1983; Beverly Hills: MGM, 1998.

Warner, Michael. *Publics and Counterpublics*. Cambridge, MA: Zone/MIT, 1992.

Warrick, Joby, and Peter Finn. "Internal Rifts on Road to Torment." *Washington Post,* July 19, 2009. http://www.washingtonpost.com/wp-dyn/content/article/2009/07/18/AR2009071802065.html.

Wegner, Phillip. *Life between Two Deaths, 1989–2001: U.S. Culture in the Long Nineties*. Durham: Duke University Press, 2009.

Weiner, Tim. *Legacy of Ashes: The History of the CIA*. New York: Anchor, 2008.

Weinstein, Philip. *Unknowing: The Work of Modernist Fiction*. Ithaca, NY: Cornell University Press, 2005.

Weisberg, Jacob. "All the President's Accomplices: How the Country Acquiesced to Bush's Torture Policy." *Slate,* May 2, 2009. http://www.slate.com/id/2217359/.

Westerfield, H. Bradford. *Inside CIA's Private World: Declassified Articles from the Agency's Internal Journal, 1955–1992*. New Haven, CT: Yale University Press, 1995.

Wexley, John. *The Judgment of Julius and Ethel Rosenberg*. New York: Cameron and Kahn, 1955.

White, Hayden. *The Content of the Form: Narrative Discourse and Historical Representation*. Baltimore: Johns Hopkins University Press, 1987.

———. *Tropics of Discourse*. Baltimore: Johns Hopkins University Press, 1978.

The White House. "First Lady Michelle Obama to Surprise Visitors on White House Tour at 10:45 AM ET." Press release. White House Press Office. January 20, 2010. http://www.whitehouse.gov/the-press-office/first-lady-michelle-obama-surprise-visitors-white-house-tour-1045-am-et-livestream-.

———. "National Security Action Memorandum 273." November 26, 1963. John McAdams, The Kennedy Assassination, http://mcadams.posc.mu.edu/viet16.htm.

Whitfield, Stephen. *The Culture of the Cold War*. 2nd ed. Baltimore: Johns Hopkins University Press, 1996.

Whyte, William. *The Organization Man*. New York: Simon and Schuster, 1956.

Wiegman, Robyn. *American Anatomies: Theorizing Race and Gender*. Durham: Duke University Press, 1995.

Wilson, Joseph. *The Politics of Truth: Inside the Lies That Led to War and Betrayed My Wife's CIA Identity: A Diplomat's Memoir*. New York: Carroll and Graf, 2004.

———. "What I Didn't Find in Africa." *New York Times,* July 6, 2003. http://www.nytimes.com/2003/07/06/opinion/what-i-didn-t-find-in-africa.html?src=pm.

Wise, David, and Thomas B. Ross. *The Invisible Government*. New York: Random House, 1964.

Wolff, Geoffrey. "An American Epic." *New Times,* August 19, 1977, 48–57.

Wood, Michael. "The New Journalism." Review of *The New Journalism,* by Tom Wolfe, edited by Tom Wolfe and E. W. Johnson. *New York Times,* July 22, 1973. http://www.nytimes.com/books/98/11/08/specials/wolfe-journalism.html.

Wubben, H. H. "American Prisoners of War in Korea: A Second Look at the 'Something New in History' Theme." *American Quarterly* 22, no. 1 (1970): 3–19.

Wyatt, Edward. "New Era in Politics, New Focus for *24.*" *New York Times,* January 8, 2009, C1.

Wylie, Phillip. *A Generation of Vipers.* New York: Farrar and Rhinehart, 1942.

XIII: The Conspiracy. TV miniseries. DVD. Directed by Duane Clark. 2008; Toronto: 2010.

Yoo, John. *War by Other Means.* Boston: Atlantic Monthly Press, 2006.

Zakaria, Fareed. "What America Has Lost." *Newsweek,* September 13, 2010, 18.

Žižek, Slavoj. *Looking Awry: An Introduction to Jacques Lacan through Popular Culture.* Cambridge, MA: MIT Press, 1992.

——. *The Plague of Fantasies.* London: Verso, 1997.

——. *Welcome to the Desert of the Real: Five Essays on September 11 and Related Dates.* London: Verso, 2002.

——. "Welcome to the Desert of the Real!" *South Atlantic Quarterly* 101, no. 2 (2002): 385–89.

INDEX

Note: Page numbers in *italics* indicate illustrations.